SALEM-VILLAGE WITCHCRAFT   A D
OCUMENTARY RECORD OF LOCAL CON
FLICT IN COLONIAL NEW ENGLAND

BOYER, PAUL S

Salem-Village Witchcraft

A Documentary Record of Local Conflict in Colonial New England

Salem-Village Witchcraft

A Documentary Record of Local Conflict in Colonial New England

edited by PAUL BOYER *and* STEPHEN NISSENBAUM

with a new preface by the editors

Northeastern University Press

BOSTON

Northeastern University Press

Library of Congress Cataloging-in-Publication Data
Salem-village witchcraft : a documentary record of local conflict in
colonial New England / edited by Paul Boyer and Stephen Nissenbaum,
with a new preface by the editors.
p. cm.
Originally published: Belmont, Calif. : Wadsworth Pub. Co., 1972,
in series: American history research series.
Includes bibliographical references.
ISBN 1-55553-164-4 (alk. paper) — ISBN 1-55553-165-2 (pbk. : alk. paper)
1. Witchcraft—Massachusetts—Salem—History—Sources. 2. Trials
(Witchcraft)—Massachusetts—Salem. 3. Salem (Mass.)—History—
Sources. I. Boyer, Paul S. II. Nissenbaum, Stephen.
BF1575.S25 1993
133.4'3'097445—dc20   93-16009

Printed and bound by Maple Press, York, Pennsylvania.
The paper is Maple Eggshell, an acid-free sheet.

MANUFACTURED IN THE UNITED STATES OF AMERICA
97 96 95 94 93   5 4 3 2 1

Preface to the 1993 Edition

This book was out of print for almost two decades, but it continued to have an active, though shadowy, afterlife (a *spectral* afterlife, it is tempting to say). We know this from the stream of letters we have received over the years, generally from college faculty, asking for legal permission to reprint the materials, in whole or in part, for use in their classes. (The copyright had reverted to us after the book went out of print.) We were pleased, therefore, when (on the occasion of the tercentenary of the Salem witchcraft trials) Northeastern University Press offered to reprint the book. You hold the result in your hands.

The book began life as a collection of documents we generated for an undergraduate course we started to teach in 1969 at the University of Massachusetts, Amherst. The course was an experimental introductory-level one, in which our students spent an entire semester studying a single dramatic episode in American history, using only primary sources. Our aim was to offer students an introduction to the study of history that resembles the kind of work historians actually *do*, in much the way introductory courses in science offer the experience of hands-on laboratory work, or even the way courses in literature use the works themselves rather than textbooks about those works.

The first episode we chose was Salem witchcraft. It seemed a good candidate because it was a "local" event for our Massachusetts students, one that promised to have considerable appeal to undergraduates. (In addition, Stephen Nissenbaum had helped teach the Salem episode in an earlier version of the same course while a graduate student at the University of Wisconsin, under the direction of William R. Taylor, who had actually conceived the "laboratory" method there in the mid-1960s.) That first year, about thirty students enrolled for the course (eventually, the number rose to as high as three hundred and involved several of our colleagues as well as some half-dozen graduate teaching assistants each semester). With the help of those first students we began to look for new documentary materials—and to find them.

We still remember the way we came upon some of these documents, and our excitement when we realized how new, and how useful, they were: a phone call to the First Church of Danvers inquiring whether, by any chance, the early records of the church still survived, produced the petitions for and against Rev. Samuel Parris; a letter to the Connecticut Historical Society (acting on a lead from nineteenth-century local historian Charles Upham) produced Rev. Parris's manuscript sermon book; many trips from Amherst to the Massachusetts Archives and the Essex County Registries of Probate and Deeds produced, among so much else, the story of the estates of Thomas Putnam, Sr., and his second wife, Mary Veren Putnam, and the battles over them.

Even before the end of that first semester, we had begun to realize the value of this veritable treasure trove, not only for teaching purposes, but as the basis for a new interpretation of the historical context in which the Salem witchcraft trials took place. Sometime during the following year we decided to write that new interpretation ourselves. The result, published in 1974 (two years after this collection of primary source materials) was our book *Salem Possessed: The Social Origins of Witchcraft.*

Salem-Village Witchcraft contains the sources on which *Salem Possessed* was substantially based. The book's subtitle makes clear our underlying purpose: we chose materials that offer "a documentary record of *local conflict* in colonial New England." These materials include the very kinds of data that record the mundane public life of any community in early New England: tax lists, minutes of town meetings, and annals of the local Congregational church. They also include the personal records (and trial transcripts) of five people executed as witches in 1692. We chose these five because they were all local residents, and also in part because their pre-1692 lives reveal something about local issues. (The elusive John Willard, for example, was one of the very few accused witches who lived in the western part of Salem Village.)

As we wrote in the preface to the original edition of this book, we had become more interested in what the events of 1692 revealed about the history of the community in which they took place than about what that history revealed about 1692; our interest had shifted "from Salem-Village *witchcraft* to *Salem-Village.*" In retrospect, one can clearly see that the years around 1970 marked the creative heyday of colonial "community studies," and of what had begun to be called the "new" social history. Our impulse to pursue the "normal" life of Salem Village's inhabitants was palpably a part of that development.

Little could we have known then that scholarly interest in early American witchcraft was just beginning. Over the last dozen years alone, John Demos and Richard Weisman have published important books about the politics and sociology of New England witchcraft. David Konig has explored the relationship between witchcraft and law in early Essex County society. Christine Heyrmann has unearthed important links between Salem witchcraft and Quakerism. Larry Gragg has published an illuminating biography of Samuel Parris. Carol Karlsen has shown precisely how witchcraft accusations were frequently related to gender roles. David Hall and, most recently, Richard Godbeer have demonstrated in a new way the importance of magic in understanding not only witchcraft but early New England culture as a whole. The 1992 tercentenary of the Salem witchcraft trials generated a three-day scholarly conference held in Salem and devoted to new work on the subject. (Ten of the papers read at that conference have been published in two volumes of the *Essex*

Institute Historical Collections.) The scholarship of Salem witchcraft has passed into the hands of new generations of historians.

So, too, these documents now pass into the hands of new generations of readers. The republication of *Salem-Village Witchcraft* allows easy access to anyone interested in exploring at first hand the lives of early New Englanders—their lives before, after, and at the moment when the ordinary, mundane details of village life converged upon an extraordinary episode that brought to this unlikely community such unexpected and lasting infamy. In the documents that follow, men and women such as accused witch Rebecca Nurse, afflicted girl Ann Putnam and her embittered parents, and unhappy minister Samuel Parris all appear—and reappear—in one context after another: now in witchcraft testimonies, and then again in petitions, tax lists, probate disputes, even narrative accounts. By poring over and interlinking this varied material in different ways, the analytic possibilities are almost literally endless.

As for the original manuscript copies of the documents contained in this book, we are pleased to report that several of the most important are now better preserved, and more easily accessible, than they were when we first discovered them. Both the Salem Village community records and the records of its church are preserved in Danvers, thanks to the untiring efforts of Richard Trask, who is now serving as the town archivist of Danvers (it was he, back in 1970, who graciously monitored our initial encounter with the Village Church records). Finally, the sermon book of Rev. Samuel Parris (from which five sermons were first printed in *Salem-Village Witchcraft*) is about to be published in its entirety. All in all, we have much reason to feel good about the ongoing history of Salem Village witchcraft, a history of which this book is itself a part.

Paul Boyer
Stephen Nissenbaum

April 1993

Preface

Few episodes of American history have aroused such intense and continuing interest as the trials and executions for witchcraft which occurred in Massachusetts in 1692. Historians have scrutinized the event from many perspectives; novelists and playwrights from Nathaniel Hawthorne to Arthur Miller have capitalized upon its inherent dramatic possibilities. The value, then, of a collection of primary documents relating to this event would seem to be clear.

In *Salem-Village Witchcraft* we have included transcripts of the preliminary proceedings and much of the testimony against five accused witches. (Unfortunately the actual trial records have not survived.) We selected these five because the documents in their cases are comparatively extensive and also because all five individuals are linked to Salem Village, a settlement near the town of Salem, on the site of present-day Danvers, Massachusetts. We have included two contemporary narratives of the 1692 witchcraft outbreak and several sermons occasioned by the event.

Salem-Village Witchcraft also contains extensive documentation relating to the history of Salem Village and the lives of its residents. At first glance this additional material may seem somewhat tangential to the witchcraft outbreak, but its inclusion represents a conscious decision on our part, for we are convinced that these documents make possible an understanding of the witchcraft episode which would otherwise be impossible. The accused and accusers of 1692 did not suddenly materialize to play their assigned roles and then fade into the wings. For the most part they had been living together for years as part of a functioning village—an "ordinary" community which was nevertheless capable of exploding with dramatic force. Any attempt to understand the explosion must take into account the nature of the community and its history *before* the community achieved notoriety.

On the other hand the deliberate localism of our editorial approach has obvious limitations. By focusing so narrowly upon a single village, our collection fails to place the witchcraft trials in a variety of historical contexts. For example the documents do not convey the extent to which the belief in witchcraft was nearly universal in this period, as is suggested by the thousands of witchcraft trials and executions which took place in England and on the Continent during the sixteenth and seventeenth centuries. Indeed by 1692 the "witch craze" which had begun in Europe around 1500 was distinctly on the wane so that the trials in Salem Village were among the last of the major outbreaks—if the execution of only twenty persons entitles this outbreak to be called "major" in the history of European witchcraft.

Even within the more limited context of American colonial history, these documents touch only lightly, if at all, on important aspects of the event. We have ignored the occasional witchcraft cases which occurred both before and after 1692. Before the outbreak at Salem Village, trials for witchcraft had been fairly common events in colonial America, but they had not invariably resulted in executions or even in conviction; in fact one such case is recorded in this book. Even more striking is the fact that these earlier trials had rarely involved more than a single accused witch. Only in 1692 did the accusations multiply so quickly and envelop an entire community. Thus although the trials of 1692 were significantly different from those which had preceded them and from the few which followed, our collection provides no easy way of explaining this uniqueness.

We have devoted relatively little space to the purely theological ramifications of the witchcraft episode, even though some of the most prominent ministers in New England (most of whom lived in Boston, some fifteen miles south of Salem Village) spent much of their time in 1692 arguing about precisely these ramifications and how they might judge the fairness of the procedures with which the trials were being conducted. (The ministers at Salem Village were by no means speaking for the majority of their colleagues in Massachusetts when they wholeheartedly endorsed the trials.) We have similarly devoted relatively little space to the wider political context of the outbreak: how the political climate of the colony in 1692 affected the trials; how certain individuals, in and out of power, attempted to turn the trials to their own benefit; or how others viewed the events as a threat to their own careers. Finally, perhaps, we have not documented the extent to which individuals in other towns of Massachusetts became involved, as either accusers or accused, as the shock waves from the Salem-Village meetinghouse radiated outward.

We are aware of these varied facets of the subject and recognize that any one of them could provide grist for another collection of documents at least as long as the present one. Our defense for the documents we have included must simply be that as we studied the outbreak of 1692, our interest increasingly shifted from Salem-Village *witchcraft* to *Salem-Village*. The supernatural afflictions which plagued the village in 1692 have become significant to us primarily as the particular (and particularly dramatic) outlet through which the almost unbearable conflicts and tensions generated within this small agricultural settlement found expression. The widespread belief in witchcraft and perhaps even the existence of witchcraft cults in New England made possible the Salem-Village outbreak in its particular form. But more interesting, it seems to us, are the circumstances which underlay that outbreak and which helped to determine the roles that specific individuals played.

It was some time before we came to see the subject in this way. It may be helpful to users of this collection if we describe the history of its preparation. The idea was conceived, in fact, out of the exigencies of an experimental introductory course in American history, which we taught together at the University of Massachusetts in the fall of 1969 (and, in the case of Stephen Nissenbaum, earlier at the University of Wisconsin). Having originally chosen Salem witchcraft to illustrate some of the problems which historians confront in studying and interpreting their evidence, we found that both we and our students were becoming impatient and frustrated—even bored—after a few weeks in which we limited our attention to the witchcraft episode itself. Furthermore the all-too-easy game of "explaining" the event by reference to some sweeping generalization did not seem to diminish our discontent. Some students suggested that the whole affair be swept under a carpet labeled "Puritanism." Others insisted that the "afflicted girls" were simply sensation-starved adolescents in need of a good spanking. Still other students concluded that the executed persons were, in fact, practicing witches who merely received their just deserts by the laws of the day.

We soon recognized that such speculations were actually masking our vast ignorance about the persons whose behavior we were so glibly "explaining." At this point we began to ask ourselves hard questions, and at once our interest revived. Our curiosity about Salem Village was aroused as we studied the community in its moment of crisis. We found that we wanted more biographical data on the shadowy individuals whose names appear in the testimony. In short we and our students began exploring—and in the process discovered a wealth of material on Salem Village and its residents.

We learned, for example, that the Salem-Village Book of Record had been published in several issues of the *Historical Collections of the Danvers Historical Society* in the 1920s, only to be ignored by historians and historical popularizers in the succeeding forty years. We found the manuscript church records in the library of the First Church of Danvers—the direct institutional descendant of the "witchcraft" parish of 1692. Fragments of these records had appeared in various nineteenth-century historical publications, but never the complete text. At the Connecticut Historical Society in Hartford we found in manuscript the sermons of Samuel Parris (minister at Salem Village from 1689 to 1696) written in Parris's own hand. In the published and unpublished court, probate, and land records of Essex County (in which Salem Village lay) and in the Massachusetts State Archives in Boston, we and our students located quantities of material about the residents of the village. In the extensive genealogical collections of Salem's Essex Institute several of our students came upon much information about the principal families of Salem Village, including the ubiquitous Putnams, who figure so prominently in village affairs and in the witchcraft episode. From these varied sources began to emerge a picture of the historical context of the events of 1692—a picture more complex, and hence more revealing, than we had anticipated.

We have not attempted in this book to interpret these documents or point out their "significance." Neither have we tried to formulate a new explanation of the witchcraft outbreak—although some of our hunches, to be sure, have influenced our choice and arrangement of the documents. Not only would such interpolations have diminished the classroom value of this book, but they would have implied that there is only *one* use to which the documents can be put, *one* interpretation toward which all the documents inexorably point. As we scrutinized and transcribed the faded manuscripts, we had ample time to speculate on details which seemed intensely suggestive; but we would prefer to let the documents speak for themselves. Hence we leave it to each student—or preferably to groups of students working together—to discover in these materials what they will.

Some preliminary comments may, however, be helpful in this process. The reader will observe that the same names occur over and over again in these documents, often in quite different contexts: in the witchcraft records, tax rolls, deeds, wills, census, maps, and petitions. Similarly the same incident may be referred to and amplified in various kinds of documents, often in different parts of the book. This recurrence suggests that the documents must not only be read carefully but often more than once. While some of them are highly dramatic, most take on meaning only in the context of other documents. Any given document is thus more like a piece in a jigsaw puzzle than a Rosetta Stone which in itself offers great revelations. Often a single document (a petition, for instance, or a tax list) will suggest little or nothing of interest. But when they are juxtaposed, the petition and the tax list may yield fascinating relationships and correlations. It is surprising how even the simplest operation, such as alphabetizing a list of names, will sometimes make even a difficult document clearer and more usable.

In these days when national leaders bank on the assumption that an individual's memory—and indeed his concern—do not extend beyond this morning's *Times* or last night's Cronkite show, the ability to examine evidence deliberately and comparatively and to link up seemingly unrelated bits of data is surely worth cultivating.

We hope that *Salem-Village Witchcraft* will have varied uses. As a collection of documents relating to a rather neatly circumscribed and yet inherently fascinating event, the book readily lends itself to courses which try to teach history by permitting students actually to take part in the historiographical process—as in a laboratory course—instead of merely reading the polished final products of other men's research. We have found that the documents included in this book are more than sufficient to provide assignments for an entire semester devoted to Salem Village, but we also believe that through careful selection the book can be used with equal success in a course which spends only a few weeks on the witchcraft episode.

Since the circumscribed nature of the subject has paradoxically allowed us to include a broad range of materials not ordinarily in an anthology, we suspect that the book will provide valuable sources (preserved, as it were, in their natural state) for students in such diverse fields as legal and economic history and even historical demography.

In preparing these documents for publication we have been mindful both of the obligation to be as faithful to the originals as possible and of the fact that this book is not a definitive scholarly edition but rather a working source book for students. Thus we have modernized spelling and punctuation (except for proper names, for which we have retained the Salem Villagers' rather appealing habit of endless variation) and revised paragraphing when it seemed to promote clarity. In legal documents we have often deleted standardized and formulaic expressions (such as *Jurat in Curia* at the end of a deposition). We have omitted boundary descriptions in deeds unless the descriptions include significant information not otherwise available. All omissions, of course, have been indicated by ellipses.

The dating of some documents may be a source of confusion. Until 1752 the English calendar officially began the new year on March 25th, and the period from January 1 to March 24 belonged to the old year. But popular usage was beginning to favor January 1 as New Year's Day, and beginning in the 1670s the inclusion of both the old *and* the new year in reference to dates within this interval became customary. Thus, "March 10, 1691/92" is "March 10, 1692" by present reckoning. In addition, since March was the first rather than the third month of the year, the formulation "17, 9th month, 1689" (or the terser "17.9.89"), for example, means *November* 17, 1689.

We wish to thank those individuals whose helpfulness facilitated our work, including Reverend Edward H. Glennie of the First Church of Danvers; Richard Trask of the Danvers Historical Society; Leo Flaherty, Curator of the Massachusetts State Archives; and the staffs of the Essex Institute, the Connecticut Historical Society, and the Essex County Courthouse. We are also indebted to our colleagues in History 185: Patricia Behenna, Patricia Tracy, William Valvo, and Robert Wilson. Judy Nissenbaum provided extensive transcribing and typing assistance.

We would like to add a special word of appreciation to our students, whose enthusiasm and insights helped us reach the initial decision to undertake this collection and guided us in the choice of materials. In particular we are grateful to Richard Henderson, Abbey Miller, and Catherine Leonard Hopkins, who played equally important roles in the initial conceptualization of this book and its subsequent preparation.

Finally we should acknowledge the birth of Daniel Andrew Nissenbaum during the last stages of our own labor. This is not the only place at which his given names will greet the careful reader of the book.

Paul Boyer
Stephen Nissenbaum

Amherst, Massachusetts
September 1971

A Note on Sources

This list includes the sources for the documents which appear in *Salem-Village Witchcraft*. The sources are arranged in the sequence in which the documents appear and are indicated by the following abbreviations:

Essex Co. Reg. Deeds: The Essex County Registry of Deeds, County Courthouse, Salem, Massachusetts.

Essex Co. Reg. Prob.: Essex County Registry of Probate, County Courthouse, Salem, Massachusetts.

Suffolk Co. Reg. Prob.: Suffolk County Registry of Probate, County Courthouse, Cambridge, Massachusetts.

Mass. Arch.: Massachusetts State Archives, Boston.

Essex Co. Ct. Rec.: Manuscript volumes of Essex County Court Records, County Courthouse, Salem.

EQC: *Records and Files of the Quarterly Courts of Essex County, Massachusetts.* (8 vols., Salem, 1911-21), published by the Essex Institute and covering the years 1636-83.

PR: *The Probate Records of Essex County, Massachusetts.* (3 vols., Salem, 1916-20), published by the Essex Institute and covering the years 1635-81.

The Trials (pp. 1-136)

The five trial records and the additional testimony are from a three-volume typescript of the surviving Salem-Village witchcraft documents prepared in 1938 by the Works Progress Administration and on file at the Essex Institute, Salem, Massachusetts.

Robert Calef, *More Wonders* . . . , and Deodat Lawson, "Brief and True Narrative," in George L. Burr, ed., *Narratives of the Witchcraft Cases, 1648-1706* (New York: Barnes and Noble, 1914).

"The Return of Several Ministers Consulted," in Cotton Mather, *The Wonders of the Invisible World* (London, 1862).

Cotton Mather to John Foster: *Transactions of the Literary and Historical Society of Quebec*, II (1831), 313-16, reprinted in Chadwick Hansen, *Witchcraft at Salem* (New York: George Braziller, 1969), pp. 183-86.

William Phips to the Earl of Nottingham, in David Levin, ed., *What Happened in Salem?* (New York: Harcourt Brace Jovanovich, 1959), pp. 92-94.

The 1711 "Restitution" document, in W. E. Woodward, *Records of Salem Witchcraft* (Roxbury, Mass., 1864), II, 220-21.

Deodat Lawson, "Christ's Fidelity . . . ," in Charles W. Upham, *Salem Witchcraft* (Boston, 1967; reprinted, New York: Frederick Ungar Publishing Company, 1966), II, 78-87.

Samuel Parris, "Christ Knows . . ." and "These Shall Make War . . ." in Parris's Sermon Book, manuscript volume in the Connecticut Historical Society, Hartford, Connecticut.

The Accused (pp. 137-179)

Sarah Good:
John Solart's Estate: *EQC*, V, 89-90, 124; VIII, 432-33; *PR*, II, 283-85.

Cromwell v. Good: Essex Co. Ct. Rec., XXXV, 70-71; Essex Co. Ct. Rec., "County Court, Ipswich, 1682-92," p. 51 (verdict).

William Good to Freeborn Balch: Essex Co. Reg. Deeds, VIII, 441.

Rebecca Nurse:
Christopher Waller to Francis Nurse: Essex Co. Reg. Deeds, II, 52.

James Allen to Francis Nurse: Essex Co. Reg. Deeds, IV, 189.

Estate of William Towne: *PR*, II, 358.

Francis Nurse to Samuel Nurse: Essex Co. Reg. Deeds, VIII, 151.

Francis Nurse's Will: Essex Co. Prob. Rec., Envelope 1968.

Bridget Bishop:	Brought to Court for Fighting: *EQC*, IV, 90.
	Brought to Court for Foul Language: *EQC*, VI, 386-87.
	Estate of Thomas Oliver: *PR*, III, 319.
	Witchcraft Case of 1679: *EQC*, VII, 329-30.
	Bridget Oliver to Daniel Epes: Essex Co. Reg. Deeds, VI, 57.
	Stacey v. *Bishop*: Essex Co. Ct. Rec., XXXXVII, 99-101.
John Willard:	Bray Wilkins to His Sons: Essex Co. Reg. Deeds, IX, 136.
	General Court Order of May 1681: Nathaniel B. Shurtleff, *Records of The Governor and Company of Massachusetts Bay*, V (Boston, 1854), p. 310.
	John Willard *et al.* to Zacheus and Ephraim Curtis: Essex Co. Reg. Deeds, IX, 5.
	Nashaway Town Action, 1692: *History of Lancaster, Massachusetts, 1643-1725.* p. 307.
	Will of Bray Wilkins: William C. Hill, *The Family of Bray Wilkins* (Milford, 1943), pp. 16-19.
	Administrators Appointed for John Willard's Estate: Essex Co. Reg. Prob., CCCXII, 51.
George Burroughs:	Jeremy Watts Case: *EQC*, VIII, 293-94.
	Salem Village v. *Burroughs*: Essex Co. Ct. Rec., XXXIX, 81-82.
	Putnam v. *Burroughs:* Essex Co. Ct. Rec., XXXIX, 104-5; Upham, *Salem Witchcraft*, I, 258-59.
	Burroughs to the General Court (1691): 37 Mass. Arch., p. 144.

The Accusers (pp. 181-225)

S. Parris:	Deposition: Charles W. Upham, *Salem Witchcraft*, I, 287-91.
	Three sermons: Parris's Sermon Book, manuscript volume in the Connecticut Historical Society, Hartford, Connecticut.
	Deeds: Essex Co. Reg. Deeds, IX, 71; IX, 70; X, 35; XI, 212; XII, 42; XIV, 210.
	Will and Estate Inventory: Suffolk Co. Reg. Prob., Docket No. 16951.
The Wilkinses:	*Bellingham* v. *Wilkins and Gingell: EQC*, III, 322-24.
The Putnams:	Thomas Putnam, Sr., Deeds: Essex Co. Reg. Deeds: I, 117; II, 12; III, 74; VII, 68; XXXIII, 174.

Estate of Thomas Putnam, Sr.: Eben Putnam, *History of the Putnam Family* (Salem, 1891).

Estate of Mary Putnam: Essex Co. Reg. Prob: Docket 23077.

Thomas Putnam, Jr., to Topsfield Men: Essex Co. Reg. Deeds, XXXIII, 174.

Estate of Thomas Putnam, Jr.: Essex Co. Prob. Rec.

The Community: Salem Village (pp. 227-372).

Petition (1667): 112 Mass. Arch., 175-77.

Salem Town Meeting Vote (1670): *EQC*, V, 272.

Salem Farmers Petition (1670): *EQC*, V, 273.

Testimony of John Putnam and Joseph Hutchinson: *EQC*, V, 274.

Salem Farmers Petition to General Court (1670): 10 Mass. Arch., 105.

Salem Town Meeting Vote (1672): Salem Village Book of Record.

Order of the General Court (1672): Salem Village Book of Record.

Topsfield Dispute Documents: *EQC*, VIII, 319-23; Nathaniel B. Shurtleff, *Records of the Governor and Company of Massachusetts Bay*, V, 415.

Salem Village v. *Salem Town*: 11 Mass. Arch. 57-60.

Bayley Dispute: 10 Mass. Arch. 140-50; *EQC*, VII, 248-49 (H. Kenney case); Putnam et al., Deed to Bayley: Essex Co. Reg. Deeds, VII, 79.

Parris Dispute:

Salem Village Petition to Court (1692): Salem Village Church Record.

Salem-Village Church Complaint to Court, and the Court's Response (1693): Essex Co. Ct. Rec., "General Sessions Record Volume, 7/92–3/95," pp. 28-30.

Petition to the Governor (1693): 11 Mass. Arch., 76.

Petition to the General Court, and Response (1695): 113 Mass. Arch., 103, 103a.

Pro- and Anti-Parris Petitions (1695): Salem-Village Church Record.

A Paper "Handed About": Charles W. Upham, *Salem Witchcraft*, II, 495.

Salem Village and Samuel Parris Counter-Suits (1697): Essex Co. Ct. Rec., "Court of Common Pleas, 1692-1719," XXVIII; Charles W. Upham, *Salem Witchcraft*, I, 295-96.

Petition of John Tarbell et al. to the Aribtrators (July 1697): Charles W. Upham, *Salem Witchcraft*, II, 497-98.

Vote of Salem-Village Inhabitants (September 1697): Salem-Village Book of Record.

Parris Deed to Salem Village: *Historical Collections of the Danvers Historical Society*, XVI (1928), p. 8.

Salem-Village Church Records, 1689-96: Manuscript volume in Samuel Parris's handwriting in the Library of the First Church of Danvers, Massachusetts.

Salem-Village Book of Record, 1672-97: Original in the Library of the First Church, Danvers, Massachusetts. The version printed in this book was drawn from the aforementioned source and from the *Historical Collections of the Danvers Historical Society*, XIII (1925); XIV (1926); and XVI (1928).

Danvers, Massachusetts, Act of Incorporation: J. W. Hanson, *History of the Town of Danvers From Its Earliest Settlement to the Year 1848* (Danvers, 1848), pp. 51-52.

Map of Salem Village in 1692 by W. P. Upham, in Charles W. Upham, *Salem Witchcraft*, Vol. I, following p. xvii.

Maps of Salem-Village Land Holdings in 1700 by Sidney Perley: *Essex Institute Historical Collections* (Salem, Mass.), April, July, and October 1915; April 1916; October 1917; April, July, and October 1918; and January 1919.

Contents

Part Four: The Community: Salem Village   227

Appendices

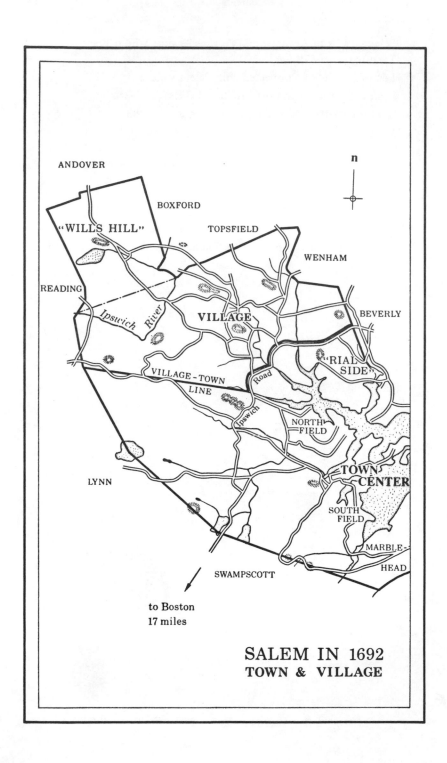

ANDOVER

BOXFORD

"WILLS HILL"

TOPSFIELD

WENHAM

READING

Ipswich River

VILLAGE

BEVERLY

"RIAL SIDE"

VILLAGE - TOWN LINE

Road

Ipswich

NORTH FIELD

LYNN

TOWN CENTER

SOUTH FIELD

MARBLE-HEAD

SWAMPSCOTT

to Boston
17 miles

n

SALEM IN 1692
TOWN & VILLAGE

Part One

The Trials: Records of Five Witchcraft Cases

In each of these five trials we have included all the relevant documents. There were, of course, a number of other persons accused and tried in 1692. We selected these five individuals for inclusion because each was a Salem Villager and because the documentation of these particular cases, as compared to some others, was quite extensive.

Chapter One

Sarah Good

Testimony of Ann Putnam, Junior

The deposition of Ann Putnam, Junior, who testifieth and saith that on the 25th of February, 1691/92, I saw the apparition of Sarah Good, which did torture me most grievously. But I did not know her name till the 27th of February, and then she told me her name was Sarah Good, and then she did prick me and pinch me most grievously, and also since, several times urging me vehemently to write in her book.

And also, on the first day of March, being the day of her examination, Sarah Good did most grievously torture me, and also several times since. And also, on the first day of March, 1692, I saw the apparition of Sarah Good go and afflict and torture the bodies of Elizabeth Parish [i.e., Parris], Abigail Williams, and Elizabeth Hubbard. Also I have seen the apparition of Sara Good afflicting the body of Sarah Vibber [i.e., Bibber].

mark

Ann ☾ Putnam

Ann Putnam owned this her testimony to be the truth on her oath, before the Jurors of Inquest this 28 of June, 1692.

And further says that she verily believes that Sarah Good doth bewitch and afflict her.

Testimony of Elizabeth Hubbard

The deposition of Elizabeth Hubbard, aged about 17 years, who testifieth and saith that on the 28 February, 1691/92, I saw the apparition of Sarah Good, who did most grievously afflict me by pinching and pricking me, and so she continued hurting of me till the first day of March, being the day of her examination. And then she did also most grievously afflict and torture me also during the time of her examination. Also several times since, she hath afflicted me and urged me to write in her book. Also on the day of her examination I saw the apparition of Sarah Good go and hurt and afflict the bodies of Elizabeth Parish, Abigail Williams, and Ann Putnam, junr., also I have seen the apparition of Sarah Good afflicting the body of Sarah Vibber.

mark
Elizabeth   ⅎ   Hubbard

Also in the night after Sarah Good's examination, Sarah Good came to me barefoot and barelegged, and did most grievously torment me by pricking and pinching me. And I verily believe that Sarah Good hath bewitched me. And also that night Samuell Sibly, that was then attending me, struck Sarah Good on her arm.

Warrant for Sarah Good's Arrest

Salem, February the 29th, 1691/92

Whereas Messrs. Joseph Hutchinson, Thomas Putnam, Edward Putnam, and Thomas Preston, yeoman of Salem Village in the County of Essex, personally appeared before us and made complaint on behalf of their Majesties against Sarah Good, the wife of William Good of Salem Village abovesaid, for suspicion of witchcraft by her committed, and thereby much injury done by Eliz. Paris, Abigail Williams, Anne Putnam, and Elizabeth Hubert, all of Salem Village aforesaid, sundry times within this two months and lately also done at Salem Village, contrary to the peace of our Sovereign Lord and Lady William and Mary, King and Queen of England, etc.—You are therefore in their Majesties' names hereby required to apprehend and bring before us the said Sarah Good tomorrow about ten of the clock in the forenoon at the house of Lt. Nathaniele Ingersall in Salem Village, or as soon as may be, then and there to be examined relating to the abovesaid premises, and hereof you are not to fail at your peril.

Dated Salem, February 29th 1691/92

John Hathorne   }   Assistants
Jonathan Corwin

To Constable George Locker

Return of the Constable

I brought the person of Sarah Good, the wife of William Good, according to the tenor of the within warrant, as is attest by me.

George Locker, Constable

1 March, 1691/92

Examination of Sarah Good as Recorded
by Ezekiel Cheever

The examination of Sarah Good before the worshipful Assistants John Hathorne [and] Jonathan Curran.

Q. Sarah Good, what evil spirit have you familiarity with?

A. None.

Q. Have you made no contract with the devil?

Good answered no.

Q. Why do you hurt these children?

A. I do not hurt them. I scorn it.

Q. Who do you employ, then, to do it?

A. I employ nobody.

Q. What creature do you employ then?

A. No creature. But I am falsely accused.

Q. Why did you go away muttering from Mr. Parris's house?

A. I did not mutter, but I thanked him for what he gave my child.

Q. Have you made no contract with the devil?

A. No.

H[athorne] desired the children, all of them, to look upon her and see if this were the person that had hurt them, and so they all did look upon her and said this was one of the persons that did torment them. Presently they were all tormented.

Q. Sarah Good, do you not see now what you have done? Why do you not tell us the truth? Why do you thus torment these poor children?

A. I do not torment them.

Q. Who do you employ then?

A. I employ nobody. I scorn it.

Q. How came they thus tormented?

A. What do I know? You bring others here and now you charge me with it.

Q. Why, who was it?

A. I do not know but it was some you brought into the meeting house with you.

Q. We brought you into the meeting house.

A. But you brought in two more.

Q. Who was it, then, that tormented the children?

A. It was Osborne.

Q. What is it you say when you go muttering from persons' houses?

A. If I must tell, I will tell.

Q. Do tell us then.

A. If I must tell, I will tell. It is the commandments. I may say my commandments, I hope.

Q. What commandment is it?

A. If I must tell you, I will tell. It is a psalm.

Q. What psalm?

After a long time, she muttered over some part of a psalm.

Q. Who do you serve?

A. I serve God.

Q. What God do you serve?

A. The God that made heaven and earth—though she was not willing to mention the word God. Her answers were in a very wicked, spiteful manner, reflecting and retorting against the authority with base and abusive words, and many lies she was taken in.

It was here said that her husband had said that he was afraid that she either was a witch or would be one very quickly. The worshipful Mr. Hathorne asked him his reason why he said so of her, whether he had ever seen anything by her. He answered no, not in this nature, but it was her bad carriage to him. And indeed, said he, I may say with tears that she is an enemy to all good.

Salem Village, March the 1st, 1691/92
Written by Ezekiel Cheever

Examination of Sarah Good as Abstracted by Joseph Putnam

What Sarah Good saith

1. With no one.
2. She saith that she did do them no harm.
3. She employed nobody to do the children [harm].
4. She saith that she hath made no contract or covenant.
5. She saith that she never did hurt the children.
6. She saith that she never had familiarity with the Devil.
7. She saith that she never saw the children in such a condition.

She saith that she came not to meeting for want of clothes.

Who is it she usually discourseth with? Nobody: but it is a psalm or a commandment: her God is the God that made heaven and earth, she hopes: she saith that she never did no harm to Mr. Parris.

She saith it was not she, it is grandma Osborne that doth pinch and afflict the children.

William Good saith that she is an enemy to all good. She saith she is clear of being a witch.

[There follow two similar summaries of the examinations of "grandma" Osborne and the "Indian woman" Tituba, which were held the same day.]

Written by Jos. Putnam

Salem Village
March the 1st, 1691/92

Examination of Sarah Good as Summarized
by John Hathorne and Jonathan Corwin

Salem Village, March the 1st, 1691/92

Sarah Good, the wife of Wm. Good of Salem Village, labourer, brought before us by George Locker, Constable in Salem, to answer Joseph Hutcheson, Thomas Putnam, &c., of Salem Village, yeomen (complainants on behalf of their Majesties against said Sarah Good for suspicion of witchcraft by her committed and thereby much injury done to the bodies of Elizabeth Parris, Abigaile Williams, Anna Putnam, and Elizabeth Hubert, all of Salem Village aforesaid), according to their complaints as per warrants.

Dated Salem March 29th, 1691/92

Sarah Good, upon examination, denieth the matter of fact, *viz.*, that she ever used any witchcraft or hurt the abovesaid children, or any of them.

The abovenamed children, being all present, positively accused her of hurting of them sundry times within this two months, and also that morning.

Sarah Good denied that she had been at their houses in said time, or near them, or had done them any hurt. All the abovesaid children then present accused her face to face upon which they were all dreadfully tortured and tormented for a short space of time, and the affliction and tortures being over, they charged said Sarah Good again that she had then so tortured them, and came to them and did it, although she was personally then kept at a considerable distance from them.

Sarah Good, being asked if that she did not then hurt them, who did it, and the children being again tortured, she looked upon them, and said that it was one of them we brought into the house with us. We asked her who it was. She then answered and said it was Sarah Osburne; and Sarah Osburne was then under custody and not in the house. And the children, being quickly after recovered out of their fit, said that it was Sarah Good and also Sarah Osburne that then did hurt and torment or afflict them—although both of them at the same time at a distance or remote from them personally.

There were also sundry other questions put to her, and answers given thereunto by her, according as is also given in.

[John Hathorne, Jonathan Corwin]

Abstract of Tituba's Confession and Examination

Charges Sarah Good to hurt the children and would have had her do it. Five were with her last night, and would have had her hurt the children, which she refused, and that Good was one of them.

Good with others are very strong and pull her with them to Mr. Putnam's and made her hurt the child. Good there rode with her upon a pole behind her, taking hold of one another. Doth not know how they go, for she never sees trees nor path, but are presently th[ere].

Good there tell her she must kill somebody with a knife, and would have had her kill Tho: Putnam's child last night. The child at the same time affirmed she would have had her cut off her own head; if not, Titabe would do it. And complained of a knife cutting her.

Good came to her last night when her Mr. [master, i.e., Samuel Parris] was at prayer, and would not let her hear. Hath one yellow bird, and stopped her ears in prayer time. The yellow bird hath been seen by the children, and Titabee saw it suck Good between the forefinger and long finger on the right hand.

Saw Good there practice witchcraft.

Saw Good have a cat besides the bird and a thing all over hairy there.

Sarah Good appeared like a wolf to Hubbard going to Proctors, and saw it sent by Good to Hubbard.

Good there hurt the children again, and the children affirmed the same. Hubbard knew them not, being blinded by them, and was once or twice taken dumb herself.

Good caused her to pinch the children, all in their own persons.

Saw Good's name in the book, and the devil told her they made these marks, and said to her, she made this mark, and it was the same day she went to prison.

Good there came to ride abroad with her, and the man showed Good's mark in the book.

Good there pinched her on the legs, and being searched, found it so after confession.

Testimony of Abigail Williams

The testimony of Abigail Williams, testifieth and saith that several times last February she hath been much afflicted with pains in her head and other parts, and often pinched by the apparition of Sarah Good, Sarah Osburne, and Tituba Indian, all of Salem Village, and also excessively afflicted by the said apparition of Good, Osburne, and Tituba at their examination before authority the 1st of March last past, 1691/92.

Further, the said Abigail Williams testifieth that she saw the apparition of Sarah Good at her examination pinch Eliz. Hubbard and set her into fits, and also Eliz. Parris, and Ann Putman.

The mark of
Abigail   A. W.   Williams

Testified before us by Abigaile Williams. Salem, May the 23d, 1692

John Hathorne
Jonathan Corwin
per order of the Governor and Council

Abstract of Testimony (?) of Dorothy Good

Dorathy Good's charge against her mother, Sarah Good: That she had three birds, one black, one yellow, and that these birds hurt the children and afflicted persons.

Testimony of Joseph and Mary Herrick

The deposition of Joseph Herrick, senior, who testifieth and saith that on the first day of March, 1691/92, I being the Constable for Salem, there was delivered to me by warrant from the worshiful Jno. Hathorne and Jonathan Corwin, Esqrs., Sarah Good, for me to carry to their majesties's jail at Ipswich. And that night, I set a guard to watch her at my own house, namely Samuel Braybrook, Michaell Dunell, [and] Jonathan Baker. And the aforenamed persons informed me in the morning that that night Sarah Good was gone for some time from them, both barefooted and barelegged. And I was also informed that that night Elizabeth Hubbard, one of the afflicted persons, complained that Sarah Good came and afflicted her, being barefoot and barelegged. And Samuell Sibley, that was one that was attending of Eliza Hubbard, struck Sarah Good on the arm, as Elizabeth Hubbard said.

And Mary Herrick, the wife of the abovesaid Joseph Herrick, testifieth that on the 2nd March, 1691/92, in the morning, I took notice of Sarah Good in the morning, and one of her arms was bloody from a little below the elbow to the wrist. And I also took notice of her arms on the night before, and then there was no sign of blood on them.

Joseph Herrick, senior, and Mary Herrick appeared before us, the Jury for Inquest, and did on the oath which she had taken, own this their evidence to be the truth, this 28 of June, 1692.

Testimony of William Allen, John Hughes, William Good, and Samuel Braybrook

March 5th, 1691/92

Wm. Allin saith that on the 1st of March, at night, he heard a strange noise not usually heard, and so continued for many times, so that he was affrighted. And coming nearer to it, he there saw a strange and unusual beast lying on the ground so that going up to it, the said beast vanished away. And in the said place starte[d] up 2 or 3 women, and fled from me, not after the manner of other women, but swiftly vanished away out of our sight. Which women we took to be Sarah Good, Sarah Osburne, and Tittabe. The time was about an hour within night.

And I, John Hughes, saith the same, being in company then with said Allen, as witness our hands.

William Allen
John Hughes

William Allen further saith that on the 2nd day of March, the said Sarah Good visibly appeared to him in his chamber, said Allen being in bed, and brought an unusual light in with her. The said Sarah came and sat upon his foot. The said Allen went to kick at her, upon which she vanished and the light with her.

William Good saith that the night before his said wife was examined he saw a wart or tit a little below her right shoulder, which he never saw before, and asked Goodwife Engersol whether she did not see it when she searched her.

John Hughes further saith, that on the 2nd day of March that coming from Goodman Sibley's about eight of the clock in the night he saw a great white dog whom he came up to, but he would not stir. But when he was passed he, the said dog, followed him about 4 or 5 pole,* and so disappeared.

The same night, the said John Hughes being in bed in a closed room, and the door being fast so that no cat nor dog could come in, the said John saw a great light appear in the said chamber. And rising up in his bed he saw a large gray cat at his bed's foot.

March the 2nd. Saml. Braybrook saith, that carrying Sarah Good to Ipswich, the said Sarah leapt off her horse 3 times, which was between 12 and 3 of the clock of the same day which the daughter of Thomas Puttman declared the same at her father's house. The said Brabrook further saith that said Sarah Good told him that she would not own herself to be a witch unless she is proved one. She saith that there is but one evidence, and that an Indian, and therefore she fears not. And so continued railing against the magistrates, and she endeavored to kill herself.

Warrant for the Arrest of Dorcas Good

To the Marshall of Essex or his Deputy

You are in their Majesties' names hereby required to bring before us Dorcas Good, the daughter of William Good of Salem Village, tomorrow morning upon suspicion of acts of witchcraft by her committed, according to complaints made against her by Edward Putnam and Jonathan Putnam of Salem Village, and hereof fail not.

Dated Salem, March 23rd, 1691/92

p. us.   John Hathorne   } Assistants
                 Jonathan Corwin

*[A pole is a unit of linear measurement equal to 16½ feet.]

March 23rd, 1691/92. I do appoint Mr. Sam[ll]. Brabrook to be my lawful Deputy to serve this summons and to make a true return.

per George Herrick, Marshall of Essex

Indictment of Sarah Good

Anno: Regis et Reginee William et Mariae nunc Anglice ec. Quarto

Essex Ss. [Sessions]

The Jurors for our Sovereign Lord and Lady the King and Queen, present, that Sarah Good, the wife of William Good of Salem Village in the County of Essex, husbandman, the second day of May in the fourth year of the reign of our Sovereign Lord and Lady William and Mary, by the Grace of God of England, Scotland, France and Ireland, King and Queen, Defenders of the Faith, &c., and divers other days and times as well, before and after, certain detestable arts called witchcrafts and sorceries, wickedly and feloniously hath used, practiced, and exercized, at and within the township of Salem in the County of Essex aforesaid, in, upon, and against one Sarah Vibber, wife of John Vibber of Salem aforesaid, husbandman, by which said wicked arts she, the said Sarah Vibber, the said second day of May in the fourth year abovesaid and divers other days and times as well, before as after, was and is tortured, afflicted, pined, consumed, wasted and tormented, and also for sundry other acts of witchcraft by said Sarah Good committed and done before and since that time against the peace of our Sovereign Lord and Lady the King and Queen, their Crown and dignity, and against the form of the statute in that case made and provided.

Witnesses
Sarah Vibbers, Jurat
Abigail Williams, Jurat
Elizabeth Hubbard, Jurat
Ann Putnam, Jurat
Jno. Vibber, Sworne.

[Two additional indictments against Sarah Good, similar in form, name, respectively, Elizabeth Hubbard and Ann Putnam as the victim. The second indictment is dated June 28, 1692.]

Testimony of Sarah Bibber

The deposition of Sarah Vib[b]er, aged about 36 years, who testifieth and saith that since I have been afflicted I have often seen the apparition of Sarah

Good, but she did not hurt me till the 2 day of May, 1692, though I saw her apparition most grievously torture Mercy Lewis and Jno Indian at Salem on the 11th of April, 1692. But on the 2 May, 1692, the apparition of Sarah Good did most grievously torment me by pressing my breath almost out of my body, and also she did immediately afflict my child by pinching of it, that I could hardly hold it. And my husband, seeing of it, took hold of the child, but it cried out and twisted so dreadfully, by reason of the torture, that the apparition of Sarah Good did afflict it withal, that it got out of its father's arms, too. Also, several times since, the apparition of Sarah Good has most grievously tormented me by beating and pinching me and almost choking me to death, and pricking me with pins after a most dreadful manner.

Sarah Viber owned this her testimony to be the truth on the oath she had taken, before us, the Jurors for Inquest, this 28 day of June, 1692.

And further adds that she verily believes, upon her oath, that Sarah Good had bewitched her.

Testimony of Sarah Bibber

The deposition of Sarah Viber, aged 36 years, testifieth and saith that the Saturday night before Goody Dustin of Reading was examined, I saw the apparition of Sarah Good standing by my bedside, and she pulled aside the curtain and turned down the sheet and looked upon my child 4 years old, and presently, upon it, the child was struck into a great fit that my husband and I could hardly hold it.

Sarah Viber on her oath did own this her testimony before the jurors for inquest, this 28 of June, 1692.

Jurat, Sarah Viber

Testimony of Mary Walcott

The deposition of Mary Wolcott, aged about 17 years, who testifieth and saith that since I have been afflicted I have often seen the apparition of Sarah Good amongst the witches, who has also afflicted me and urged me to write in her book.

The mark of
Mary Walcot
m w

Mary Welcott owned this her testimony to be the truth on her oath before the Jurors for Inquest, this 28 of June, 1692.

Also, Mary Walcott testifieth that I have seen Sarah Good afflicting Mercy Lewes and Elizabeth Hubberd and Abigail Williams, and I verily believe she bewitched me.

Sarah Good and Tituba Committed
to Boston Jail

To the Keeper of their Majesties' Jail in Boston

You are, in their Majesties' names, hereby required to take into your care and safe custody the bodies of Sarah Good, the wife of William Good of Salem Farms, husbandman, and Tituba, an Indian woman belonging unto Samuel Parris of Salem Village, minister, who stand charged on behalf of their Majesties for their feloniously committing sundry acts of witchcraft at Salem Village on the bodies of Elizabeth Parris, Eliz. Hubbert, Abigail Williams, and Ann Putnam of Salem Village, whereby great hurt hath been done to their body contrary to the peace of our Sovereign Lord and Lady William and Mary of England &c, King and Queen.

Whom you are well to secure until they shall thence be delivered by due order of law, and hereof you are not to fail.

Dated Boston, May the 25th, 1692.

per us   John Hathorne   }   Assistants
                           Jonathan Corwin

Testimony of Johanna Childen

The deposition of Johanna Childen, testifieth and saith that upon 2nd of June, 1692, that the apparition of Sarah Good and her least child did appear to her, and the child did tell its mother that she did murder it, to which Sarah Good replied that she did it because that she could not attend it. And the child told its mother that she was a witch, and then Sarah Good said she did give it to the devil.

Testimony of Susannah Sheldon

The deposition of Susannah Sheldon, aged about 18 years, who testifieth and saith that since I have been afflicted I have very often been most grievously tortured by [the] apparition of Sarah Good, who has most dreadfully afflicted me by biting, pricking, and pinching me, and almost choking me to death. But on the 26 June, 1692, Sarah Good most violently pulled down my head behind a chest and tied my hands together with a whale band, and almost choked me to death. And, also, several times since, the apparition of Sarah Good has most grievously tortured me by biting, pinching, and almost choking me to death. Also, William Battin and Thomas Buffington, junior, were forced to cut the whale band from off my hands, for they could not untie it.

And farther, said Shelden, upon giving in this testimony to the grand jury, was seized with sundry fits which, when she came to herself, she told the said jury, being asked, that it was the said Good that afflicted her. And a little after, Mary Warren falling into a fit, said Sheldon affirmed to the Grand jury that she saw said Good upon her. And also, a saucer being by invisible hands taken off from a table and carried out of doors, said Sheldon affirmed she saw said Sarah Good carry it away and put it where it was found abroad.

Susannah Sheldon owned this her testimony to be the truth before the Jurors of Inquest on the oath which she had taken this 28 of June, 1692.

Testimony of William Batten, William Shaw, and Deborah Shaw

The testimony of William Batten, aged 76 years or thereabouts, and William Shaw, aged about 50 years, and Deborah his wife, aged about 40 years. These all testify and say that this day was a week ago, Susannah Shelding being at the house of William Shaw, she was tied her hands across in such a manner we were forced to cut the string before we could get her hand loose. And when she was out of her fit she told us it was Goody Dustin that did tie her hands after that manner. And 4 times she hath been tied in this manner in two weeks time. The 2 first times she saith it was Goody Dustin, and the 2 last times it was Sarah Goode that did tie her. We further testify that whenever she doth but touch this string she is presently bit.

We further testify that in this time there was a broom carried away out of the house invisible to us and put in a apple tree two times, and a shirt once, and a milk tub once was carried out of the house three poles from the house into the woods, and she saith that it [words missing].

This persons abovenamed upon their oath owned this their testimony to be the truth before us, Jurors for Inquest, this 28 of June, 1692.

Testimony of Samuel and Mary Abbey

Samuel Abbey of Salem Village, aged 45 years or thereabouts, and Mary Abbey, his wife, aged 38 years or thereabouts, deposeth and saith that about this time three years past, Wm. Good and his wife Sarah Good being destitute of an house to dwell in, these deponents out of charity, they being poor, let them live in theirs some time, until that the said Sarah Good was of so turbulent a spirit, spiteful, and so maliciously bent, that these deponents could not suffer her to live in their house any longer, and was forced for quietness' sake to turn she, the said Sarah, with her husband, out of their house ever since, which is about two and one-half years ago.

The said Sarah Good hath carried it very spitefully and maliciously towards them. The winter following after the said Sarah was gone from our house, we began to lose cattle, and lost several after an unusual manner, in a drooping condition, and yet they would eat. And your deponents have lost after that manner 17 head of cattle within this two years, besides sheep and hogs, and both do believe they died by witchcraft.

The said William Good, on the last of May was twelve months, went home to his wife, the said Sarah Good, and told her what a sad accident had fallen out. She asked what. He answered that his neighbor Abbey had lost two cows, both dying within half an hour of one another. The said Sarah Good said she did not care if he, the said Abbey, had lost all the cattle he had, as the said Jno. [*sic.*] Good told us.

Just that very day that the said Sarah Good was taken up [i.e., arrested] , we, your deponents, had a cow that could not rise alone. But since, presently after she was taken up, the said cow was well and could rise so well as if she had ailed nothing.

She, the said Sarah Good, ever since these deponents turned her out of their house, she hath behaved herself very crossly and maliciously to them and their children, calling their children vile names and hath threatened them often.

Testimony of Thomas and Sarah Gadge

The deposition of Sarah Gadge, the wife of Thomas Gadge, aged about 40 years. This deponent testifieth and saith that about two years and a half ago, Sarah Good came to her house and would have come into the house, but said Sarah Gadge told her she should not come in, for she was afraid she had been with them that had the smallpox. And with that she fell to muttering and scolding extremely, and she told said Gadge if she would not let her in, she should give her something. And she answered she would not have anything to do with her; and the next morning after, to said deponent's best remembrance, one of said Gadge's cows died in a sudden, terrible, and strange unusual manner, so that some of the neighbors, and said deponent, did think it to be done by witchcraft, and further saith not.

And Thomas Gadge, husband of said Sarah, testifieth that he had a cow so died about the time abovementioned, and though he and some neighbors opened the cow, yet they could find no natural cause of said cow's death, and further saith not.

Thomas Gadge and Sarah Gadge owned this to be the truth on their oath before us, the Jurors for Inquest, this 28 of June, '92.

Testimony of Henry Herrick and Jonathan Batchelder

The deposition of Henery Herrick, aged about 21 years, this deponent testifieth and saith that in last March was two year, Sarah Good came to his father's house and desired to lodge there, and his father forbid it and she went away grumbling. And my father bid us follow her and see that she went away clear, lest she should lie in the barn and by smoking of her pipe should fire the barn. And said deponent with Jonathan Batchelor, seeing her make a stop near the barn, bid her be gone, or we would set her further off. To which she replied that then it should cost his father (Zechariah Herick) one or two of the best cows which he had.

And Jonathan Batchelor, aged 14 year, testifieth the same above written, and doth further testify that about a week after, two of his grandfather's master cattle were removed from their places and other, younger, cattle put in their rooms. And since that, several of their cattle have been set loose in a strange manner.

Samuel Rea Posts Bail for Dorcas Good

Memorandum

That on the tenth day of December 1692, Samuel Ray of Salem appeared before me underwritten, one of the Council for Their Majesties' Province of the Massachusetts Bay in New England and acknowledged himself indebted unto Our Sovereign Lord and Lady, the King and Queen, the sum of fifty pounds current money of New England, on the condition hereafter named:

vidt., that [Dorcas] Good, daughter of [William] Good of Salem, laborer, being imprisoned on suspicion of her being guilty of the crime of witchcraft and being now let to bail, that if the said [Dorcas] Good shall appear at the next assize and general jail delivery to be holden at Salem and abide the court's judgment, then the above recognisance to be void, else to remain in force and virtue.

Petition of William Good (September 1710)

To the Honourable Committee:

The humble representation of William Good of the damage sustained by him in the year 1692 by reason of the sufferings of his family upon the account of supposed witchcraft.

1. My wife, Sarah Good, was in prison about four months and then executed.
2. A sucking child died in prison before the mother's execution.
3. A child of 4 or 5 years old was in prison 7 or 8 months and, being chained in the dungeon, was so hardly used and terrified that she hath ever since been very chargeable, having little or no reason to govern herself.

And I leave it unto the Honourable Court to judge what damage I have sustained by such a destruction of my poor family.

And so rest

Your Honours' humble servant

William Good

Salem, Sept. 13, 1710

Request of William Good (1711 or 1712)

To the Committee appointed by the Governor and Council for the distribution of the money allowed by the General Court to the sufferers in the year 1692.

Please to pay my part and proportion allowed me by the said court unto Deacon Benjamin Putnam, who I have desired to pay my part of the necessary charge. And his receipt shall be your full discharge.

From your servant,

Wm. Good   X   his mark

Chapter Two

Rebecca Nurse

Testimony of Ann Putnam, Junior

The deposition of Ann Putnam, junior, who testifieth and saith that on the 13th March, 1691/92, I saw the apparition of Goody Nurse, and she did immediately afflict me, but I did not know what her name was then, though I knew where she used to sit in our meetinghouse. But since that, she hath grievously afflicted by biting, pinching, and pricking me, [and] urging me to write in her book. And, also, on the 24th of March, being the day of her examination, I was grievously tortured by her during the time for her examination, and also several times since. And, also, during the time of her examination, I saw the apparition of Rebekah Nurs go and hurt the bodies of Mercy Lewis, Mary Wolcott, Elizabeth Hubbard, and Abigail Williams.

Ann Putnam, Junr, did own the oath which she hath taken: this her evidence to be truth, before us, the Jurors for Inquest, this 4 day of June, 1692.

Testimony of Ann Putnam, Senior, and Ann Putnam, Junior

The deposition of Ann Putnam, the wife of Thomas Putnam, aged about 30 years, who testifieth and saith that on the 18th March 1692, I being wearied out in helping to tend my poor afflicted child and maid, about the middle of the afternoon I lay me down on the bed to take a little rest; and immediately I was almost pressed and choked to death, that, had it not been for the mercy of a gracious God and the help of those that were with me, I could not have lived many moments; and presently I saw the apparition of Martha Corey, who did torture me so as I cannot express, ready to tear me all to pieces, and then departed from me a little while; but before I could recover strength or well take breath, the apparition of Martha Corey fell upon me again with dreadful tortures, and hellish temptations to go along with her. And she also brought to me a little red book in her hand and a black pen, urging me vehemently to write in her book; and several times that day she did most grievously torture me, almost ready to kill me.

And on the 19th March, Martha Corey again appeared to me; and also Rebecca Nurse, the wife of Francis Nurse, Sr.; and they both did torture me a great many times this day with such tortures as no tongue can express, because I would not yield to their hellish temptations, that, had I not been upheld by an Almighty arm, I could not have lived [the] night. The 20th March being sabbath-day, I had a great deal of respite between my fits. 21st March being the day of the examination of Martha Corey I had not many fits, though I was very weak, my strength being, as I thought, almost gone.

But on the 22nd March, 1692, the apparition of Rebecca Nurse did again set upon me in a most dreadful manner, very early in the morning, as soon as it was well light. And now she appeared to me only in her shift, and brought a little red book in her hand, urging me vehemently to write in her book; and because I would not yield to her hellish temptations, she threatened to tear my soul out of my body, blasphemously denying the blessed God and the power of the Lord Jesus Christ to save my soul, and denying several places of Scripture which I told her of, to repel her hellish temptations. And for near two hours together, at this time, the apparition of Rebecca Nurse did tempt and torture me, and also the greater part of this day with but very little respite. 23d March, am again afflicted by the apparitions of Rebecca Nurse and Martha Corey, but chiefly by Rebecca Nurse. 24th March being the day of the examination of Rebecca Nurse, I was several times in the morning afflicted by the apparition of Rebecca Nurse, but most dreadfully tortured by her in the time of her examination, insomuch that the honored magistrates gave my husband leave to carry me out of the meetinghouse; and as soon as I was carried out of the meetinghouse doors, it pleased Almighty God, for his free grace and mercy's sake, to deliver me out of the paws of those roaring lions, and jaws of those tearing bears [so] that ever since that time they have not had power so to afflict me, until this 31st May 1692. At the same moment that I was hearing my evidence read by the honored magistrates, to take my oath, I was again re-assaulted and tortured by my before-mentioned tormentor, Rebecca Nurse.

> Sworn Salem Villiage, May the 31st, 1692
> Before us   John Hathorne   } Assistants
>   Jonathan Corwin }

Ann Putnam, Senior, appeared before us, the Jurors of Inquest, and owned this her evidence this 3rd day of June, 1692.

The testimony of Ann Putnam, Jr., witnesseth and saith that being in the room when her mother was afflicted, she saw Martha Corey, Sarah Cloyse and Rebecca Nurse, or their apparition, upon her mother.

> Testified to the truth thereof by
> Ann Putnam, Salem, May 31st, 1692
> Before us   John Hathorne   ⎫
>   Jonathan Corwin ⎬ Assistants

Testimony of Mary Walcott

The deposition of Mary Walcott, aged about 17 years, who testifieth and saith, that on the 20th March, 1691/92, I saw the apparition of Rebekah Nurs, the wife of Frances Nurs, senr., but she did not hurt me till the 24 March, being the day of her examination. But then the apparition of Rebekah Nurs did most grievously torment me during the time of her examination. And also several times since she hath most grievously afflicted me by biting, pinching, and almost choking me, urging me vehemently to write in her book or else she would kill me. And on the 3d of May, in the evening, the apparition of Rebekah Nurse told me she had a hand in the deaths of Benjamin Holton, John Harrod, Rebekah Sheppard, and several others. And also at the time of her examination I saw the apparition of Rebekah Nurs go and hurt the bodies of Ann Putnam, Mircy Lewes, Elizabeth Hubbard, and Abigail Williams.

Mary Wowlcot, on the oath which she hath taken, did own this her testimony to be truth, before us, the Jurors of Inquest, this 3d of June, 1692.

Testimony of Elizabeth Hubbard

The deposition of Elizabeth Hubburd, aged about 17 years, who testifieth and saith that about the 20th March, 1692, I saw the apparition of Rebekah Nurs, the wife of Francis Nurs, senr, though she did not hurt me till the 24th March, being the day of her examination, and then she did hurt me most grievously during the time of her examination, for if she did but look upon me she would strike me down or almost choke me. And also several times since, the apparition of Rebekah Nurs has most grievously afflicted me by pinching, pricking, and almost choking, and urging me to write in her book. And also on the day of her examination I saw the apparition of Rebekah Nurs go and hurt the bodies of Ann Putnam, senr and Mary Walcott and Abigail Williams and Ann Putnam Junr.

Elizabeth Hubbard, upon her oath she had taken, did own this testimony before us, the Jurors of Inquest, this 3rd of June, 1692.

Testimony of Abigail Williams

[This deposition has been torn. Probable missing words have been inserted in brackets.]

The testimony of Abigail Williams witnesseth and saith that divers times in [the month] of March last past, particularly on the 15, 16, 19, 20, 21, 23, 31 days of that m[onth and] in the month of April following, at several times, particularly on the 13 and 1 [days of] that month, and also in this present month of May, the 4th and 29 days, she [the said] Abigail, has been exceedingly perplexed with the apparition of Rebek[a Nurse of] Salem Village, by which apparition she hath been pulled violently [and] often pinched and almost choked and tempted, sometimes to leap into the [fire and] sometimes to subscribe a book the said apparition brought. And als[o she saith] that she hath seen this apparition at a sacrament, sitting next to [a man?] with an high crowned hat, at the upper end of the table. And f[arther saith that] said apparition hath sometimes confessed to her, the said Abigail, its gu[ilt in] committing several murders, together with her sister Cloyse, as upon old Goodman Hanvood, Benj[n] Porter and Rebek: Shepard and saith Shepard's [words missing] .

May 31st, 1692, attested before [words missing] .

Abigail Williams did own this her testimony, [on the] oath which she had taken, to be the truth, before us [the] Jurors of Inquest, this 3 day of June, '92.

Testimony of Israel and Elizabeth Porter, Daniel Andrew, and Peter Cloyse

We whose names are underwritten, being desired to go to Goodman Nurse's house to speak with his wife and to tell her that several of the afflicted persons mentioned her; and accordingly we went, and we found her in a weak and low condition in body as she told us, and had been sick almost a week.

And we asked her how it was, otherwise, with her. And she said she blessed God for it, she had more of his presence in this sickness than sometime she have had, but not so much as she desired. But she would, with the apostle, press forward to the mark, and many other places of Scripture to the like purpose.

And then, of her own accord, she began to speak of the affliction that was amongst them, and in particular of Mr. Parris's family, and how she was grieved for them, though she had not been to see them by reason of fits that she formerly used to have, for people said it was awful to behold. But she pitied them with all her heart, and went to God for them. But she said she heard that there was persons spoke of that were as innocent as she was, she believed.

And after much to this purpose, we told her we heard that she was spoken of also. Well, she said, if it be so, the will of the Lord be done. She sat still a while, being as it were amazed, and then she said, Well, as to this thing, I am as innocent as the child unborn. But surely, she said, what sin hath God found out in me unrepented of, that he should lay such an affliction upon me in my old age? And, according to our best observation, we could not discern that she knew what we come for before we told her.

Israel Porter
Elizabeth Porter

To the substance of what is above we, if called thereto, are ready to testify on oath.

Daniel Andrew
Peter Cloyse

Warrant for Arrest of Rebecca Nurse

To the Marshall of Essex, or his deputy.

There being complaint this day made before us by Edward Putnam and Jonathan Putnam, yeomen, both of Salem Village, against Rebecca Nurse, the wife of Frances Nurce of Salem Village, for vehement suspicion of having committed sundry acts of witchcraft and thereby having done much hurt and injury to the bodies of Ann Putnam, the wife of Thomas Putnam of Salem Village, and Ann Putnam, the daughter of said Thomas Putnam, and Abigail Williams, &c.

You are therefore in their Majesties' names hereby required to apprehend and bring before us Rebecca Nurce, the wife of ffron^c Nurce of Salem Village, tomorrow about eight of the clock in the aforenoon, at the house of Lieut. Nathaniell Ingersoll in Salem Village in order to her examination relating to the abovesaid premises, and hereof you are not to fail. Salem, March the 23d 1691/92.

John Hathorne   } Assistants
Jonathan Corwin

Return of the Marshall

March 24th, 1691/92. I have apprehended the body of Rebecca Nurse and brought her to the house of Lieut. Nath: Ingersal where she is in custody.

per George Herrick, Marshall of Essex

[Reverse] In the meeting house Mary Walkott, Marcy Lewis, Eliz. Hubberd. All these accused Goody Nurce, then, to her face that she then hurt them &c. and they saw, besides the others on contra side.

Examination of Rebecca Nurse

The examination of Rebeckah Nurse at Salen Village, 24 Mar., 1691/92.

Mr. Harthorn. What do you say (speaking to one afflicted), have you seen this woman hurt you?

Yes, she beat me this morning.

Abigail, have you been hurt by this woman?

Yes.

Ann Putnam, in a grievous fit, cried out that she hurt her.

Goody Nurse, here are two—Ann Putnam the child and Abigail Williams— complains of your hurting them. What do you say to it?

N. I can say before my Eternal Father, I am innocent, and God will clear my innocency.

Here is never a one in the assembly but desires it. But if you be guilty, pray God discover you.

Then Hen: Kenney rose up to speak.

Goodman Kenney, what do you say?

Then he entered his complaint and farther said that since this Nurse came into the house he was seized twice with an amazed condition.

Here are not only these, but here is the wife of Mr. Tho Putnam who accuseth you by creditable information, and that both of tempting her to iniquity and of greatly hurting her.

N. I am innocent and clear, and have not been able to get out of doors these 8 or 9 days.

Mr. Putman, give in what you have to say.

Then Mr. Edward Putnam gave in his relate.

Is this true, Goody Nurse?

I never afflicted no child, never in my life.

You see these accuse you. Is it true?

No.

Are you an innocent person, relating to this witchcraft?

Here Tho: Putnam's wife cried out: Did you not bring the Black man with you? Did you not bid me tempt God and die? How oft have you eat and drunk your own damnation? What do you say to them?

Oh Lord, help me, and spread out her hands, and the afflicted were grievously vexed.

Do you see what a solemn condition these are in? When your hands are loose, the persons are afflicted.

Then Mary Walcott (who often heretofore said she had seen her, but never could say, or did say, that she either bit or pinched her, or hurt her) and also

Elis. Hubbard, under the like circumstances, both openly accused her of hurting them.

Here are these 2 grown persons now accuse you. What say you? Do not you see these afflicted persons, and hear them accuse you?

The Lord knows. I have not hurt them. I am an innocent person.

It is very awful for all to see these agonies, and you, an old professor, thus charged with contracting with the devil by the effects of it, and yet to see you stand with dry eyes when there are so many wet.

You do not know my heart.

You would do well, if you are guilty, to confess. Give Glory to God.

I am as clear as the child unborn.

What uncertainty there may be in apparitions I know not, yet this with me strikes hard upon you, that you are, at this very present, charged with familiar spirits. This is your bodily person they speak to. They say now they see these familiar spirits come to your bodily person. Now what do you say to that?

I have none, sir.

If you have confessed, and give Glory to God, I pray God clear you, if you be innocent. And if you be guilty, discover you. And therefore give me an upright answer: have you any familiarity with these spirits?

No. I have none but with God alone.

How came you sick, for there is an odd discourse of that in the mouths of many.

I am sick at my stomach.

Have you no wounds?

I have not but old age.

You do know whether you are guilty, and have familiarity with the devil, and now when you are here present, to see such a thing as these testify: a black man whispering in your ear and birds about you. What do you say to it?

It is all false. I am clear.

Possibly you may apprehend you are no witch, but have you not been led aside by temptations that way?

I have not.

What a sad thing it is that a church member here, and now another of Salem, should be thus accused and charged.

Mrs. Pope fell into a grievous fit and cried out: a sad thing sure enough. And then many more fell into lamentable fits.

Tell us, have you had visible appearances more than what is common in nature?

I have none, nor never had in my life.

Do you think these suffer voluntary or involuntary?

I cannot tell.

That is strange: everyone can judge.

I must be silent.

They accuse you of hurting them, and if you think it is not unwilling but by design, you must look upon them as murderers.

I cannot tell what to think of it.   Afterwards, when this was somewhat insisted on, she said: I do not think so. She did not understand aright what was said.

Well then, give an answer now, do you think these suffer against their wills or not?

I do not think these suffer against their wills.

Why did you never visit these afflicted persons?

Because I was afraid I should have fits, too.

Note: Upon the motion of her body, fits followed upon the complainants, abundantly and very frequently.

Is it not an unaccountable case that when you are examined these persons are afflicted?

I have got nobody to look to but God.

Again, upon stirring her hands, the afflicted persons were seized with violent fits of torture.

Do you believe these afflicted persons are bewitched?

I do think they are.

When this witchcraft came upon the stage, there was no suspicion of Tituba (Mr. Parris's Indian woman). She professed much love to that child, Betty Parris. But it was her apparition did the mischief, and why should not you also be guilty, for your apparition doth hurt also?

Would you have me belie myself?

She held her neck on one side, and accordingly so were the afflicted taken.

Then, authority requiring it, Sam: Parris read what he had in characters taken from Mr. Tho: Putman's wife in her fits.

What do you think of this?

I cannot help it, the Devil may appear in my shape.

This is a true account of the sum of her examination, but by reason of great noise, by the afflicted and many speakers, many things are pretermitted.

Memorandum

Nurse held her neck on one side and Eliz. Hubbard (one of the sufferers) had her neck set in that posture. Whereupon another patient, Abigail Williams, cried out: Set up Goody Nurse's head, the maid's neck will be broke. And when some set up Nurse's head, Aaron Wey observed that Betty Hubbard's was immediately righted.

Salem Village, March 24th, 1691/92.

The Rev. Mr. Samuell Parris, being desired to take in writing the examination of Rebeckah Nurse, hath returned it as aforesaid.

Upon hearing the aforesaid, and seeing what we then did see, together with the charge of the persons then present, we committed Rebekah Nurse, the wife of ffran^S Nurse of Salem Village, unto their Majesties' jail in Salem, as per a *mittimus* then given out, in order to farther examination.

John Hathorne   }
Jonathan Corwin   Assistants

Testimony of Thomas and Edward Putnam

The deposition of Tho: Putnam, aged about 40 years, and Edward Putman, aged about 38 years, witnesseth and saith that having been several times present with Ann Putman, junr., in and after her fits, and saw her much afflicted, being bitten, pinched, her limbs distorted, and pins thrust into her flesh, which she charges on Rebekah Nurse, that she was the actor thereof, and that she saw her do it.

The deponents farther testify that on the 24 March last past, at the public examination of said Nurs, we saw the said Ann Putman, Abigail Williams, and Elis Hubbard, often struck down upon the glance of the said Nurse's eye upon said Williams Putman, and Hubbard several times. And the said Putman, Williams, and Hubbard was then afflicted according to the various motions of said Nurse her body, in time of examination, as when said Nurse did clench her hands, bite her lips, or hold her head aside, the said Putman, Hubbard, and Williams was set in the same posture to her great torture and affliction.

Thomas Putnam
Edward Putnam

Testimony of Samuel Parris,
Nathaniel Ingersoll, and Thomas Putnam

The deposition of Sam: Parris, aged about 39 years, and Nathaniel Ingersoll, aged about fifty and eight years, and Thomas Putnam, aged about forty years, all of Salem, testifieth and saith that Ann Putnam, sen^r, and her daughter, Ann, and Mary Walcot, and Abigail Williams were several times and grievously tortured at the examination of Rebekah Nurse, wife to Francis Nurse of Salem, before the Honoured Magistrates the 24 March, 1691/92, and particularly that when her hands were at liberty some of the afflicted were pinched, and upon the motion of her head and fingers, some of them were tortured, and farther that some of the afflicted then and there affirmed that they saw a black man whispering in her ear, and that they saw birds fluttering about her.

Indictment of Rebecca Nurse

The jurors for our Sovereign Lord and Lady the King and Queen present that Rebecca Nurse, the wife of ffrancis Nurse, sen[ior], of Salem Village in the County of Essex, husbandman, the four and twentieth day of March, [1692] ... and divers other days and times as well before as after, certain detestable arts called Witchcraft and Sorceries wickedly and feloniously hath used, practiced, and exercised at and within the Township of Salem, in the County of Essex aforesaid, in, upon, and against one Ann Puttnam, Junr, of Salem Village aforesaid, in the County aforesaid, single-woman, by which said wicked arts the said Ann Puttnam, Junr, ... is hurt, tortured, afflicted, consumed, pined, wasted, and tormented against the peace of our said Sovereign Lord and Lady, the King & Queen, and against the form of the statute in that case made and provided.

Witnesses

Ann Puttnam Junr Mary Walcott
Abigail Williams   Elizabeth Hubbard

[Three additional indictments, identical in form, charge Rebecca Nurse with practicing witchcraft upon Mary Walcott, Elizabeth Hubbard, and Abigail Williams. They are all identified as being of Salem Village, while Hubbard and Williams are further characterized as "singlewoman."]

Testimony of Edward Putnam

The deposition of Edward Putman, aged about 30 years, he testifieth and saith upon the 25 day of March, 1692, Ann Putnam, senior, was bitten by Rebekah Nurse, as she said [she] did; about 2 of the clock the same day she was struck with her chain—the mark being in a kind of a round ring and 3 strokes across the ring. She had 6 blows with a chain in the space of half an hour, and she had one remarkable one with 6 strokes across her arm. I saw the mark both of bite and chain.

Testimony of John and Hannah Putnam

The deposition of John Putnam, weaver, and Hannah, his wife, who testifieth and saith that our child which died about the middle of April, 1692, was as well and as thriving a child as most was, till it was about eight weeks old, but a while after that I, the said Jno. Putnam, had reported something which I had heard concerning the mother of Rebekah Nurs, Mary Estich [Eastey], and Sarah

Cloyes, I myself was taken with strange kinds of fits, but it pleased Almighty God to deliver me from them, but quickly after this, our poor young child was taken about midnight with strange and violent fits which did most grievously affright us, acting much like to the poor bewitched persons, when we thought they would indeed have died. Whereupon we sent for our mother Putnam in the night. Immediately, as soon as she came and see our child, she told us that she feared there was an evil hand upon it. And also, as fast as possibly could be, we got a doctor to it, but all he did give it could do it no good, but it continued in strange and violent fits for about two days and two nights, and then departed this life by a cruel and violent death, being enough to pierce a stony heart, for to the best of our understanding it was near five hours a-dying.

Testimony of Sarah Bibber

The deposition of Sharah Viber, aged about 36 years, who testifieth and saith that on the 2 day of May, 1692, I saw the apparition of Rebekah Nurs, the wife of ffrances Nurs, sen[r], most grievously torture and afflict the bodies of Mary Walcott, Mercy lewes, and Abigaill williams, by pinching them and almost choking them to death, but I do not know that she hurt me till the 27th June, 1692, and then the apparition of Rebekah Nurs did most grievously torment me by pinching me and almost choking me several times.

Testimony of Sarah Nurse

[The deposition of Sarah Nurse,] aged 28 years or thereabouts, [who] testifieth and saith that being in the Court this 29th of June, 1692, I saw Goodwife Bibber pull pins out of her clothes, and held them between her fingers, and clasped her hands round her knee, and then she cried out and said Goody Nurse pinched her.

Testimony of Ann Putnam, Senior

The deposition of Ann Putnam, the wife of Thomas Putnam, who testifieth and saith that on the first day of June, 1692, the apparition of Rebekah Nurs did again fall upon me and almost choke me, and she told me that now she was come out of prison she had power to afflict me, and that now she would afflict me all this day long and would kill me if she could, for she told me she had killed Benjamin Holton and John Fuller and Rebekah Shepard, and she also told me that she and her sister, Cloyce, and Ed: Bishop['s] wife of Salem Village had killed young Jno. Putnam's child because young Jno. Putnam had said that ιt was no wonder they were witches, for their mother was so before them, and because they could not avenge themselves on him they kill[ed] his child. And immediately there did appear to me six children in winding sheets which called me aunt, which did most grievously affright me, and they told me that they were my sister Baker's children of Boston, and that Goody Nurs, and Mistress Cary of Charlestown, and an old deaf woman at Boston had murdered them, and charged me to go and tell these things to the magistrates or else they would tear me to pieces, for their blood did cry out for vengeance. Also there appeared to me my own sister Bayley and three of her children in winding sheets, and told me that Goody Nurs had murdered them.

Testimony of Johanna Childen

The deposition of Johannah Childen, testifieth and saith that upon the 2d of June, 1692, that the apparition of Goody Nurs, and Goodman Harrwood, did appear to her, and the said Harrwood did look Goody Nurs in the face, and said to her that she did murder him by pushing him off the cart and struck the breath out of his body.

Testimony of Samuel Parris
and John Putnam, Senior

The deposition of Sam: Parris, aged about 39 years, and John Putnam, sen^r, aged about 63 years, both of Salem Village, testifieth and saith that this 18 instant June, being at the house of Jonathan Putman, whom we found very ill, after a little while Mercy Lewes, sent for on purpose, came into said Jonathan Putman's house and was presently struck dumb, but being bid to hold up her hand if she saw any of the witches afflict said Jonathan, whereupon she presently lifted up her hand and after fell into a trance. And when said Mercy came to herself she saith she saw Goody Nurse and Goody Carrier, holding said Jonathan's head, and further saith not.

Testimony of Sarah Houlton

The deposition of Sarah Holton, relique of Benjamin Holton, deceased, who testifieth and saith that about this time three years, my dear and loving husband, Benjamin Holton, deceased, was as well as ever I knew him in my life, till one Saturday morning that Rebekah Nurs, who now stands charged for witchcraft, came to our house and fell a railing at him, because our pigs got into her field, though our pigs were sufficiently yoked, and their fence was down in several places, yet all we could say to her could no ways pacify her, but she continued railing and scolding a great while together, calling to her son Benj. Nurs to go and get a gun and kill our pigs and let none of them go out of the field, though my poor husband gave her never a misbeholding word.

And within a short time after this, my poor husband, going out very early in the morning, as he was a coming in again he was taken with a strange fit in the entry, being struck blind and struck down two or three times, so that when he came to himself he told me he thought he should never have come into the house anymore. And all summer after, he continued in a languishing condition, being much pained at his stomach and often struck blind. But about a fortnight before he died he was taken with strange and violent fits, acting much like to our poor bewitched persons when we thought they would have died. And the doctor that was with him could not find what his distemper was. And the day before he died he was very cheerly, but about midnight he was again most violently seized upon with violent fits till the next night about midnight he departed this life by a cruel death.

Testimony of Nathaniel and Hannah Ingersoll

The deposition of Nathaniell Ingersoll and Hannah his wife, who testify and say that we were conversant with Benjamin Holton for above a week before he died and was acted in a very strange manner with most violent fits, acting much like to our poor bewitched persons when we thought they would have died, though then we had no suspicion of witchcraft amongst us; and he died a most violent death with dreadful fits, and the doctor that was with him said he could not tell what his distemper was, and he died about two days before Rebekah Sheepard.

Testimony of John Putnam, Senior, and Rebecca Putnam

The testimony of John Putnam, senior, and Rebeccah, his wife, saith that our son-in-law John Fuller and our daughter Rebecca Shepard did both of them die a most violent death and die acting very strangely at the time of their death. Further saith that we did judge then that they both died of a malignant fever, and had no suspicion of witchcraft of any, neither can we accuse the prisoner at the bar of any such thing.

Physical Examination of Rebecca Nurse, Bridget Bishop, Sarah Good, and Others

1692. Salem, June 2$^\text{d}$, about 10 in morning.

We whose names are underwritten, being commanded by Capt. George Corwin, Esq$^\text{r.}$, Sheriff of the County of Essex, this 2d day of June 1692, for to view the bodies of Bridgett Bishop, alias Oliver

Rebecca Nurse   Elizabeth Proctor
Alice Parker   Susanna Martine
Sarah Good

The first three, namely Bishop, Nurse, Proctor, by diligent search have discovered a preternatural excrescence of flesh between the pudendum and anus, much like to teats, and not usual in women, and much unlike to the other three that hath been searched by us, and that they were in all the three women near the same place.

J. Barton, Surgeon

Alice		Pickering
her		mark
Jane		Woolings
her		mark
Margery		Wettiams
her		mark
Anna		Stephens
her		mark
Elizabeth		Hill
her		mark
Elanor		Henderson
her		mark
Rebeccah		Sharpe
her		mark
Lydia		Peckman
her		mark
Hannah		Kezeir

Sworn in court, June 2^d, 1692

Attest, Step. Sewall, Clerk

Second Physical Examination of
Bridget Bishop, Rebecca Nurse, and Others

Salem, about 4 afternoon, June 2^d, 1692

We whose names are subscribed to the within mentioned, upon a second search about 3 or 4 hours distance, did find the said Bridget Bishop, alias Oliver, in a clear and free state from any preternatural excrescence as formerly seen by us. As also, Rebecah Nurse, instead of that excrescence within mentioned, it appears only as a dry skin without sense [i.e., without sensation]. And as for Elizabeth Procter, which excrescence like a teat, red and fresh, not anything appears, but only a proper *procedeulia ani*. And as for Susanna Martine, whose breast in the morning search appeared to us very full, the nipples fresh and starting, now at this searching all lanche and pendant, which is all at present from the within mentioned subscribers. And that piece of flesh of

Goodwife Nurse's, formerly seen, is gone, and only a dry skin nearer to the anus in another place.

J. Barton, Surgeon

Rebecah Sharpe
mark

Eli zabeth Hill

the mark of

Lidia Pickman
her mark

Eleanor Henderson
her mark

Alice Pickering
mark

Hannah Kezar

Marjery Williams
mark

Anna Stephens

Jane Wollings
mark

Sworn in court, June 2ᵈ, 1692.

Petition of Rebecca Nurse

To the Honoured Court of Oyer and Terminer now sitting in Salem this 28th of June, *Anno* 1692.

The humble petition of Rebeccah Nurse of Salem Village humbly sheweth that whereas some women did search your petitioner at Salem, as I did then conceive for some supernatural mark, and then one of the said women, which is known to be the most ancient, skillful, prudent person of them all, as to any such concern, did express herself to be of a contrary opinion from the rest, and did then declare that she saw nothing in or about your Honour's poor petitioner but what might arise from a natural cause. And I then rendered the said persons a sufficient known reason as to myself of the moving cause thereof, which was by exceeding weakness descending partly from an overture of nature and difficult exigencies that hath befallen me in the times of my travails.

And therefore your petitioner humbly prays I that your Honours would be pleased to admit of some other women to enquire into this great concern, those that are most grand, wise, and skillful; namely, Ms. [Mistress] Higginson, Ms. Buxton, Ms. Woodbery, two of them being midwives, Ms. Porter, together with such others as may be chosen on that account before I am brought to my trial.

All which I hope your Honours will take into your prudent consideration and find it requisite so to do, for my life lies now in your hands, under God. And being conscious of my own innocency, I humbly beg that I may have liberty to manifest it to the world, partly by the means abovesaid. And your poor petitioner shall evermore pray as in duty bound, &c.

Rebecca Nurse:
her mark

Testimony of Rebecca Preston
and Mary Tarbell

We whose names are underwritten can testify, if called to it, that Goody Nurs have been troubled with an infirmity of body for many years, which the jury of women seem to be afraid it should be something else.

Rebecah Preston   Mary Tarbel

Excommunication of Rebecca Nurse from the
First Church of the Town of Salem

1692, July 3—After sacrament, the elders propounded to the church, and it was, by an unanimous vote, consented to,—that our sister Nurse, being a convicted witch by the Court, and condemned to die, should be excommunicated; which was accordingly done in the afternoon, she being present.

Testimony of Nathaniel Putnam, Senior

Nathaniel Putnam, Senior, being desired by Francis Nurse, Senior, to give information of what I could say concerning his wife's life and conversation, I, the abovesaid, have known this said aforesaid woman forty years, and what I have observed of her, human frailties excepted, her life and conversation have been according to her profession. And she hath brought up a great family of children and educated them well, so that there is in some of them apparent savor of godliness. I have known her [to] differ with her neighbors, but I never know or heard of any that did accuse her of what she is now charged with.

Testimony of John Tarbell

John Tarbell, being at the house of Thomas Putnam's upon the 28 day of this instant March, being the year 1692, upon discourse of many things, I asked them some questions, and among others I asked this question: whether the girl that was afflicted did first speak of Goody Nurs before others mentioned her to her. They said she told them she saw the apparition of a pale-faced woman that sat in her grandmother's seat, but did not know her name. Then I replied and said: but who was it that told her that it was Goody Nurs. Mercy Lewes said it was Goody Putnam that said it was Goody Nurs. Goody Putnam said it was Mercy Lewes that told her. Thus they turned it upon one another, saying it was you and it was you that told her. This was before any was afflicted at Thomas Putnam's beside his daughter, that they told his daughter it was Goody Nurs.
Samuel Nurs doth testify to all above written

Petition on Behalf of Rebecca Nurse

We whose names are hereunto subscribed, being desired by Goodman Nurse to declare what we know concerning his wife's conversation for time past, we can testify to all whom it may concern, that we have known her for many years and according to our observation her life and conversation was according to her profession, and we never had any cause or grounds to suspect her of any such thing as she is now accused of.

Israel Porter	Job Swinerton	Elizibeth Buxtston
Elizibeth Porter	Esther Swinerton	Samuel Aborn, senr.
Edward Beshep, sen.	Joseph Herrick, sen.	Isaack Cooke
Hana Beshep	Samuell Sibley	Elisabeth Cooke
Joshua Rea	Hephzibah Rea	William Osborne
Sarah Rea	Daniell Andrew	Hanah Osborne
Sarah Leach	Sara Andrew	Daniell Rea
John Putnam, sen.	Jonathan Putnam	Sarah Putnam
Rebeckh Putnam	Lydia Putnam	Joseph Putnam
Joseph Hucheson, sen.	Walter Phillips, senior	
Leda [Lydia] Hucheson	Nathaniel Felton, Sen.	
Joseph Holten, sen.	Margaret Philips	
Sarah Holten	Taitha [Tabitha?] Phillips	
Benjaman Putnam	Joseph Houlton, Junior	
Sarah Putnam	Sam[ll]. Endecott	

Memorandum by Stephen Sewell

Memorandum

In this trial are twenty papers, besides this judgment, and there were in this trial, as well as other trials of the same nature, several evidences *viva voce* which were not written and so I can give no copies of them, some for and some against the parties. Some of the confessions did also mention this and other persons in their several declarations. Which being premised and considered, the said 20 papers herewith filed is the whole trial.

Attest   Steph. Sewell, Clerk

Copy of the above wrote on the judgment which I gave out to the Nurses.

Petition of Samuel Nurse (September 1710)

To the Honourable Committee appointed to make inquiry with respect to the sufferings in the trials in the year 1692.

The humble representation of Samuel Nurse of the damage sustained by our family in the year 1692 by reason of the imprisonment, condemnation, and execution of my honoured mother, Rebekah Nurse, for supposed witchcraft.

1. We were at the whole charge of providing for her during her imprisonment in Salem and Boston for the space of almost four months.
2. And also we spent much time and made many journies to Boston and Salem and other places in order to have vindicated her innocency.
3. And although we produced plentiful testimony that my honoured and dear mother had led a blameless life from her youth up, yet she was condemned and executed upon such evidence as is now generally thought to be insufficient, which may be seen in the court record of her trial.
4. And so her name and the name of her posterity lies under reproach, the removing of which reproach is the principal thing wherein we desire restitution.
5. And as we know not how to express our loss of such a mother in such a way, so we know not how to compute our charge, but shall leave it to the judgment of others, and shall not be critical, but ready to receive such a satisfaction as shall be by the Honourable Court judged sufficient.

So, praying God to guide unto such methods as may be for his glory and the good of this land, I rest,

> Your Honours, in all Christian obedience,
> Samuel Nurse
> In the name of my brethren

Salem, Septem. 13, 1710

Although forty pounds would not repair my loss and damage in my estate, yet I shall be satisfied if may be allowed five and twenty pounds, provided the attainder be taken off.

Chapter Three

Bridget Bishop

Complaint Against
Bridget Bishop and Others

Salem, April the 18th, 1692

There being complaint this day made before us by Ezekiell Chevers and John Putnam, Junior, both of Salem Village, yeomen, in behalf of their Majesties, for themselves and also for their neighbors, against Giles Cory and Mary Waren, both of Salem Farms, and Abigaile Hobs, the daughter of William Hobs of the town of Topsfield, and Bridgett Bishop, the wife of Edward Bishop of Salem, sawyer, for high suspicion of sundry acts of witchcraft done or committed by them upon the bodies of Ann Putnam, Marcy Lewis, and Abigail Williams, and Mary Walcot, and Elis Hubert of Salem Village, whereby great hurt and damage hath been done to the bodies of said persons abovenamed, therefore craved justice.

You are therefore in their Majesties' names hereby required to apprehend and bring before us Giles Cory and Mary Waren of Salem Farms, and Abigail Hobs, the daughter of William Hobs of the town of Topsfield, and Bridgett Bishop, the wife of Edward Bishop of Salem, tomorrow about eight of the clock in the forenoon at the house of Lt. Nathaniell Ingersalls in Salem Village in order to their examination relating to the premises abovesaid, and hereof you are not to fail.

Dated Salem, April 18th, 1692

> John Hathorne   } Assistants
> Jonathan Corwin

To George Herrick, Marshall of the County of Essex

You are likewise required to summon Margaret Knight, Lydya Nichols, Elisabeth Nichols, and Elezabeth Hubert, Jonathan Putnam, and Hepzibah Rea and John Hewes, all and every one of them, to appear before us at the abovesaid time and place to give in what evidence they know relating to the abovesaid or like cases depending.

Salem, April 18th, 1692

Examination of Bridget Bishop
as Recorded by Ezekiel Cheever

The examination of Bridget Bishop before the worshipful John Hathon and Jonathan Curren, Esq^{rs}.

Bridget Bishop, being now coming in to be examined relating to her accusation of suspicion of sundry acts of witchcraft, the afflicted persons are now dreadfully afflicted by her, as they do say.

(Mr. Hathon) Bishop, what do you say? You here stand charged with sundry acts of witchcraft by you done or committed upon the bodies of Mercy Lews and Ann Putnam and others.

(Bishop) I am innocent. I know nothing of it. I have done no witchcraft.

(Mr. Hathen) Look upon this woman and see if this be the woman that you have seen hurting you.

Mercy Lewes and Ann Putnam and others do now charge her to her face with hurting of them.

(Mr. Hathen) What do you say now you see they charge you to your face?

(Bish.) I never did hurt them in my life. I did never see these persons before. I am as innocent as the child unborn.

(Mr. Hath.) Is not your coat cut?

(Bish.) Answers no, but her garment being looked upon, they find it cut or torn two ways. Jonathan Walcoate saith that the sword that he struck at Goody Bishup with was not naked, but was within the scabbard, so that the rent may very probably be the same that Mary Walcoate did tell that she had in her coat by Jonathan's striking at her appearance.

The afflicted persons charge her with having hurt them many ways, and by tempting them to sign the Devil's book. At which charge she seemed to be very angry, and shaking her head at them, saying it was false. They are all greatly tormented (as I conceive) by the shaking of her head.

(Mr. Har.) Goody Bishop, what contract have you made with the devil?

(Bish.) I have made no contract with the devil. I never saw him in my life.

Ann Putnam saith that she calls the devil her God.

(Mr. Har.) What say you to all this that you are charged with? Can you not find in your heart to tell the truth?

(Bish.) I do tell the truth. I never hurt these persons in my life. I never saw them before.

(Mercy Lewes) Oh, Goody Bishop, did you not come to our house the last night, and did you not tell me that your master made you tell more than you were willing to tell.

(Mr. Har.) Tell us the truth in this matter. How come these persons to be thus tormented and to charge you with doing?

(Bish.) I am not come here to say I am a witch, to take away my life.

(Mr. H) Who is it that doth it, if you do not? They say it is your likeness that comes and torments them and tempts them to write in the book. What book is that you tempted them with?

(Bish.) I know nothing of it. I am innocent.

(Mr. Harth.) Do you not see how they are tormented? You are acting witchcraft before us. What do you say to this? Why have you not an heart to confess the truth?

(Bsh.) I am innocent. I know nothing of it. I am no witch. I know not what a witch is.

(Mr. H) Have you not given consent that some evil spirit should do this in your likeness?

(B) No, I am innocent of being a witch. I know no man, woman, or child here.

(Marshall Herrick) How came you into my bed chamber one morning, then, and asked me whether I had any curtains to sell?

She is by some of the afflicted persons charged with murder.

(Mr. Harth.) What do you say to these murders you are charged with?

(B) I am innocent. I know nothing of it.

Now she lifts up her eyes and they are greatly tormented again.

(Mr. Har.) What do you say to these things here, horrible acts of witchcraft?

(Bish.) I know nothing of it. I do not know whether [there] be any witches or no.

(Mr. Har.) Have you not heard that some have confessed?

(Bish.) No I did not.

Two men told her to her face that they had told her. Here she is taken in a plain lie.

Now she is going away, they are dreadfully afflicted. Five afflicted persons do charge this woman to be the very woman that hurts them.

This is a true account of what I have taken down at her examination according to best understanding and observation. I have also in her examination taken notice that all her actions have great influence upon the afflicted persons and that have been tortured by her.

Ezekiel Cheever

Examination of Bridget Bishop
as Recorded by Samuel Parris

The examination of Bridget Bishop at Salem Village, 19 April, 1692.
By John Hathorn and Jonath. Corwin, Esq[rs.]

As soon as she came near, all fell into fits.

Bridget Bishop, you are now brought before authority to give account of what witchcrafts you are conversant in.

I take all this people (turning her head and eyes about) to witness that I am clear.

Hath this woman hurt you? (Speaking to the afflicted.)

Eliz. Hubbard, Ann Putnam, Abigail Williams, and Mercy Lewes affirmed that she had hurt them.

You are here accused by 4 or 5 for hurting them. What do you say to it?

I never saw these persons before, nor I never was in this place before.

Mary Walcot said that her brother Jonathan struck her appearance, and she saw that he had torn her coat in striking, and she heard it tear.

Upon some search in the court, a rent that seems to answer what was alleged was found.

They say you bewitched your first husband to death.

If it please your worship, I know nothing of it.

---- She shook her head, and the afflicted were tortured.

---- The like again upon the motion of her head.

Sam: Braybrook affirmed that she told him today that he had been accounted a witch these 10 years, but she was no witch. The Devil cannot hurt her.

I am no witch.

Why, if you have not wrote in the book, yet tell me how far you have gone?

Have you not to do with familiar spirits?

I have no familiarity with the devil.

How is it, then, that your appearance doth hurt these?

I am innocent.

Why you seem to act witchcraft before us by the motion of your body, which seems to have influence upon the afflicted?

I know nothing of it. I am innocent to a witch. I know not what a witch is.

How do you know, then, that you are not a witch?

I do not know what you say.

How can you know you are no witch, and yet not know what a witch is?

I am clear. If I were any such person you should know it.

You may threaten, but you can do no more than you are permitted.

I am innocent of a witch.

What do you say of those murders you are charged with?

I hope I am not guilty of murder.

Then she turned up her eyes, and the eyes of the afflicted were turned up.

It may be you do not know that any have confessed today, who have been examined before you, that they are witches.

No. I know nothing of it.

John Hutchinson and John Lewis in open court affirmed that they had told her.

Why look you, you are taken now in a flat lie.

I did not hear them.

Note: Sam: Gold saith that after this examination he asked said Bridget Bishop if she were not troubled to see the afflicted persons so tormented. Said Bishop answered no, she was not troubled for them. Then he asked her whether she thought they were bewitched. She said she could not tell what to think about them. Will Good and John Buxton, Jun[r.], were by, and he supposeth they heard her also.

Salem Village, April 19, 1962.

Mr. Sam[l] Parris, being desired to take in writing the examination of Bridget Bishop, hath delivered it as aforesaid. And upon hearing the same and seeing what we did then see, together with the charge of the afflicted persons then present, we committed said Bridget Olliver.

John Hathorne

Indictment of Bridget Bishop

The jurors for our Sovereign Lord and Lady the King and Queen, present that Briget Bishop, alias Oliver, the wife of Edward Bishop of Salem in the County of Essex, sawyer, the nineteenth day of April, [1692] . . . and divers other days and times as well before as after, certain detestable arts called witchcraft and sorceries, wickedly and feloniously hath used, practiced and exercised at and within the Township of Salem in the County of Essex aforesaid, in, upon, and against one Mercy Lewis of Salem Village in the county aforesaid, singlewoman, by which said wicked arts the said Mercy Lewis . . . was and is hurt, tortured, afflicted, pined, consumed, wasted and tormented, against the peace of our said Sovereign Lord and Lady the King and Queen, and against the form of the statute in that case made and provided.

Witnesses

Mercy Lewis	Nathaniel Ingersoll
Mr. Samuel Parris	Thomas Putnam, Jun[r]
Mary Walcott	Ann Putnam, Jun[r]
Elizabeth Hubbard	Abigail Williams

[Three additional indictments, similar in form, were returned against Bridget Bishop. They named as victims Abigail Williams, Elizabeth Hubbard, and Ann Putnam, Jr. The same group of witnesses appear in all four indictments, but in the second indictment the following witnesses are also listed: John Bligh and Rebekah his wife, Samuel Shattuck and Sarah his wife, William Bligh, William Stacey, and John Londer.]

Testimony of William Stacey

William Stacey of the Town of Salem, aged thirty six years or thereabouts, deposeth and saith that about fourteen years ago, this deponent was visited with the smallpox. Then Bridget Bishop did give him a visit, and withal professed a great love for this deponent in his affliction, more than ordinary, at which this deponent admired [i.e., wondered]. Some time after this deponent was well, the said Bishop got him to do some work for her, for which she gave him three pence, which seemed to this deponent as if it had been good money. But he had not gone not above 3 or 4 rods before he looked in his pocket where he put it, for it, but could not find any.

Sometime after, this deponent met the said Bishop in the street going to mill. She asking this deponent whether his father would grind her grist, he put it to the said Bishop why she asked. She answered, because folks counted her a witch. This deponent made answer, he did not question but that his father would grind it. But being gone about 6 rod from her, the said Bishop, with a small load in his cart, suddenly the off wheel plumped or sunk down into a hole upon plain ground, that this deponent was forced to get one to help him get the wheel out. Afterwards, this deponent went back to look for said hole where his wheel sunk in, but could not find any hole.

Sometime after, in the winter, about midnight, this deponent felt something between his lips, pressing hard against his teeth, and withal was very cold, in so much that it did awake him, so that he got up and sat upon his bed. He at the same time seeing the said Bridget Bishop sitting at the foot of the bed, being to his seeming (it was then as light as if it had been day) or one in the said Bishop's shape, she having then a black cape and a black hat, and a red coat with two eakes [?] of two colors. Then she, the said Bishop or her shape, clasped her coat close to her legs and hopped upon the bed and about the room, and then went out, and then it was dark.

Again, some time after, the said Bishop went to this deponent and asked him whether that which he had reported was true, that he had told to several. He answered that it was true, and that it was she, and bid her deny it if she dare. The said Bishop did not deny it, and went away very angry and said that this deponent did her more mischief than any other body. He asked why. She answered, because folks would believe him before anybody else.

Sometime after, the said Bishop threatened this deponent, and told him he was the occasion of bringing her out about the brass she stole. Some time after, this deponent in a dark night was going to the barn who was suddenly taken or hoisted from the ground and threw against a stone wall [and] after that taken up again and throwed down a bank at the end of his house.

Some time after, this deponent met the said Bishop by Isaac Stone's brick kiln. After he had passed by her, this deponent's horse stood still with a small load going up the hill, so that the horse striving to draw, all his gears and tacking flew in pieces, and the cart fell down.

Afterward, this deponent went to lift a bag of corn of about 2 bushels, but could not budge it with all his might.

This deponent hath met with several other of her pranks at several times, which would take up a great time to tell of.

This deponent doth verily believe that the said Bridget Bishop was instrumental to his daughter Precilla's death about two years ago. The child was a likely, thriving child, and suddenly screeched out and so continued in an unusual manner for about a fortnight, and so died in that lamentable manner.

Sworn, Salem, May the 30th, 1692,
before us

John Hathorne
Jonathan Corwin } Assistants

June 2^d, 1692

Testimony of Samuel Gray

Samuel Gray of Salem, aged about 42 years, testifieth and saith that about fourteen years ago, he going to bed well one Lord's Day at night, and after he had been asleep some time, he awakened. And look[ing] up, saw the house light as if a candle or candles were lighted in it, and the door locked and that little fire there was, raked up. He did then see a woman standing between the cradle in the room and the bedside, and seemed to look upon him. So he did rise up in his bed, and it vanished or disappeared. Then he went to the door and found it locked, and unlocking and opening the door, he went to the entry door and looked out, and then again did see the same woman he had a little before seen in the room, and in the same garb she was in before. Then he said to her, in the name of God, what do you come for? Then she vanished away.

So he locked the door again and went to bed. And between sleeping and waking, he felt something come to his mouth or lips, cold, and thereupon started and looked up, and again did see the same woman with something between both her hands holding before his mouth. Upon which she moved, and the child in the cradle gave a great screech out, as if it was greatly hurt, and she disappeared. And taking the child up, could not quiet it in some hours. From which time, the child, that before was a very likely, thriving child, did pine away and was never well, although it lived some months after, yet in a sad condition, and so died.

Some time after, within a week or less, he did see the same woman, in the same garb and clothes, that appeared to him as aforesaid. And, although he knew not her nor her name before, yet both by her countenance and garb, doth testify that it was the same woman that they now call Bridget Bishop, alias Oliver, of Salem.

Samuel Gray

Sworn, Salem, May 30th, 1692
before me

John Hathorne, Assistant

Testimony of Samuel and Sarah Shattuck

Sam[ll] Shattoch, aged 41 years, testifieth, that in the year 1680, Bridget
Oliver, formerly wife to old Goodman Oliver, now wife to Edward Bishop, did
come to my house pretending to buy an old hh[d] which, though I asked very
little for, and for all her pretended want, she went away without it. And sundry
other times she came in a smooth, flattering manner in very slightly errands, we
have thought since on purpose to work mischief.

At, or very near, this time, our eldest child, who promised as much and
understanding, both by countance and actions, as any other children of his
years, was taken in a very drooping condition. And as she came oftener to the
house, he grew worse and worse. As he would be standing at the door [he]
would fall out and bruise his face upon a great stepstone, as if he had been thrust
out by an invisible hand, oftentimes falling and hitting his face against the sides
of the house, bruising his face in a very miserable manner.

After this, the abovesaid Oliver brought me a pair of sleeves to dye, and after
that, sundry pieces of lace, some of which were so short that I could not judge
them fit for any use. She paid me 2 d. for dyeing them, which 2 d. I gave to
Henery Williams which lived with me. He told me [he] put it in a purse among
some other money, which he locked up in a box, and that the purse and money
was gone out of the box, he could not tell how, and never found it after.

Just after the dyeing of these things, this child [was] taken in a terrible fit,
his mouth and eyes drawn aside, and gasped in such a manner as if he was upon
the point of death. After this, he grew worse in his fits and, out of them, would
be almost always crying. That for many months he would be crying, till nature's
strength was spent, and then would fall asleep and then awake and fall to crying
and moaning, that his very countenance did bespeak compassion. And at length
we perceived his understanding decayed so that we feared (as it has since proved)
that he would be quite bereft of his wits. Forever since, he has been stupefied
and void of reason, his fits still following of him. After he had been in this kind
of sickness some time, he has gone into the garden and has got upon a board of
an inch thick which lay flat upon the ground, and we have called him. He would
come to the edge of the board and hold out his hand and make as if he would
come, but could not until he was helped off the board. Other times, when he has
got upon a board as aforesaid, my wife has said she has offered him a cake and
money to come to her, and he has held out his hand and reached after it, but
could not come till he had been helped off the board. By which I judge some
enchantment kept him on.

About 17 or 18 months after the first of this illness, there came a stranger to
my house and pitied this child, and said, among other words, we are all born,
some to one thing and some to another. I asked him, and what do you say this
child is born to? He replied, he is born to be bewitched and is bewitched. I told
him he did not know. He said he did know, and said to me, you have a neighbor
that lives not far off that is a witch. I told him we had no neighbor but what was
honest folk. He replied, you have a neighbor that is a witch and she has had a

falling out with your wife and said in her heart your wife is a proud woman, and she would bring down her pride in this child.

I paused in myself and did remember that my wife had told me that Goodwife Oliver had been at the house and spoke to her to beat Henery Williams that lived with us, and that she went away muttering and, she thought, threatening, but little before our child was taken ill. I told the aforesaid stranger that there was such a woman as he spoke of. He asked where she lived, for he would go and see her if he knew how. I gave him money and bid him ask her for a pot of cider. Away he went, and I sent my boy with him, who after a short time both returned, the boy's face bleeding. And I asked what was the matter. They told me the man knocked at the door, and Goody Olivier came to the door and asked the stranger what he would have. He told her a pot of cider. She said he should have none and bid him get out, and took up a spade and made him go out. She followed him and when she came without the porch she saw my boy and ran to him and scratched his face and made it bleed, saying to him, thou rogue, what dost thou bring this fellow here to plague me. Now this man did say, before he went, that he would fetch blood of her.

And ever since, this child hath been followed with grievous fits as if he would never recover more, his head and eyes drawn aside so as if they would never come to rights more, lying as if he were in a manner dead, falling anywhere, either into fire or water, if he be not constantly looked to, and generally in such an uneasy and restless frame, almost always running to and fro, acting so strange that I cannot judge otherwise but that he is bewitched, and by these circumstances do believe that the aforesaid Bridget Oliver, now called Bishop, is the cause of it. And it has been the judgment of doctors such as lived here, and ferrugriers[?], that he is under an evil hand of witchcraft.

Sam^{ll} Shattuck and
Sarah Shattock

affirmeth upon the oath they have taken to the truth of what is abovewritten.

Attest, Stephen Sewall, Clerk

June 2^d, 1692

Testimony of Richard Coman

Richard Coman, aged about 32 years, testifieth that sometime about eight years since, I then being in bed with my wife at Salem, one fifth day of the week, at night, either in the latter end of May [or] the beginning of June, and a light burning in our room, I, being awake, did then see Bridget Bishup of Salem, alias Olliver, come into the room we lay in, and two women more with her, which two women were strangers to me, I knew them not. But said Bishop came in her red paragon bodice and the rest of her clothing that she then usually did wear. And I, knowing of her well, also the garb she did use to go in, did clearly and plainly know her.

And testifieth that as he locked the door of the house when he went to bed, so he found it afterwards, when he did rise. And quickly after, they appeared. The light was out, and the curtains at the foot of the bed opened where I did see her. And presently came and lay upon my breast or body, and so oppressed him that he could not speak nor stir, no not so much as to awake his wife, although he endeavored much so to do it.

The next night they all appeared again in like manner, and the said Bishop, alias Oliver, took hold of him by the throat and almost hauled him out of the bed. The Saturday night following, I having been that day telling of what I had seen and how I suffered the two nights before, my kinsman William Coman told me he would stay with me and see if they would come again, and advised me to lay my sword athwart my body. Quickly after we went to bed that said night, and both well awake and discoursing together, in came all the three women again. And said Bishop was the first, as she had been the other two nights. So I told him, William, here they be, all come again. And he was immediately struck speechless, and could not move hand or foot. And immediately they got hold of my sword and strived to take it from me, but I held so fast as they did not get it away.

And I had then liberty of speech, and called William, also my wife and Sarah Phillips that lay with my wife, who all told me afterwards they heard me but had not power to speak or stir afterwards. And the first that spoke was Sarah Phillips and said, in the name of God, Goodman Coman, what is the matter with you. So they all vanished away.

Sworn, Salem, June 2d, 1692. Before me

John Hathorne

Testimony of John Londer

John Londer of Salem, aged about thirty two years, testifieth and saith that about seven or eight years since, I then living with Mr. John Gedney in Salem and having had some controversy with Bridget Bishop, the wife of Edw. Bushop of Salem, sawyer, about her fowls that used to come into our orchard or garden, some little time after which, I going well to bed, about the dead of the night felt a great weight upon my breast, and awakening, looked, and it being bright moonlight, did clearly see said Bridget Bushop, or her likeness, sitting upon my stomach. And putting my arms off of the bed to free myself from that great oppression, she presently laid hold of my throat and almost choked me. And I had no strength or power in my hands to resist or help myself. And in this condition she held me to almost day.

Some time after this, my mistress, Susannah Gedney, was in our orchard, and I was then with her, and said Bridget Bishop being then in her orchard, which was next adjoining to ours, my mistress told said Bridget that I said or affirmed that she came one night and sat upon my breast, as aforesaid, which she denied and I affirmed to her face to be true and that I did plainly see her. Upon which discourse with her, she threatened me.

And some time after that, I being not very well stayed at home on a Lord's Day. And on the afternoon of said day, the doors being shut, I did see a black pig in the room coming towards me, so I went towards it to kick it, and it vanished away. Immediately after, I sat down in a narrow bar and did see a black thing jump into the window and came and stood just before my face, upon the bar. The body of it looked like a monkey, only the feet were like a cock's feet, with claws, and the face somewhat more like a man's than a monkey. And I being greatly affrighted, not being able to speak or help myself, by reason of fear, I suppose. So the thing spoke to me and said, I am a messenger sent to you, for I understand you are troubled in mind, and if you will be ruled by me you shall want for nothing in this world. Upon which, I endeavored to clap my hands upon it, and said, you devil, I will kill you. But [I] could feel no substance, and it jumped out of the window again, and immediately came in by the porch, although the doors were shut, and said, you had better take my counsel. Whereupon, I struck at it with a stick, but struck the groundsill and broke the stick, but felt no substance. And that arm with which I struck was presently disenabled. Then it vanished away, and I opened the back door and went out.

And going towards the house end, I espied said Bridget Bishop in her orchard, going towards her house. And seeing her, [I] had no power to set one foot forward, but returned in again. And going to shut the door, I again did see that, or the like creature, that I before did see, within doors, in such a posture as it seemed to be agoing to fly at me. Upon which I cried out, the whole armour of God to be between me and you. So it sprang back and flew over the apple tree, flinging the dust with its feet against my stomach. Upon which I was struck dumb, and so continued for about three day's time, and also shook many of the apples off from the tree which it flew over.

[Reverse] John Lowder appeared before us this 2 day of June, 1692, and on the oath that he had taken, did own this testimony to be the truth before us, the Jurors of Inquest.

Bridget Bishop, alias Oliver, on her trial denied that she knew this deponent, though the orchard of this deponent and the orchard of said Bishop joined and they often had differences for some years.

Testimony of John and William Blye

June 2^d, 1692. John Blye, Senior, aged about 57 years, and William Blye, aged about 15 years, both of Salem, testifieth and saith that being employed by

Bridgitt Boshop, alias Oliver, of Salem, to help take down the cellar wall of the old house she formerly lived in, we, the said deponents, in holes in the said old wall belonging to the said cellar found several puppets made up of rags and hogs' bristles, with headless pins in them with the points outward, and this was about seven years last passed.

Testimony of John Cooke

John Cooke, aged about 18 years, testifieth that about five or six years ago, one morning about sun rising, as I was in bed before I rose, I saw Goodwife Bishop, alias Oliver, stand in the chamber by the window. And she looked on me and grinned on me, and presently struck me on the sides of the head, which did very much hurt me. And then I saw her go out under the end window, at a little crevice about so big as I could thrust my hand into.

I saw her again the same day, which was the Sabbath Day, about noon, walk across the room. And having at the time an apple in my hand, it flew out of my hand into my mother's lap, who sat six or eight feet distance from me. And then she disappeared. And though my mother and several others were in the same room, yet they affirmed they saw her not.

John Cooke appeared before us, the Jurors of Inquest, and did own this to be his testimony on the oath that he hath taken, this 2 day of June, '92.

Testimony of John and Rebecca Bly

John Bly, Senior, and Rebecka Bly, his wife, of Salem, both testify and say that said Jno. Bly bought a sow of Edwd. Bishop of Salem, sawyer, and by agreement with said Bushop was to pay the price agreed upon unto Lt. Jeremiah Neale of Salem. And Bridgett, the wife of said Edward Bushop, because she could not have the money or value agreed for paid unto her, she came to the house of the deponents in Salem and quarrelled with them about it.

Soon after which, the sow having pigged, she was taken with strange fits, jumping up and knocking her head against the fence, and seemed blind and deaf, and would not eat, neither let her pigs suck, but foamed at the mouth, which Goody Hinderson hearing of, said she believed she was overlooked, and that they had their cattle ill in such a manner at the eastward when she lived there, and used to cure them by giving of them red ocre and milk, which we also gave the sow. Quickly after eating of which she grew better, and then for the space of near two hours together she, getting into the street, did set off jumping and running between the house of said deponents and said Bishops as if she were stark mad. And after that, was well again. And we did then apprehend or judge, and do still, that said Bishop had bewitched said sow.

Testimony of Susanna Sheldon

The deposition of Susannah Sheldon, aged about 18 years, who testifieth and saith that on the 2 June, 1692, I saw the apparition of Bridget Bishop, and immediately appeared two little children and said that they were Thomas Green's two twins, and told Bridget Bishop to her face that she had murdered them, in setting them into fits whereof they died.

Testimony of Susanna Sheldon Against
Bridget Bishop and Others

On the fourth day, at night, came Goody Olliver, and Mrs. English, and Goodman Corie, and a black man with a high crowned hat, with books in their hands. Goody Olliver bade me touch her book. I would not. I did not know her name. She told me her name was Goody Olliver, and bid me touch her book now. I bid her tell me how long she had been a witch. She told me she had been a witch above twenty years. Then there came a stretched snake creeping over her shoulder, and crept into her bosom.

Mrs. English had a yellow bird in her bosom, and Goodman Corie had two turtles hang[ing] to his coat, and he opened his bosom and put his turtles to his breast and gave them suck. Then Goodman Core and Goody Olliver kneeled down before the black man and went to prayer. And then the black man told me Goody Olliver had been a witch twenty years and an half. Then they all set to biting me and so went away. The next day came Goodman Corie [and] Mrs. English, in the morning, and told me I should not eat no vittles. I took a spoon and put one spoonful in my mouth, and Goodman Corie gave me a blow on the ear and almost choked me. Then he laughed at me and told me I would eat when he told me I should not. Then he clenched my hands that they could not be opened for more than a quarter of an hour. Then came Phillip English and told me if I would touch his book he would not bite me, but if I refused then he did bite me, and went away.

The sixth day, at night, came Goody Olliver and Mrs. English, Goodman Core and his wife. Goodwife Core presented me a book. I refused it and asked her where she lived. She told me she lived in Boston prison. Then she pulled out her breast and the black man gave her a thing like a black pig. It had no hairs on it, and she put it to her breast and gave it suck, and when it had sucked one breast she put it to the other, and gave it suck there. Then she gave it to the black man. Then they went to prayer to the black man. Then Goody Olliver told me she had killed four women. Two of them were the Fosters' wives, and John Traske's wife, and did not name the other.

Then they did all bite me and went away. Then the next day came Goody Core [who] choked me and told me I would not eat when my dame bid me, but now I should eat none.

Testimony of the Reverend Mr. John Hale

John Hale of Beverly, aged about 56 years, testifieth and saith that about 5 or 6 years ago, Christian, the wife of John Trask (living in Salem bounds bordering on the abovesaid Beverly), being in full communion in our church, came to me to desire that Goodwife Bishop, her neighbor, wife of Edw. Bishop, Jun., might not be permitted to receive the Lord's Supper in our church till she had given her, the said Trask, satisfaction for some offences that were against her, *viz.*, because the said Bishop did entertain people in her house at unseasonable hours in the night to keep drinking and playing at shuffleboard, whereby discord did arise in other families, and young people were in danger to be corrupted. And that the said Trask knew these things, and has once gone into the house and finding some at shuffleboard had taken the pieces they played with and thrown them into the fire, and had reproved the said Bishop for promoting such disorders, but received no satisfaction from her about it.

I gave said Christian Trask direction how to proceed farther in this matter, if it were clearly proved. And indeed, by the information I have had otherwise, I do fear that if a stop had not been put to those disorders, said Edward Bishop's house would have been a house of great profaneness and iniquity.

But as to Christian Trask, the next news I heard of her was that she was distracted. And asking her husband, Trask, when she was so taken, [he told] me she was taken distracted that night after she [came from] my house when she complained against Goody Bishop.

She continuing some time distracted, we sought the Lord by fasting and prayer, and the Lord was pleased to restore the said [Trask] to the use of her reason again. I was with her often in [her] distraction (and took it then to be only distraction, yet fearing sometimes some [thing] yet worse), but since I have seen the fits of those bewitched at Salem Village, I call to mind some of hers to be much like some of theirs.

The said Trask, when recovered, as I understood it, did manifest strong suspicion that she had been bewitched by the said Bishop's wife, and showed so much averseness from having any converse [with] her that I was then troubled at it, as hoping better of Goody Bishop at that time, for we have since [torn]. At length, said Christian Trask fell [?] again in a distracted fit on a Sabbath day, in the forenoon at the public meeting, to our public disturbance, and so continued, sometimes better, sometimes worse, unto her death, manifesting that she [torn] under temptation to kill herself or somebody else.

I enquired of Margt. King, who kept at or nigh the house, what she had observed of said Trask before this last distraction. She told [me] Goody Trask was much given to reading and search[ing] the prophecies of scripture.

The day before she made that disturbance in the meeting house, she came home and said she had been with Goody Bishop and that they two were now friends, or to that effect.

I was off praying with and counselling of Goody Trask before her death, and not many days before her end, being there, she seemed more rational, and earnestly desired Edw. Bishop might be sent for that she might make friends with him. I asked her if she had wronged Edw. Bishop. She said, not that she knew of, unless it were in taking his shuffleboard pieces when people were at play with them and throwing them into the fire. And if she did evil in it, she was very sorry for it, and desired he would be friends with her or forgive her. This was the very day before she died, or a few days before.

Her distraction (or bewitching) continued about a month, and in those intervals wherein she was better, she earnestly desired prayers. And the Sabbath before she died, I received a note for prayers on her behalf, which her husband said was written by herself, and I judge was her own handwriting, being well acquainted with her hand.

As to the wounds she died of, I observed 3 deadly ones: a piece of her windpipe cut out, and another wound above that, through the windpipe and gulle[t] to the vein they call jugular. So that I then judged and still do apprehend it impossible for her with so short a pair of scissors to mangle herself so, without some extraordinary work of the devil or witchcraft.

Signed, 20 May 1692, by John Hale

To several parts of this testimony can witness Maj^r. Gedney, Mr. Paris, Joseph Herrick, junr., and his wife, Thomas Raiment and his wife, John Traske, Marget King, Hannah, wife of Colonel Baker, [illegible] Miles, and others.

As also, about the said Goody Bishop: Capt. William Raiment, his son Wm. Raiment, about creatures strangely dying. James Kettle, and the abovesaid Jos. Herrick and Tho. Rayment about sundry actions that have the appearance of witchcraft.

Death Warrant Against Bridget Bishop

To George Corwin, Gent^m., High Sheriff of the County of Essex.

Greeting.

Whereas Bridgett Bishop, alias Olliver, the wife of Edward Bishop of Salem in the County of Essex, sawyer, at a special court of Oyer and Terminer held at Salem the second day of this instant month of June for the Counties of Essex, Middlesex, and Suffolk, before William Stoughton, Esqr., and his Associate Justices of the said court, was indicted and arraigned upon five several indictments for using, practicing, and exercising on the nineteenth day of April last past, and divers other days and time before and after, certain acts of witchcraft in and upon the bodies of Abigail Williams, Ann Puttnam, Junr., Mercy Lewis, Mary Walcott, and Elizabeth Hubbard of Salem Village, single-women, whereby their bodies were hurt, afflicted, pined, consumed, wasted, and tormented contrary to the form of the statute in that case made and provided.

To which indictments the said Bridgett Bishop pleaded not guilty and for trial thereof put herself upon God and her country, whereupon she was found guilty of the felonies and witchcrafts whereof she stood indicted, and sentence of death accordingly passed against her as the law directs.

Execution whereof yet remains to be done.

These are therefore in the name of their Majesties William and Mary, now King and Queen over England &c. to will and command you that upon Friday next, being the tenth day of this instant month of June, between the hours of eight and twelve in the forenoon of the same day, you safely conduct the said Bridget Bishop, alias Oliver, from their Majesties' jail in Salem aforesaid to the place of execution, and there cause her to be hanged by the neck until she be dead, and of your doings herein make return to the clerk of the said court and p^scept.

And hereof you are not to fail at your peril.

> And this shall be your sufficient warrant. Given under my hand and seal at Boston the eighth day of June in the fourth year of the reign of our sovereign Lord and Lady William and Mary, now King and Queen over England &c., *Anno Dom.* 1692.

> Wm. Stoughton

Execution of Bridget Bishop

June 10th, 1692

According to the within written precept, I have taken the body of the within named Brigett Bishop out of their Majesties' jail in Salem and safely conveyed her to the place provided for her execution, and caused the said Brigett to be hanged by the neck until she was dead and buried in the place. All which was according to the time within required. And so I make return by me.

> George Corwin, Sheriff

Nehemiah Jewett to Stephen Sewall of the Committee Chosen by the General Court to Make Restitution (1711)

Mr. Sewall,

Sir, I thought good to return to you the names of several persons that were condemned and executed that not any person or relations appeared in the behalf of, for the taking off the attainder, or for other expenses. They I supposed were returned to the General Court's consideration for to act about according to their best prudence: Bridget Bishop, alias Oliver; Susanna Martin; Alice Parker; Ann Pudeter; Welmot Read; Marget Scott.

Sir, I am your Honour's to serve,

Neh. Jewet.

Chapter Four

John Willard

Testimony of Phillip Knight
and Thomas Nichols

The deposition of Phillip Knight, aged 46 years, and of Thomas Nicols, 22 years, who do testify and say that sometimes in April last, there was discourse at the house of the said Phillip Knight about several of the village that were taken up upon suspicion of witchcraft. John Willard, being present, then replied, hang them, they are all witches.

Testimony of Henry Wilkins, Senior

The deposition of Henery Wilknes, Sen., aged 41 years, who testifieth and saith that upon the third of May last, John Willard came to my house and very earnestly entreated me to go with him to Boston, which I at length consented to go with him. My son Daniel coming and understanding I was going with him to Boston and seemed to be much troubled that I would go with the said Willard, and he said he thought it were well if the said Willard were hanged, which made me admire, for I never heard such an expression come from him to any one being, since he came to years of discretion.

But after I was gone, in a few days he was taken sick, and grew every day worse and worse. Whereupon we made application to a physician who affirmed his sickness was by some preternatural cause, and would make no application of any physick. Sometimes after this, our neighbors coming to visit my son, Mercy Lewis came with them and affirmed that she saw the apparition of John Willard afflicting him. Quickly after came Ann Putnam, and she saw the same apparition. And then my eldest daughter was taken in a sad manner and the said An saw the said Willard afflicting her. At another time Mercy Lewes and Mary Walcott came to visit him and they saw the same apparition of Willard afflicting him, and this not but a little time before his death.

Testimony of Benjamin Wilkins and Thomas Flint

The testimony of Benjamin Wilkins, aged about 36 years, and Thomas Flint, aged about 46 years, testifieth that on the 16 day of May last, 1692, we being at the house of Henry Wilkins where we saw his son Daniell Wilkins [torn] as we judged at the point of death, and Marcy Lues and Mary Wolcot being with us, told us that John Willard and Goody Buckly were upon his throat and upon his breast and pressed him and choked him. And to our best judgment he was pressed and choked from the time we saw him almost to death, [torn] and the said Benjamin Wilkins continued with him till [torn] was about 3 hours after, and he altered not in the manner [torn] condition, only grew worse and worse till he died.

Testimony of Bray Wilkins

The deposition of Bray Wilkins of Salem Village, aged about eighty and one years, with reference to John Willard of said Salem, lately charged with witchcraft. When he was at first complained of by the afflicted persons for afflicting of them, he came to my house greatly troubled, desiring me with some other neighbors to pray for him. I told him I was then going from home and could not stay, but if I could come home before night I should not be unwilling, but it was near night before I came home, and so I did not answer his desire. But I heard no more of him upon that account. Whether my not answering his desire did not offend him I cannot tell, but I was jealous afterward that it did.

A little after, my wife and I went to Boston at the last election, when I was as well in health as in many years before. And [on] the election day, coming to my brother Lieut. Richard Way's house at noon, there were many friends to dine there. They were sat down at the table, Mr. Lawson and his wife and several more. John Willard came into the house with my son Henry Wilkins before I sat down, and said Willard, to my apprehension, looked after such a sort upon me as I never before discerned in any. I did but step into the next room and I was presently taken in a strange condition so that I could not dine nor eat anything. I cannot express the misery I was in, for my water was suddenly stopped and I had no benefit of nature, but was like a man on a rack, and I told my wife immediately that I was afraid that Willard had done me wrong. My pain continuing, and finding no relief, my jealously continued. Mr. Lawson and others there were all amazed and knew not what to do for me. There was a woman accounted skillful came, hoping to help me, and after she had used means she asked me whether none of those evil persons had done me damage. I said I could not say they had, but I was sore afraid they had. She answered she did fear so too.

As near as I remember, I lay in this case 3 or 4 days at Boston, and afterwards, with the jeopardy of my life (as I thought), I came home. And then, some of my friends coming to see me (and at this time John Willard was run away), one of the afflicted persons, Mercy Lewes, came in with them, and they asked whether she saw anything. She said, yes, they are looking for John Willard but there he is upon his grandfather's* belly (and at that time I was in grievous pain in the small of my belly). I continued so in grievous pain, and my water much stopped, till said Willard was in chains, and then, as near as I can guess, I had considerable ease. But, on the other hand, in the room of a stoppage I was vexed with a flowing of water so that it was hard to keep myself dry. On the 5 July last, talking with some friends about John Willard, some pleading his innocency, and myself and some others arguing the contrary, within about 1/4 of an hour after that (I had said it was not I nor my son Benj. Wilkins, but the testimony of the afflicted persons, and the jury, concerning the murder of my grandson, Dan Wilkins, that would take away his life, if anything did), and within about 1/4 hour after this, I was taken in the sorest distress and misery, my water being turned into real blood, or of a bloody color, and the old pain returned excessively as before, which continued for about 24 hours together.

Testimony of Benjamin Wilkins and John Putnam

The testimony of Benjamin Wilkens, aged about 36 years, saith that about the 12 of May last, Mercy Lues, being at my father's house, told us that she saw John Wilard and Goody Buckly upon my father Wilknes, pressing his belly. And my father complained of extreme pain in his belly at the same time. Then John Putnam struck at the apparitions, then Marcy Lues fell down, and my father had ease immediately.

John Putnam testifieth to the same abovewritten.

Testimony of Susanna Sheldon

The 9th of May, 1692. This is the first to be read.
The testimony of Susannah Shelton, aged 18 years or thereabout, testifieth and saith, the day of the date hereof I saw at Natt Ingerson's [i.e., Ingersoll's]

*[*In this period, terms such as "brother," "grandfather," "mother" were commonly used to designate in-laws as well as blood relatives.]*

house the apparition of these 4 persons: William Shaw's first wife, the widow Cooke, Goodman Jons, and his child. And among these came the apparition of John Willard, to whom these 4 said, you have murdered us. These 4 having said thus to Willard they turned as red as blood, and turning about to look on me they turned as pale as death. These 4 desired me to tell Mr. Hathorn. Willard, hearing them, pulled out a knife saying if I did he would cut my throat.

The second to be read.

The same day there appeared to me Eleasabath Colson, and she took a book and would have me to set my hand to it, and I would not. And then she proffered me a black purse [?] of money and said I might touch it and I shall be well. May the 10, on Tuesday, there appeared to me the same apparitions and another with them in the likeness of a man, and they said I should go and tell Mr. Hathorn of it. Then the said Willard said he would break my head and stop my legs that I should not go. There did appear to me a Shining Man who told [me] I should go and tell what I had heard and seem to Mr. Hathorn. This Willard, being there present, told me if I did, he would cut my throat. At this same time and place, this shining man told me that if I did go to tell this to Mr. Hathorn that I should be well, going and coming, but I should be afflicted there. Then said I to the shining man, hunt Willard away and I would believe what he said, that he might not shock me. With that, the shining man held up his hand and Willard vanished away.

About two hours after, the same appeared to me again, and the said Willard with them, and I asked them where their wounds were, and they said there would come an angel from heaven and would show them, and forthwith the angel come. I asked what the man's name was that appeared to me last, and the angel told his name was Southerek. And the angel lifted up his winding sheet, and out of his left side he pulled out a pitchfork tine and put it in again. And likewise he opened all their winding sheets and showed all their wound. And the white man told me to tell Mr. Hathorne of it, and I told him to hunt Willard away and I would. And he held up his hand and he vanished away.

The second [i. e., third] to be read.

The evening of the same day came to me the apparition of these three: John Willard, Elizabeth Colson, and one old man which I knew not, who tempted her with their books and money and afflicted her sorely all the fore part of the night. I saw this Willard suckle the apparition of two black pigs on his breast, and this Colson suckled, as it appeared, a yellow bird. This old man, which I knew not, suckled a black snake. Then Willard tempted me again with his book. I said to Willard, how long have you been a wizard. He told me twenty years. And forthwith they kneeled to prayer to the black man with a long-crowned hat which then was with them, and then they vanished away.

May the 11, being on Wednesday, 1692

As I was coming to the bound by the bridge, I saw the said Willard and the old man coming over the waters. They landed by George Hacker's in a dish, and at the present writing these three appeared with a book tempting me after the same manner.

Susannah Shelton did this 3 day of June own this her testimony before us, the Jurors of Inquest, to be the truth.

Testimony of Elizabeth Hubbard

The deposition of Elizabeth Hubburd, aged about 17 years, who testifieth and saith that on the 11 May, 1692, I saw the apparition of John Willard of Salem Village, who did immediately torment me and urged me to write in his book. But on the 18th of May, being the day of his examination, John Willard did most grievously torture me during the time of his examination, for if he did but look upon me he would immediately strike me down, or almost choke me. And also during the time of his examination I saw the apparition of John Willard go from him and afflict the bodies of Mary Walcott, Mircy Lewes, Abigaill Williams, and Ann Putnam, Jun[r].

Elizabeth Hubburt did own this testimony after the reading of it before us, the Jurors for Inquest, this 3 day of June, '92.

Testimony of Mercy Lewis

The deposition of Mircy Lewes, who testifieth and saith that I have often seen the apparition of John Willard amongst the witches within this three weeks, but he did not do me much hurt till the 11th of May, 1692, and then he fell upon me most dreadfully and did most grievously afflict me, almost ready to kill me, urging me most vehemently to write in his book. And so he hath continued ever since, at times torturing me most dreadfully, beating and pinching me and almost ready to choke me, threatening to kill if I would not write in his book.

Also, I being carried to Will's Hill on the 14th of May at evening, to see the afflicted persons there, I saw there the apparition of John Willard grievously afflicting his grandfather Wilknes, and I also saw the apparition of John Willard there grievously afflicting the body of Daniell Wilknes who laid speechless and in a sad condition, and John Willard told me he would kill Daniell Wilknes within two days if he could.

Also, I was at Henry Wilknes' the 16 May, a little before night, and there I saw the apparition of John Willard choking Daniell Wilknes. Also on the 18th May, being the day of his examination, I was most grievously tortured by him during the time of his examination. For if he did but look upon me, he struck me down or almost choked me to death. And several times since, the apparition of John Willard has most grievously afflicted me by beating, pinching, and almost choking me to death. Also, during the time of his examination, I saw the apparition of John Willard go from him and afflict the bodies of Mary Wolcott, Abigail Williams, Elizabeth Hubbard, and Ann Putnam, Jun[r].

Warrant for the Arrest of John Willard

To the Constables of Salem

You are in their Majesties' Names required to apprehend and bring before us the body of John Willard of Salem Village, husbandman, tomorrow, being the eleventh day of this instant May, by one of the clock afternoon, at the house of Thomas Beadle in Salem, who stands accused of high suspicion of several acts of witchcraft done or committed upon the bodies of sundry persons in Salem Village to their great hurt and injury, and hereof you are not to fail.

Dated, Salem, May 10th, 1692

John Hathorne } Assistants
Jonathan Corwin

Return of the Constable

In prosecution of this warrant I went to the house of the usual abode of John Willard's and made search for him, and in several other houses and places, but could not find him, and his relations and friends then gave me account that to their best knowledge he was fled.

Salem, May 12th, 1692

John Putnam, Jun., Constable, Salem

Second Warrant for the Arrest of John Willard

To the Marshall of the County of Essex, or to the Constables in Salem or any other Marshall or Marshalls, Constable or Constables, with this their Majesties' Colony or Territory of the Massachusetts in New England.

You are, in their Majesties' names, hereby required to apprehend John Willard of Salem Village, husbandman, if he may be found in your precincts, who stands charged with sundry acts of witchcraft by him done or committed on the bodies of Bray Wilkins and Daniel Wilkins, the son of Henery Wilkins, both of Salem Village, and others according to complaint made before us by Thomas Fuller, Jun[r], and Benj. Wilkins, Sen[r], both of Salem Village aforesaid, yeoman; who, being found, you are to convey from town to town, from Constable to Constable, until he be brought before us or such as may be authority here in Salem, and hereof you are not to fail.

Dated Salem, May the 15th, 1692,

John Hathorne } Assistants
Jonathan Corwin

P. us.

To be prosecuted according to the direction of Constable John Putnam of Salem Village, who goes with the same.

Return of the Constable

I have apprehended John Willard of Salem Village according to the tenor of this warrant, and brought him before your worships.

Date 18 May, 1692.

by me   John Putnam, Constable of Salem.

Testimony of Sarah Bibber

June the 3, 1692

Sarah Vibber, aged 36 years or thereabouts, testifieth and saith, the day before Jno. Willard was examined at the village, I being in Lieut. Ingersol's chamber, I saw the apparition of John Willard come to Mary Wolcot and Mercy Luis and hurt them grievously and almost choked them. Then I told of it, and immediately the said Willard fell upon me and tormented me grievously and pinched me and threw me down.
Sarah Vibber owned this her testimony before us, the Jurors for Inquest, this 3 of June. 1692.

Testimony of Samuel Parris, Nathaniel Ingersoll, and Thomas Putnam

The deposition of Samuel Parris, aged about 39 years, and Nathaniell Ingersoll, aged about fifty and eight years, and also Thomas Putnam, aged about forty years, all of Salem, testifieth and saith, that Eliz. Hubbard, Mary Warren, and Ann Putnam, and John Indian, were exceedingly tortured at the examination of John Willard of Salem, husbandman, before the honoured Magistrates the 18 May, 1692, and also, that upon his looking upon Eliz. Hubbard she was knocked down, and also that some of the afflicted, and particularly Susannah Sheldon, then and there testified that they saw a black man whispering him in the ear, and that said Sheldon could not come near to said Willard but was knocked down, and also that Mary Warren in a fit, being carried to him, the said Willard, the said was presently well upon his grasping her arm. And further, that several of the afflicted also then testified that divers of those he had murdered then rose up against him, and further that he could by no means rightly repeat the Lord's Prayer, though he made manifold assays.
Mr. Samuel Parris and Nathaniel Ingersoll and Thomas Putnam did upon the oath which they had taken did before us the Juries of Inquest own this their testimony this 3d day of June '92.
Sworn in Court by Mr. Parris and Tho. Putnam

Testimony of Thomas and Edward Putnam

The deposition of Thomas Putnam, aged about 40 years, and Edward Putnam, aged 38 years, who testify and say that, we having been conversant with several of the afflicted persons, as namely, Mary Walcott, Mercy Lewes, Elizabeth Hubbert, Abigail Williams, and Ann Putnam, Junr, and we have seen them most grievously tormented by pinching and pricking and being almost choked to death, most grievously complaining of John Willard for hurting them. But on the 18th day of May, 1692, being the day of his examination, the aforesaid afflicted persons were most grievously tormented during the time of his examination, for if he did but cast his eyes upon them they were struck down or almost choked. Also, several times since, we have seen the aforesaid afflicted persons most grievously tormented, as if their bones would have been disjoined, grievously complaining of John Willard for hurting them. And we verily believe that John Willard, the prisoner at the bar, has several times tormented and afflicted the aforesaid persons with acts of witchcraft.

Thomas Putnam
Edward Putnam

Indictment of John Willard

The Jurors for our Sovereign Lord and Lady, the King and Queen, present, that John Willard of Salem Village in the County of Essex, husbandman, the eighteenth day of May, [1692] . . . and divers other days and times as well, before and after, certain detestable arts called witchcrafts and sorceries wickedly and feloniously hath used, practiced, and exercised at and within the town of Salem in the County of Essex aforesaid in, upon, and against one Mercy Lewis of Salem Village aforesaid in the county aforesaid, singlewoman, by which said wicked arts the said Mercy Lewis . . . was and is hurt, tortured, afflicted, consumed, pined, wasted, and tormented against the peace of our Sovereign Lord and Lady, the King and Queen, and against the form of the statute in that case made and provided.

Witnesses   Mercy Lewis

Abigail Williams
Mary Walcott
Susanna Sheldon
Ann Puttnam Senr
Ann Putnam Junr
Elizabeth Hubbard

[A total of seven indictments, identical in form to the one printed above, were returned against Willard. Two are missing. The remaining four charge him

with practicing witchcraft upon Ann Putnam, Jr., Susannah Sheldon, Abigail Williams, and Elizabeth Hubbard. The date of the alleged sorcery is the same in all the indictments: May 18, 1692.]

Physical Examination of John Willard

We whose names under written, having searched the bodies of John Proctor, sen^r, and John Willard, now in the jail, and do not find anything to farther suspect them.

Dated June 2, 1692

N. Roudel, Apprentice
John Rogers
Joshua Rea, Junr
John Cooke

J. Barton, Chyrg^e. [Surgeon]
John Gyles
William Hyne
Ezekel Cheever

Testimony of Ann Putnam, Senior

Hannah [Ann] Putnam, aged 30 years, saith that the shape of Sam^ll Fuller and Lidia Wilkins this day told me, at my own house by the bedside, who appeared in winding sheets, that if I did not go and tell Mr. Hathorne that John Willard had murdered them, they would tear me to pieces. I knew them when they were living, and it was exactly their resemblance and shape.

And at the same time the apparition of John Willard told me that he had killed Sam^ll Fuller, Lidia Wilkins, Goody Shaw, and Fuller's second wife, and Aron Way's child, and Ben Fuller's child, and this deponent's child, Sarah, 6 weeks old, and Phillip Knight's child, with the help of Wm Hobbs, and Johnathan Knight's child and 2 of Ezch: Cheever's children with the help of Wm Hobbs. Anne Eliot and Isaac Nichols with the help of Williams Hobbs. And that if Mr. Hathorne would not believe them, Sam Fuller and Lida Wilkins, perhaps they would appear to the magistrates.

Joseph Fuller's apparition the same day also came to me and told me that Goody Corey had killed him. The specter aforesaid told me that vengeance, vengeance, was cried by said Fuller.

This relation is *true*.

mark
Ann   an   Putnam

Sworn in Court, June 2^d, 1692

Testimony of Samuel Wilkins

The deposition of Samuell Wilknes, aged about 19 years, who testifieth and saith, that since Jno. Willard has been in prison I have been afflicted in a strange kind of manner, for about the latter end of June or beginning of July, as I was a weaving, the yarn broke exceeding fast, and as I was a tying a thread I had a stroke on my hand like a knife, the blood being almost ready to come out. And I was also pinched several times by an unseen hand. Also, riding to Marblehead, just as I came to Forest River Bridge, I was immediately seized with a violent weight on my back, and I saw a black hat, and was immediately pulled off my horse or mare and almost pulled into the river. But holding fast at last I got up again. A while after, as I was once in the woods and agoing home, and a little boy with me, I thought I must run, and I said to the boy: Let us run. And as soon as I ran, there was a black hat run along by me. A while after, one morning about an hour by sun, I was afflicted and I saw John Willard, or his appearance, with a dark-colored coat and a black hat very like that hat which I formerly saw. A little while after this, one night as soon as I was a bed, John Willard, whom I very well knew, or his appearance, came into the room where I was a bed, and another man and woman along with him which I did not know, and they told me they would carry me away before morning.

Testimony of Elizabeth Booth
and Susanna Sheldon

The deposition of Eliz. Booth, aged about 18 years, who testifieth and saith, that several times since the latter end of June, 1692, I have been most grievously afflicted and tormented by John Willard, or his appearance, by pinching, pricking, and almost choking me to death. Also I have often seen John Willard, or his appearance, most grievously tormenting and afflicting my brother George Booth, almost ready to kill him.

Susannah Shelden also testifieth that within this fortnight she hath seen John Willard, or his appearance, most grievously torment and afflict George Booth, almost ready to press him to death.

Examination of Richard Carrier

Richard Carrier's Confession, July 22, 1692

Q. Have you been in the devil's snare?
A. Yes.
Q. Is your brother Andrew ensnared by the devil's snare?
A. Yes.
Q. How long has your brother been a witch?

A. Near a month.
Q. How long have you been a witch?
A. Not long.
Q. Have you joined in afflicting the afflicted persons?
A. Yes.
Q. You helped to hurt Timo. Swan, did you?
A. Yes.
Q. How long have you been a witch?
A. About five weeks.
Q. Who was in company when you convenanted with the devil?
A. Mrs. Bradbery.
Q. Did she help you afflict?
A. Yes.
Q. What was the occasion Mrs. Bradbery would have to afflict Timo. Swan?
A. Because her husband and Timo. Swan fell out about a scythe, I think.
Q. Did they not fall out about thatching a barn, too?
A. No, not as I know of.
Q. Who was at the village meeting when you was there?
A. Goodwife How, Goodwife Nurs, Goodwife Wildes, Proctor and his wife, Mrs. Bradbery, and Gory's [Cory's] wife.
Q. Was any of Boston there?
A. No.
Q. How many was there in all?
A. A dozen, I think.
Q. Was John Willard there?
A. I think he was.
Q. What kind of man is John Willard? A young man or an old man?
A. He is not an old man. He had black hair.
Q. What meeting was this meeting? Was this that that was near Ingersal's?
A. Yes, I think.
Q. What did they do then?
A. They ate and drank wine.
Q. Was there a minister there?
A. No, not as I know of.
Q. From whence had you your wine?
A. From Salem, I think it was.
Q. Goodwife Olliver there?
A. Yes, I knew her.

Testimony of Rebecca Wilkins

The testimony of Rebeckah Wilkins, aged nineteen years, do testify that 29th July, at night, she see John Willard setting in the corner, and he said that he would afflict me that night, and forthwith he did afflict me. And the next day I did see him afflict me sore by choking and pulling me [my] ear into pieces. The next day being the Lord's Day, I being going to meeting I see John Willard, and he afflicted me very sore.

Rebecca Wilkins

Testimony of Lydia Nichols and Margaret Knight

The deposition of Lydia Nicoles, aged 46 years, and of Margeret Knight, aged 20 years, who testify and say that the wife of John Willard, being at her father's house when the said Willard lived at Groton, she made a lamentable complaint how cruelly her husband had beaten her. She thought herself that she should never recover of the blows he had given her. The next morning he was got into a little hole under the stairs, and then she thought something extraordinary had befallen him. Then he ran out at the door and ran up a steep hill almost impossible for any man to run up, as she said. Then she took her mare and rode away, fearing some evil had been intended as against her. And when she came to the house of Henery or Benjamin Willard she told how it was with her, and the said Henery Willard, or both, went to look after him and met him running in a strange, distracted frame.

Testimony of Thomas Bailey

The deposition of Thomas Baly, aged 36 years, who testifieth and saith that I, being at Groton some short time after John Willard, as the report went, had beaten his wife, I went to call him home, and coming home with him in the night, I heard such a hideous noise of strange creatures I was much affrighted, for I never had heard the like noise. I fearing they might be some evil spirits, I enquired of the said Willard what might it be that made such a hideous noise. The said Willard said they were locust. The next day, as I suppose, the said Willard's wife, with a young child and her mother, being upon my mare riding between Groton mill and Chelmsford, they being willing to go on foot a little, desired me to ride. Then I taking my mare, being willing to let her feed a little there, as I remember I apprehend I heard the same noise again, whereat my mare started and got from me.

Testimony of Benjamin and John Wilkins and Nathaniel Richardson

The deposition of Benjamin Wilkins, aged 36 years, and John Wilkins, aged 36 years.

These deponents testify and say that Lidia Wilkins, wife of John Wilkins, was well delivered with child, and was well the next day after. But the second day after she was delivered, she was taken with a violent fever and flux, as we supposed [she] had. In a little time the flux abated, but the fever continued till she died, which was about four days.

Nath. Richison tells of a Nashway man that speaks of a profound sleep that Willard was in.

Testimony of Elizabeth Bailey

The testimony of Elizabeth Bayly, aged twenty seven years or thereabouts, testifieth and saith, that John Willard looking [for?] his oxen met with this deponent and told her that all the way from Francis Elliott's house to his own home he verily thought that the Devil came before him or behind him all the way, which dreadfully frighted him. The said deponent asked him why he thought so, he answered he could not tell and immediately fell a singing.

The mark of ⟂ Elizabeth Bayley

Petition of John Willard's Widow
(September 1710)

Topsfield, September 13, 1710

To the Honoured Committee appointed by the Honoured General Court to make inquiry into the damage sustained by any persons in the year 1692 by reason of the great disturbance in our land from the powers of darkness, the committee aforesaid being to meet at Salem, September the 14th.

Margaret Town of Topsfield in the County of Essex in New England, formerly Margaret Willard, relict of John Willard, late of Salem, who suffered death in that hour of the power of darkness as if he had been quilty of one of the greatest crimes that ever any of the sons of Adam have been left of God to fall into, having been notified by order of the General Court to appear before your Honours to give an account, as near as I can, what damage myself together with my aforesaid former husband did sustain in our estate, besides the fearful odium cast on him by imputing to him and causing him to suffer death for such a piece of wickedness as I have not the least reason in the world to think he was guilty of, I say besides that reproach and the grief and sorrow I was exposed to by that means, I do account our damage as to our outward estate to have been very considerable, for by reason of my said former husband being seized by order of the civil authority and imprisoned, all our husband's concerns were laid by. For that summer we had not opportunity to plant or sow, whereas we were wont to raise our own bread corn.

I reckon (which your Honours may please more certainly to inform yourselves from the records of those unhappy times and things that happened), I say, according to my best remembrance, from the time of his first imprisonment to the time of his suffering was near upon half a year, all of which time I was at the trouble and charge to provide for him in prison what he stood in need of, out of our own estate. My aforesaid husband was 3 weeks a prisoner at Boston, which occasioned me to be at yet more charge and trouble. And although I had, after his sentence of death was passed upon him, obtained a replevin for him for a little time, which was not coming as was expected at the time appointed, I was forced to hire a horse at Salem and go to Boston to see what was the reason of the failure.

I have nothing further to add, but only to pray your Honours to guess at the damage as well as you can by the information I have here given, and that God will direct you in and about what you are now concerned about, and so take leave to subscribe myself your Honours' humble and

sorrowful servant,

The mark of
Margaret X Town

I judge that my loss and damage in my estate hath not been less than thirty pounds, but I shall be satisfied if I may have twenty pounds allowed me.

Chapter Five

George Burroughs

First Examination of Abigail Hobbs

Abigail Hobbs's Examination 20 April 1692 in Salem Prison.

This examinant declares that Judah White, a Jersey maid that lived with Joseph Ingersoll at Casco but now lives at Boston, with whom this examinant was very well formerly acquainted, came to her yesterday in apparition together with Sarah Good (as this examinant was going to examination) and advised her to fly, and not to go to be examined. She told them that she would go. They charged her (if she did go to examination) not to confess anything. She said that she would confess all that she knew. They told her also that Goody Osborn was a witch. This Judah White came to her in fine clothes, in a red-colored silk mantle with a top knot and an hood.

She confesseth further that the Devil in the shape of a man came to her and would have her to afflict Ann Putnam, Mercy Lewis and Abigail Williams, and brought their images with him in wood like them, and gave her thorns, and bid her prick them into these images: which she did accordingly into each one of them. And then the Devil told her they were afflicted, which accordingly they were and cried out they were hurt by Abigail Hobbs.

She confesseth she was at the great meeting in Mr. Parris's pasture when they administered the sacrament and did eat of the red bread and drink of the red wine at the same time.

Testimony of Ann Putnam

The deposition of Ann Putnam, who testifieth and saith that on 20th of April, 1692, at evening, she saw the apparition of a minister, at which she was grievously affrighted and cried out, oh, dreadful, dreadful, here is a minister come. What, are ministers witches, too? Whence come you, and what is your name? For I will complain of you, though you be a minister, if you be a wizard. And immediately I was tortured by him, being racked and almost choked by him. And he tempted me to write in his book, which I refused with loud outcries, and said I would not write in his book though he tore me all to pieces, but told him that it was a dreadful thing that he, which was a minister that should teach children to fear God, should come to persuade poor creatures to give their souls to the devil. Oh, dreadful, dreadful. Tell me your name that I may know who you are. Then again he tortured me and urged me to write in his book, which I refused.

And then presently he told me that his name was George Burroughs, and that he had had three wives, and that he had bewitched the two first of them to death, and that he killed Mistress Lawson because she was so unwilling to go from the village, and also killed Mr. Lawson's child because he went to the eastward with Sir Edmond [Andros] and preached so to the soldiers, and that he had bewitched a great many soldiers to death at the eastward when Sir Edmond was there, and that he had made Abigail Hobbs a witch, and several witches more. And he has continued ever since, by times tempting me to write in his book and grievously torturing me by beating, pinching, and almost choking me several times a day. And he also told me that he was above a witch, he was a conjurer.

Testimony of Thomas Putnam, Peter Prescott, Robert Morrell, and Ezekiel Cheever

We whose names are underwritten, being present with Ann Putnam at the time above mentioned, heard her declare what is abovewritten, what she said she saw and heard from the apparition of Mr. George Burroughs, and also beheld her tortures and perceived her hellish temptations by her loud outcries, I will not, I will not write though you torment me all [the] days of my life. And, being conversant with her ever since, have seen her tortured and complaining that Mr. Burroughs hurt her and tempts her to write in his book.

Thomas Putnam   Peter Prescott

Robert Morrell

Ann Putnam declared her abovewritten evidence to be the truth before the Jury of Inquest. August 3, '92, upon her oath.

Ezekiel Cheever made oath to the latter part of this paper.

Letter of Thomas Putnam

These to the honored John Hathorne and Jonathan Corwin, Esqs., living at Salem, present.

Salem Village, this 21st of April, 1692

Much honored:

After most humble and hearty thanks presented to your Honors for the great care and pains you have already taken for us, for which we are never able to make you recompense (and we believe you do not expect it of us; therefore a full reward will be given you of the Lord God of Israel, whose cause and interest you have espoused, and we trust this shall add to your crown of glory in the day of the Lord Jesus); and we, beholding continually the tremendous works of divine providence—not only every day but every hour—thought it our duty to inform your Honors of what we conceive you have not heard, which are high and dreadful: of a wheel within a wheel, at which our ears do tingle.

Humbly craving continually your prayers and help in this distressed case, so praying almighty God continually to prepare you, that you may be a terror to evil-doers and a praise to them that do well, we remain yours to serve in what we are able.

Thomas Putnam

Statement by Benjamin Hutchinson

Benjemin Huchenson said that on the 21st April, '92, Abegeral Wiluams said that there was a little black minister that lived at Casco Bay, he told me so and said that he had killed three wives, two for himself and one for Mr. Losen [Lawson], and that he had made nine witches in this place, and said that he could hold out the heaviest gun that is in Casco Bay with one hand which no man can scarce hold out with both hands.

This is about 11 o'clock. And I asked her whereabout this little man stood. Said she, just where the cart wheel went along. I had a three-tined iron fork in my hand and I threw it where she said he stood. And she presently fell into a little fit, and when it was over said she, you have torn his coat, for I heard it tear. Whereabouts, said I. On one side, said she. Then we came into the house of Lieut. Ingersall, and I went into the great room and Abigle came in and said, there he stands. I said, where, where, and presently drew my rapier. But he was immediately gone, as she said. Then said she, there is a gray cat. Then I said, whereabouts doth she stand. There, said she, there. Then I struck with my rapier. Then she fell in a fit, and when it was over she said, you killed her. And immediately Sary Good come and carried her away. This was about 12 o'clock.

The same day, after lecture, in the said Ingersoll's chamber, Abigaill Williams [and] Mary Walcot said that Goody Hobs of Topsfield bit Mary Walcot by the foot, then both falling into a fit. As soon as it was over, the said William Hobs and his wife go both of them along the table. The said Hucheson took his rapier [and] stabbed Goody Hobs on the side, as Abigail Williams and Mary Walcot said. The said Abigaill and Mary said the room was full of them. Then the said Hucheson and Eli Putnam stabbed with their rapiers at a ventor. Then said Mary and Abigell, you have killed a great black woman of Stonington and an Indian that come with her, for the floor is all covered with blood. Then the said Mary and Abigaill looked out of doors and said they saw a great company of them on a hill, and there was three of them lay dead, the black woman and the Indian, and one more that they knew not.

This being about 4 o'clock in the afternoon.

Confession of Deliverance Hobbs

Deliverance Hobs's Confession.

That they were both at the general meeting of the witches in Mr. Parishes. Mr. Burroughs preached and administered to them.

Examination of Deliverance Hobbs

The first examination of Deliverance Hobbs in prison.

She continued in the free acknowledging herself to be a covenant witch, and further confesseth she was warned to a meeting yesterday morning, and that there was present [John] Proctor and his wife, Goody Nurse, Giles Cory and his wife, Goody Bishop alias Oliver, and Mr. Burroughs was the preacher, and pressed them to bewitch all in the village, telling them they should do it gradually and not all at once, assuring them they should prevail.

He administered the sacrament unto them at the same time with red bread, and red wine like blood. She affirms she saw Osburn, Sarah Good, [and] Goody Wilds. Goody Nurse and Goody Wilds distributed the bread and wine, and a man in a long-crowned white hat sat next [to] the minister, and they sat seemingly at a table, and they filled out the wine in tankards. The notice of this meeting was given her by Goody Wilds. She herself affirms [that she] did not nor would not eat or drink, but all the rest did who were there present, therefore they threatened to torment her.

The meeting was in the pasture by Mr. Parris's house, and she saw when Abigail Williams ran out [to] speak with them. But that time Abigail was come a little distance from the house, this examinant was struck blind so that she saw not with whom Abigail spake.

She further saith that Goody Wilds, to prevail with her to sign, told her that if she would put her hand to the book she would give her some clothes, and would not afflict her anymore.

Her daughter Abigail Hobbs, being brought in at the same time while her mother was present, was immediately taken with a dreadful fit. And her mother, being asked who it was that hurt her daughter, answered it was Goodman Cory, and she saw him and the gentlewoman of Boston striving to break her daughter's neck.

Testimony of Abigail Hobbs, Deliverance Hobbs, and Mary Warren

1st June, 1692

Abigaile Hobbs then confessed before John Hathorn and Jonathan Corwin, Esq^{rs}, that at the general meeting of the witches in the field near Mr. Parrisse's house she saw Mr. George Burroughs, Sarah Good, Sarah Osborne, Bridgett Bishop, alias Oliver, and Giles Cory, two or three nights ago. Mr. Burrough came and sat at the window and told her he would terribly afflict her for saying so much against him, and then pinched her. Deliverance Hobbs then saw said Burroughs, and he would have tempted her to set her hand to the book and almost shook her to pieces because she would not do it.

Mary Warren testifieth that when she was in prison in Salem, about a fortnight ago, Mr. George Burroughs, Goody Nurse, Goody Procter, Goody Parker, Goody Pudeator, Abigail Soames, Goodman Proctor, Goody Darling, and others unknown came to this deponent and Mr. Burroughs had a trumpet and sounded it, and they would have had this deponent to have gone up with them to a feast at Mr. Parrisses. And Goody Nurse and Goody Proctor told her, this deponent, they were deacons and would have her eat some of their sweet bread and wine. And she asking them what wine that was, one of them said it was blood, and better than our wine. But this deponent refused to eat or drink with them, and they then dreadfully afflicted her at that time.

Sworn the first of June, 1692.

John Hathorne
Jonathan Corwin } Assistants

M[emorandum], that at the time of the taking of this deposition, Goody Nurse appeared in the room and afflicted the deponent Mary and Deliverance Hobbs as they attested, and also almost choked Abigail Hobbs as [she] also testified, and Mr. English then run a pin into Mary's hand as she attested.

Complaint Against George Burroughs

Salem, April the 30th, 1692

There being complaint this day made (before us) by Capt. Jonathan Walcot and Serjt. Thomas Putnam of Salem Village, in behalf of their Majesties, for themselves, and also for several of their neighbors, against George Burroughs, minister in Wells in the province of Maine, Lydia Dasting in Reading, widow Susanah Martin of Amesbury, widow Dorcas Hoar of Beverly, widow, and Sarah Murrell of Beverly, and Phillip English of Salem, merchant, for high suspicion of sundry acts of witchcraft done or committed by them upon the bodies of Mary Walcot, Marcy Lewis, Abigail Williams, Ann Putnam, and Eliz Hubert, and Susanah Sheldon (*viz.*) upon some or all of them, of Salem Village or farms, whereby great hurt and damage been done to the bodies of said persons above named, therefore craved justice.

Signed by both the Complainers abovesaid } Jonathan Walcott　Thomas Putnam

The abovesaid complaint was exhibited before us this 30th April, 1692.

John Hathorne　Jonathan Corwin } Assistants

Arrest and Extradition of George Burroughs

To John Partredg, field marshal

You are required in their Majesties' names to apprehend the body of Mr. George Burroughs, at present preacher at Wells in the province of Maine, and convey him with all speed to Salem before the magistrates there, to be examined, he being suspected for a confederacy with the devil in oppressing of sundry about Salem, as they relate. I having received order from the Governor and Council of their Majesties' Colony of the Massachusetts, for the same, you may not fail herein.

Dated in Portsmouth in the province of Hampshire, April 30th, 1692.

Elisha Hutchinson, Maj[r].

By virtue of this warrant I apprehended said George Burroughs and have brought him to Salem and delivered him to the authority there this fourth day of May, 1962.

John Partridge, field marshal of the
province of New Hampshire
and Maine.

Portsmouth, May 2, 1691

Gentlemen,

I received an order from the Governor and Council to apprehend Mr. George Buroughs, at present preacher at Wells, to be sent to Salem, there to be examined, being suspected to have confederacy with the devil in oppressing sundry persons about your town of Salem. Accordingly I have sent him by John Partredg, marshall of this province, except he meet with any other authority that will commit him to some other officer to be conveyed as above, he pleading it will be to his damage to go so far. I am

Your humble servant,
Elisha Hutchinson

Testimony of Mary Walcott

The deposition of Mary Walcott, aged about 17 years, who testifieth and saith that on the latter end of April, 1692, Mr. George Burroughs, or his appearance, came to me, whom I formerly knew well, and he did immediately most grievously torment me by biting, pinching, and almost choking me, urging me to write in his book. Which I refusing to do, he did again most grievously torment me and told me if I would but touch his book I should be well. But I told him I would not for all the world, and then he threatened to kill me and said I should never witness against him.

But he continued torturing and tempting me until the 8 May, and then he told me he would have killed his first wife and child, when his wife was in travail, but he kept her in the kitchen until he gave her her death wound. But he charged me in the name of his God I should not tell of it. But immediately there appeared to me Mr. Burroughs's two first wives in their winding sheets, whom I formerly well knew, and told me that Mr. Burroughs had murdered them, and that their blood did cry for vengeance against him.

Also, on the 9th May, being the day of his examination, he did most grievously torment me during the time of his examination, for if he did but look on me he would strike me down or almost choke me. Also during his examination I saw Mr. George Burroughs, or his appearance, most grievously torment Mercy Lewes, Eliz. Hubbrt, Abigail William, and Ann Putnam, and I believe in my heart that Mr. George Burroughs is a dreadful wizard, and that he had often afflicted and tormented me and the aforesaid persons by his acts of witchcraft.

Mary Walcot declared this writing to be a true evidence to the Jury of Inquest, August 3, 1692, upon the oath she has taken.

Testimony of Ann Putnam

The deposition of Ann Putnam, who testifieth and saith, that on the 3rd of May, 1692, at evening, I saw the apparition of Mr. George Burroughs who grievously tortured me and urged me to write in his book, which I refused. Then he told me that his two first wives would appear to me presently and tell me a great many lies, but I should not believe them. Then immediately appeared to me the form of two women in winding sheets and napkins about their heads, at which I was greatly affrighted. And they turned their faces towards Mr. Burroughs and looked very red and angry and told him that he had been a cruel man to them, and that their blood did cry for vengeance against him, and also told him that they should be clothed with white robes in heaven, when he should be cast into hell. And immediately he vanished away, and as soon as he was gone the two women turned their faces towards me and looked as pale as a white wall and told me that they were Mr. Burroughs's two first wives, and that he had murdered them. And one told me that she was his first wife, and he stabbed her under the left arm and put a piece of sealing wax on the wound. And she pulled aside the winding sheet and showed me the place, and also told me that she was in the house Mr. Parish now lives when it was done. And the other told me that Mr. Burrough and that wife which he hath now killed her in the vessel as she was coming to see her friends, because they would have one another.

And they both charged me that I should tell these things to the Magistrates before Mr. Burroughs's face, and if he did not own them they did not know but they should appear there. This morning also, Mistress Lawson and her daughter Ann appeared to me, whom I knew, and told me that Mr. Burroughs murdered them. This morning also appeared to me another woman in a winding sheet and told me that she was Goodman Fuller's first wife, and Mr. Burroughs killed her because there was some difference between her husband and him.

Also, on the 9th May, during the time of his examination, he did most grievously torment and afflict Mary Walcott, Mercy Lewes, Eliz. Hubberd, and Abigail Williams by pinching, pricking, and choking them.

Testimony of Edward and Thomas Putnam

We whose names are underwritten, being present with Ann Putnam at the times abovementioned, saw her tortured and heard her refuse to write in the book, also heard her declare what is abovewritten what she said she saw and heard from the apparition of Mr. George Burroughs, and from those which accused him for murdering of them.

Edward Putnam   Thomas Putnam

Ann Putnam owned this her testimony to be the truth upon her oath before the Jurors of Inquest, this 3d of August, '92.

Testimony of Eliazer Keysar and Elizabeth Wardwell

Elizer Keysar, aged about forty-five years, saith that on Thursday last passed, being the fifth day of this instant month of May, I was at the house of Thomas Beadle's in Salem, and Capt. Daniell King being there also, at the same time, and in the same room. Said Capt. Daniell King asked me whether I would not go up and see Mr. Burroughs and discourse with him, he being then in one of the chambers in said house. I told him it did not belong to me and I was not willing to meddle or make with it. Then said King said, are you not a Christian, if you are a Christian go see him and discourse with him. But I told him I did believe it did not belong to such as I was to discourse [with] him, he being a learned man. Then said King said, I believe he is a Child of God, a choice Child of God, and that God would clear up his innocency. So I told him my opinion or fear was that he was the chief of all the persons accused for witchcraft, or the ringleader of them all, and told him also that I believed if he was such an one, his Master, meaning the devil, had told him before now what I said of him. And said King seeming to me to be in a passion, I did afterwards forbear. *The same evening, after these words, being alone in one room of my house, and no candle or light being in the said room** The same afternoon, I having occasion to be at the said Beadle's house and in the chamber where Mr. George Burroughs kept, I observed that said Burroughs did stedfastly fix [his] eyes upon me.

The same evening, being in my own house, in a room without any light, I did see very strange things appear in the chimney, I suppose a dozen of them, which seemed to me to be something like jelly that used to be in the water and quaver with a strange motion and then quickly disappeared. Soon after which, I did see a light up in the chimney, about the bigness of my hand, something above the bar, which quivered and shaked and seemed to have a motion upward. Upon which, I called the maid, and she looking up into the chimney saw the same, and my wife looking up could not see anything. So I did and do *very certainly** [illegible] it was some diabolical apparition.

Notation on side of paper;

Mr. Elizer Keyzer declared to the Jury of Inquest that the evidence in this paper is the truth upon oath, August 3, 1692. Mercy Lewis also said that he made lights in Mr. Keyzer's chimney.

Sworne also by
Eliz. Wardwell
as to the last night.

*[*A line is drawn through the italicized words in the original.]*

Testimony of Mercy Lewis

The deposition of Mercy Lewes, who testifieth and saith that on the 7th of May, 1692, at evening, I saw the apparition of Mr. George Burroughs, whom I very well knew, which did grievously torture me, and urged me to write in his book. And then he brought me a new fashion book, which he did not use to bring, and told me I might write in that book, for that was a book that was in his study when I lived with them. But I told him I did not believe him, for I had been often in his study but I never saw that book there. But he told me that he had several books in his study which I never saw in his study, and he could raise the devil, and now had bewitched Mr. Sheppard's daughter. And I asked him how he could go to bewitch her now he was kept at Salem. And he told me that the devil was his servant and he sent him in his shape to do it.

Then he again tortured me most dreadfully and threatened to kill me, for he said I should not witness against him. Also, he told me that he had made Abigaill Hobbs a witch, and several more. Then again he did most dreadfully torture me, as if he would have racked me all to pieces, and urged me to write in his book or else he would kill me. But I told him I hoped my life was not in the power of his hand, and that I would not write though he did kill me. The next night he told me I should not see his two wives if he could help it, because I should not witness against him.

This 9th May, Mr. Burroughs carried me up to an exceeding high mountain and showed me all the kingdoms of the earth, and told me that he would give them all to me if I would write in his book, and if I would not, he would throw me down and break my neck. But I told him they were none of his to give, and I would not write if he throwed me down on 100 pitchforks. Also, on the 9th May, being the time of his examination, Mr. George Burroughs did most dreadfully torment me, and also several times since.

Marce Lewis upon her oath did own this her testimony to be the truth before the Jurors for Inquest, August 3, '92.

Testimony of Thomas and Edward Putnam

We whose names are underwritten, being present, heard Mircy Lewes declare what is abovewritten, what she said she saw and heard from the apparition of Mr. George Burroughs, and also beheld her tortures which we cannot express, for sometimes we were ready to fear that every joint of her body was ready to be displaced. Also we perceived her hellish temptations by her loud outcries, Mr. Burroughs, I will not write in your book though you do kill me.

                                   Thomas Putnam   Edward Putnam

Statement by Susannah Sheldon

The complaint of Susannah Shelden against Mr. Burros which brought a book to me and told me if I would not set my hand to it he would tear me to pieces. I told him I would not, then he told me he would starve me to death. Then the next morning he told me he could not starve me to death, but he would choke me, that my vittles should do me but little good. Then he told me his name was Borros, which had preached at the village.

The last night he came to me and asked me whether I would go to the village tomorrow to witness against him. I asked him if he was examined then. He told [me] he was. Then I told him I would go. Then he told me he would kill me before morning. Then he appeared to me at the house of Nathanniel Ingolson [Ingersoll] and told me he had been the death of three children at the eastward and had killed two of his wives, the first he smothered and the second he choked, and killed two of his own children.

Summary of the Examination of George Burroughs

The examination of Geo: Burrough, 9 May, 1692.

By the
Honoured
$\left\{ \begin{array}{l} \text{Wm. Stoughton} \\ \text{John Hathorne} \\ \text{Sam. Sewall} \\ \text{Jonath. Corwin} \end{array} \right\}$ Esq$^{\text{s.}}$

Being asked when he partook of the Lord's Supper, he being (as he said) in full communion at Roxbury, he answered it was so long since, he could not tell. Yet he owned he was at meeting one Sabbath at Boston part of the day, and the other at Charlestown part of a Sabbath, when that sacrament happened to be at both, yet did not partake of either. He denied that his house at Casco was haunted, yet he owned there were toads. He denied that he made his wife swear that she could not write to his father [-in-law] Ruck without his approbation of her letter to her father. He owned that none of his children but the eldest was baptized.

The above was in private, none of the bewitched being present. At his entry into the room, many, if not all, of the bewitched were grievously tortured.

1. Sus. Sheldon testified that Burroughs's two wives appeared in their winding sheets, and said that man killed them.
   He was bid to look upon Sus. Sheldon.
   He looked back and knocked down all (or most) of the afflicted who stood behind him.
   Sus. Sheldon [one line gone] the soldiers.

2. Mary Lewes deposition going to be read and he looked upon her, and she fell into a dreadful and tedious fit.

3. Mary Walcot
4. Eliz. Hubbard   }   Testimony going to be read
   Susan Sheldon   and they all fell into fits.

5. Susan Sheldon   }   Affirmed, each of them, that he
   Ann Putman jun^r.   brought the book and would have
                                     them write.

Being asked what he thought of these things, he answered it was an amazing and humbling providence, but he understood nothing of it. And he said, some of you may observe that when they begin to name my name, they cannot name it.

Ann Putman jun^r.   }   Testified that his 2 wives and
Susan Sheldon   2 children were destroyed by him.

The bewitched were so tortured that authority ordered them to be taken away, some of them.

6. Sarah Bibber testified that he had hurt her, though she had not seen him personally before, as she knew.

Abig. Hobbs
Deliverance Hobbs   }   Testimony read
Elizar Keiser

Capt. Willard   }
Jno. Brown   }   Testimony about his great
Jno. Wheldon   strength and the gun.

Capt. Putman testified about the gun.

Capt. Wormwood testified about the gun and the molasses. He denied that about the molasses. About the gun, he said he took it before the lock and rested it upon his breast.

John Brown testified about a barrel cider.

He denied that his family was affrighted by a white calf in his house.

Capt. Putman testified that he made his wife enter into a covenant. 11 May 1692.

Abig. Hobbs in prison affirmed that Geo. Burroughs in his shape appeared to her and urged her to set her hand to the book, which she did, and afterwards, in his own person, he acknowledged to her that he had made her set her hand to the book.

Testimony of Thomas and Edward Putnam

The deposition of Tho. Putnam, aged 40 years, and Edward Putnam, aged 38 years, who testifieth and saith that, we having been conversant with several of the afflicted persons, as Mary Wolcott, Mercy Lewes, Eliz. Hubburt, and we have seen them most dreadfully tormented, and we have seen dreadful marks in their flesh which they said Mr. Burroughs did make by hurting them. But on 9th May, 1692, the day of the examination of Mr. George Burroughs, the aforesaid persons were most dreadfully tormented during the time of his examination, as if they would have been torn all to pieces, or all their bones put out of joint, and with such tortures as no tongue can express. Also, several times since, we have seen the aforesaid afflicted persons most dreadfully tormented and grievously complaining of Mr. Burroughs for hurting them, and we believe that Mr. George Burroughs, the prisoner at the bar, has several times afflicted and tormented the aforesaid persons by acts of witchcraft.

Testimony of Sarah Bibber

The deposition of Sarah Biber, who testifieth and saith, that on the 9th day of May, 1692, as I was agoing to Salem Village, I saw the apparition of a little man, like a minister, with a black coat on, and he pinched me by the arm and bid me go along with him, but I told him I would not. But when I came to the village I saw there Mr. George Burroughs, or his appearance, most grievously torment and afflict Mary Wallcott, Mercy Luis, Elizabeth Hubbert, Ann Putnam, and Abigaill Williams, by pinching, twisting, and almost choking them to death. Also, several times since, Mr. George Burroughs, or his appearance, has most grievously tormented me with a variety of tortures, and I believe in my heart that Mr. George Burroughs is a dreadful wizard, and that he has most grievously tormented me and the abovementioned persons by his acts of witchcraft.

Sarah Biber declared to the Jury of Inquest that the abovewritten evidence is the truth, August 3, 1692, the which she owned on her oath.

Testimony of Elizabeth Hubbard

May the 9, 1692. Elizabeth Hubord, aged about 17 years, saith that the last second day, at night, there appeared a little blackbearded man to me in blackish apparel. I asked him his name, and he told me his name was Borrous. Then he took a book out of his pocket and opened it and bid me set my hand to it. I told him I would not. The lines in this book was red as blood. Then he pinched me twice and went away.

The next morning he appeared to me again and told me he was above a wizard, for he was a conjurer, and so went away. But since that he hath appeared to me every day and night very often and urged me very much to set my hand to his book, and to run away, telling me if I would do so I should be well, and that I should need fear nobody, and withal tormented me several ways every time he came, except that time he told me he was a conjurer.

This night he asked me very much to set my hand to his book or else, he said, he would kill me, withall torturing me very much by biting and pinching, squeezing my body, and running pins into [it]. Also, on the 9th May, 1692, being the time of his examination, Mr. George Burroughs, or his appearance, did most grievously afflict and torment the bodies of Mary Walcott, Mercy Lewes,

Ann Putnam, and Abigail Williams, for if he did but look upon them he would strike them down or almost choke them to death. Also, several times since, he has most dreadfully afflicted and tormented me with [a] variety of torments, and I believe in my heart that Mr. George Burroughs is a dreadful wizard and that he has very often tormented me and also the abovenamed persons by his acts of witchcraft.

Eliz. Hubbard declared the abovewritten evidence to be the truth, upon her oath, that she had taken. This she owned before the Jury of Inquest, August 3, 1692.

Indictment of George Burroughs

Essex Ss. The jurors for our Sovereign Lord and Lady, the King and Queen, presents that George Burroughs, late of Falmouth within the province of the Massachusetts Bay in New England, clerk, the ninth day of May, [1692] . . . and divers other days and times as well, before and after, certain detestable arts called witchcraft and sorceries, wickedly and feloniously hath used, practiced, and exercised at and within the Township of Salem in the County of Essex and aforesaid, in, upon, and against one Elizabeth Hubbard of Salem in the County of Essex, singlewoman, by which said wicked arts the said Elizabeth Hubbard . . . was, and is, tortured, afflicted, pined, consumed, wasted and tormented. Also for sundry other acts of witchcrafts by said George Burroughs committed and done against the peace of our Sovereign Lord and Lady, the King and Queen, their crown and dignity, and against the form of the statute in that case made and provided.

Witnesses   Elizabeth Hubbard
                       Mary Wolcott
                       Ann Putman

[Three additional indictments, identical in form, were issued against Burroughs, naming, respectively, Mercy Lewis, Ann Putnam, and Mary Walcott as the victim. The three girls signing this indictment also signed the three additional indictments. In addition, Mercy Lewis signed the indictment naming her as sufferer, Mary Warren signed the indictment naming Ann Putnam as sufferer, and Sarah Bibber and Mercy Lewis signed the indictment naming Mary Walcott as sufferer.]

Second Examination of Abigail Hobbs

Abigail Hobbs's Examination at Salem Prison, May 12, 1692.

Q. Did Mr. Burroughs bring you any of the puppets of his wives to stick pins into?

Ans. I do not remember that he did.

Q. Did he [illegible] off any of his children or of the eastward soldiers?

A. No.

Q. Have you known of any that have been killed by witchcraft?

A. No, nobody.

Q. How came you to speak of Mr. Burroughs's wives yesterday?

A. I don't know.

Q. Is that true about Davis's son of Casco, and of those of the Village?

A. Yes, it is true.

Q. What service did he put you upon? And who are they you afflicted?

A. I cannot tell who. Neither do I know whether they died.

Q. Were they strangers to you that Burroughs would have you afflict?

A. Yes.

Q. And were they afflicted accordingly?

A. Yes.

Q. Can't you name some of them?

A. No, I cannot remember them.

Q. Where did they live?

A. At the eastward.

Q. Have any vessels been cast away by you?

A. I do not know.

Q. Have you consented to the afflicting any other besides those at the Village?

A. Yes.

Q. Who were they?

A. I cannot tell, but it was such who lived at the fort side of the river about half a mile from the fort, toward Capt. Brackett's.

Q. What was the hurt you gave to them by consent?

A. I don't know.

Q. Was there anything brought to you like them?

A. Yes.

Q. What did you stick into them?

A. Thorns.

Q. Did some of them die?

A. Yes. One of them was Mary Laurence that died.

Q. Where did you stick the thorns?

A. I do not know.

Q. Was it about the middle of her body?

A. Yes, and I stuck it right in.

Q. What provoked you? Had she displeased you?

A. Yes, by some words she spoke of me.

Q. Who brought the image to you?

A. It was Mr. Burroughs.

Q. How did he bring it to you?

A. In his own person, bodily.

Q. Where did he bring it to you?

A. Abroad, a little way off from our house.

Q. And what did he say to you then?

A. He told me he was angry with that family.

Q. How many years since was it?

A. Before this Indian war.

Q. How did you know Mr. Burroughs was a witch?

A. I don't know.

She owned again she had made two covenants with the Devil, first for two years and after that for four years, and she confesseth herself to have been a witch these six years.

Q. Did the maid complain of pain about the place you stuck the thorn in?

A. Yes, but how long she lived I don't know.

Q. How do you know Burroughs was angry with Laurence's family?

A. Because he told me so.

Q. Where did any other live that you afflicted?

A. Just by the other, toward James Andrews's, and they died also.

Q. How many were they? More than one?

A. Yes.

Q. And who brought those puppets to you?

A. Mr. Burroughs.

Q. What did you stick into them?

A. Pins. And he gave them to me.

Q. Did you keep those puppets?

A. No, he carried them away with him.

Q. Was he there with you himself in bodily person?

A. Yes, and so he was when he appeared to tempt me to set my hand to the book. He then appeared in person, and I felt his hand at the same time.

Q. Were they men, women or children you killed?

A. They were both boys and girls.

Q. Was you angry with them yourself?

A. Yes, though I don't know why now.

Q. Did you know Mr. Burroughs's wife?

A. Yes.

Q. Did you know of any puppets pricked to kill her?

A. No, I don't.

Q. Have you seen several witches at the eastward?

A. Yes, but I don't know who they were.

Testimony of Mary Warren

The testimony of Mary Warren, aged twenty years or thereabouts, testifieth and saith that sometime in July last, Mr. Burroughs pinched me very much and choked me almost to death, and I saw and heard him sound a trumpet and immediately I saw several come to him, as namely, Capt. Allding, Mis[tress] Cory, and Goody Pudeator, and several others, and they urged me to go along with them to their sacramental meeting. And Mr. Burroughs brought to me bread to eat and wine to drink, which I refusing, he did most grievously torment me, urging me vehemently to write in his book. Also, I have seen Mr. George Burroughs, or his appearance, most grievously tormenting Mary Walcott and Ann Putnam, and I verily believe in my heart that Mr. George Burroughs is a dreadful wizard and that he has several times tormented me and the aforesaid persons by his acts of witchcraft.

Mary Warrin declared upon her oath to the Jury of Inquest that the abovewritten evidence is the truth. August 3, 1692.

Testimony of John and Rebecca Putnam

The deposition of John Putnam, and Rebecah, his wife, testifieth and saith that in the year '80, Mr. Burros lived in our house nine month, there being a great difference betwixt said Barros and his wife, the difference was so great that they did desire us, the deponents, to come into their room to hear their differences. The controversy that was betwixt them was that the aforesaid Burros did require his wife to give him a written covenant, under her hand and seal, that she would never reveal his secrets. Our answer was that they had once made a covenant before God and men, which covenant we did conceive did bind each other to keep their lawful secrets. And further saith that all the time that said Burros did live at our house he was a very sharp man to his wife, notwithstanding to our observation she was a very good and dutiful wife to him.

Testimony of Hannah Harris

The deposition of Hannah Harris, aged twenty seven years or thereabouts, testifieth and saith, that she lived at the house of Georg Burros at Falmouth, and the abovesaid Hannah Harres many times hath taken notice that when she hath had any discourse with the abovesaid Burros's wife when the abovesaid Burros was from home, that upon his return he hath often scolded [his] wife and told her that he knew what they said when he was abroad.

And further saith that upon a time when his wife had lain-in not above one week, that he fell out with his wife and kept her by discourse at the door till she fell sick in the place and grew worse at night, so that the abovesaid Hannah Harres was afraid she would die. And they called in their neighbors, and the abovesaid Burros's daughter told one of the women that was there the cause of her mother's illness. And the abovesaid Burros chided his daughter for telling, and the abovesaid Burros came to the abovesaid Hannah Harres and told her that if his wife did otherwise than well she should not tell of it. And the abovesaid Hannah Harres told him that she would not be confined to any such thing.

Testimony of Samuel Webber

Samuel Webber, aged about 36 years, testifieth and saith that about seven or eight years ago, I lived at Casco Bay and George Burroughs was then minister there. And having heard much of the great strength of him, said Burroughs, he coming to our house, we were in discourse about the same, and he then told me that he had put his fingers into the bung of a barrel of molasses and lifted it up and carried it round him and set it down again.

Salem, August 2d, 1692.

Samuell Webber

Testimony of Simon Willard

The deposition of Simon Willard, aged about forty two years, saith, I being at the house of Mr. Robert Lawrence at Falmouth, in Casco Bay, in September 1689, said Mr. Lawrence was commenting [upon] Mr. George Borroughs's strength, saying that we, none of us, could do what he could do. For said Mr. Borroughs can hold out this gun with one hand. Mr. Borroughs, being there, said, I held my hand here behind the lock and took it up and held it out.

I, said deponent, saw Mr. Borroughs put his hand on the gun to show us how he held it and where he held his hand, and saying there he held his hand when he held said gun out. But I saw him not hold it out then. Said gun was about seven-foot barrel, and very heavy. I then tried to hold out said gun with both hands, but could not do it long enough to take sight.

Simon Willard

Simon Willard owned to the Jury of Inquest that the abovewritten evidence is the truth,
August 3, 1692

Capt. Wm. Wormall sworn to the above, and that he saw him raise it from the ground himself.

Testimony of Simon Willard

The deposition of Simon Willard, aged about 42 years, saith, I being at Saco in the year 1689, some in Capt. Ed Sarjant's garrison was speaking of Mr. George Borroughs's great strength, saying he could take a barrel of molasses out of a canoe or boat alone, and that he could take it in his hands or arms out of the canoe or boat and carry it and set it on the shore. And Mr. Burroughs, being there, said that he had carried one barrel of molasses or cider out of a canoe that had like to have done him a displeasure. Said Mr. Borroughs intimated as if he did not want [i.e., lack] strength to do it, but the disadvantage of the shore was such that his foot slipping in the sand he had liked to have strained his leg.

Simon Willard

Simon Willard owned to the Jury of Inquest that the abovewritten evidence is the truth.

Testimony of Thomas Greenslit

The deposition of Thomas Greinslitt, aged about forty years, testifieth that about the breaking out of this last Indian war, being at the house of Capt. Scottow's, at Black Point, he saw Mr. George Burroughs lift and hold out a gun of six foot barrel or thereabouts, putting the forefinger of his right hand into the muzzle of said gun, and so held it out at arm's end, only with that finger. And further this deponent testifieth that at the same time he saw the said Burroughs take up a full barrel of molasses with but two fingers of one of his hands in the bung, and carry it from the stage head to the door at the end of the stage, without letting it down, and that Lieut. Richard Hunniwell and John Greinslitt and some other persons that are since dead were then present.

Salem, September 15, 1692. Thomas Greinslitt appeared before their Majesties' Justices of Oyer and Terminer in open court and made oath that the above mentioned particulars, and every part of them, were true.

attest   Step. Sewall, Clerk

Summary of Oral Testimony Against
George Burroughs

Memorandum
In Mr. George Burroughs trial, besides the written evidences that was sworn, several who gave theirs by word of mouth.
Major Browne: holding out a heavy gun with one hand.
Thomas Ruck: of his sudden coming in after them, and that he could tell his thoughts.
Thomas Evans: that he carried out barrels [of] molasses and meat, &c. out of a canoe whilst his mate went to the fort for hands to help out with them.
Sarah Wilson confessed that the night before Mr. Burroughs was executed that there was a great meeting of the witches nigh Sarjt. Chandler's. That

Mr. Burroughs was there, and they had the sacrament, and after they had done he took leave and bid them stand to their faith, and not own anything.

Martha Tyler saith the same with Sarah Wilson and several others.

Physical Examination of George Burroughs and George Jacobs

We whose names are underwritten, having received an order from the sheriff for to search the bodies of George Burroughs and George Jacobs, we find nothing upon the body of the above said Burroughs but what is natural.

But upon the body of George Jacobs we find 3 teats which according to the best of our judgments we think is not natural, for we run a pin through 2 of them and he was not sensible of it, one of them being within his mouth, upon the inside of his right cheek, and the 2nd upon his right shoulder blade, and a 3rd upon his right hip.

Ed. Welch, sworn	Tom Flint, jurat
Will. Gill, sworn	Tom West, sworn
Zeb. Hill, jurat	Sam Morgan, sworn

John Bare, jurat

Declaration of Margaret Jacobs to the Special Witchcraft Court Appointed by the Governor

[For more information on Margaret Jacobs, see pp. 107-108.]

The humble declaration of Margaret Jacobs unto the honoured court now sitting at Salem, sheweth

That whereas your poor and humble declarant being closely confined here in Salem jail for the crime of witchcraft, which crime, thanks be to the Lord, I am altogether ignorant of, as will appear at the great day of judgment. May it please the honoured court, I was cried out upon by some of the possessed persons, as afflicting of them; whereupon I was brought to my examination, which persons at the sight of me fell down, which did very much startle and affright me. The Lord above knows I knew nothing, in the least measure, how or who afflicted them; they told me, without doubt I did, or else they would not fall down at me; they told me if I would not confess, I should be put down into the dungeon and would be hanged, but if I would confess I should have my life; the which did so affright me, with my own vile wicked heart, to save my life made me make the confession I did, which confession, may it please the honoured court, is altogether false and untrue. The very first night after I had made my confession, I was in such horror of conscience that I could not sleep, for fear the Devil should carry me away for telling such horrid lies. I was, may it please the honoured court, sworn to my confession, as I understand since, but then, at that time, was ignorant of it, not knowing what an oath did mean. The Lord, I hope, in whom I trust, out of the abundance of his mercy, will forgive me my false forswearing myself.

What I said was altogether false, against my grandfather, and Mr. Burroughs, which I did to save my life and to have my liberty; but the Lord, charging it to my conscience, made me in so much horror, that I could not contain myself before I had denied my confession, which I did, though I saw nothing but death before me, choosing rather death with a quiet conscience, than to live in such horror, which I could not suffer. Whereupon my denying my confession, I was committed to close prison, where I have enjoyed more felicity in spirit a thousand times than I did before in my enlargement.

And now, may it please your honours, your poor and humble declarant having, in part, given your honours a description of my condition, do leave it to your honours' pious and judicious discretions to take pity and compassion on my young and tender years; to act and do with me as the Lord above and your honours shall see good, having no friend but the Lord to plead my cause for me; not being guilty in the least measure of the crime of witchcraft, nor any other sin that deserves death from man; and your poor and humble declarant shall forever pray, as she is bound in duty, for your honours' happiness in this life, and eternal felicity in the world to come. So prays your honours' declarant.

Margaret Jacobs

Extract from the Diary of Judge Samuel Sewall, Merchant of Boston and a Judge of the Special Witchcraft Court Appointed by Governor Phips

August 19, 1692

This day George Burrough, John Willard, Jno. Proctor, Martha Carrier and George Jacobs were executed at Salem, a very great number of spectators being present. Mr. Cotton Mather was there, Mr. Sims, Hale, Noyes, Chiever, etc. All of them said they were innocent, Carrier and all. Mr. Mather says they all died by a Righteous sentence. Mr. Burrough by his speech, prayer, protestation of his innocence, did much move unthinking persons, which occasions their speaking hardly concerning his being executed.

[Later marginal note: "Doleful Witchcraft!"]

John Ruck Becomes Guardian of George Burroughs' Children (June 1693)

Know all men by these presents that we John Ruck of Salem, merchant [?], and Thomas Jacob and John Appleton, parties of Ipswich, yeomen, are held and

firmly bound unto Bartholmew Gedney Esq. or his successors in the office of
judge of the probate of wills and granting letters of Administration in the county
of Essex, and unto Charles Borroughs, George Borroughs, Jeremiah Borroughs
and Josiah Borroughs now of Salem, minors and children of George Borroughs
late of Falmouth [illegible], in the sum of two hundred pounds current money
of New England to be paid unto the said Bartholomew Gedney Esq. or his
successors in the office aforesaid, or unto the said Charles Borroughs, George
Borroughs, Jeremiah Burroughs and Josiah Borroughs, the said payment well and
truly to be made. . . .

Sealed with our seals this sixth day of June 1693. . . .

The condition of this obligation is such that whereas the said John Ruck
above bounden is admitted and appointed guardian to the said Charles
Borroughs, George Borroughs, Jeremiah Borroughs and Josiah Borroughs, if the
said Ruck shall well and faithfully discharge his trust according to law relating
thereunto and render above amount to the judge of the probate, the time being
when called thereunto, or unto the said Charles, George, Jeremiah and Josiah or
any one of them when they shall come to full age, then the above obligation to
be void and of no effect; else to remain in full force. . . .

Signed, sealed and delivered   John Ruck
in presence of us.   Thomas Jacob
Samuel Southworth   John Appleton
Stephen Sewall

Petition of George Burroughs' Children (1710 or 1711)

To the Honoured Committee appointed by the General Court to inquire into
the names of such as may be meet for taking off the attainder for the making of
some restitution,

And these humbly and sorrowfully show that our dear and honoured father,
Mr. George Burroughs, was apprehended in April 1692 at Wells and imprisoned
several months in Boston and Salem jails, and at last condemned and executed
for witchcraft, which we have all the reason in the world to believe he was
innocent of, by his careful catechizing his children and upholding religion in his
family, and by his solemn and savory written instructions from prison.

We were left, a parcel of small children of us, helpless, and a mother-in-law
[i.e., stepmother] with one small child of her own to take care of, whereby she
was not so capable to take care of us. By all which, our father's small estate was
most of it lost and expended, and we scattered.

We cannot tell certainly what the loss may be, but the least we can judge by
best information was fifty pounds; besides the damage that hath accrued to us
many ways thereby is some hundreds of pounds. We earnestly pray that the

attainder may be taken off, and, if you please, the fifty pounds may be restored.

Charles Burroughs,
elder son, in the name of the rest

Petition of George Burroughs' Children
(December 1712)

Boston,
December 16th, 1712

To the Honourable Gentlemen appointed for a committee relating to the affair of witchcraft in the year 1692.

Gentlemen,

We the subscribers and children of Mr. George Burroughs, late of Wells, who suffered at Salem in the trouble there, humbly offer for your Honours' consideration a few lines relating our case and circumstances upon account of our mother-in-law's conduct and carriage toward us. After our father was apprehended and taken away, our mother-in-law laid hands upon all she could secure (the children were generally unable to shift for themselves), and what she could lay hands on was her own, without any person but her own daughter to share with her, whom she says was to bring up.

But may it please your Honours to consider there was seven children more besides that were to bring up, the eldest of which was but sixteen years old at that time. But [we], instead of sharing in what our father left and she had secured, were turned to shift for ourselves without anything for so much as a remembrance of our father, though some of us can remember of considerable in the house, besides his library, which she sold and received the money for, then let it out at interest, and was afterward received by another husband, and not one farthing bestowed upon any child but her own.

This being matter of fact, we humbly leave it with your Honours to consider whether, of what the Honourable General Court allowed etc., she have not already received too much and the children too little. We subscribe ourselves your Honours' humble servants.

Rebaker Fowl	Jeremi Burrough
The ✕ mark of	Charles Burrough
Eliz. Thomas	Hannah Fox

Response of the Committee (January 1713)

For as much as it is made manifest that the children of Mr. George Burroughs, deceased, by his former wives, did in the time of his imprisonment administer unto him necessary things, and were at considerable charge thereabout, and for his interment, and that the widow had most or all of the personal estate.

In consideration whereof, we the subscribers, a committee appointed by the General Court, consent and agree and order that the six pounds, 6 d., money yet remaining of the fifty pounds allowed by the government shall be paid to the said children in equal shares.

January 3rd, 1712/13.

John Appleton	Stephen Sewall
Thomas Noyes	Neh. Jewett

Chapter Six

Additional Testimony

[The following testimony and other documents, although not specifically related to these five cases, are nevertheless relevant.]

Warrant for the Arrest of Daniel Andrew and Others

To the Constable in Salem

You are in their Majesties' names hereby required to apprehend and bring before us on Tuesday next, being the seventeenth day of this instant month of May, about ten of the clock in the forenoon at the house of Lt. Nathaniell Ingerson's of Salem Village, Daniel Andrew of Salem Village, bricklayer; George Jacobs, Junior, of Salem Village, husbandman; and Rebecka Jacobs, the wife of said George Jacobs; and Sarah Buckley, the wife of Wm. Buckley of Salem Village, cordwainer; and Mary Withridge, the daughter of said Buckley, who all stand charged in behalf of their Majesties with high suspicion of sundry acts of witchcrafts by them done or committed on the bodies of Ann Putnam, Marcy Lewis, Mary Walcot, and Abigail Williams, and others of Salem Village lately, whereby great hurt hath been done them. And hereof you are not to fail.

Dated Salem, May the 14th, 1692.

John Hathorne } Assistants
Jonathan Corwin

Return of the Constable to the Above Warrant

In prosecution of this warrant I have apprehended and brought the bodies of Sarah Buckley and Mary Withridg and Rebekah Jacobs, all of Salem Village, according to the tenor of the within written warrant, and have likewise made diligent search at the house of Daniell Andrew and at the house of George Jacobs for them likewise, but cannot find them.

p. me.   Jonathan Putnam, Constable in Salem.

Testimony of Sarah Ingersoll

The deposition of Sarah Ingelson [Ingersoll], aged about 30 years, saith that seeing Sarah Church[ill] after her examination, she came to me crying and wringing her hands, seeming to be much troubled in spirit. I asked her what she ailed. She answered she had undone herself. I asked her in what. She said, in belying herself and others in saying she had set her hand to the Devil's Book, whereas, she said, she never did. I told her I believed she had set her hand to the Book. She answered, crying, and said no, no, no, I never, I never did.

I asked then what made her say she did. She answered, because they threatened her and told her they would put her into the dungeon and put her along with Mr. Borows. And thus several times she followed on, up and down telling me that she had undone herself in belying herself and others. I asked her why she did [not] right it. She told me, because she had stood out for so long in it that now she durst not. She said also that if she told Mr. Noys but once she had set her hand to the Book he would believe her, but if she told the truth and said she had not set her hand to the Book a hundred times, he would not believe her.

Sarah Ingersol

Testimony of Samuel Sibley

The morning after the examination of Goody Nurse, Sam Sibley met John Proctor about Mr. Phillips's. He called to said Sibley as he was going to said Phillips's and asked how the folks did at the village. He answered he heard they were very bad last night, but he had heard nothing this morning. Proctor replied he was going to fetch home his jade. He left her there last night, and had rather given 40c than let her come up. Said Sibley asked why he talked so. Proctor replied, if they were let alone, then we should all be devils and witches quickly. They should rather be had to the whipping post. But he would fetch his jade home and thrust the Devil out of her, and more to the like purpose, crying, hang them, hang them. And also added that when she was first taken with fits he kept her close to the wheel and threatened to thrash her, and then she had no more fits till the next day [after] he was gone forth, and then she must have her fits again, forsooth, &c.

Proctor owns he meant Mary Warren.

Attest.   St. Sewall, Clerk.

Testimony of Edward and Sarah Bishop
and Mary Easty

Edward Bishop, aged about 44 years, Sarah Bishop, aged about 41 years, and Mary Estey, aged about 56 years, all testify and say that about three weeks ago, [that is] to say, when we was in Salem jail, then and there we heard Mary Warrin several times say that the Magistrates might as well examine Keysar's daughter, that had been distracted many years, and take notice of what she said, as well as any of the afflicted persons. For, said Mary Warrin, when I was afflicted I thought I saw the apparitions of a hundred persons. For she said her head was distempered that she could not tell what she said. And the said Mary told us that when she was well again she could not say that she saw any of the apparitions at the time aforesaid.

Testimony of James Kettle

The testimony of James Cetel [Kettle], being of age, who testify and saith, I being at Doctor Grigs's on a Sabbath day about the last of May in 1692, having some discourse with Elizabeth Hubberd, and I found her to speak several untruths in denying the Sabbath Day and saying she had not been to meeting that day, but had only been up to James Houlton's.
This I can testify to if called, as witness my hand.

James Ketle

Testimony of Clement Coldum

The deposition of Clement Coldum, aged 60 years or thereabouts, saith that on the 29th of May, 1692, being at Salem Village [and] carrying home Elizabeth Hubbard from the meeting behind me, she desired me to ride faster. I asked her why. She said, the woods were full of devils, and said, there they are, there they be. But I could see none. Then I put on my horse, and after I had rode a while she told me I might ride softer, for we had outrid them. I asked her if she was not afraid of the Devil. She answered me, no, she could discourse with the Devil as well as with me.

Further saith not. This I am ready to testify on oath if called thereto, as witness my hand.

Testimony of Thomas and Mary Jacobs

The testimony of Thomas Jacob and Mary, his wife, doth testify and say that Goodwife Bibbor, now that is now counted [an] afflicted person, she did for a time surgeon [i.e., practice medicine or midwifery?] in our house, and Goody Bibber would be very often speaking against one and another very obscenely and those things that were very false, and wishing very bad wishes. And very often and she wishes that when her child fell into the river that she had never pulled her child out. And Goody Bibber used to wish ill wishes to herself and her children and also to others [in] the neighborhood where she lived amongst. After she [?] her first husband he told us that this John Bibber's wife could fall into fits as often as she pleased.

Testimony of Richard Walker

The testimony of Richard Walker, who testifieth that Goodwife Bibber, some time living near to me, I did observe to be a woman of an unruly, turbulent spirit, and would often fall into strange fits when anything crossed her humor.

Testimony of Joseph Fowler

The testimony of Joseph Fowler, who testifieth that Goodman Bibber and his wife lived at my house, and I did observe and take notice that Goodwife Bibber was a woman who was very idle in her calling, and very much given to tattling and tale bearing, making mischief amongst her neighbors, and very much given to speak bad words, and would call her husband bad names, and was a woman of a very turbulent, unruly spirit.

Testimony of John and Lydia Porter

The testimony of John Porter and Lidia Porter, these:

The testimony of John Porter, who testifieth and saith that Goodwife Biber some time living amongst us, I did observe her to be a woman of an unruly, turbulent spirit, and she would often fall into strange fits when she was crossed of her humor.

Likewise, Lidea Porter testifieth that Goodwife Bibber and her husband would often quarrel, and in their quarrels she would call him very bad names, and would have strange fits when she was crossed, and a woman of an unruly spirit and double-tongued.

Testimony of Robert Moulton, Senior

The testimony of Robert Moulton, Senior, who testifieth and saith that, I watching with Susannah Sheldon since she was afflicted, I heard her say that the witches hauled her upon her belly through the yard like a snake and hauled her over the stone walls. And presently I heard her contradict her former discourse and said that she came over the stone wall herself, and I heard her say that she rode upon a pole to Boston, and she said the devil carried the pole.

Robart Mouelton

Samuel Nurs and Joseph Trumball saw Robert Moulton sign this writing.

Testimony of Daniel Eliot

The testimony of Daniel Elet, aged 27 years or thereabouts, who testifieth and saith that, I being at the house of Lieutenant Ingason's [Ingersoll's] on the 28th of March in the year 1692, there being present one of the afflicted persons which cried out and said, there's Goody Proctor, William Raiment being there present told the girl he believed she lied, for he saw nothing. Then Goody Ingerson told the girl she told a lie, for there was nothing. Then the girl said that she did it for sport, they must have some sport.

Chapter Seven

Contempory Accounts and Reactions

From Robert Calef, *More Wonders*
of the Invisible World (1700)

[In 1693 Cotton Mather, a prominent Boston clergyman and son of Increase Mather, the leading minister of the colony, published Wonders of the Invisible World *in defense of the witchcraft trials. Seven years later Robert Calef, a Boston merchant, responded with* More Wonders of the Invisible World, *designed as much to embarrass Mather personally as to attack the trials. The following narrative extract forms the concluding section of Calef's work.]*

An Impartial Account of the Most Memorable Matters
of Fact, Touching the Supposed Witchcraft in
New England

Mr. Parris had been some years a Minister in Salem-Village, when this sad Calamity (as a deluge) overflowed them, spreading itself far and near: He was a Gentlemen of Liberal Education, and not meeting with any great Encouragement, or Advantage in Merchandizing, to which for some time he apply'd himself, betook himself to the work of the Ministry; this Village being then vacant, he met with so much Encouragement, as to settle in that Capacity among them.

After he had been there about two years, he obtained a Grant from a part of the Town, that the House and Land he Occupied, and which had been Allotted by the whole People to the Ministry, should be and remain to him, etc. as his own Estate in Fee Simple. This occasioned great Divisions both between the

Inhabitants themselves, and between a considerable part of them and their said Minister, which Divisions were but as a beginning or Praeludium to what immediately followed.

It was the latter end of February 1691 [i.e., 1692 by present reckoning] when divers young Persons belonging to Mr. Parris's Family, and one or more of the Neighbourhood, began to Act, after a strange and unusual manner, *viz.* as by getting into Holes, and creeping under Chairs and Stools, and to use sundry odd Postures and Antick Gestures, uttering foolish, ridiculous Speeches, which neither they themselves nor any others could make sense of; the Physicians that were called could assign no reason for this; but it seems one of them [probably William Griggs] having recourse to the old shift, told them he was afraid they were Bewitched; upon such suggestions, they that were concerned applied themselves to Fasting and Prayer, which was attended not only in their own private Families, but with calling in the help of others.

March the 11th. Mr. Parris invited several Neighbouring Ministers to join with him in keeping a Solemn day of Prayer at his own House; the time of the exercise those Persons were for the most part silent, but after any one Prayer was ended, they would Act and Speak strangely and Ridiculously, yet were such as had been well Educated and of good Behaviour, the one, a Girl of 11 or 12 years old [Abigail Williams, Parris's niece] would sometimes seem to be in a Convulsion Fit, her Limbs being twisted several ways, and very stiff, but presently her Fit would be over.

A few days before this Solemn day of Prayer, Mr. Parris's Indian Man and Woman made a Cake of Rye Meal, with the Childrens' Water, and Baked it in the ashes, and as is said, gave it to the Dog; this was done as a means to Discover Witchcraft, soon after which those ill affected or afflicted Persons named several that they said they saw, when in their Fits, afflicting of them.

The first complain'd of, was the said Indian Woman, named Tituba. She confessed that the Devil urged her to sign a Book, which he presented to her, and also to work Mischief to the Children, etc. She was afterwards Committed to Prison, and lay there till Sold for her Fees [i.e., to pay for her prison expenses]. The account she since gives of it is, that her Master did beat her and otherways abuse her, to make her confess and accuse (such as he call'd) her Sister-Witches, and that whatsoever she said by way of confessing or accusing others, was the effect of such usage; her Master refused to pay her Fees, unless she would stand to what she had said.

The Children complained likewise of two other Women, to be the Authors of their Hurt, *Viz.* Sarah Good, who had long been counted a Melancholy or Distracted Woman, and one Osburn, an Old Bed-rid Woman; which two were Persons so ill thought of, that the accusation was the more readily believed; and after Examination before two Salem Magistrates, were committed:

March the 19th. Mr. Lawson (who had been formerly a Preacher at the said Village) came thither, and hath since set forth in Print an account of what then passed, about which time, as he saith, they complained of Goodwife Cory, and

Goodwife Nurse, Members of the Churches at the Village and at Salem, many others being by that time Accused.

March the 21st. Goodwife Cory was examined before the Magistrates of Salem, at the Meeting House in the Village, a throng of Spectators being present to see the Novelty. Mr. Noyes, one of the Ministers of Salem, began with Prayer, after which the Prisoner being call'd, in order to answer to what should be Alleged against her, she desired that she might go to Prayer, and was answered by the Magistrates, that they did not come to hear her pray, but to examine her.

The number of the Afflicted were at that time about Ten, *Viz.* Mrs. Pope, Mrs. Putman, Goodwife Bibber, and Goodwife Goodall, Mary Wolcott, Mercy Lewes (at Thomas Putmans) and Dr. Griggs's Maid, and three Girls, *Viz.* Elizabeth Parris, Daughter to the Minister, Abigail Williams his Niece, and Ann Putman, which last three were not only the beginners, but were also the chief in these Accusations. These Ten were most of them present at the Examination, and did vehemently accuse her of Afflicting them, by Biting, Pinching, Strangling, etc. And they said, they did in their Fits see her likeness coming to them, and bringing a Book for them to Sign; Mr. Hathorn, a Magistrate of Salem, asked her, why she Afflicted those Children? she said, she did not Afflict them; he asked her, who did then? she said, "I do not know, how should I know?" she said, they were Poor Distracted Creatures, and no heed to be given to what they said; Mr. Hathorn and Mr. Noyes replied that it was the Judgment of all that were there present, that they were bewitched, and only she (the Accused) said they were Distracted: She was Accused by them, that the Black Man Whispered to her in her Ear now (while she was upon Examination) and that she had a Yellow Bird, that did use to Suck between her Fingers, and that the said Bird did Suck now in the Assembly; order being given to look in that place to see if there were any sign, the Girl that pretended to see it said that it was too late now, for she had removed a Pin and put it on her Head, it was upon search found, that a Pin was there sticking upright. When the Accused had any motion of their Body, Hands or Mouth, the Accusers would cry out, as when she bit her Lip, they would cry out of being bitten, if she grasped one hand with the other, they would cry out of being Pinched by her, and would produce marks, so of the other motions of her Body, as complaining of being Prest, when she lean'd to the seat next her, if she stirred her Feet, they would stamp and cry out of Pain there. After the hearing the said Cory was committed to Salem Prison, and then their crying out of her abated.

March the 24th. Goodwife Nurse was brought before Mr. Hathorn and Mr. Curwin (Magistrates) in the Meeting House. Mr. Hale, Minister of Beverly, began with Prayer, after which she being Accus'd of much the same Crimes made the like answers, asserting her own Innocence with earnestness. The Accusers were mostly the same, Tho. Putman's Wife, etc. complaining much. The dreadful Shrieking from her and others, was very amazing, which was heard at a great distance; she was also Committed to Prison.

A Child of Sarah Good's was likewise apprehended, being between 4 and 5 years Old. The Accusers said this Child bit them, and would shew such like marks, as those of a small Sett of Teeth upon their Arms; as many of the Afflicted as the Child cast its Eye upon, would complain they were in Torment; which Child they also Committed.

Concerning these that had been hitherto Examined and Committed, it is among other things observed by Mr. Lawson (in Print) that they were by the Accusers charged to belong to a Company that did muster in Arms, and were reported by them to keep Days of Fast, Thanksgiving and Sacraments; and that those Afflicted (or Accusers) did in the Assembly Cure each others, even with a touch of their Hand, when strangled and otherways tortured, and would endeavour to get to the Afflicted to relieve them thereby (for hitherto they had not used the Experiment of bringing the Accused to touch the Afflicted, in order to their Cure) and could foretell one another's Fits to be coming, and would say, look to such a one, she will have a Fit presently and so it happened, and that at the same time when the Accused person was present, the Afflicted said they saw her Spectre or likeness in other places of the Meeting House Suckling of their Familiars.

The said Mr. Lawson being to Preach at the Village, after the Psalm was Sung, Abigail Williams said, "Now stand up and name your Text"; after it was read, she said, "It is a long Text." Mrs. Pope in the beginning of Sermon said to him, "Now there is enough of that." In Sermon, he referring to his Doctrine, Abigail Williams said to him, "I know no Doctrine you had, if you did name one I have forgot it." Ann Putman, an afflicted Girl, said, There was a Yellow Bird sat on his Hat as it hung on the Pin in the Pulpit.

March 31, 1692. Was set apart as a day of Solemn Humiliation at Salem, upon the Account of this Business, on which day Abigail Williams said, That she saw a great number of Persons in the Village at the Administration of a Mock Sacrament, where they had Bread as red as raw Flesh, and red Drink.

April 1. Mercy Lewis affirmed, That she saw a man in white, with whom she went into a Glorious Place, *viz.* In her fits, where was no Light of the Sun, much less of Candles, yet was full of Light and Brightness, with a great Multitude in White Glittering Robes, who Sang the Song in 5. Rev. 9. and the 110 and 149 Psalms; And was grieved that she might tarry no longer in this place. This White Man is said to have appeared several times to others of them, and to have given them notice how long it should be before they should have another Fit.

April the 3d. Being Sacrament Day at the Village, Sarah Cloys, Sister to Goodwife Nurse, a Member to one of the Churches, was (tho' it seems with difficulty prevail'd with to be) present; but being entred the place, and Mr. Parris naming his Text, 6 John, 70. *Have not I chosen you Twelve, and one of you is a Devil* (for what cause may rest as a doubt whether upon the account of her Sister's being Committed, or because of the choice of that Text) she rose up and went out, the wind shutting the Door forcibly, gave occasion to some to suppose whe went out in Anger, and might occasion a suspicion of her; however she was soon after complain'd of, examin'd and Committed.

April the 11th. By this time the number of the Accused and Accusers being much encreased, was a Publick Examination at Salem, Six of the Magistrates with several Ministers being present; there appeared several who complain'd against others with hidious clamours and Screechings. Goodwife Proctor was brought thither, being Accused or cryed out against; her Husband coming to attend and assist her, as there might be need, the Accusers cryed out of him also, and that with so much earnestness, that he was Committed with his Wife. About this time besides the Experiment of the Afflicted falling at the sight, etc., they put the Accused upon saying the Lord's Prayer, which one among them performed, except in that petition, *Deliver us from Evil,* she exprest it thus, *Deliver us from all Evil.* This was lookt upon as if she Prayed against what she was now justly under, and being put upon it again, and repeating those words, *Hallowed be thy Name,* she exprest it, *Hollowed be thy Name,* this was counted a depraving the words, as signifying to make void, and so a Curse rather then a Prayer, upon the whole it was concluded that she also could not say it, etc. Proceeding in this work of examination and Commitment, many were sent to Prison.

[Calef here reproduces the warrants ordering the arrest and imprisonment of eight of the accused.]

The occasion of [Edward] Bishop's being cry'd out of was, he being at an Examination in Salem, when at the Inn an afflicted Indian [i.e., Parris's John] was very unruly, whom he undertook, and so managed him, that he was very orderly, after which in riding home, in company of him and other Accusers, the Indian fell into a fit, and clapping hold with his Teeth on the back of the Man that rode before him, thereby held himself upon the horse. But said Bishop striking him with his stick, the Indian soon recovered, and promised he would do so no more, to which Bishop replied that he doubted not but he could cure them all, with more to the same effect. Immediately after he was parted from them, he was cried out of, etc.

May 14, 1692. Sir William Phips arrived with Commission from Their Magesties to be Governour, pursuant to the New-Charter; which he now brought with him;* the Ancient Charter having been vacated by King Charles, and King

*[*Some political history will help clarify the following two paragraphs. Until 1684 Massachusetts Bay was governed under a Royal charter which allowed the colony to choose its own leaders. However, in 1684 King James II revoked this charter in an effort to increase royal control. From 1686 to 1689 the unpopular Edmund Andros governed the colony (along with the rest of New England and New York). A bloodless coup made possible by the overthrow of King James II several months earlier resulted in Andros' removal in 1689. Massachusetts now resumed control of her own affairs but this time without a charter or other legal justification. The colony sent Increase Mather and others to London in 1690 in what proved an unsuccessful effort to convince the new monarchs, William and Mary, to restore the old charter. In 1691 they issued a new charter which preserved a few of the colony's old privileges but provided for the appointment of its governors in England. William Phips, a self-made Massachusetts ship captain and a good friend of Increase Mather's, was the first governor named under the new charter. Mather and Phips arrived back in Massachusetts in May 1692, just as the witchcraft troubles were reaching their height.]*

James (by which they had a power not only to make their own Laws; but also to chuse their own Governour and Officers;) and the Country for some years was put under an absolute Commission-Government, till the Revolution, at which time tho' more than two-thirds of the People were for reassuming their ancient Government, (to which they had encouragement by His then Royal Highness's Proclamation) yet some that might have been better imployed (in another Station) made it their business (by printing, as well as speaking) to their utmost to divert them from such a settlement; and so far prevailed, that for about seven Weeks after the Revolution, here was not so much as a face of any Government; but some few Men upon their own Nomination would be called a Committee of Safety; but at length the Assembly prevailed with those that had been of the Government, to promise that they would reassume; and accordingly a Proclamation was drawn, but before publishing it, it was underwritten, that they would not have it understood that they did reassume Charter-Government; so that between Government and no Government, this Countrey remained till Sir William arrived; Agents being in this time impowered in England, which no doubt did not all of them act according to the Minds or Interests of those that impowered them, which is manifest by their not acting jointly in what was done; so that this place is perhaps a single Instance (even in the best of Reigns) of a Charter not restored after so happy a Revolution.

This settlement by Sir William Phips, his being come Governour, put an end to all disputes of these things, and being arrived, and having read his Commission, the first thing he exerted his Power in, was said to be his giving Orders that Irons should be put upon those in Prison; for tho' for some time after these were Committed, the Accusers ceased to cry out of them, yet now the cry against them was renewed, which occasioned such Order; and tho' there was partiality in the executing it (some having taken them off almost as soon as put on) yet the cry of these Accusers against such ceased after this Order.

May 24. Mrs. Cary of Charlestown, was Examined and Committed.

[There follows Nathaniel Cary's account, here ommitted, of his wife's examination, imprisonment, and eventual escape.]

May 31. Captain John Aldin [a wealthy and prominent Boston merchant, son of John and Priscilla Alden of Plymouth Colony.] was Examined at Salem, and Committed to Boston Prison. The Prison-Keeper seeing such a Man Committed, of whom he had a good esteem, was after this the more Compassionate to those that were in Prison on the like account; and did refrain from such hard things to the Prisoners, as before he had used. Mr. Aldin himself has given account of his Examination, in these Words.

An Account How John Aldin, Senior, was Dealt with at Salem-Village

John Aldin Senior, of Boston, in the County of Suffolk, Marriner, on the 28th Day of May, 1692, was sent for by the Magistrates of Salem, in the County of Essex, upon the Accusation of a company of poor distracted, or possessed

Creatures or Witches; and being sent by Mr. Stoughton, arrived there the 31st of May, and appeared at Salem-Village, before Mr. Gidney, Mr. Hathorn, and Mr. Curwin.

Those Wenches being present, who plaid their juggling tricks, falling down, crying out, and staring in Peoples Faces; the Magistrates demanded of them several times, who it was of all the People in the Room that hurt them? one of these Accusers pointed several times at one Captain Hill, there present, but spake nothing; the same Accuser had a Man standing at her back to hold her up; he stooped down to her Ear, then she cried out, Aldin, Aldin afflicted her; one of the Magistrates asked her if she had ever seen Aldin, she answered no, he asked her how she knew it was Aldin? She said, the Man told her so.

Then all were ordered to go down into the Street, where a Ring was made; and the same Accuser cried out, "there stands Aldin, a bold fellow with his Hat on before the Judges, he sells Powder and Shot to the Indians and French, and lies with the Indian Squaws, and has Indian Papooses." Then was Aldin committed to the Marshal's Custody, and his Sword taken from him; for they said he afflicted them with his Sword. After some hours Aldin was sent for to the Meeting-house in the Village before the Magistrates; who required Aldin to stand upon a Chair, to the open view of all the People.

The Accusers cried out that Aldin did pinch them, then, when he stood upon the Chair, in the sight of all the People, a good way distant from them, one of the Magistrates bid the Marshal to hold open Aldin's hands, that he might not pinch those Creatures. Aldin asked them why they should think, that he should come to that Village to afflict those persons that he never knew or saw before? Mr. Gidney bid Aldin confess, and give glory to God; Aldin said he hoped he should give glory to God, and hoped he should never gratifie the Devil; but appealed to all that ever knew him, if they ever suspected him to be such a person, and challenged any one, that could bring in any thing upon their own knowledge, that might give suspicion of his being such an one. Mr. Gidney said he had known Aldin many Years, and had been at Sea with him, and always look'd upon him to be an honest Man, but now he did see cause to alter his judgment: Aldin answered, he was sorry for that, but he hoped God would clear up his Innocency, that he would recall that judgment again, and added that he hoped that he should with Job maintain his Integrity till he died. They bid Aldin look upon the Accusers, which he did, and then they fell down. Aldin asked Mr. Gidney, what Reason there could be given, why Aldin's looking upon *him* did not strike *him* down as well; but no reason was given that I heard. But the Accusers were brought to Aldin to touch them, and this touch they said made them well. Aldin began to speak of the Providence of God in suffering these Creatures to accuse Innocent persons. Mr. Noyes asked Aldin why he would offer to speak of the Providence of God. God by his Providence (said Mr. Noyes) governs the World, and keeps it in peace; and so went on with Discourse, and stopt Aldin's mouth, as to that. Aldin told Mr. Gidney, that he could assure him that there was a lying Spirit in them, for I can assure you that there is not a word of truth in all these say of me. But Aldin was again committed to the Marshal, and his Mittimus written, which was as follows. [*Omitted*]

To Boston Aldin was carried by a Constable, no Bail would be taken for him; but was delivered to the Prison-keeper, where he remained Fifteen Weeks, and then observing the manner of Tryals, and Evidence then taken, was at length prevailed with to make his Escape, and being returned, was bound over to Answer at the Superior Court at Boston, the last Tuesday in April, Anno 1693. And was there cleared by Proclamation, none appearing against him.

Per John Aldin

At Examination, and at other times, 'twas usual for the Accusers to tell of the black Man, or of a Spectre, as being then on the Table, etc. The People about would strike with Swords, or sticks at those places. One justice broke his Cane at this Exercise, and sometimes the Accusers would say, they struck the Spectre, and it is reported several of the accused were hurt and wounded thereby, though at home at the same time.

The Justices proceeding in these works of Examination, and Commitment, to the end of May, there was by that time about a Hundred persons Imprisoned upon that Account.

June 2. A special Commission of Oyer and Terminer having been Issued out, to Mr. Stoughton, the New Lieutenant Governor, Major Saltonstall, Major Richards, Major Gidny, Mr. Wait Winthrop, Captain Sewall, and Mr. Sergeant; These (a Quorum of them) sat at Salem this day;* where the most that was done this Week, was the Tryal of one Bishop, *alias* Oliver, of Salem; who having long undergone the repute of a Witch, occasioned by the Accusations of one Samuel Gray: he about 20 Years since, having charged her with such Crimes, and though upon his Death-bed he testified his sorrow and repentance for such Accusations, as being wholly groundless; yet the report taken up by his means continued, and she being accused by those afflicted, and upon search a Tet, as they call it, being found, she was brought in guilty by the Jury; she received her Sentence of Death, and was Executed, June 10, but made not the least Confession of any thing relating to Witchcraft.

June 15. Several Ministers in and near Boston, having been to that end consulted by his Excellency, exprest their minds to this effect, *viz.*

[Calef here summarizes the "Return of Several Ministers Consulted," reprinted in full on pages 117-118.]

The *30th of June,* the Court according to Adjournment again sat; five more were tried, *viz.* Sarah Good and Rebecca Nurse, of Salem-Village; Susanna Martin of Amesbury; Elizabeth How of Ipswich; and Sarah Wildes of Topsfield; these were all condemned that Sessions, and were all Executed on the 19th of July.

At the Tryal of Sarah Good, one of the afflicted fell in a Fit, and after coming out of it, she cried out of the Prisoner for stabbing her in the breast with

[*One of Governor Phips's first actions was to appoint a special Court of Oyer and Terminer (i.e., "to hear and to determine") to judge the accused witches, who were by this time beginning to fill the jails. The chief justice of this court was William Stoughton, lieutenant governor of the Province. The first sitting of the court was on June 2, 1692.]

a Knife, and that she had broken the Knife in stabbing of her, accordingly a piece of the blade of a Knife was found about her. Immediately information being given to the Court, a young Man was called, who produced a Haft and part of the Blade, which the Court having viewed and compared, saw it to be the same. And upon inquiry the young Man affirmed, that yesterday he happened to break that Knife, and that he cast away the upper part, this afflicted person being then present. The young Man was dismist, and she was bidden by the Court not to tell lyes; and was improved (after as she had been before) to give Evidence against the Prisoners.

At Execution, Mr. Noyes urged Sarah Good to Confess and told her she was a Witch, and she knew she was a Witch, to which she replied, "you are a lyer; I am no more a Witch than you are a Wizard, and if you take away my Life, God will give you Blood to drink."

At the Tryal of Rebecka Nurse, this was remarkable that the Jury brought in their Verdict not Guilty, immediately all the accusers in the Court, and suddenly after all the afflicted out of Court, made an hideous out-cry, to the amazement, not only of the Spectators, but the Court also seemed straangely surprized; one of the Judges exprest himself not satisfied, another of them as he was going off the Bench, said they would have her Indicted anew. The chief Judge said he would not Impose upon the Jury; but intimated, as if they had not well considered one Expression of the Prisoners, when she was upon Tryal, *viz.* That when one Hobbs, who had confessed her self to be a Witch, was brought into the Court to witness against her, the Prisoner turning her head to her, said, "What, do you bring her? she is one of us," or to that effect; this together with the Clamours of the Accusers, induced the Jury to go out again, after their Verdict, not Guilty. But not agreeing, they came into the Court, and she being then at the Bar, her words were repeated to her, in order to have had her explanation of them, and she making no Reply to them, they found the Bill, and brought her in Guilty; these words being the Inducement to it, as the Foremen has signified in writing, as follows.

July 4, 1692. I Thomas Fisk, the Subscriber hereof, being one of them that were of the Jury the last week at Salem-Court, upon the Tryal of Rebecka Nurse, etc., being desired by some of the Relations to give a Reason why the Jury brought her in Guilty, after her Verdict not Guilty; I do hereby give my Reasons to be as follows, *viz.*

When the Verdict not Guilty was, the honoured Court was pleased to object against it, saying to them, that they think they let slip the words, which the Prisoner at the Bar spake against her self, which were spoken in reply to Goodwife Hobbs and her Daughter, who had been faulty in setting their hands to the Devils Book, as they have confessed formerly; the words were "What, do these persons give in Evidence against me now, they used to come among us." After the honoured Court had manifested their dissatisfaction of the Verdict, several of the Jury declared themselves desirous to go out again, and thereupon the honoured Court gave leave; but when we came to consider of the Case, I could not tell how to take her words, as an Evidence against her, till she had a further opportunity to put her Sense upon them, if she would take it; and then going into Court, I mentioned the words aforesaid, which by one of the Court were affirmed to have been spoken by her, she being then at the Bar, but made no reply, nor interpretation of them; whereupon these words were to me a principal Evidence against her.

Thomas Fisk

When Goodwife Nurse was informed what use was made of these words, she put in this following Declaration into the Court.

These presents do humbly shew, to the honoured Court and Jury, that I being informed, that the Jury brought me in Guilty, upon my saying that Goodwife Hobbs and her Daughter were of our Company; but I intended no otherways, then as they were Prisoners with us, and therefore did then, and yet do judge them not legal Evidence against their fellow Prisoners. And I being something hard of hearing, and full of grief, none informing me how the Court took up my words, and therefore had not opportunity to declare what I intended, when I said they were of our Company.

Rebecka Nurse

After her Condemnation she was by one of the Ministers of Salem excommunicated; yet the Governour saw cause to grant a Reprieve, which when known (and some say immediately upon granting) the Accusers renewed their dismal outcries against her, insomuch that the Governour was by some Salem Gentleman prevailed with to recall the Reprieve, and she was Executed with the rest.

The Testimonials of her Christian behaviour, both in the course of her Life, and at her Death, and her extraordinary care in educating her Children, and setting them good Examples, etc., under the hands of so many, are so numerous, that for brevity they are here omitted.

It was at the Tryal of these that one of the Accusers cried out publickly of Mr. Willard, Minister in Boston [not John Willard of Salem Village], as afflicting of her; she was sent out of the Court, and it was told about she was mistaken in the person.

August 5. The Court again sitting, six more were tried on the same Account, *viz.* Mr. George Burroughs, sometime minister of Wells, John Procter, and Elizabeth Procter his Wife, with John Willard of Salem-Village, George Jacobs Senior, of Salem, and Martha Carryer of Andover, these were all brought in Guilty and Condemned; and were all Executed Aug. 19, except Procter's Wife, who pleaded Pregnancy.

Mr. Burroughs was carried in a Cart with the others through the streets of Salem to Execution; when he was upon the Ladder, he made a Speech for the clearing of his Innocency, with such Solemn and Serious Expressions, as were to .he Admiration of all present; his Prayer (which he concluded by repeating the Lord's Prayer,) was so well worded, and uttered with such composedness, and such (at least seeming) fervency of Spirit, as was very affecting, and drew Tears from many (so that it seemed to some, that the Spectators would hinder the Execution). The accusers said the black Man stood and dictated to him; as soon as he was turned off, Mr. Cotton Mather, being mounted upon a Horse, addressed himself to the People, partly to declare, that he was no ordained Minister, and partly to possess the People of his guilt; saying, That the Devil has often been transformed into an Angel of Light; and this did somewhat appease the People, and the Executions went on; when he was cut down, he was dragged by the Halter to a Hole, or Grave, between the Rocks, about two foot deep, his Shirt and Breeches being pulled off, and an old pair of Trousers of one Executed, put on his lower parts, he was so put in, together with Willard and Carryer, one of his Hands and his Chin, and a Foot of one [of] them being left uncovered.

John Willard had been imployed to fetch in several that were accused; but taking dissatisfaction from his being sent to fetch up some that he had better thoughts of, he declined the Service, and presently after he himself was accused of the same Crime, and that with such vehemency, that they sent after him to apprehend him; he had made his Escape as far as Nashawag [Nashaway; now Lancaster, Massachusetts], about 40 Miles from Salem; yet 'tis said those Accusers did then presently tell the exact time, saying, now Willard is taken.

John Procter and his Wife being in Prison, the Sheriff came to his House and seized all the Goods, Provisions, and Cattle that he could come at, and sold some of the Cattle at half price, and killed others, and put them up for the West-Indies; threw out the Beer out of a Barrel, and carried away the Barrel; emptied a Pot of Broath, and took away the Pot, and left nothing in the House for the support of the Children: No part of the said Goods are known to be returned. Procter earnestly requested Mr. Noyes to pray with and for him, but it was wholly denied, because he would not own himself to be a Witch.

During his Imprisonment he sent the following Letter, in behalf of himself and others.

Salem-Prison, July 23, 1692.

Mr. [Increase] Mather, Mr. Allen,
Mr. Moody, Mr. Willard, and
Mr. Bailey.

Reverend Gentlemen.

The innocency of our Case with the Enmity of our Accusers and our Judges, and Jury, whom nothing but our Innocent Blood will serve their turn, having Condemned us already before our Trials, being so much incensed and engaged against us by the Devil, makes us bold to Beg and Implore your Favourable Assistance of this our Humble Petition to his Excellency, That if it be possible our Innocent Blood may be spared, which undoubtedly otherwise will be shed, if the Lord doth not mercifully step in. The Magistrates, Ministers, Jewries [juries], and all the People in general, being so much inraged and incensed against us by the Delusion of the Devil, which we can term no other, by reason we know in our own Consciences, we are all Innocent Persons. Here are five Persons who have lately confessed themselves to be Witches, and do accuse some of us; of being along with them at a Sacrament, since we were committed into close Prison, which we know to be Lies. Two of the 5 are ([Martha] Carrier's Sons) Young-men, who would not confess any thing till they tyed them Neck and Heels till the Blood was ready to come out of their Noses, and 'tis credibly believed and reported this was the occasion of making them confess that they never did, by reason they said one had been a Witch a Month, and another five Weeks, and that their Mother had made them so, who has been confined here this nine Weeks. My son William Procter, when he was examin'd, because he would not confess that he was Guilty, when he was Innocent, they tyed him Neck and Heels till the Blood gushed out at his Nose, and would have kept him so 24 Hours, if one more Merciful than the rest, had not taken pity on him, and caused him to be unbound. These actions are very like the Popish Cruelties. They have already undone us in our Estates, and that will not serve their turns, without our Innocent Bloods.

If it cannot be granted that we have our Trials at Boston, we humbly beg that you would endeavour to have these Magistrates changed, and others in their rooms, begging also and beseeching you would be pleased to be here, if not all, some of you, at our Trials, hoping thereby you may be the means of saving the shedding our Innocent Bloods, desiring your Prayers to the Lord in our behalf, we rest your Poor Afflicted Servants,

John Procter, etc.

He pleaded very hard at Execution, for a little respite of time, saying that he was not fit to Die; but it was not granted.

Old Jacobs being Condemned, the Sheriff and Officers came and seized all he had, his Wife had her Wedding Ring taken from her, but with great difficulty obtained it again. She was forced to buy Provisions of the Sheriff, such as he had taken, towards her own support, which not being sufficient, the Neighbours, of Charity, relieved her.

Margaret Jacobs being one that had confessed her own Guilt, and testified against her Grand-Father Jacobs, Mr. Burroughs, and John Willard, She the day before Executions, came to Mr. Burroughs, acknowledging that she had belyed them, and begged Mr. Burroughs Forgiveness, who not only forgave her, but also Prayed with and for her. She wrote the following Letter to her Father.

From the Dungeon in Salem-Prison, August 20, '92.

Honoured Father,

After my Humble Duty Remembered to you, hoping in the Lord of your good Health, as Blessed be God I enjoy, tho' in abundance of Affliction, being close confined here in a loathsome Dungeon, the Lord look down in mercy upon me, not knowing how soon I shall be put to Death, by means of the Afflicted Persons; my Grand-Father having Suffered already, and all his Estate Seized for the King. The reason of my Confinement is this, I having, through the Magistrates Threatnings, and my own Vile and Wretched Heart, confessed several things contrary to my Conscience and Knowledge, tho' to the Wounding of my own Soul, the Lord pardon me for it; but Oh! the terrors of a wounded Conscience who can bear. But blessed be the Lord, he would not let me go on in my Sins, but in mercy I hope so my Soul would not suffer me to keep it in any longer, but I was forced to confess the truth of all before the Magistrates, who would not believe me, but tis their pleasure to put me in here, and God knows how soon I shall be put to death. Dear Father, let me beg your Prayers to the Lord on my behalf, and send us a Joyful and Happy meeting in Heaven. My Mother poor Woman is very Crazy, and remembers her kind Love to you, and to Uncle, *viz.* D. A. [Daniel Andrew]. So leaving you to the protection of the Lord, I rest your Dutiful Daughter,

Margaret Jacobs

At the time appointed for her Tryal, she had an Imposthume [i.e., abcess or cyst] in her head, which was her Escape.

September 9. Six more were tried, and received Sentence of Death, *viz.* Martha Cory of Salem-Village, Mary Easty of Topsfield, Alice Parker and Ann Pudeater of Salem, Dorcas Hoar of Beverly, and Mary Bradberry of Salisbury.

September 16, Giles Cory was prest to Death.

September 17 Nine more received Sentance of Death, *viz.* Margaret Scot of Rowly, Goodwife Redd of Marblehead, Samuel Wardwell, and Mary Parker of Andover, also Abigail Falkner of Andover, who pleaded Pregnancy, Rebecka Eames of Boxford, Mary Lacy, and Ann Foster of Andover, and Abigail Hobbs of Topsfield. Of these, Eight were Executed, *September 22, viz.* Martha Cory, Mary Easty, Alice Parker, Ann Pudeater, Margaret Scot, Willmet Redd, Samuel Wardwell, and Mary Parker.

Giles Cory pleaded not Guilty to his Indictment, but would not put himself upon Tryal by the Jury (they having cleared none upon Tryal) and knowing there would be the same Witnesses against him, rather chose to undergo what Death they would put him to. In pressing, his Tongue being prest out of his Mouth, the Sheriff with his Cane forced it in again, when he was dying. He was the first in New-England, that was ever prest to Death.

The Cart going up the Hill with these Eight to Execution, was for some time at a sett; the afflicted and others said, that the Devil hindred it, etc.

Martha Cory, Wife to Giles Cory, protesting her Innocency, concluded her Life with an Eminent Prayer upon the Ladder.

Wardwell having formerly confessed himself Guilty, and after denied it, was soon brought upon his Tryal; his former Confession and Spectre Testimony was all that appeared against him. At Execution while he was speaking to the People, protesting his Innocency, the Executioner being at the same time smoaking Tobacco, the smoak coming in his Face, interrupted his Discourse, those Accusers said, the Devil hindred him with smoak.

Mary Easty, Sister also to Rebecka Nurse, when she took her last farewell of her Husband, Children and Friends, was, as is reported by them present, as Serious, Religious, Distinct, and Affectionate as could well be exprest, drawing Tears from the Eyes of almost all present. It seems besides the Testimony of the

Accusers and Confessors, another proof, as it was counted, appeared against her, it having been usual to search the Accused for Tets; upon some parts of her Body, not here to be named, was found an Excrescence, which they called a Tet. Before her Death she put up the following Petition:

To the Honourable Judge and Bench now sitting in Judicature in Salem and the Reverend Ministers, humbly sheweth, That whereas your humble poor Petitioner being Condemned to die, doth humbly beg of you, to take it into your Judicious and Pious Consideration, that your poor and humble Petitioner knowing my own Innocency (blessed be the Lord for it) and seeing plainly the Wiles and Subtilty of my Accusers, by my self, cannot but judge charitably of others, that are going the same way with my self, if the Lord step not mightily in. I was confined a whole Month on the same account that I am now condemned for, and then cleared by the Afflicted persons, as some of your Honours know, and in two days time I was cried out upon by them, and have been confined, and now am condemned to die. The Lord above knows my Innocency then, and likewise doth now, as at the great day will be known to Men and Angels. I Petition to your Honours not for my own Life, for I know I must die, and my appointed time is set; but the Lord he knows it is, if it be possible, that no more Innocent Blood be shed, which undoubtedly cannot be avoided in the way and course you go in. I question not, but your Honours do to the utmost of your powers, in the discovery and detecting of Witchcraft and Witches, and would not be guilty of Innocent Blood for the World; but by my own Innocency I know you are in the wrong way. The Lord in his infinite Mercy direct you in this great work, if it be his blessed will, that Innocent Blood be not shed; I would humbly beg of you, that your Honours would be pleased to Examine some of those confessing Witches, I being confident there are several of them have belyed themselves and others, as will appear, if not in this World, I am sure in the World to come, whither I am going; and I question not, but your selves will see an alteration in these things: They say, my self and others have made a league with the Devil, we cannot confess. I know and the Lord he knows (as will shortly appear) they belye me, and so I question not but they do others; the Lord alone, who is the searcher of all hearts, knows that as I shall answer it at the Tribunal Seat, that I know not the least thing of Witchcraft, therefore I cannot, I durst not belye my own Soul. I beg your Honours not to deny this my humble Petition, from a poor dying Innocent person, and I question not but the Lord will give a blessing to your Endeavours.

Mary Esty

After Execution Mr. Noyes turning him to the Bodies said, what a sad thing it is to see Eight Firebrands of Hell hanging there.

In *October 1692,* One of Wenham complained of Mrs. Hale, whose Husband, the Minister of Beverly, had been very forward in these Prosecutions, but being fully satisfied of his wife's sincere Christianity, caused him to alter his Judgment; for it was come to a stated Controversie, among the New-England Divines, whether the Devil could Afflict in a good Man's shape; it seems nothing else could convince him: yet when it came so near to himself, he was soon convinc'd that the Devil might so Afflict. Which same reason did afterwards prevail with many others; and much influenced to the succeeding change at Tryals.

October 7. (Edward Bishop and his Wife having made their Escape out of Prison) this day Mr. Corwin the Sheriff, came and Seiz'd his Goods, and Cattle, and had it not been for his second Son (who borrowed Ten Pound and gave it him) they had been wholly lost, the Receipt follows; but it seems they must be content with such a Receipt as he would give them.

Received this 7th day of October 1692, of Samuel Bishop of the Town of Salem, of the County of Essex, in New-England, Cordwainer, in full satisfaction, a valuable Summ of Money, for the Goods and Chattels of Edward Bishop, Senior, of the Town and County aforesaid, Husbandman; which Goods and Chattels being seized, for that the said Edward Bishop, and Sarah his Wife, having been committed for Witchcraft and Felony, have made their Escape; and their Goods and Chattles were forfeited unto their Majesties, and now being in Possession of the said Samuel Bishop; and in behalf of Their Majesties, I do hereby discharge the said Goods and Chattles, the day and year above written, as witness my hand,

George Corwin, *Sheriff.*

But before this the said Bishop's Eldest Son, having Married into that Family of the Putmans, who were chief Prosecutors in this business; he holding a Cow to be branded lest it should be seiz'd, and having a Push or Boyl upon his Thigh, with his straining it broke; this is that that was pretended to be burnt with the said Brand; and is one of the bones thrown to the Dogmatical to pick, in [Cotton Mather's] *Wonders of the Invisible World* [1693], p. 143. The other, of a Corner of a Sheet, pretended to be taken from a Spectre, it is known that it was provided the day before, by that Afflicted person, and the third bone of a Spindle is almost as easily provided, as the piece of the Knife; so that Apollo needs not herein be consulted, etc.

[In a section here omitted, Calef relates further experiences and sufferings of some of the accused, including Dorcas Hoar, Philip English and his wife, and George Jacobs Junior and his wife. He also describes a flurry of witchcraft excitement which agitated Andover, Massachusetts, at this time.]

And now Nineteen persons having been hang'd, and one prest to death, and Eight more condemned, in all Twenty and Eight, of which above a third part were Members of some of the Churches in N. England, and more than half of them of a good Conversation in general, and not one clear'd; About Fifty having confest themselves to be Witches of which not one Executed; above an Hundred and Fifty in Prison, and above Two Hundred more accused; The Special Commission of Oyer and Terminer comes to a period, which has no other foundation than the Governours Commission, and had proceeded in the manner of swearing Witnesses, *viz.* By holding up the hand, (and by receiving Evidences in writing) according to the Ancient Usage of this Country; as also having their Indictments in English. In the Trials, when any were Indicted for Afflicting, Pining, and wasting the Bodies of particular persons by Witchcraft, it was usual to hear Evidence of matter foreign, and of perhaps Twenty or Thirty years standing, about over-setting Carts, the death of Cattle, unkindness to Relations, or unexpected Accidents befalling after some quarrel. Whether this was admitted by the Law of England, or by what other Law, wants to be determined; the Executions seemed mixt, in pressing to death for not pleading, which most agrees with the Laws of England, and Sentencing Women to be hanged for Witchcraft, according to the former practice of this Country, and not by burning, as is said to have been the Law of England. And though the confessing Witches were many; yet not one of them that confessed their own guilt, and abode by their Confession, were put to Death.

Extracts From Deodat Lawson, *A Brief and True Narrative* (1692)

[Deodat Lawson was a former Salem Village minister who returned for a timely visit in March 1692. A sermon which he delivered during his visit is reprinted on pp. 124-128.]

On the Nineteenth day of March last, I went to Salem Village, and lodged at Nathaniel Ingersol's near to the Minister Mr. P's. house, and presently after I came into my Lodging, Capt. Walcut's Daughter Mary came to Lieut. Ingersol's and spake to me, but, suddenly after as she stood by the door, was bitten, so that she cried out of her Wrist, and looking on it with a Candle, we saw apparently the marks of Teeth both upper and lower set, on each side of her wrist.

In the beginning of the Evening, I went to give Mr. P. a visit. When I was there, his Kins-woman, Abigail Williams, (about 12 years of age,) had a grievous fit; she was at first hurryed with Violence to and fro in the room, (though Mrs. Ingersol endeavoured to hold her,) sometimes makeing as if she would fly, stretching up her arms as high as she could and crying "Whish, Whish, Whish!" several times; Presently after she said there was Goodw. N. [i.e., Rebecca Nurse] and said "Do you not see her? Why, there she stands!" And then said Goodw. N. offered her The Book, but she was resolved she would not take it, saying Often, "I won't, I won't, I won't, take it, I do not know what Book it is: I am sure it is none of God's Book, it is the Devils Book, for ought I know." After that, she run to the Fire, and begun to throw Fire Brands about the house; and run against the Back, as if she would run up Chimney, and, as they said, she had attempted to go into the Fire in other Fits.

On Lord's Day, the Twentieth of March, there were sundry of the afflicted Persons at Meeting, as, Mrs. Pope, and Goodwife Bibber, Abigail Williams, Mary Walcut, Mary Lewes, and Doctor Griggs' Maid. There was also at Meeting, Goodwife C. [i.e., Martha Cory] (who was afterward Examined on suspicion of being a Witch:) They had several Sore Fits, in the time of Publick Worship, which did something interrupt me in my First Prayer; being so unusual. After Psalm was Sung, Abigail Williams said to me, "Now stand up, and Name your Text": And after it was read, she said, "It is a long Text." In the beginning of Sermon, Mrs. Pope, a Woman afflicted, said to me, "Now there is enough of that." And in the afternoon, Abigail Williams upon my referring to my Doctrine said to me, "I know no Doctrine you had, If you did name one, I have forgot it."

In Sermon time, when Goodw. C was present in the Meetinghouse, Ab. W. called out, "Look where Goodw. C sits on the Beam suckling her Yellow bird betwixt her fingers"! Anne Putnam, another Girle afflicted, said there was a Yellow-bird sat on my hat as it hung on the Pin in the Pulpit: but those that were by, restrained her from speaking loud about it.

On Monday the 21st of March, The Magistrates of Salem appointed to come to Examination of Goodw C. And about twelve of the Clock, they went into the Meeting House, which was Thronged with Spectators: Mr. Noyes began with a very pertinent and pathetic Prayer; and Goodwife C. being called to answer to what was Alleged against her, she desired to go to Prayer, which was much wondred at, in the presence of so many hundred people: The Magistrates told her, they would not admit it; they came not there to hear her Pray, but to Examine her, in what was Alleged against her. The Worshipful Mr. Hathorne asked her, Why she Afflicted those Children? she said, she did not Afflict them. He asked her, who did then? she said, "I do not know; How should I know?"

The Number of the Afflicted Persons were about that time Ten: *viz.* Four Married Women, Mrs. Pope, Mrs. Putman, Goodw. Bibber, and an Ancient Woman, named Goodall; three Maids, Mary Walcut, Mercy Lewes, at Thomas Putman's, and a Maid at Dr. Grigg's; there were three Girls from 9 to 12 Years of Age, each of them, or thereabouts, *viz.* Elizabeth Parris, Abigail Williams and Ann Putman. These were most of them at G. C.'s Examination, and did vehemently accuse her in the Assembly of afflicting them, by Biting, Pinching, Strangling, etc. And that they did in their Fit see her Likeness coming to them, and bringing a Book to them, she said, she had no Book. They affirmed, she had a Yellow-Bird, that used to suck betwixt her Fingers, and being asked about it, if she had any Familiar Spirit, that attended her, she said, She had no Familiarity with any such thing. She was a Gospel Woman: which Title she called her self by; and the Afflicted Persons told her, ah! She was, A Gospel Witch. Ann Putman did there affirm, that one day when Lieutenant Fuller was at Prayer at her Father's House, she saw the shape of Goodw. C. and she thought Goodw. N. Praying at the same time to the Devil; she was not sure it was Goodw. N., she thought it was; but very sure she saw the Shape of G. C. The said C. said, they were poor, distracted Children, and no heed to be given to what they said. Mr. Hathorne and Mr. Noyes replyed, it was the judgment of all that were present, they were Bewitched, and only she, the Accused Person said, they were Distracted.

It was observed several times, that if she did but bite her Under lip in time of Examination the persons afflicted were bitten on their arms and wrists and produced the Marks before the Magistrates, Ministers and others. And being watched for that, if she did but Pinch her Fingers, or Grasp one hand hard in another, they were Pinched and produced the Marks before the Magistrates, and Spectators. After that, it was observed, that if she did but lean her Breast against the Seat, in the Meeting House, (being the Barr at which she stood,) they were afflicted. Particularly Mrs. Pope complained of grievous torment in her Bowels as if they were torn out. She vehemently accused said C. as the instrument, and first threw her Muff at her; but that flying not home, got off her Shoe, and hit Goodwife C. on the head with it. After these postures were watched, if said C. did but stir her feet, they were afflicted in their Feet, and stamped fearfully. The afflicted persons asked her why she did not go to the company of Witches which were before the Meeting house mustering? Did she not hear the Drum beat? They accused her of having Familiarity with the Devil, in the time of Examination, in the shape of a Black man whispering in her ear; they affirmed, that her Yellow-Bird sucked betwixt her Fingers in the Assembly; and order being given to see if there were any sign, the Girl that saw it said, it was too late now; she had removed a Pin, and put it on her head; which was found there sticking upright.

They told her, she had Covenanted with the Devil for ten years, six of them were gone, and four more to come. She was required by the Magistrates to answer that Question in the Catechism, "How many persons be there in the God-Head?" she answered it but oddly, yet was there no great thing to be gathered from it: she denied all that was charged upon her and said, They could not prove a Witch; she was that Afternoon Committed to Salem Prison; and after she was in Custody, she did not so appear to them, and afflict them as before.

On Wednesday the 23 of March, I went to Thomas Putman's, on purpose to see his Wife: I found her lying on the Bed, having had a sore fit a little before. She spake to me, and said, she was glad to see me; her Husband and she both desired me to pray with her, while she was sensible; which I did, though the Apparition said, I should not go to Prayer. At the first beginning she attended; but after a little time, was taken with a fit; yet continued silent, and seemed to be Asleep. When Prayer was done, her Husband going to her, found her in a Fit; he took her off the Bed, to set her on his Knees; but at first she was so stiff, she could not be bended; but she afterwards set down; but quickly began to strive violently with her Arms and Legs; she then began to Complain of, and as it were to Converse personally with, Goodw. N., saying, "Goodw. N. Be gone! Be gone! Be gone! are you not ashamed, a Woman of your Profession, to afflict a poor Creature so? what hurt did I ever do you in my life! you have but two years to live, and then the Devil will torment your Soul, for this your Name is blotted out of God's Book, and it shall never be put in God's Book again, be gone for shame, are you not afraid of that which is coming upon you? I Know, I know, what will make you afraid; the wrath of an Angry God, I am sure that will make you afraid; be gone, do not torment me, I know what you would have (we judged she meant, her Soul) but it is out of your reach; it is Clothed with the white Robes of Christ's Righteousness."

After this, she seemed to dispute with the Apparition about a particular Text of Scripture. The Apparition seemed to deny it, (the Woman's eyes being fast closed all this time); she said, She was sure there was such a Text; and she would tell it; and then the Shape would be gone, for said she, "I am sure you cannot stand before that Text!" then she was sorely Afflicted; her mouth drawn on one side, and her body strained for about a minute, and then said, "I will tell, I will tell; it is, it is, it is!" three or four times, and then was afflicted to hinder her from telling, at last she broke forth and said, "It is the third Chapter of the Revelations." I did something scruple the reading it, and did let my scruple appear, lest Satan should make any Superstitious lie to improve the Word of the Eternal God. However, tho' not versed in these things, I judged I might do it this once for an Experiment. I began to read, and before I had near read through the first verse, she opened her eyes, and was well; this fit continued near half an hour. Her Husband and the Spectators told me, she had often been so relieved by reading Texts that she named, something pertinent to her Case; as Isa. 40. 1, Isa. 49. 1, Isa. 50. 1, and several others.

On Thursday the Twenty fourth of March, (being in course the Lecture Day, at the Village,) Goodwife N. was brought before the Magistrates Mr. Hathorne and Mr. Corwin, about Ten of [the] Clock, in the Fore Noon, to be Examined in the Meeting House; the Reverend Mr. Hale begun with Prayer, and the Warrant being read, she was required to give answer, Why she aflicted those persons? she pleaded her own innocency with earnestness. Thomas Putman's Wife, Abigail Williams and Thomas Putman's daughter accused her that she appeared to them, and afflicted them in their fits: but some of the other said, that they had seen her, but knew not that ever she had hurt them; amongst which was Mary Walcut, who was presently after she had so declared bitten, and cryed out of her in the Meeting House; producing the Marks of teeth on her wrist.

It was so disposed, that I had not leisure to attend the whole time of Examination, but both Magistrates and Ministers told me, that the things alleged by the afflicted, and defences made by her, were much after the same manner, as the former was. And her Motions did produce like effects as to Biting, Pinching, Bruising, Tormenting, at their Breasts, by her Leaning, and when, bended Back, were as if their Backs was broken. The afflicted persons said, the Black Man whispered to her in the Assembly, and therefore she could not hear what the Magistrates said unto her. They said also that she did then ride by the Meeting-house, behind the Black Man. Thomas Putman's wife had a grievous Fit, in the time of Examination, to the very great Impairing of her strength, and wasting of her spirits, insomuch as she could hardly move hand, or foot, when she was carryed out. Others also were there grievously afflicted, so that there was once such an hideous screetch and noise, (which I heard as I walked, at a little distance from the Meeting house,) as did amaze me, and some that were within told me the whole assembly was struck with consternation, and they were afraid, that those that sat next to them, were under the influence of Witchcraft. This woman also was that day committed to Salem Prison.

The Magistrates and Ministers also did inform me, that they apprehended a child of Sarah G. [Good] and Examined it, being between 4 and 5 years of Age, And as to matter of Fact, they did Unanimously affirm, that when this Child did but cast its eye upon the afflicted persons, they were tormented, and they held her Head, and yet so many as her eye could fix upon were afflicted. Which they did several times make careful observation of: the afflicted complained, they had often been Bitten by this child, and produced the marks of a small set of teeth, accordingly, this was also committed to Salem Prison; the child looked hail and well as other Children. I saw it at Lieut. Ingersol's. After the commitment of Goodw. N., Tho: Putman's wife was much better, and had no violent fits at all from that 24th of March to the 5th of April. Some others also said they had not seen her so frequently appear to them, to hurt them.

On the 25th of March, (as Capt. Stephen Sewal, of Salem, did afterwards inform me) Eliza. Paris had sore Fits, at his house, which much troubled himself, and his wife, so as he told me they were almost discouraged. She related, that the great Black Man came to her, and told her, if she would be ruled by him, she should have whatsoever she desired, and go to a Golden City. She relating this to Mrs. Sewall, she told the child, it was the Divel, and he was a Lyar from the Beginning, and bid her tell him so, if he came again: which she did accordingly, at the next coming to her, in her fits.

On the 26th of March, Mr. Hathorne, Mr. Corwin, and Mr. Higison were at the Prison-Keeper's House, to Examine the Child, and it told them there, it had a little Snake that used to Suck on the lowest Joint of it[s] Fore-Finger; and when they inquired where, pointing to other places, it told them, not there, but there, pointing on the Lowest point of Fore-Finger; where they Observed a deep Red Spot, about the Bigness of a Flea-bite, they asked who gave it that Snake? whether the great Black man, it said no, its Mother gave it.

The 31 of March there was a Publick Fast kept at Salem on account of these Afflicted Persons. And Abigail Williams said, that the Witches had a Sacrament that day at an house in the Village, and that they had Red Bread and Red Drink. The first of April, Mercy Lewis, Thomas Putman's Maid, in her fit, said, they did eat Red Bread like Man's Flesh, and would have had her eat some: but she would not; but turned away her head, and Spit at them, and said, "I will not Eat, I will not Drink, it is Blood," etc. She said, "That is not the Bread of Life, that is not the Water of Life; Christ gives the Bread of Life, I will have none of it!" This first of April also Marcy Lewis aforesaid saw in her fit a White man and was with him in a Glorious Place, which had no Candles nor Sun, yet was full of Light and Brightness; where was a great Multitude in White glittering Robes, and they Sung the Song in the fifth of Revelation the Ninth verse, and the 110 Psalm and the 149 Psalm; and said with her self, "How long shall I stay here? let me be along with you": She was loth to leave this place, and grieved that she could tarry no longer. This White man hath appeared several times to some of them, and given them notice how long it should be before they had another Fit, which was sometimes a day, or day and half, or more or less: it hath fallen out accordingly.

The third of April, the Lord's-Day, being Sacrament-day, at the Village, Goodw. C. [i.e., Sarah Cloyse] upon Mr. Parris's naming his Text, John 6, 70, *One of them is a Devil,* the said Goodw. C. went immediately out of the Meeting House, and flung the door after her violently, to the amazement of the Congregation: She was afterward seen by some in their Fits, who said, "O Goodw. C., I did not think to see you here!" (and being at their Red bread and drink) said to her, "Is this a time to receive the Sacrament, you ran-away on the Lord's-Day, and scorned to receive it in the Meeting-House, and, Is this a time to receive it? I wonder at you!"

This is the sum of what I either saw my self, or did receive Information from persons of undoubted Reputation and Credit.

Chapter Eight

Comment by Outside Authorities:
Civil and Ecclesiastical

The Return of Several Ministers
Consulted (June 15, 1692)

[After Bridget Bishop was sentenced to hang, one of the judges of the Court of Oyer and Terminer resigned. At this point Governor Phips requested the leading ministers of Massachusetts Bay to advise him on the issues raised by by the witchcraft prosecutions. Their "Return," probably written by Cotton Mather, was delivered on June 15.]

Boston, June 15, 1692

I. The afflicted state of our poor neighbors that are now suffering by molestations from the Invisible World, we apprehend so deplorable that we think their condition calls for the utmost help of all persons in their several capacities.

II. We cannot but with all thankfulness acknowledge the success which the merciful God has given unto the sedulous and assiduous endeavors of our honorable rulers to detect the abominable witchcrafts which have been committed in the country, humbly praying that the discovery of these mysterious and mischievous wickednesses may be perfected.

III. We judge that in the prosecution of these and all such witchcrafts, there is need of a very critical and exquisite caution, lest by too much credulity for things received only upon the Devil's authority, there be a door opened for a long train of miserable consequences, and Satan get an advantage over us; for we should not be ignorant of his devices.

IV. As in complaints upon witchcrafts there may be matters of inquiry which do not amount unto matters of presumption, and there may be matters of presumption which yet may not be reckoned matters of *conviction*, so 'tis necessary that all proceedings thereabout be managed with an exceeding tenderness towards those that may be complained of, especially if they have been persons formerly of an unblemished reputation.

V. When the first inquiry is made into the circumstances of such as may lie under any just suspicion of witchcrafts, we could wish that there may be admitted as little as is possible of such noise, company, and openness, as may too hastily expose them that are examined, and that there may nothing be used as a test, for the trial of the suspected, the lawfulness whereof may be doubted among the people of God; but that the directions given by such judicious writers as *Perkins* and *Bernard* be consulted in such a case.

VI. Presumptions whereupon persons may be committed, and, much more, convictions whereupon persons may be condemned as guilty of witchcrafts, ought certainly to be more considerable than barely [i.e., merely] the accused person being represented by a spector unto the afflicted, inasmuch as 'tis an undoubted and a notorious thing that a Demon may, by God's permission, appear, even to ill purposes, in the shape of an innocent, yea, and a virtuous man. Nor can we esteem alterations made in the sufferers by a look or touch of the accused to be an infallible evidence of guilt, but frequently liable to be abused by the Devil's legerdemains.

VII. We know not whether some remarkable affronts given to the Devils by our disbelieving of those testimonies whose whole force and strength is from them alone, may not put a period [i.e., a stop] unto the progress of the dreadful calamity begun upon us, in the accusation of so many persons whereof we hope some are yet clear from the great transgression laid unto their charge.

VIII. Nevertheless, we cannot but humbly recommend unto the Government the speedy and vigorous prosecution of such as have rendered themselves obnoxious, according to the direction given in the laws of God, and the wholesome statutes of the *English* nation, for the detection of witchcrafts.

Cotton Mather to John Foster, a Member of the Governor's Council (August 17, 1692)

Sir:

You would know whether I still retain my opinion about the horrible witchcrafts among us, and I acknowledge that I do.

I do still think that when there is no further evidence against a person but only this, that a specter in their shape does afflict a neighbor, that evidence is not enough to convict the [person] of witchcraft.

That the Devils have a natural power which makes them capable of exhibiting what shape they please I suppose nobody doubts, and I have no absolute promise of God that they shall not exhibit *mine.*

It is the opinion generally of all Protestant writers that the Devil may thus abuse the innocent; yea, 'tis the confession of some Popish ones. And our honorable judges are so eminent for their justice, wisdom, and goodness, that whatever their own particular sense may be, yet they will not proceed capitally against any upon a principle contested with great odds on the other side in the learned and Godly world.

Nevertheless, a very great use is to be made of the spectral impressions upon the sufferers. They justly introduce and determine an inquiry into the circumstances of the person accused, and they strengthen other presumptions.

When so much use is made of those things, I believe the use for which the great God intends them is made. And accordingly you see that the excellent judges have had such an encouraging presence of God with them as that scarce any, if at all any, have been tried before them against whom God has not strangely sent in other, and more human, and most convincing testimonies.

If any persons have been condemned about whom any of the judges are not easy in their minds that the evidence against them has been satisfactory, it would certainly be for the glory of the whole transaction to give that person a reprieve.

It would make all matters easier if at least bail were taken for people accused only by the invisible tormentors of the poor sufferers, and not blemished by any further grounds of suspicion against them.

The odd effects produced upon the sufferers by the look or touch of the accused are things wherein the Devils may as much impose upon some harmless people as by the representation of their shapes.

My notion of these matters is this. A suspected and unlawful communion with a familiar spirit is the thing inquired after. The communion on the Devil's part may be proved while, for aught I can say, the man may be innocent. The Devil may impudently impose his communion upon some that care not for his company. But if the communion on the man's part be proved, then the business is done.

I am suspicious lest the Devil may at some time or other serve us a trick by his constancy for a long while in one way of dealing. We may find the Devil using one constant course in nineteen several actions, and yet he be too hard for us at last, if we thence make a rule to form an infallible judgment of a twentieth. It is our singular happiness that we are blessed with judges who are aware of this danger.

For my own part, if the Holy God should permit such a terrible calamity to befall myself as that a specter in my shape should so molest my neighborhood as that they can have no quiet, although there should be no other evidence against me, I should very patiently submit unto a judgment of transportation [i.e., exile], and all reasonable men would count our judges to act as they are, like the fathers of the public, in such a judgment. What if such a thing should be ordered for those whose guilt is more dubious and uncertain, whose presence yet perpetuates the miseries of our sufferers? They would cleanse the land of witchcrafts and yet also prevent the shedding of innocent blood, whereof some are so apprehensive of hazard. If our judges want any good bottom to act thus upon, you know that besides the usual power of governors to relax many judgments of death our General Court can soon provide a law.

Sir,

You see the incoherency of my thoughts, but I hope you will also find some reasonableness in those thoughts.

In the year 1645 a vast number of persons in the county of Suffolk [England] were apprehended as guilty of witchcraft, whereof some confessed. The Parliament granted a Special Commission of Oyer and Terminer for the trial of those witches, in which commission there were a famous divine or two, Mr. Fariclough particularly, inserted. That excellent man did preach two sermons to the court before his first sitting on the bench, wherein having first proved the existence of witches he afterwards showed the evil of endeavoring the conviction of any upon defective evidence. The sermon had the effect that none were condemned who could be saved without an express breach of the law. And then, though 'twas possible some guilty did escape, yet the troubles of those places were, I think, extinguished.

Our case is extraordinary. And so you and others will pardon the extraordinary liberty I take to address you on this occasion. But after all, I entreat you that whatever you do, you strengthen the hands of our honorable judges in the great work before them. They are persons for whom no man living has a greater veneration than

Sir,
Your servant
C. Mather

Governor William Phips to the Earl of Nottingham (February 21, 1693)

Boston in New England Febry 21st, 1692-93

May it please your Lordship

By the Capn. of the *Samuel and Henry* I gave an account that at my arrival here I found the prisons full of people committed upon suspicion of witchcraft, and that continual complaints were made to me that many persons were grievously tormented by witches, and that they cried out upon several persons by name, as the cause of their torments. The number of these complaints increasing every day, by advice of the Lieut. Govr. and the Council I gave a Commission of Oyer and Terminer to try the suspected witches and at that time the generality of the people represented the matter to me as real witchcraft and gave very strange instances of the same. The first in Commission was the Lieut. Govr. and the rest persons of the best prudence and figure that could then be pitched upon, and I depended upon the Court for a right method of proceeding in cases of witchcraft.

At that time I went to command the army at the eastern part of the Province, for the French and Indians had made an attack upon some of our frontier towns. I continued there for some time but when I returned I found people much dissatisfied at the proceedings of the Court, for about twenty persons were condemned and executed of which number some were thought by many persons to be innocent. The Court still proceeded in the same method of trying them, which was by the evidence of the afflicted persons who, when they were brought into the Court—as soon as the suspected witches looked upon them, instantly fell to the ground in strange agonies and grievous torments, but when touched by them upon the arm or some other part of their flesh they immediately revived and came to themselves, upon [which] they made oath that the prisoner at the bar did afflict them and that they saw their shape or specter come from their bodies which put them to such pains and torments. When I inquired into the matter I was informed by the Judges that they began with this, but had human testimony against such as were condemned and undoubted proof of their being witches. But at length I found that the Devil did take upon him the shape of Innocent persons and some were accused of whose innocency I was well assured and many considerable persons of unblameable life and conversation were cried out upon as witches and wizards.

The Deputy Govr., notwithstanding, persisted vigorously in the same method, to the great dissatisfaction and disturbance of the people, until I put an end to the Court and stopped the proceedings, which I did because I saw many innocent persons might otherwise perish and at that time I thought it my duty to give an account thereof that their Majesties' pleasure might be signified, hoping that for the better ordering thereof the Judges learned in the law in England might give such rules and directions as have been practiced in England for proceedings in so difficult and so nice a point. When I put an end to the Court there were at least fifty persons in prison in great misery by reason of the extreme cold and their poverty, most of them having only specter evidence against them, and their *mittimusses* being defective, I caused some of them to be let out upon bail and put the Judges upon considering of a way to relieve others and prevent them from perishing in prison, upon which some of them were convinced and acknowledged that their former proceedings were too violent and not grounded upon a right foundation but that if they might sit again, they would proceed after another method, and whereas Mr. Increase Mathew [Mather] and several other Divines did give it as their Judgment that the Devil might afflict in the shape of an innocent person and that the look and the touch of the suspected persons was not sufficient proof against them, these things had not the same stress laid upon them as before. And upon this consideration I permitted a special Superior Court to be held at Salem in the County of Essex on the third day of January, the Lieut. Govr. being Chief Judge. Their method of proceeding being altered, all that were brought to trial, to the number of fifty two, were cleared saving [except] three, and I was informed by the King's Attorney General that some of the cleared and the condemned were under the same circumstances or that there was the same reason to clear the three condemned as the rest according to his Judgment. The Deputy Govr. signed a Warrant for their speedy execution and also of five others who were condemned at the former Court of Oyer and Terminer, but considering how the matter had been managed I sent a reprieve whereby the execution was stopped until their Maj. pleasure be signified and declared. The Lieut. Gov. upon this occasion was enraged and filled with passionate anger and refused to sit upon the bench in a Superior Court then held at Charlestown, and indeed hath from the beginning hurried on these matters with great precipitancy and by his warrant hath caused the estates, goods and chattels of the executed to be seized and disposed of without my knowledge or consent.

The stop put to the first method of proceedings hath dissipated the black cloud that threatened this Province with destruction; for whereas this delusion of the Devil did spread and its dismal effects touched the lives and estates of many of their Majesties' subjects and the reputation of some of the principal persons here, and indeed unhappily clogged and interrupted their Majesties' affairs which hath been a great vexation to me, I have no new complaints but people's minds before divided and distracted by differing opinions concerning this matter are now well composed.

I am

Your Lordship's most faithful

humble Servant

William Phips

The Massachusetts General Court
Makes Restitution (1711)

By His Excellency the Governor

Whereas the General Assembly in their last session accepted the report of their committee appointed to consider of the damages sustained by sundry persons prosecuted for witchcraft in the year 1692, *vizt.*

	£	s.	d.		£	s.	d.
To Elizabeth How	12	0	0	John Proctor			
George Jacobs	79	0	0	and wife	150	0	0
Mary Eastey	20	0	0	Sarah Wild	14	0	0
Mary Parker	8	0	0	Mary Bradbury	20	0	0
George Burroughs	50	0	0	Abigail Faulkner	10	0	0
Giles Cory and wife	21	0	0	Abigail Hobbs	10	0	0
Rebeccah Nurse	25	0	0	Anne Foster	6	10	0
John Willard	20	0	0	Rebeccah Eames	10	0	0
Sarah Good	30	0	0	Dorcas Hoar	21	17	0
Martha Carrier	7	6	0	Mary Post	8	14	0
Samuel Wardwell				Mary Lacey	8	10	0
and wife	36	15	0		269	11	0
	309	1	0		309	1	0
					578	12	0

The whole amounting unto five hundred seventy eight pounds and twelve shillings.

I do by and with the advice and consent of Her Majesty's council hereby order you to pay the above sum of five hundred seventy eight pounds and twelve shillings to Stephen Sewall, Esq., who, together with the gentlemen of the committee that estimated and reported the said damages, are desired and directed to distribute the same in proportion as above to such of the said persons as are living, and to those that legally represent them that are dead, according as the law directs, and for which this shall be your warrant.

Given under my hand at Boston, the 17th day of December, 1711.

J. Dudley

Chapter Nine

Three Sermons on Salem-Village Witchcraft

Deodat Lawson, "Christ's Fidelity the Only Shield Against Satan's Malignity"*

Zech. 3:2. "And the Lord said unto Satan, the Lord rebuke thee O Satan; even the Lord that hath chosen Jerusalem rebuke thee. Is this not a brand plucked out of the fire?"

[Deodat Lawson published "Christ's Fidelity" in 1693, a year after he delivered it. Since the printed version comes to more than fifty pages, Lawson more than probably expanded his original text for publication. We have reprinted the final section (the "Application") of the printed version.]

The application of this doctrine to ourselves remains now to be attended. Let it be for solemn warning and awakening to all of us that are before the Lord at this time, and to all others of this whole people, who shall come to the knowledge of these direful operations of Satan, which the holy God hath permitted in the midst of us.

The Lord doth terrible things amongst us, by lengthening the chain of the roaring lion in an extraordinary manner, so that the Devil is come down in great wrath (Rev. xii. 12), endeavoring to set up his kingdom, and, by racking torments on the bodies, and affrightening representations to the minds of many amongst us, to force and fright them to become his subjects. I may well say, then, in the words of the prophet (Mic. vi. 9), 'The Lord's voice crieth to the city,' and to the country also, with an unusual and amazing loudness. Surely, it

*[*A sermon preached at Salem Village, March 24, 1692.]*

warns us to awaken out of all sleep, of security or stupidity, to arise, and take our Bibles, turn to, and learn that lesson, not by rote only, but by heart (1 Pet. v. 8): 'Be sober, be vigilant; because your adversary the Devil goes about as a roaring lion, seeking whom amongst you he may distress, delude, and devour.'. . .

Awake, awake then, I beseech you, and remain no longer under the dominion of that prince of cruelty and malice, whose tyrannical fury we see thus exerted against the bodies and minds of these afflicted persons! . . . This warning is directed to all manner of persons, according to their condition of life, both in civil and sacred order; both high and low, rich and poor, old and young, bond and free. Oh, let the observation of these amazing dispensations of God's unusual and strange Providence quicken us to our duty, at such a time as this, in our respective places and stations, relations and capacities! The great God hath done such things amongst us as to make the ears of those that hear them to tingle (Jer. xix. 3); and serious souls are at a loss to what these things may grow, and what we shall find to be the end of this dreadful visitation, in the permission whereof the provoked God as a lion hath roared, who can but fear? the Lord hath spoken, who can but prophesy? (Amos iii. 8.) The loud trumpet of God, in this thundering providence, is blown in the city, and the echo of it heard through the country, surely then the people must and ought to be afraid (Amos iii. 6). . .

You are therefore to be deeply humbled, and sit in the dust, considering the signal hand of God in singling out this place, this poor village, for the first seat of Satan's tyranny, and to make it (as 'twere) the rendezvous of devils, where they muster their infernal forces; appearing to the afflicted as coming armed to carry on their malicious designs against the bodies, and, if God in mercy prevent not, against the souls, of many in this place. . . . Be humbled also that so many members of this church of the Lord Jesus Christ should be under the influences of Satan's malice in these his operations; some as the objects of his tyranny on their bodies to that degree of distress which none can be sensible of but those that see and feel it, who are in the mean time also sorely distressed in their minds by frightful representations made by the devils unto them. Other professors and visible members of this church are under the awful accusations and imputations of being the instruments of Satan in his mischievous actings. It cannot but be matter of deep humiliation, to such as are innocent, that the righteous and holy God should permit them to be named in such pernicious and unheard-of practices, and not only so, but that he who cannot but do right should suffer the stain of suspected guilt to be, as it were, rubbed on and soaked in by many sore and amazing circumstances.

And it is a matter of soul-abasement to all that are in the bond of God's holy covenant in this place, that Satan's seat should be amongst them, where he attempts to set up his kingdom in opposition to Christ's kingdom, and to take some of the visible subjects of our Lord Jesus, and use at least their shapes and appearances, instrumentally, to afflict and torture other visible subjects of the same kingdom. Surely his design is that Christ's kingdom may be divided against itself, that, being thereby weakened, he may the better take opportunity to set up his own accursed powers and dominions. It calls aloud then to all in this place in the name of the blessed Jesus and words of his holy apostle (1 Peter v. 6), 'Humble yourselves under the mighty hand of God.'

It is matter of terror, amazement, and astonishment, to all such wretched souls (if there be any here in the congregation; and God, of his infinite mercy, grant that none of you may ever be found such!) as have given up their names and souls to the Devil; who by covenant, explicit or implicit, have bound themselves to be his slaves and drudges, consenting to be instruments in whose shapes he may torment and afflict their fellow-creatures (even of their own kind) to the amazing and astonishing of the standers-by. I would hope I might have spared this use, but I desire (by divine assistance) to declare the whole counsel of God; and if it come not as conviction where it is so, it may serve for warning, that it may never be so. For it is a most dreadful thing to consider that any should change the service of God for the service of the Devil, the worship of the blessed God for the worship of the cursed enemy of God and man. But, oh! (which is yet a thousand times worse) how shall I name it? if any that are in the visible covenant of God should break that covenant, and make a league with Satan; if any that have sat down and eat at Christ's Table, should so lift up their heel against him as to have fellowship at the table of devils, and (as it hath been represented to some of the afflicted) eat of the bread and drink of the wine that Satan hath mingled. Surely, if this be so, the poet is in the right, "Audax omnia perpeti. Gens humana ruit per vetitum nefas": audacious mortals are grown to a fearful height of impiety; and we must cry out in Scripture language, and that emphatical apostrophe of the Prophet Jeremy (chap. ii. 12), 'Be astonished, O ye heavens, at this, and be horribly afraid: be ye very desolate, saith the Lord.' . . .

If you are in covenant with the Devil, the intercession of the blessed Jesus is against you. His prayer is for the subduing of Satan's power and kingdom, and the utter confounding of all his instruments. If it be so, then the great God is set against you. The omnipotent Jehovah, one God in three Persons; Father, Son, and Holy Ghost, in their several distinct operations and all their divine attributes,—are engaged against you. Therefore KNOW YE that are guilty of such monstrous iniquity, that He that made you will not save you, and that He that formed you will show you no favor (Isa. xxvii. 11). Be assured, that, although you should now evade the condemnation of man's judgment, and escape a violent death by the hand of justice; yet, unless God shall give you repentance (which we heartily pray for), there is a day coming when the secrets of all hearts shall be revealed by Jesus Christ (Rom. ii. 16). Then, then, your sin will find you out; and you shall be punished with everlasting destruction from the presence of the Lord, and doomed to those endless, easeless, and remediless torments prepared for the Devil and his angels (Matt. xxv. 41). . . .

If you have been guilty of such impiety, the prayers of the people of God are against you on that account. It is their duty to pray daily, that Satan's kingdom may be suppressed, weakened, brought down, and at last totally destroyed;

hence that all abettors, subjects, defenders, and promoters thereof, may be utterly crushed and confounded. They are constrained to suppress that kindness and compassion that in their sacred addresses they once bare unto you (as those of their own kind, and framed out of the same mould), praying with one consent, as the royal prophet did against his malicious enemies, the instruments of Satan (Ps. cix. 6), 'Set thou a wicked man over him, and let Satan stand at his right hand' (i.e.), to withstand all that is for his good, and promote all that is for his hurt; and (verse 7) 'When he is judged, let him be condemned, and let his prayer become sin.'

Be we exhorted and directed to exercise true spiritual sympathy with, and compassion towards, those poor, afflicted persons that are by divine permission under the direful influence of Satan's malice. There is a divine precept enjoining the practice of such duty: Heb. xiii. 3, 'Remember them that suffer adversity, as being yourselves also in the body.' Let us, then, be deeply sensible, and, as the elect of God, put on bowels of mercy towards those in misery (Col. iii. 12). Oh, pity, pity them! for the hand of the Lord hath touched them, and the malice of devils hath fallen upon them.

Let us be sure to take unto us and put on the whole armor of God, and every piece of it; let none be wanting. Let us labor to be in the exercise and practice of the whole company of sanctifying graces and religious duties. This important duty is pressed, and the particular pieces of that armor recited Eph. vi. 11 and 13 to 18. Satan is representing his infernal forces; and the devils seem to come armed, mustering amongst us. I am this day commanded to call and cry an alarm unto you: ARM, ARM, ARM! handle your arms, see that you are fixed and in a readiness, as faithful soldiers under the Captain of our salvation, that, by the shield of faith, ye and we all may resist the fiery darts of the wicked; and may be faithful unto death in our spiritual warfare; so shall we assuredly receive the crown of life (Rev. ii. 10). Let us admit no parley, give no quarter: let none of Satan's forces or furies be more vigilant to hurt us than we are to resist and repress them, in the name, and by the spirit, grace, and strength of our Lord Jesus Christ. Let us ply the throne of grace, in the name and merit of our Blessed Mediator, taking all possible opportunities, public, private, and secret, to pour out our supplications to the God of our salvation. Prayer is the most proper and potent antidote against the old Serpent's venomous operations. When legions of devils do come down among us, multitudes of prayers should go up to God. Satan, the worst of all our enemies, is called in Scripture a dragon, to note his malice; a serpent, to note his subtilty; a lion, to note his strength. But none of all these can stand before prayer. The most inveterate malice (as that of Haman) sinks under the prayer of Esther (chap. iv. 16). The deepest policy (the counsel of Achitophel) withers before the prayer of David (2 Sam. xv. 31); and the vastest army (an host of a thousand thousand Ethiopians) ran away, like so many cowards, before the prayer of Asa (2 Chron. xiv. 9 to 15).

What therefore I say unto one I say unto all, in this important case, PRAY, PRAY, PRAY.

To our honored magistrates, here present this day, to inquire into these things, give me leave, much honored, to offer one word to your consideration. Do all that in you lies to check and rebuke Satan; endeavoring, by all ways and means that are according to the rule of God, to discover his instruments in these horrid operations. You are concerned in the civil government of this people, being invested with power by their Sacred Majesties, under this glorious Jesus (the King and Governor of his church), for the supporting of Christ's kingdom against all oppositions of Satan's kingdom and his instruments. Being ordained of God to such a station (Rom. xiii. 1), we entreat you, bear not the sword in vain, as ver. 4; but approve yourselves a terror of and punishment to evil-doers, and a praise to them that do well (1 Peter ii. 14); ever remembering that ye judge not for men, but for the Lord (2 Chron. xix. 6); and, as his promise is, so our prayer shall be for you, without ceasing, that he would be with you in the judgment, as he that can and will direct, assist, and reward you. Follow the example of the upright Job (chap. xxix. 16): Be a father to the poor; to these poor afflicted persons, in pitiful and painful endeavors to help them; and the cause that seems to be so dark, as you know not how to determine it, do your utmost, in the use of all regular means, to search it out.

There is comfort in considering that the Lord Jesus, the Captain of our salvation, hath already overcome the Devil. Christ, that blessed seed of the woman, hath given this cursed old serpent called the Devil and Satan a mortal and incurable bruise on the head (Gen. iii. 15). He was too much for him in a single conflict (Matt. iv.). He opposed his power and kingdom in the possessed. He suffered not the devils to speak, because they knew him (Mark i. 34). He completed his victory by his death on the cross, and destroyed his dominion (Heb. ii. 14), that through death he might destroy death, and him that had the powers of death, that is the Devil; and by and after his resurrection made show openly unto the world, that he had spoiled principalities and powers, triumphing over them (Col. ii. 15). Hence, if we are by faith united to him, his victory is an earnest and prelibation of our conquest at last. All Satan's strugglings now are but those of a conquered enemy. It is no small comfort to consider, that Job's exercise of patience had its beginning from the Devil; but we have seen the end to be from the Lord (James v. 11). That we also may find by experience the same blessed issue of our present distresses by Satan's malice, let us repent of every sin that hath been committed, and labor to practise every duty which hath been neglected. Then we shall assuredly and speedily find that the kingly power of our Lord and Savior shall be magnified, in delivering his poor sheep and lambs out of the jaws and paws of the roaring lion.

Samuel Parris, "Christ Knows How Many Devils There Are"*

Christ knows how many Devils there are.

27 March 1691/92, Sacrament day.

Occasioned by dreadful Witchcraft broke out here a few weeks past, and one Member of this Church, and another of Salem, upon public examination by Civil Authority vehemently suspected for she-witches, and upon it committed.
    John 6: 70. "Have not I chosen you twelve, and one of you is a Devil."

This Chapter consists of 3 principal parts:
    Part 1 consists of a declaration of Christ's miraculous feeding of 5000 with 5 loaves and 2 small fishes (verses 1-15).
    Part 2 treats of Christ's miraculous walking upon the sea (v. 15-22).
    Part 3 consists of Christ's sermon to the Capernates (v. 22-end) concerning the heavenly, or truly vivified, bread. This part consists of sundry particles, *viz:* 1. The occasion of this sermon (v. 22-25); 2. The sermon itself (v. 26-59); 3. The event of this sermon (v. 59-end). Now this event consists of: 1. The offence of many (v. 59 etc.); 2. A reprehension of their error from whence this their offence arose: in which reprehension he shows them that it was not the eating of his flesh carnally but spiritually that he spoke of (v. 61 etc.); 3. Christ's complaint of the incredulity of many (v. 64-65); 4. Another event which was worse than the former; namely, the total departure of several of his disciples from him (v. 66).
    Whereupon note: 1. Our Lord takes occasion to ask his disciples whether they also would desert him (v. 67). 2. Peter in the name of the rest answers by confessing the excellency both of Christ's doctrine and his person (v. 68-69). 3. (Last) This confession Christ so approves of that in the meanwhile he doth admonish them that there is an hypocrite among them, a Devil among them (v. 70-71). "Have not I chosen you twelve, and one of you is a Devil": i.e., I have chosen twelve of you to familiarity with me, to be my Apostle, and for all one of you is a devil.

Doctrine: *Our Lord Jesus Christ knows how many Devils there are in his Church, and who they are.*

1. There are devils as well as saints in Christ's Church.
2. Christ knows how many of these devils there are.
3. Christ knows who these devils are.

Proposition 1: There are devils as well as saints in Christ's church. Here three things may be spoken to: (1) Show you what is meant here by *devils*; (2) That

[*A sermon preached at Salem Village, March 27, 1692.]

there are such devils in the church; (3) That there are also true saints in such churches.

(1). What is meant here by *devils*? "One of you is a devil." Answer: By *devil* is ordinarily meant any wicked angel or spirit. Sometimes it is put for the prince or head of the evil spirits, or fallen angels. Sometimes it is used for vile and wicked persons—the worst of such, who for their villainy and impiety do most resemble devils and wicked spirits. Thus Christ in our text calls Judas a devil: for his great likeness to the devil. "One of you is a devil": i.e., a devil for quality and disposition, not a devil for nature—for he was a man, etc.—but a devil for likeness and operation (John 8: 38, 41, 44—"Ye are of your father the devil.")

(2). There are such devils in the church. Not only sinners, but notorious sinners; sinners more like to the devil than others. So here in Christ's little Church. (Text.) This also Christ teacheth us in the parable of the tares (Matth. 13: 38), where Christ tells us that such are the children of the wicked one—i.e., of the devil. Reason: Because hypocrites are the very worst of men—*corruptio optimi est pessima*. Hypocrites are the sons and heirs of the devil, the free-holders of hell—whereas other sinners are but tenants. When Satan repossesseth a soul, he becomes more vile and sinful (Luke 11: 24-26). As the jailer lays loads of iron on him that hath escaped. None are worse than those who have been good, and are naught; and might be good, but will be naught.

(3). There are also true saints in the church. The church consists of good and bad: as a garden that has weeds as well as flowers, and as a field that has wheat as well as tares. Hence that gospel is compared to a net that taketh good and bad (Matth. 13: 47-50). Here are good men to be found—yea, the very best; and here are bad men to be found—yea, the very worst. Such as shall have the highest seat in glory, and such also as shall be cast into the lowest and fiercest flames of misery. Saints and devils, like Jeremiah's basket of figs (Jer. 24: 1-4).

Proposition 2: Christ knows how many of these devils there are in his churches. As in our text there was one among the twelve. And so in our churches God knows how many devils there are: whether one, two, three, or four in twelve—how many devils, how many saints. He that knows whom he has chosen (John 13: 18), he also knows who they are that have not chosen him, but prefer farms and merchandise above him and above his ordinances (2 Tim. 4: 10).

Proposition 3: Christ knows who these devils are. There is one among you, says Christ to the twelve: Well, who is that? Why, it is Judas. Why, so Christ knows how many devils among us—whether one, or ten, or twenty; and also who they are. He knows us perfectly; and he knows those of us that are in his church, that we are either saints or devils, true believers or hypocrites and dissembling Judases that would sell Christ and his kingdom to gratify a lust. We do not think we are such (II Kings 8: 12-13).

Use 1. Let none then build their hopes of salvation merely upon this: that they are church members. This you and I may be, and yet devils for all that

(Matth. 8: 11-12—"Many shall come from the east and west, and shall sit down, etc. And however we may pass here, a true difference shall be made shortly, etc.").

Use 2. Let none then be stumbled at religion, because too often there are devils found among the saints. You see, here was a true church, sincere converts and sound believers; and yet here was a devil among them.

Use 3. Terror to hypocrites who profess much love to Christ but indeed are in league with their lusts, which they prefer above Christ. Oh! remember that you are devils in Christ's account. Christ is lightly esteemed of you, and you are vilely accounted for by Christ. Oh! if there be any such among us, forbear to come this day to the Lord's table, lest Satan enter more powerfully into you—lest while the bread be between your teeth, the wrath of the Lord come pouring down upon you (Psalm 78: 30-31).

Use 4. Exhort in two branches:

(1). To be deeply humbled for the appearances of devils among our churches. If the church of Corinth were called to mourn because of one incestuous person among them (1 Cor. 5: 1), how much more may New England churches mourn, that such as work witchcraft, or are vehemently suspected so to do, should be found among them.

(2). To be much in prayer that God would deliver our churches from devils; that God would not suffer devils in the guise of saints to associate with us. One sinner destroys much good: how much more one devil. Pray we also that not one true saint may suffer as a devil, either in name or body. The devil would represent the best saints as devils if he could, but it is not easy to imagine that his power is of such extent, to the hazard of the church.

Use 5. Examine we ourselves well, what we are—what we church members are. We are either saints or devils: the Scripture gives us no medium. The Apostle tells us we are to examine ourselves (2 Cor. 13: 5). Oh! it is a dreadful thing to be a devil, and yet to sit down at the Lord's table (1 Cor. 10: 21). Such incur the hottest of God's wrath (as follows—v. 22). Now, if we would not be devils, we must give ourselves wholly up to Christ, and not suffer the predominancy of one lust—and particularly that of covetousness, which is made so light of, and which so sorely prevails in these perilous times. Why, this one lust made Judas a devil (John 12: 6, Matth. 26: 15). And no doubt it has made more devils than one. For a little pelf, men sell Christ to his enemies, and their souls to the devil. But there are certain sins that make us devils; see that we be not such:

1. A liar or murderer (John 8: 44)
2. A slanderer or an accuser of the godly
3. A tempter to sin
4. An opposer of godliness, as Elymos (Acts 13: 8 etc.)
5. Envious persons as witches
6. A drunkard (I Sam. 1: 15-16)
7. A proud person

Finis textus

Samuel Parris, "These Shall Make War With the Lamb"*

11 September 1692. 'After the condemnation of six witches at a court in Salem: one of the witches (*viz.* Martha Kory) in full communion with our Church.

Rev. 17: 14. "These shall make war with the lamb, and the lamb shall overcome them: For he is the Lord of Lords, and king of kings. And they that are with him are called, and chosen, and faithful."

In these words two things are observable:
I.   A war prophesied of.
II. The victory that this war shall issue in.

I. Here is mention made of a war: "These shall make war, etc." Now, in all wars are two parties. And so here:
1. Here is the offending party—namely, these: *viz.* Antichrist (the spiritual whore) and all her assistants, instruments of Satan, and instigated by that dragon to this war (Rev. 13: 1-2). Namely, by sorceries and witchcrafts (plentiful among the Papacy) doing lying wonders, whereby multitudes were deluded.
2. Here is the offended party: *viz.* the lamb and his followers. (Text.) With these they make war.

II. Here is the victory, and the reason of the victory:
1. The victory. Devils and idolators will make war with the lamb and his followers. But who shall have the victory? Why, the lamb (i.e., Christ) and his followers. (Text.)
2. Here is the reason of it, and that is twofold:
1st and main reason is taken from the lamb (Christ), for he is Lord of Lords, etc.
2nd reason is taken from the saints. Three victorial properties: 1. They are chosen. 2. They are called. 3. They are faithful. Of all which hereafter.

First doctrine: *The devil and his instruments will be making war with the lamb and his followers as long as they can.*

Second doctrine: *The lamb and his followers shall overcome the devil and his instruments in this war against them.*

First doctrine (The devil and his instruments will be making war as long as they can with the lamb and his followers.) Here are two things in this doctrine, namely:

[*A sermon preached at Salem Village, September 11, 1692.]

I. The devil and his instruments will be warring against Chrise and his followers.

II. This war will be as long as they can. It will not be forever. There will be a time when they shall war no longer.

I. The devil and his instruments will be warring against Christ and his followers. (Text.) These shall make war with the lamb (Rev. 11: 7). The beast shall make war against them (Rev. 12: 7, 17). War in heaven: the dragon fought, and his angels (Rev. 13: 7). It was given to him to make war with the saints, etc. (Rev. 19: 19). We may farther confirm this point by instances and reasons:

1. For instances. We find the devil assaulting the lamb as soon as he was born [and] to the end of his days. As we see in his instrument Herod (Matth. 2: 7 etc). And afterwards by his manifold temptations of Christ in the wilderness (Matth. 4). And afterwards by his stirring up the chief of the Jews to kill Christ (Matth. 26: 3-4). And to help forward that murder, the devil puts it into the heart of one of Christ's disciples to betray him (John 13: 2). And after all, though the lamb be killed, but yet liveth forever; and no advantage got by the devil by the murder of Christ—why, now he seeks to destroy his church. And for this end influenceth bloody Saul to lay all waste (Acts, 8: 3, 9: 1-2). But now when the lamb had conquered this bloody instrument, and of a Saul made him Paul, a preacher of righteousness, why, now the devil as much opposeth Paul (Acts 13: 4 etc.). Yea, the Scripture is full of such instances; church history abounds also with evidences of this truth. Yea, and in our days, how industrious and vigorous is the bloody French monarch and his confederates against Christ and his interest? Yea, and in our land—in this and some neighboring places—how many, what multitudes of witches and wizards, has the devil instigated with utmost violence to attempt the overthrow of religion?

2. The reason—and that in a word—is from the enmity of the devil and his instruments to religion (Acts 13: 10). Thou child of the devil, thou enemy of all righteousness. Now, the seed of the devil will do the works of the devil. (John 8: 44) "Ye are of your father the devil, and the lusts of your father ye will do," etc. Satan (says one: Trapp *in loco*) is called the god of this world, because as God at first did but speak the word and it was done, so if the devil do but hold up his finger—give the least hint of his mind—his servants and slaves will obey.

II. This war shall be as long as they can. It shall not be forever and always. For:

1. Sometimes the devil loseth his volunteers in war. The lawful captive, the captives of the mighty, are sometimes delivered (Isa. 49: 24—25). We have an instance in bloody Saul (Acts 9: 3 etc.).

2. Sometimes the devil is chained up, so that he cannot head and form an army as otherwise he would, against the saints (Rev. 20: 1-3).

3. After this life the saints shall no more be troubled with war from devils and their instruments. The city of heaven, provided for the saints, is well-walled and

well-gated, so that no devils nor their instruments shall enter therein (Rev. 21: 10 etc.).

Use 1. It may serve to reprove such as seem to be amazed at the war the devil has raised amongst us by wizards and witches against the lamb and his followers, that they altogether deny it. If ever there were witches—men and women in covenant with the devil—here are multitudes in New England. Nor is it so strange a thing there should be such; no, nor that some church members should be such. The Jews, after the return of their captivity, woefully degenerated even unto the horrible sin of sorcery and witchcraft (Mal. 3: 5). Pious Bishop Hall saith: The devil's prevalency in this age is most clear in the marvelous number of witches abounding in all places. Now hundreds (says he) are discovered in one shire; and if fame deceive us not, in a village of fourteen houses in the North are found so many of this damned brood. Heretofore only barbarous deserts had them, but now the civilest and religious parts are frequently pestered with them. Heretofore some silly ignorant old woman, etc., but now we have known those of both sexes who possessed much knowledge, holiness and devotion, drawn into this damnable practice. (Baxter's *Apparitions and Witches*, page 122.)

Also the same Mr. Baxter speaks of a woman who pretended to have the holy ghost, and had a gift of prayer, and did many wonders, proved to be a witch (p. 123).

Use 2. We may see here who they are that war against the lamb and his followers. Why, they are devils, or devils' instruments. Here are but two parties in the world: the lamb and his followers, and the dragon and his followers. And these are contrary one to the other. Well, now they that are aginst the lamb, against the peace and prosperity of Zion, the interest of Christ: they are for the devil. Here are no neuters. Everyone is on one side or the other.

Use 3. It calls on us all—especially those that would be accounted followers of the lamb—to mourn that the devil has had so many assistants from amongst us; especially that he should find or make such in our churches. If so be [that] churches are deeply to mourn the dishonor done to Christ and religion by fornication among them (1 Cor. 5: 1 etc.), how much more, when witches and wizards are amongst them.

Use 4. It may show us the vileness of our natures, and that we should be ever praying that we be left not to our own lusts: for then we shall, by and by, fall in with devils, and with the dragon make war with the lamb and his followers.

[At this point Parris concluded the first section of his sermon. Later the same day, after a brief summation of what he had already said, the minister resumed where he had left off.]

Use 5. Caution and admonition to all and every one of us to beware of making war with the lamb.

1. Consider [that] so to do is to fight for the devil. 'Tis to fight for an enemy. 'Tis to fight for him who will pay you no other wages than of being your eternal torturer (I Pet. 5: 8).

2. Consider [that] it is to take the weakest side. The lamb shall most certainly overcome (Text: Rev. 19: 17 etc.).

3. Consider [that] this will aggravate sin above the sin of devils. To fight against the lamb is to fight against thy Savior, which the damned devils never had an offer of (Heb. 2: 16) "He took not on him the nature of angels."

4. It is the way to utter ruin. I say it is the way, the high-way, to utter ruin. It is true [that] Christ may conquer thee when thou art hot in the battle, as he did Saul, and make thee throw away thy weapons of rebellion. But who can tell that he will do so? This is not ordinary; and if thou shoudst die a rebel in the fight, then thou art damned forever. Therefore be we cautioned against making war with the lamb.

Objection: But you may say, what is it to make war with the lamb? And when do men make war with the lamb?

Answer 1: In general, all disobedience to Christ is a making war against him. As:

1. Disobedience to his laws. You know those that do not obey the king's laws are justly called rebels (I Kings 12: 19). So here, not to do what Christ commands is to rebel against him, and to make war with him (Deut. 9: 22-24, Isa. 1: 19-20).

2. Disobedience to Christ's ordinances is rebellion against Christ, and making war with him. As warring against magistrates, opposing them in their duties. In this sense Aaron and his company are called rebels (Num. 20: 10). Hence resisters of authority are resisters of God, because they resist the ordinance of God (Rom. 13: 1 etc). But:

Answer 2: More especially, to fight against the lamb, and so to side with the devil, is:

1. To fight against the Gospel, or to war against the Gospel. When men will not receive the Gospel, and do what they can to hinder the course of the Gospel, this is to make war with the lamb.

(1). When men will not receive the Gospel themselves, then they fight against the lamb—as the Jews (Acts 13: 46). Not to accept of terms of peace, is to proclaim war, etc.

(2). When they will not suffer others to receive it, as those Jews (Acts 13: 44 etc.), and the sorcerer (v. 8), and those (2 Tim. 3: 8). And they that forbid preaching (Acts 5: 28).

2. They make war against the lamb who oppose the holy spirit (Acts 7: 51): "Ye do always resist the holy ghost."

3. They make war against the lamb who do oppose the doctrine of Christ. As:

(1). Either the person of Christ: his deity or his humanity. He must be man that he might die for us; he must be God that he might conquer death for us. Now, to deny either of these is to deny the lamb, and so to make war with the lamb.

(2). Or the offices of Christ as a saviour, both prophetical, sacerdotal, or regal. His office of prophet to teach; of priest to atone for us; of king to govern us. As might in particular be shown.

Use 6. May be of encouragement to all Christians, in the words of the Apostle, to endure hardness as good soldiers of Christ (2 Tim. 2: 3). For encouragement hereto, devils and [their] instruments shall not war against us always (Rev. 2: 10): "Fear none of those things which thou shalt suffer: behold, the devil shall cast some of you into prison, that you may be tried: and ye shall have tribulation ten days: be thou faithful unto death, and I will give you a crown of life."

Finis textus

[The only extant record of Parris's other sermons during these months is a listing of the dates on which they were delivered and the Biblical texts on which they were based, as follows:

Sacrament day, 8 May, 1692. I Corinthians 10: 21. "Ye cannot drink the cup of the Lord, and the cup of devils: ye cannot be partakers of the Lord's table, and of the table of devils."

19 June, 1692. Canticles 2: 1. "I am the rose of Sharon, and the lily of the valleys."

31 July, 1692. John 6: 48. "I am the bread of life."]

Part Two

The Accused

This section includes a variety of documents which shed light on the lives of the accused witches outside the limited context of the witchcraft trials. These documents reveal information about the accused persons in the years before 1692, when they were functioning as ordinary members of the Salem-Village community.

A word of warning is in order at this point. Many of the following documents relate to episodes of dispute and litigation which happened to array the five subjects against other residents of the community. It is tempting to infer from these episodes a ready-made explanation of the witch trials—to conclude, for example, that the five individuals were accused of witchcraft in 1692 because they were particularly disputatious persons and had therefore acquired an obnoxious reputation among their fellow villagers. Tempting as it may be, this kind of reasoning is dangerous. From our own examination of the Essex County court records in this period, we can give reasonable assurances that it would be possible to pick almost any inhabitant of Salem Village—or any other community in the area, for that matter—and come up with a similar picture of chronic litigation and conflict. This is true of people on both sides of the witchcraft controversy (see, for instance, section III, which deals with the accusers) as well as of those Villagers who never publicly got involved in the controversy in any capacity. The fact of the matter seems to be that New Englanders of this period went to court a great deal. These five accused witches may appear to be particularly litigious simply because we are placing them under particularly close scrutiny.

Chapter Ten

Sarah Good

[Sarah Good was one of the more difficult accused witches to track down. Records of her life are all too sparse. Aside from a lengthy dispute concerning the final disposition of her father's estate, the following documents are the only ones relating to Sarah Good or her immediate family that we have been able to locate.]

Documents Relating to the Disposition of the Estate of John Solart, the Father of Sarah Good

Report of a Jury of Inquest upon the Death of John Solart (1672)

Report of a jury of inquest, dated 29: 4: 1672, appointed upon the sudden death of John Soolart of Wenham, found him accessory to his own death by drowning himself on 29: 4: 1672.

Signed by Thomas Fiske in the name of the rest: James Moulton, senior; William Geare; Alexander Brauerder; Henry Kemball; Walter Fairefield; Mark Batchelder; James Moulton, junior; William Fiske; Charles Gott; James Bette; and Samuel Fiske.

Inventory of John Solart's Estate (1672)

Inventory taken 7 August, 1672, by Nathaniel Putnam and Thomas Fiske:

Houses and about twenty acres of land with orchard thereunto joining, £165; twenty acres of upland joining to Richard Kemball's farm, and four acres of meadow adjoining, £ 38; one acre [and] one-half of meadow in the Great Meadow, £ 6; about four acres [and] one-half of upland at Lord's hill, £ 5; about six acres of meadow called Thorndicke meadow, £ 30; seventeen acres of upland in the neck, £ 34; five acres upland bought of John Batchelder, £ 30 . . .

[Here follows an itemization of Solart's livestock, grain, farm equipment, and household goods.]

Total: £ 575, 13 s.

Debts: To Mr. Browne of Salem to be paid in money, £ 43, 16 s., 3 d.; Stephen Hasket, £ 2, 2 s.; John Batchelder, £ 25; Joseph Lovet, £ 2, 10 s.; Total: £ 73, 8 s., 3 d.

Attested in Ipswich court, September 24, 1672, by Elizabeth Soolart, administratrix of the estate of her late husband.

Testimony of Abraham Martin and Lewis Ford
as to the Will of John Solart (1672)

The verbal will of John Soolart of Wenham in the County of Essex, ordinary keeper, about three or four months before his death, as attests Abraham Martine and Lewis Ford this 25th September, 1672:

We, the abovesaid deponents; I, Lewis Ford, being in the room where my master and dame was, he spake to me to call in Abraham Martin, which I did. And when we were both come in, he said, I being often troubled with fainting fits and do apprehend I have not long to live, my will, therefore, is that after my decease my wife shall have the use of my whole estate for herself during the time of her widowhood (and for the bringing up of the children that were with her, as Lewis saith, which clause only Abraham doth not remember), and if she should marry, he did then give her a third part of all his estate, and [as to] the rest of the estate, his will was that it should be divided amongst the children, as he said.

Testimony of Elizabeth Solart
as to Her Late Husband's Will (1672)

This Honoured Court may be pleased to understand that when the abovementioned will was declared by my husband, John Solart, as the witnesses do avouch, that my eldest son, John, was not then in the country, but my husband had given him a parcel of land, in writing, which according to his declared intent, should be his portion. But he, by the providence of God coming home again between the time of the abovesaid will and his decease, John did deliver up the writing again, expressing his desire rather unto some other gratuity, his intentions being to follow the sea, and should not so well be able to improve land.

Whereupon my husband did again say to me, and declared it to me as his very will, that if he died, I should have the use of his whole estate for myself and the bringing up of the children during the time of my widowhood, and if I should marry, then I should have one-third part of the estate to myself, and my eldest son, John, should have a double portion out of the remainder, and the rest of the estate should be equally divided amongst the rest of the children.

This, as also that which is abovewritten as the witnesses do declare, I do desire to commit with myself and the whole case unto your Wisdoms to consider and determine as your Worships shall judge equal.

Elesebeth Solart

Apportionment of John Solart's Estate among His Survivors

John Sorlah [Solart] dying intestate, court granted administration upon the estate to Elizabeth, the relict.

An inventory of £ 500 clear estate being presented, court ordered to the widow, £ 165. And two of the daughters having received their portions, as appeared by an acquittance, and seven children yet remaining, court ordered to the eldest son, John, a double portion, £ 84, and to [the] rest of the six, £ 42 each, namely Sarah, Hanah, Martha, Joseph, Abigaill, and Bethia, as they come of age.

Upon condition that said John wait for his portion until his mother's death, he was to have his portion out of the homestead, and if he had occasion to build, he was to have one acre of land next [to] the highway, about the place where Spalden's house stood, he fencing it. He was to have all the land for his whole portion as it was appraised, the inventory and the rest of the land to be security for the payment of the other children's portions.

Petition of the Surviving Children of John Solart (1682)

Our father died intestate about eleven years since, and [on] September 24th, 1672, administration was granted to our mother, who was also deceased before the time was come that we were all of age to receive our proportions, ordered to us by the said court, of our father's estate. Our mother was not bound by the Honoured Court to pay us, but our father's land was bound for the security of our portions.

And Ezekill Woodward, that married with our mother, did refuse to enter into any obligation to pay our portions. Our brother Joseph, who would have been of age the last winter, is dead, and your Honours have declared, [at] the last court at Salem, that his portion shall be divided amongst us. But excepting your Honours will be pleased to put us into some capacity to get it, we know not well how to get it that so we may divide it.

And as to our sister Sarah, the wife of Daniel Poole, she is 28 years of age, and she is yet without her portion. And, except that she will accept of a parcel of land which our father bought at a very dear rate for his convenience, which was well fenced, and she allow the same price for it now the fence is taken off, she is not like to have anything.

That which we humbly crave of your Honours is that, seeing our mother, who was the Administratrix, is dead, and there is a considerable part of our father's estate remaining undisposed of, that your Honours would grant Administration to your petitioners, or to some of them, to such lands or estate of their deceased father as they may find that is not yet disposed of, so your poor fatherless petitioners be not wronged of that which doth belong to them.

> Joseph Lovett and wife Elizabeth
> John Trask and wife Hannah
> Daniel Poole and wife Sarah
> Thomas Kelham and wife Martha
> Mordecia Larckam and wife Abigail
> Bethiah Solart
> John Edwards, who married with Mary
> Soolart, in behalf of her children
> All children of John Solart of Wenham

Action of the Court on this Petition

Court declared that the children, having come to age, could recover their right from any person withholding it.

John Cromwell Versus Sarah Good
for Debt Incurred by Her First Husband,
Daniel Poole (1686)

Attachment Against William and Sarah Good

To the Marshall of Salem or his Deputy or Constable of Salem or Wenham Constable:

You or either of you in his Majesty's name required to attach the goods, or for want thereof, the body, of William Goode of Salem and Sarah, his wife, formerly the wife of Daniel Poole, now deceased, and to take bond of him to the value of fourteen pounds together with sufficient surety or security for their appearance at the next county court, to be holden at Ipswich on the last Tuesday of this present month, then and there to answer to the complaint of Mr. John Cromwell of Salem in action of debt of about seven pounds due by back account, it being for so much paid to Mr. William Browne senior of Salem [torn] several other persons [torn] by the said [torn]. The account of the abovesaid Daniel Poole his [torn] deceased [torn] when she was his widow; all which sum [torn] engaged by them to be paid to the plaintiff but is withheld from him to his great damage; withall other due damage, and so make a true return thereof under your hand.

Thomas Fisk

Dated March 8th, 1685/86

Per Curiam for the Town of Wenham.

Testimony of Nathaniel Houlton

The deposition of Nathaniel Holton, aged about 70 years, who testifieth and saith that I this deponent, understanding and knowing Daniel Poole to be indebted unto John Cromwell, after the decease of the said Poole I went to the said John Cromwell and informed him that there was an estate of the said Poole's sufficient to satisfy him for his debt due from the said Poole, who returned me this answer: that until there was administration granted he was afraid to meddle with it. Further I this deponent do testify that the said Poole owned he had received several goods from Mr. Browne, Senior, upon the account of John Cromwell, and to my knowledge John Cromwell defrayed the whole charge of Daniel Poole's funeral; and I do also testify that the said Poole was his own man several years before he was married unto Sarah Solah his wife, and that after the decease of the said Poole, Sarah his relict disposed of two cows, one horse and his movable goods. And further saith the said horse and cows was Daniel Poole's before he was married.

Sworn Salem, March 22, 1685/86

Before me, John Hawthorne, Asst.

Testimony of Thomas Cromwell

Deposition of Thomas Cromwell, aged about 65 years, who testifieth and saith that he being in the shop of Mr. William Browne, Senior, saw Mr. Browne deliver unto Daniel Poole and Sarah his wife several goods upon the account of

John Cromwell; and that I, the said Thomas Cromwell, did make one suit of clothes for Daniel Poole, and for Sarah his wife two petticoats with some of the abovesaid goods; and John Cromwell paid me for making the said clothes—which is about three years ago.

Sworn Salem, March 22th, 1685/86

Before me, John Hathorne, Asst.

Testimony of Nathaniel Sollsby

The deposition of Nathaniel Sollsby, aged about thirty-five, saith that he made a coffin for Daniel Poole, and John Cromwell paid me for the coffin, seven shillings in money.

Sworne Salem March 22, 1685/86

Before me John Hathorne,
Assistant

Testimony of Joanne Koad (Cody?)

The deposition of Joane Koad, aged about thirty years, who testifieth and saith that I, the deponent, being in the shop of Mr. William Browne, Senior, I saw Mr. Browne deliver several goods unto Daniel Poole and Sarah his wife upon the account of John Cromwell, and I do testify that the said Poole was his own man several years before he took up the said goods; and to my knowledge when the said Poole was dead, the said Sarah his relict did enjoy and dispose of the whole estate of Daniel Poole: *viz.* a horse, two cows and all his movables. The said horse and cows was Daniel Poole's before marriage, and the goods abovesaid was taken up by the said Daniel Poole and his wife about three years ago.

Sworn Salem, March 22, 1685/86

Before me, John Hawthorne, Asst.

Benjamin Browne's Invoice to Sarah Good
(Exhibit in Case of Cromwell versus Good)

Goode et al. Daniel Poole upon account of Mr. John Cromwell.

1682	To seven yards Korsy at nine pence	£	s.	d.
	Four yards [illegible] at two [illegible]	3:	13:	8
1 Nov.	To [illegible] thread nine	00:	2:	3
	To nine and three-fourths serge at six shillings—one yard one-half humanes to [illegible] thread	03:	03:	09
	Per Benjamin Browne	£ 06:	19:	08

Testimony of Ezekiel Woodward,
Stepfather of Sarah Good (1686)

The deposition of Ezekile Woodward of Wenham, aged about sixty years. This deponent do testify and say that about a month ago, this deponent having some [illegible] of John Solah's [i.e., John Solart's] estate in my hands, having married with his widow, who as administratrix to that estate, did deliver to William Good, who married with Sarah, daughter to the abovesaid Solah . . . .

[The rest of this testimony, largely illegible, has been omitted.]

Testimony of John Edwards (1686)

John Edwards of Wenham abovesaid, do testify that he was present when Ezekiel Woodward did [illegible] the widow to William Good, as is abovesaid. Sworn by both parties abovesaid in Court of Ipswich, March 30, 1686.

The Verdict of the Jury Against
William and Sarah Good

Mr. John Cromwell, plaintiff, against William Good and Sarah his wife, formerly the wife of Daniel Poole, now deceased, in an action of debt of about seven pounds due by book or account: it being for so much paid to Mr. Wm. Browne, Senior, of Salem and several other persons by the request and on the account of the abovesaid Daniel Poole her former husband, deceased, and [torn] she was his widow; all which sum was engaged by them to be paid to the plaintiff, but is withheld from him to his great damage, with all other due damages and as per attachment. The jury found for the plaintiff 7 pds. and 8 shillings and 9 pence to be paid in March corn and cattle, and cost. The bill of cost allowed: 34 shillings and 4 pence. Execution granted for the abovesaid judgement.

April 1, 1686

Returned satisfied, April 16, 1686

John Cromwell's Bill of Costs
Against William Good

John Cromwell's bill of cost against William Goode.

	£	s.	d.
The attachment and time to take it out, And day to carry it to Wenham Constable Paid to the constable to [torn] 12 d	00-04-00		
To [torn] the attachment	00-00-06		
To entering the action	00-10-00		
Two witnesses from Wenham one day	00-04-00		
To four witnesses sworn at Salem	00-05-00		
To six summonses	00-00-12		
To [illegible] them two at Wenham	00-03-04		
To my own time at court to come and go home	00-05-00		
	£1	12	–
To [illegible] of [illegible]	0	1	10
Allow	£1	14	–

Levy Against the Estate of
William and Sarah Good

To the Marshall of Ipswich or his Deputy

You are required in his Majesty's name by virtue hereof to levy in execution of the estate of William Goode and Sarah his wife of Wenham, the sum of seven pounds, eight shillings, and nine pence in merchantable corn or cattle and thirty-four shillings, four pence money for cost with two shillings more for this execution, and deliver the same unto Mr. John Cromwell of Salem, which is to satisfy him for so much granted to him at Ipswich court, March 30, 1686, and in want of the specie above mentioned, or other estate of the said William Goode and Sarah, his wife, to the satisfaction of the creditor, you are alike required to seize the person of the said Goode and him commit unto the safe keeping of the prison keeper in Ipswich until he make payment according to this execution or otherwise be released by the creditor or by order of law, hereof fail not, as you will answer the contrary at your peril, and make return of your doings herein under your hand as the law directs for which this shall be your sufficient warrant. Dated in Ipswich, April 1, 1686.

Per Mr. John Appleton

I under written, do deput John Edmund constable of Wenham, my lawful Deputy, for to extend this execution and make return according to the law, dated April 1, 1686.

Robert Low
Marshall of Essex

Seizure of Meadow Land Belonging
to William and Sarah Good

I have levied the execution upon a parcel of meadow in Wenham, belonging to William Goode and Sarah, his wife, called by the name of Thorndike meadow, which was appraised by Captain Thomas Fisk and Walter Fairfield, both of Wenham, who appraised one [torn] and half and thirty six poles and an half pole at the whole sum expressed in the exposition on the other side written. And the charging for viewing and measuring the said meadow, which meadow is bounded easterly on the meadow of John Porter, and southward upon the river adjoining with two stakes on the westerly side, which bounds the said meadow from the remainder of said Goode's meadow, and northerly bounded by the upland, and did deliver the said meadow to John Cromwell of Salem to satisfy the judgment expressed in the execution on the other side written by one John Edwards, Marshall's Deputy.

Dated April 12th, 1686

Thomas Fisk and Walter Fairfield make oath that their appraisal of the above mentioned meadow was to the true and just value thereof according their understanding, this eleventh of November, 1686, before me, Barth Gedney.

Thomas Fisk
Walter Fairfield   [signatures]
Who apprised the land.

William Good to Freeborn Balch (1686)

Be it known unto all men by these presents, that I, William Good of Salem Village, in the county of Essex, in New England, weaver, for and in consideration of the sum of five pounds in silver by Freeborn Balch of the town of Beverly, in the same county, yeoman, to me in hand paid . . . and do by these presents . . . sell, . . . unto the said Freeborn Balch, a certain parcel of meadow ground, situated and lying in the township of Wenham, containing one acre, three quarters of an acre and three poles of ground . . .

. . .

In witness whereof I, said William Good, have this twelfth day of August, in the year of our Lord One Thousand, Six Hundred, Eighty and Six affixed my own hand and seal.

Signed, sealed   the mark of
and delivered   William   X   Good
in the presence of us   & seal
John Ross
Samuel Hardie

William Good personally appeared and acknowledged the above written to be his act and deed this 30th of August, 1686, before me

Bartholmew Gedney
One of his Majesty's Council

Sarah, the wife of William Good, freely gave up and surrendered her right of dowry in the above written parcel of meadow, and manifested her free consent to the sale thereof, this 30th day of August, 1686,

before me Bartholmew Gedney

Chapter Eleven

Rebecca Nurse

[Documentation of the lives of Rebecca Nurse and her large family—particularly her husband—is abundant. We have, therefore, been selective in this section. Francis Nurse was involved, for instance, in more than a score of real-estate transactions; the two deeds which follow represent what was evidently his first purchase of land (from Christopher Waller) and his most significant purchase (from James Allen). In addition to the remaining property transactions, we have omitted the numerous brief references to Francis Nurse in the Essex County Court records. We have similarly omitted most of the documentation dealing with the Towne family, which is also in the County Court Records and the town records of Topsfield. Some of the material, however, is included in Part Four, "The Boundary Dispute with Topsfield."]

Towne, Nurse, and Cloyse Genealogies

Towne Family

William m. Johanna Blessing

| Rebecca m. Francis Nurse | Mary m. Isaac Estey | Sarah m. Edmund Bridges Peter Cloyse | +5 children |

Nurse Family

Francis m. Rebecca Towne

| Rebecca m. Thomas Preston | Mary m. John Tarbell | Francis m. Sarah Tarbell | +5 children |

Cloyse Family

John m. Jane [?]

Peter m. Hannah [?]   Thomas m. Susanna Lewis
Sarah Towne Bridges
Susanna Beers

Christopher Waller to Francis Nurse (1662)

Know all men by these presents that I, Christopher Waller of Salem, in the county of Essex, in New England, with the consent of my wife, for and in consideration of the sum of four pounds and twelve shillings... already paid,... by these presents do... sell... unto Frances Nurse of the same town, half an acre of salt marsh, be it more or less, together with all the fence or fences thereunto belonging, 'lying and being situated within the township of Salem aforesaid in a place called Riall's side....

. . .

In witness thereof I, the said Christopher Waller, have hereunto set my hand and seal, this fourth day of the twelfth month, in the year of our Lord, One Thousand, Six Hundred, Sixty and One. 1661/2.

Signed, sealed and delivered   Christopher Waller's   X
in the presence of us.   mark and his seal affixed.
Edw. Norrice
Elizabeth Pester

Christopher Waller acknowledged this to be his act and deed, 16: 6 mo: 1662, and his wife the same day yielded up her thirds, before me.

Wiy. Hathorne

James Allen to Francis Nurse (1678)

May the 16th, 1678

To all people to whom this deed of sale shall come: James Allen of Boston, in the county of Suffolk in New England, minister, sendeth greeting: Know ye that I, the said James Allen, for and in consideration of the sum of four hundred pounds of lawful money of New England, to me secured in the law, to be paid by Frances Nurse of Salem, in the county of Essex, yeoman, before the ensealing and delivery of these presents, the receipt whereof I do acknowledge and myself therewith fully satisfied and paid,... do by these presents... sell... unto the said

Francis Nurse, his heirs, executors, administrators and assigns forever, all
that my farm or tract of land, lying and being in the township of Salem,
containing three hundred acres of upland, be it more or less, according as
it lies butted and bounded, *viz.:* with a hemlock tree being the northeast
corner bounds, next [to] farmer Porter's land near Crane River, so called,
and from that hemlock tree running westward to the bridge upon the
brook, and so to a white oak tree in a straight line from the brook
aforesaid, a little to the westward of the orchard, between the land of
Joseph Holton and the bargained premises, and from thence to a black
oak almost at the corner of the said Holton's field, upon a straight line
from thence to a poplar tree at the northwest corner of the said farm,
from thence southward to a maple tree with a white oak near it, a
[line?] to the brook at the southwest corner, the bounds being there:
the butt end of a great old tree with a stake standing in it and two
small trees marked near it, lying a little to the westward of the old
Ipswich road being the southeast corner bounds, and from thence to the
hemlock tree, the northeast corner bounds, and bounded with the land
partly of farmer Porter, partly of Nathaniell Putnam, partly James
Hadlock's and partly Joseph Holton's on the north, and the land of the
said Holton to the west, and the lands of Mr. Zerubbabul Endicott to
the east and south, according to town grant, together with all trees,
underwoods, meadows, feedings, pastures, profits, privileges, easements,
commodities and appurtenances whatsoever, to the same belonging or in
any wise appertaining . . .

And I the said James Allen, for myself, my heirs, executors and
administrators, do covenant and promise to and with the said Frances
Nurse, his heirs, executors, administrators and assigns forever, by these
presents, that at and immediately before [the] ensealing hereof, I was the
true, lawful and sole owner of all the afore-bargained premises. . . .

And also that the said Frances Nurse, his heirs, executors, administrators and assigns, shall and may by force and virtue of these presents,
from time to time and at all times forever hereafter lawfully, peaceably
and quietly have, hold, use, occupy, possess and enjoy the above granted
premises with their appurtenances, free and clear. . . .

And further, I, the said James Allen, my executors or administrators,
shall and will from time to time and at all times forever hereafter,
warrant and defend the above-granted premises with their appurtenances
and every part and parcel thereof, unto the said Frances Nurse, his heirs,
executors, administrators and assigns, against all and every person and
persons whatsoever, anyways lawfully claiming or demanding the sum or
any part or parcel thereof; and lastly Sarah my wife do by these presents
freely yield up her right, title, dower, and interest, of and into the
bargained premises and every part and parcel thereof unto the said
Frances Nurse, his heirs and assigns forever.

In witness whereof I, the said James Allen, and Sarah, my wife, have hereunto set our hands and seals, this twenty ninth day of April, in the year of our Lord God, One Thousand, Six Hundred, Seventy and Eight. . . .

Signed, sealed and delivered	James Allen [seal]
in the presence of us,	
by Mr. James Allen	Sarah Allen [seal]
Isak Adington	
Eleazer Phillips	

Mr. James Allen and Mrs. Sarah Allen, his wife, have acknowledged this instrument to be their act and deed. April 29: 1678. before me Edward Ting, Assistant.

Terms of the Purchase of the James Allen Farm by Francis Nurse

[We have been unable to locate the agreement reached by James Allen and Francis Nurse at the time of the latter's purchase of Allen's farm in 1678, but the agreement was evidently consulted by Charles W. Upham in the preparation of his work Salem Witchcraft *(1867). The following abstract is taken from Upham, Vol. I, pp. 80-81.]*

The purchase-money was not required to be paid until the expiration of twenty-one years. In the meantime, a moderate annual rent was fixed upon; seven pounds for each of the first twelve years, and ten pounds for each of the remaining nine years. If, at the end of the time, the amount stipulated had not been paid, or Nurse should abandon the undertaking, the property was to relapse to Allen. Disinterested and suitable men, whose appointment was provided for, were then to estimate the value added to the estate by Nurse during his occupancy, by the clearing of meadows or erection of buildings or other permanent improvements, and all of that value over and above one hundred and fifty pounds was to be paid to him. If any part of the principal sum should be paid prior to the expiration of twenty-one years, a proportionate part of the farm was to be relieved of all obligation to Allen, vested absolutely in Nurse, and disposable by him.

Estate of William Towne of Topsfield, Father of Rebecca Nurse (1673)

Administration granted April 24, 1673, to Johana Towne on the estate of William Towne, her late husband, and she was to bring an inventory to the next Ipswich Court.

Petition of William Towne's Children (1682)

Petition for settlement of a small estate left the undersigned by their father, who died ten years ago leaving no will, but left his estate in the hands of their mother who was appointed administratrix, and the estate remained unsettled until her death, and now they desire that the following division may be allowed:

The land to be divided equally to his three sons, Edmond, Jacob, and Joseph; and the movables equally to the three daughters, Rebecka, Mary and Sarah. Also the three brothers to pay all debts now due, and what charges shall after arise in settlement of the estate to be equally borne by all six.

Dated Jan. 17, 1682

> Mary [her mark] Towne, relict of Edmond
> Jacob Towne
> Josep [his mark] Towne
> Francis [his mark] Nurs, with the consent of Rebeka
> Mary [her mark] Esty, formerly Mary Towne
> Sarah [her mark] Bridges

Witnesses: John How
             John Pritchet

Allowed by the Court at Ipswich, April 10, 1683.

Francis Nurse to His Son
Samuel Nurse (1689/90)

Be it known unto all men by these presents that I, Francis Nurse, Senr., of the town of Salem in the county of Essex in New England, for and in consideration of the sum of sixty pounds and ten shillings in lawful money of New England, principal money, and such sum and sums of money for the rent as are and shall be due unto Mr. James Allen of Boston, minister, for the proportion of the farm by me bought of said Allen, which my son Samuell Nurse now holdeth, paid or secured to be paid by my said son Samuel Nurse of the town and county aforesaid; for and in consideration of the condition above expressed, the said Francis Nurse, Senr., do by these presents bargain, sell, alien, assign, set over and confirm unto the said Samuel Nurse, certain parcels of land containing about fifty acres, one parcel of upland and meadow ground containing about twenty acres being bounded northerly by the land of me, the said Francis Nurse, easterly by the land of John Tarbell, southerly by Endicott's land, westerly by the lands of Thomas Preston, Jno. Tarbell, and his own land; and another parcel of about ten acres being bounded on the north by said Tarbell's land, easterly by his own, southerly by the land of Thomas Preston, westerly by Houlton's land and another parcel of about ten acres, bounded southerly by the land of Thomas Preston, westerly by the said Houlton's, northerly by said Tarbell's and easterly by his own land; and another parcel of land of about six acres, being bounded by my own land northerly, easterly by Thomas Preston's, southerly by Endicott's and westerly by John Tarbell's land, and another parcel of about two acres, being bounded northerly by my own land, easterly by said Tarbell's, southerly by Endicott's and westerly by Thomas Preston's, all the above-mentioned parcels of land, together with the security for the same by me, said Francis Nurse, received of Mr. James Allen. To have and to hold with all right, title, profits, and privileges to be to the proper use and behoof of him, the said Samuel Nurse, and his heirs, executors, administrators and assigns forever, and the said Francis Nurse, Senr., do warrant, acquit and defend the quiet and peaceable possession of all the premises abovesaid, to said Samuel Nurse and his heirs and assigns, as witness my hand and seal, this twenty-seventh day of January, in the year of our Lord God One Thousand, Six Hundred Eighty Nine, alias Ninety.

Signed, sealed and delivered in the presence of us. Jno. Tarbell Thomas Preston Samuel Hardye	The mark ⍯ of Francis Nurs senr. and a seal.

Francis Nurse Senr. acknowledged the above written instrument to be his act and deed. Salem. February 28: 1689:90.

before me

Jno. Hathorne, Assistant

[In two identical deeds of the same date, Francis Nurse also sold to his son-in-law Thomas Preston "about fifty-two acres" for sixty-three pounds and to his son-in-law John Tarbell "about fifty acres" for sixty pounds, ten shillings.]

Francis Nurse Settles His Estate (1694)

Know all men by these presents that I, Francis Nurs of Salem in the County of Essex in his Majesty's province in New England, through age imperfect in body yet competent of understanding, but through weakness not being able to manage my outward estate, I see cause to settle my estate as followeth:

That is, that my whole estate shall be to my eight children equally divided in quantity and quality to their proper use. And I choose to have and to hold [it] in fee simple to them and their heirs forever, all except so much as shall be after named. That is to say: John, Samuel, Francis, Benjamin, Michael, Thomas, John, William.

The condition of this settlement is as followeth:

Imprimus. That my eight children above named (that is to say, John Nurse, Samuel Nurse, Francis Nurse, Benjamin Nurse, Michael Bowden, Thomas Presson [Preston], John Tarbell, William Russell (all above named), shall pay all debts legally due from my said estate, and also that they pay or cause to be paid to me, the abovementioned Francis Nurse, yearly and equally each of them in proportion, fourteen pounds a year yearly in current money of New England. That is to say, the abovementioned Articles being performed, the abovementioned estate to be to my children and their heirs forever, but if not performed, this article to be void in law.

Further, this fourteen pounds above-named is to be understood to be paid between all the brothers. That is, thirty-five shillings apiece annually in specie as before mentioned. It is to be understood that he or they only that shall fail or neglect to perform their obligation shall suffer thereby, without any damage or detriment to the rest of their brethren.

Further, I, Francis Nurse, do reserve in my hands as followeth: *viz.,* my bed and bedding, woolens and linens, and my crop of corn, both Indian and English, that I have this year, and so much fodder as will sufficiently winter my mare (which I also keep in my hands), and one chest.

Further, I give to my grandson John Nurs, son of my son John Nurse, ten pounds in or as money after my decease. But if I have not enough estate left in my hands then [this bequest is] to be made up to him by my children equally.

If the abovementioned fourteen pounds be not sufficient for my comfortable maintenance, then [more] to be made up to . . . [me] by my children.

And further, my will is that my children do all of them equally contribute to my decent burial. . . .

The mark of	⊓	Francis Nurse
John Nurse		
Samuel Nurse		
Francis Nurse		
Michael Bowden		
Thomas Preston		
John Tarbell		
The mark of	W	William Russell

Signed, sealed, and delivered in presence
of us this 4th day of December, 1694.

William Raynet [Raiment]
Israel Porter
Exercise Conant

Chapter Twelve

Bridget Bishop

[Included here are virtually all the documents about Bridget Bishop that we have been able to locate. Her life before 1670—even her origin—remains obscure. On the other hand, there is a relative abundance of material on Bridget's husbands; we have omitted much of this material. The records of Salem town contain further references to Thomas Oliver; the Beverly town and church records give information about Edward Bishop, a founding member of the church in Beverly.]

Bishop Genealogy (Tentative)

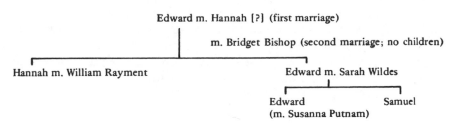

Edward m. Hannah [?] (first marriage)

m. Bridget Bishop (second marriage; no children)

Hannah m. William Rayment

Edward m. Sarah Wildes

Edward   Samuel
(m. Susanna Putnam)

Thomas and Bridget Oliver Brought to Court for Fighting (1670)

Testimony of Mary Ropes

Mary [her mark] Ropes, aged about fifty years, deposed that she had several times been called to her neighbor Thomas Oliver's, by himself, but mostly by his wife, to hear their complaints one of the other, and they both acknowledged that they had been fighting together.

Further she saw Goodwife Oliver's face at one time bloody and at other times black and blue, and the said Oliver complained that his wife had given him several blows.

Salem presentment.

Witness: Mr. Edmund Batter

Verdict

Thomas Oliver and his wife, for fighting each with the other, were fined or to be whipped ten stripes if payment be not made in one month next following.

Bridget Oliver Brought to Court for Using Foul Language Against Her Husband (January 1678)

Summons to Accused and Witnesses

Summons, dated 24: 10: 1677, to the wife of Thomas Oliver, and to witnesses, James Simonds, John Leach, Sr., and wife Sarah, and Benjamin Horne as witnesses, signed by Hilliard Veren, clerk, and served by Nathaniel Beadle, constable of Salem.

Verdict

Bridget, wife of Thomas Oliver, presented for calling her husband many opprobrious names, as old rogue and old devil, on Lord's days, was ordered to stand with her husband, back to back, on a lecture day in the public market place, both gagged, for about an hour, with a paper fastened to each of their foreheads upon which their offence should be fairly written.

Upon request of Mary West, daughter of said Thomas, who paid 20 s., he was released.

Salem, Jan. 29, 1677/78

Inventory of Thomas Oliver's Estate (1679)

Inventory of the estate of Thomas Oliver taken June 21, 1679, by Edmund Batter and Hilliard Veren Senior:

	£	s.
House and ground adjoining of about one-half an acre	45	
About ten acres of land in the north field	25	
A small old bed, bedstead, flock bolster, and pillows, with all appurtenances	2	10
His wearing apparel	1	5
A little table and three old chests		15
Two iron pots and an old iron kettle, a hanger and tongs		10
A brass skillet and some few earth[enware] dishes		5
Three or four old chairs		3
Two pigs		10
		13
Two pails and old tubs and some odd lumber		5
An old rusty sword and old bandoleers		5
Total	£76	8

The estate is in debt in England, as he said in his sickness, about £ 30; to several other men here, as he said above, 15 s.; due to the town when sick and at his burial, £ 2, 19 s., 6 d.; due to Dr. Swinerton, about £ 2, 3 s.; several other debts owing not yet known.

Attested by Bridgett, relict of Tho. Oliver, and allowed, November 28, 1679.

Disposition of Thomas Oliver's Estate (1679)

Administration upon the estate was granted November 28, 1679, to Bridget, relict of the deceased, and the estate to be for the use of the widow, she paying the two sons of her husband twenty shillings each, and her daughter, Christian, twenty shillings, and also the debts. And to have liberty to sell the ten-acre lot by advice of the selectmen of Salem, towards paying the debts and her present supply, and as need shall be, any other part of the estate.

Bridget Oliver Brought to Court on
Suspicion of Witchcraft (February 1680)

Summary of the Case

On 25: 12: 1679 [i.e., Feb. 25, 1680], Bridget Oliver being presented for suspicion of witchcraft, it was ordered that the action be presented to the next Court of Assistants at Boston.

She was to be committed to prison or give bond. She gave a bond.

Testimony of Wonn [Juan], a Negro Slave

Wonn, John Ingerson's Negro, testified that a month ago, going into the woods with the horses and sled, he took up his load of wood and came as far as

Wm. Bean's house. Going back again into the woods between Norman's rocks and Fish Brook, by the swamp side, his horses started and snorted as if they were frightened, and would not go forward but ran down into the swamp up to their bellies. They hauled the sled with them, and with much ado he got them out of their harness and from the swamp.

About a week after, deponent going into the hay-house a little after noon to get hay for his horses, and a second time for hay for the cow, he saw the shape of Goody Oliver upon the beam with an egg in her hand. He stooped down to take up the rake or pitchfork to strike her, when she vanished. It was the shape of the said Goody Oliver, as now she stands before the court. And being affrighted [I] run in presently to the house, and told my master what I saw. And afterwards, sitting at dinner, I saw two black cats, and we having one black cat of our own and no more, I said, how came two black cats here. And before my words were well out of my mouth I felt three sore grips or pinches on my side that made me cry out, and I had very much pain there, and soreness for half an hour after.

When his horses ran into the swamp there were a little distance away John Lambert, Jonathan Pickering, and some youths who noticed it and said they never saw the like, and they thought the horses were bewitched.

Sworn, 25: 12: 1679

Advice of the Salem Selectmen to Bridget Oliver (1681)

Bridgett Oliver, having desired advice from the Selectmen of Salem for the selling of a small parcel of land, about two poles more or less, lying on the back side of her house, for the relieving of her necessity in order to her present supply, hath advice granted from the Selectmen of Salem to Bridgett Oliver, for the sale of the land aforesaid unto Mr. Daniell Eppes, schoolmaster, the 9th of May, '81.

Bridget Oliver to Daniel Epes (1681)

Be it known unto all men by these presents that I, Bridgett Oliver, relict and administratrix of Thomas Oliver of Salem in the county of Essex, late deceased, for and in consideration of a valuable sum of money, *viz.:* thirty and five shillings to me in hand paid by Daniel Epes of the same town and county, schoolmaster, before the sealing and delivery of these presents; as also in consideration of a new board fence of about eight poles in length and five foot high, which said Epes hath at his own charge caused to be set up, and is bound to maintain betwixt the said Epes and Oliver, so long as she shall lawfully possess what she now enjoys, which fence *viz.:* boards, posts, nails, and setting up, together with ten shillings in money, and other considerable expense and cost, which said Epes hath been at for said Oliver's use, amounting in all to five and thirty shillings which added to the former makes up the full and just sum of three pounds, ten shillings.

In consideration of the premises, I, said Oliver, have with the consent of the Selectmen of Salem, which have underneath subscribed, in order to the further payment of debts which the estate of Thomas Oliver is liable to pay, and also for the present supply of my own necessities, ... do by these presents as administratrix aforesaid ... sell ... unto Daniel Epes, his heirs, executors, administrators, or assigns, a small parcel of land which my husband died lawfully possessed of, containing near two poles or rods, more or less, being situate in Salem town, as it lies bounded by the street on the west, by said Oliver's land on the south, by said Epes his land on the east and north. ... And in witness of all the former premises, I have hereunto set my hand and seal this fourteenth of June, in the year of our Lord, One Thousand, Six Hundred, Eighty and One. 1681.

Signed, sealed and delivered
in the presence of us.
John Hathorne
William Andrewes

The mark of

Bridgett ✕ Oliver

and a seal.

Bridgett Oliver acknowledged the above written to be her act and deed this 14th of June, 1681, before me Bartholmew Gedney, Assistant.

Thomas Stacey versus Bridget Bishop
for Stealing Brass (1688)

Testimony of Edward Dolbeare

The testimony of Edmund Dolbeare, aged forty years or thereabouts, testifieth and saith that sometime in July last, Thomas Stacey senior, miller, of this town of Salem, came to the said Dolbeare and asked of him whether he had bought a brass for a mill lately. The said Dolbeare answered, he had not. Then the said Stacey said that he had a brass taken out of the mill. And then did desire the said Dolbeare if there were any such thing brought to him to sell or to see such, that he would to stop it or to give him an account of it.

In August last, Christian Mason, daughter to Goody Bishop, brought to the said Dolbeare a brass for a mill to see such. The said Dolbeare asked of the said Christian Mason where she got that brass. The said Christian Mason answered that the said brass had lain about the house some years before her father died.

The said Dolbeare stopped the brass and did go himself and acquainted the said Thomas Stasy that there was a mill brass brought to the said Dolbeare to see such, and if he would go to the said Dolbeare's house and see whether it was his or not. Whereupon the said Stasy did presently go to the said Dolbeare's house and as soon as he saw the brass he said it was the same that he had lost. Then the said Stasy carried the same brass away with him.

December 14, 1687

attest St. Sewell, Clerk

Warrant for the Arrest of Bridget Bishop

James the Second, by the grace of God of England, Scotland, France, and Ireland, King and Defender of the Faith.

To the sheriff of our County of Essex or Deputy—greetings.

[Seal] We command you forthwith to seize the person of Bridget, the wife of Edward Bishop, and bring her before someone of our Justices of the Peace for this County of Essex to answer to what shall be objected against her on his Majesty's behalf for feloniously taking away a piece of brass sometime this last summer from Thomas Stacey. Hereof fail not.

In Court at Salem

December 14, 1687

Stephen Sewall, Clerk

I have seized the person of Bridget, the wife of Edward Bishop, and brought her before Justice John Hathorn, Esquire, this 6 day of March 1687/8.

Jeremiah Neale
Deputy Sheriff

Edward Bishop and William Reeves Post Bail
for Bridget Bishop

Edward Bishop and William Reeves, both of Salem in the County of Essex, personally appeared before me this six March, 1687/88, and acknowledged themselves jointly and severally to owe and stand bound unto our sovereign lord the King, the just and full sum of twenty pounds money.

The condition of this obligation is such that Bridgette Bishop, the wife of Edward Bishop of Salem, shall personally appear at the next session of the Peace holden at Ipswich, to answer what shall be charged or evidenced against her in the case depending and relating to the stealing of a piece of brass from Salem Mill, and to abide the judgment of the Court therein.

John Hathorn
Justice of the Peace

Testimony of Thomas Stacey

The Testimony of Thomas Stacey
Aged 66 years

Testified that sometime about August last past, coming from Mr. Dolbeir's with the brass that was taken out of the mill, he went into Edward Bishop's house and met with Bridget, his wife, and discoursing with her about the brass which he had taken with him. It was lately stolen out of the mill. Advised her to make her peace with the owner of the mill. Whereupon the said Bridget Bishop kneeled down on her knees and asked him forgiveness and said she was sorry that she had taken the brass and that she would do so no more. Further this deponent made oath that sometime after, Bridget Bishop came to the mill and there went down on her knees again and asked forgiveness and spake much after the matter as before she did at her house.

Sworne Salem March 6th, 1687/88

Before me John Hathorn,
Justice of the Peace

Testimony of William and Thomas Stacey

William Stacey of Salem testified that the brass which Bridget Bishop, the wife of Edward Bishop of Salem, sent by her daughter, Christian Mason, to Mr. Dolbeirs of Salem, as she acknowledgeth, is the very brass which was stolen out of the mill at Salem sometime in the last year.

Sworn Salem March 13th 1687/88

Before John Hathorn, Justice of the Peace

Thomas Stacey of Salem testifieth to all the abovesaid evidence.

March 14, 1687/88

Per St. Sewell, Clerk

Examination of Bridget Bishop

Salem—March 6th 1687/88

Bridget Bishop, the wife of Edward Bishop in Salem, brought before me by Lt. Jeremiah Neale, Deputy Sheriff, who having been suspected of stealing a piece of brass from the mill at Salem sometime the last summer—And Thomas Stacy of Salem, miller, being sent for, did charge her with the same, she having twice acknowledged herself guilty of the abovesaid fact unto him, according to former evidence given in by him at the last session of the peace, and now again said Stacey confirmed the same.

Upon Examination

Bridget Bishop denied the fact or that she ever acknowledged the same to Thomas Stacy, miller, and also said that Thomas Stacy never spake to her about any such thing but once, and that time was at the mill, and that she did not then nor at any other time acknowledge the same to him or to any other body. Being asked whether Thomas Stacy, miller, did not bring the brass to her house after he received the same from Mr. Dolberry, unto which she answered he did not. Being asked whether she sent it to Mr. Dolberry to sell, showing the brass now in controversy, unto which she answered that she did not send it to sell. But desired her daughter, Christian Mason, that when she went into town about any business that she would carry it with her to said Dolberry and know of him what it was, for she saw she knew not what it was. Being asked how she came by this said brass, she answered that she found it in her garden by the northwest corner of her house as her daughter and she was weeding there, but said her daughter did first see the same, and that it was a fortnight or three weeks or thereabouts before she sent it to Dolbeirs.

                                        This examination taken before
                                        John Hathorn, Justice of the Peace

Bridget Bishop, by *mittimus*, committed to Salem Jail, there to be kept in order to her trial at the next Sessions of the Peace.

[We have not discovered the final outcome of this case.]

Chapter Thirteen

John Willard

[*John Willard remains a most frustrating mystery to us. Although we spent more time tracking him down than we spent tracking down any of the four other accused persons, we still know little about him. We believe, for instance, that he was the "John Willard" born in 1655 to Simon Willard of Concord and "Nashaway," a prominent fur trader and land speculator; but we have no positive evidence. It is therefore possible that not all the following documents refer to our John or his family. For some reason the published genealogies of the Wilkins and Willard families contain no reference to our wizard; his name was evidently expunged from the family records. There does exist a 1682 tax list from the Massachusetts town of Groton, which lists a "John Wilerd" who is probably our man. At this point, then, the records of Willard's trial for witchcraft remain the best source of information about the man's life. (Further documents about the Wilkins family are included in part III.)*]

Willard Genealogies

Wilkins Family

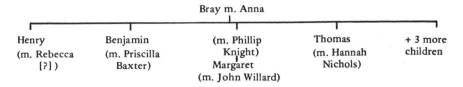

Bray m. Anna

Henry
(m. Rebecca
[?])

Benjamin
(m. Priscilla
Baxter)

(m. Phillip
Knight)
Margaret
(m. John Willard)

Thomas
(m. Hannah
Nichols)

+ 3 more
children

Nichols Family

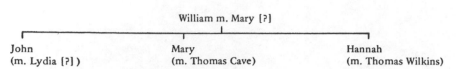

William m. Mary [?]

John	Mary	Hannah
(m. Lydia [?])	(m. Thomas Cave)	(m. Thomas Wilkins)

Bray Wilkins (Grandfather-in-Law of John Willard) Deed of Gift to His Sons (1679)

To all people whom these presents shall come: greeting. Know you that I, Bray Wilkens of Wills Hill in the limits of Salem in the County of Essex in the Colony of Massachusetts in New England plantation, for and in consideration of the good will and affection I bear toward my sons Samuell, Thomas, Henry and Benjamin Wilkens . . . do by these presents give . . . unto my said sons . . . certain parcels of upland and meadow land . . . at Wills Hill in the limits of Salem aforesaid, in manner following:

Namely, to my sons Samuel and Henry, my lots of upland containing sixty acres, more or less . . . south by the Great Pond . . . and twenty acres of meadow, more or less, at the west end of the said pond. To each of them their part both of the said upland and meadow as is now divided and possessed by each of them (excepting and always reserving liberty for myself and my said sons Thomas and Benj. to make use of any wood or timber on the said land).

To my said son Thomas, the land joining to his dwelling house, containing six acres, more or less . . . ; and also half my lot of upland on the south side [of] the pond, and all my part of meadow on the east side of Andover brook, and half my meadow up at the Great Meadow; to have all the said parts and parcels of upland and meadow as they are now divided and possessed by him. And, at or upon the division of my whole farm, his part of upland to be made up equal with his brother Samuel and Henry.

To my said son Benj., the land joining to his house, containing about half an acre, with one acre in the orchard next to Jon. Gingell, and four acres of land in the upper end of my new field next to Thomas Fuller, and also the other half part of my meadow on the south side of the pond, and the other half part of my great meadow and seven acres of meadow . . . next to Aron Way's and William Ireland's meadow: all which parts and parcels of upland and meadow he is now possessed of. And also at or upon the division of the whole farm, his part of upland to be made up equal with his brothers Samuel and Henry. . . .

In witness to all and singular [of] the within mentioned premises, I, the said Bray Wilkens, have hereunto set my hand and seal this twenty sixth day of February: Anno One Thousand Six Hundred Seventy Nine.

Signed, sealed and delivered in presence of   Bray Wilkins
William Ireland Sen[r]   [and seal]
John Gingell

Bray Wilkens acknowledges the abovewritten to be his act and deed this 20th of March 1681/82 before me

Bartho. Gedney Asst.

Examined   Steph: Sewall Reg.

Order of the Massachusetts General Court Granting 1000 Acres to the Children of Simon Willard (May 1681)

[On the assumption that John Willard was the son of Major Simon Willard of Nashaway (present-day Lancaster) we have included this document and another later one.]

In answer to the petition of Mary Noyes, relict of the late Major Simon Willard, the Court judgeth it meet [to grant] the petitioner, for and on behalf of the six youngest children of the late honored Major Simon Willard, 1,000 acres of land in any free place beyond Nashaway River, and do hereby order that the land hereby granted remain undisposed of until all the children above mentioned attain to the age of one-and-twenty years old.

[In March 1682 the General Court approved the location of this 1,000-acre grant. The land selected was in the vicinity of Hadley, Massachusetts.]

Phillip Knight, Thomas Wilkins, Henry Wilkins, and John Willard to Zacheus and Ephraim Curtis (1691)

Know all men by these presents, that we, Phillip Knight of Topsfield, and Thomas Wilkins, Henry Wilkins, and John Willard of Salem . . . , have . . . sold unto Zacheus Curtice and Ephraim Curtice of Boxford . . . , for and in consideration of thirty pounds sterling in current money of New England, in hand paid, a certain parcel of land . . . being by estimation six-score acres, be it more or less. . . . *[The bounds are then set forth, indicating that the land is on Bare Hill, adjacent to Captain John Putnam's farm.]* The abovesaid land [is] situated and lying in Boxford. . . .

Only . . . we do reserve a way for John Andrew and Joseph Andrew to go to and from the land they bought of us, the abovesaid sellers, as they shall have occasion, provided they do not damnify [any] planting nor mowing land. . . .

Signed, sealed and   Phillip   X   Knight [seal]
delivered in presence   his mark
of witnesses   Thomas T Wilkins [seal]
                                            his mark

James Smith   Henry Wilkins   [seal]
John Nichols   *H*
    his mark   his mark
Phillip Knights   Thomas Wilkins   Ruth Wilkins   John Wilard   [seal]
Henry Wilkins   John Willard   *ne*
Margaret Knights,   Hannah Wilkins   her mark
and Margret Willard   Margret   *K*   Knight   [seal]
                                             her mark
                                          Hannah   *2*   Wilkins   [seal]
                                             her mark
                                          Margret   *y*   Willard   [seal]
                                             her mark

All of them personally appeared and acknowledged the abovesaid instrument
to be their act and deed this first day of July, 1691, before me, Jonathan
Corwin, Assistant.

Examined by Stephen Sewall, Registrar

John Willard's Land in Nashaway Granted
by the Town to Benjamin Willard (1692)

John Willard's lot 30 acres all laid out herein: This day being the first of
February, 1691/92, the town confirmed the same to Benjamin Willard.

John Willard's lot, now in the possession of Benjamin Willard, is laid out in
several pieces, one part whereof lieth between the lands of Henery Willard and
Zebadiah Wheeler's land; . . . and he hath another piece on the south side of
Zebadiah Wheeler's land; . . . he hath ten acres lying near the brook meadow,
. . . which makes up his complement of thirty acres granted him by the town.
Laid out per me, Ralph Houghton. A description whereof was read before the
town the first February 1691/92 and ordered to be recorded. Recorded this first
February 1691/92.

per John Houghton, Recorder

The Will of Bray Wilkins
(Written 1697, Probated 1702)

In the name of God Amen, I Bray Wilkins of the town of Salem, in the
county of Essex, in his Majesties Province of the Massachusetts Bay in New
England, yeoman, being ancient and sensible of the declining of old age and
weakness and infirmities of mortality daily attending upon me, but being of a
sound . . . mind & memory and blessed be God for the same, Do make, ordain,
constitute and appoint this my last will and testament in manner and forms
following.

Imprimis I give and bequeath my soul into the merciful hands of Jesus Christ in whom I hope to live forever in hopes of a glorious resurrection by him when this mortal shall put on immortality and this vile body shall be made like unto his glorious body and my body to the earth to be decently by the discretion of my executors hereafter named and as for that estate that God hath given me in this world all my legal debts being once paid and disposed of as followeth, *viz:*

Item I give and bequeath to Anna Wilkins, my well beloved wife, my house, barns & orchard, improved lands and fences, together with all my moveable estate, within doors and without, for her to use and improve during the term of her natural life for her comfortable subsistance, she making no strip or waste of the same. And I do also hereby fully impower my aforesaid wife to sell and dispose of any of the aforesaid lands and moveables if she be necessitated so to do for her comfortable subsistance. Also I do hereby charge, require, & command my son Benjamin Wilkins, if he lives, to take care of his aged mother that she may not want anything for her comfortable subsistance during her natural life.

Item I give and bequeath to my son Benjamin Wilkins & to his heirs & assigns forever, after mine and my wife's decease, my home lot with my house, barns & orchard and appurtenances thereunto belonging . . . together with my thirty acres of land lying at the head of the hill, to have & to hold forever after our decease.

Item As for that lot of land that I have at the head of the fifty acres of land which I have given to my sons Samuel & Henry Wilkins, I do by these presents give & bequeath the whole of the aforesaid lot to my son Henry Wilkins & to his heirs & assigns forever after my decease.

Item I give and bequeath unto my son Benjamin Wilkins & to his heirs & assigns forever my lot of land that runs over walnut tree so called. . . .

Item Whereas I have a lot of land laying upon the neck on the north side of pout pond brook, so called, I do by these presents give & bequeath ten acres of that upland to my grandson John Wilkins & to his heirs & assigns forever. . . . And all ye rest of that aforesaid lot of upland that shall remain between the aforesaid ten acres and pout pond meadow I do by these presents give & bequeath the same, be it more or less, unto my son Thomas Wilkins. . . .

Item I give and bequeath unto my daughter Margeritt Knight, ye wife of Phillip Knight . . . , three acres of meadow laying in the tongue of pout pond meadow where the said Phillip Knight useth to mow, and all the rest of my meadow that layeth in pout pond meadow between the aforesaid three acres of meadow and Ireland's meadow & pout pond brook I do by these presents give & bequeath the same, be it more or less, unto my son Benjamin Wilkins. . . .

Item   I give and bequeath unto my daughter Lydia Nicholls, the wife of John Nicholls . . . forty shillings in money to be paid within two years after my decease.

Item   I give & bequeath unto my son Benjamin Wilkins . . . all my meadow laying in Andover meadow so called. . . .

Item   I give and bequeath unto my grandson Bray Wilkins . . . all my meadow laying in beachy meadow, so called, be it more or less.

Item   I give unto my grandson Samuel Wilkins one of my best coats for him to have quickly after my decease.

Item   All the rest of my wearing apparrel that shall be left after mine and my wife's decease I do by these presents give & bequeath the same unto my three sons, Thomas, Henry and Benjamin Wilkins equally to be divided between them.

Item   I give and bequeath to my son Benjamin Wilkins after mine and my wife's decease my great Bible and great iron kettle and all my share in carts, wheels, ploughs, yokes & chains.

Item   I give and bequeath unto my daughter Margeret Knight, and to her heirs, after mine and my wife's decease, my feather bed.

Item   All the rest of my bedding, sheets, blankets, rugs & whatsoever belongs to my bedding that shall be left after mine and my wife's decease I do by these presents give & bequeath it all to my two daughters Lydia Nicholls and Margerett Knight equally to be divided between them or their heirs.

Item   I do make, constitute, ordain & appoint my loving wife Anna Wilkins to be my executrix and my dutiful son Benjamin Wilkins executor jointly together with his mother of this my last will & testament, and I desire my loving friends Thomas Putnam & John Putnam, Junr., to be overseers of this my last will and testament as aforementioned and written in these three pages. . . . In witness whereof I have hereunto set my hand & seal the ninth day of January Anno Domini Sixteen Hundred Ninety and Six/Seven. . . .

                                                              Bray Wilkins & a seal

Signed, sealed, published, pronounced and declared by the said Bray Wilkins as his last will and testament in the presence of us the subscribers, *viz.*

                    Thomas Putnam
                    Thomas Fuller Tertius
                    Jonathan Fuller

    Essex Ss before the Hon. Jonathan Corwin, Esq. Judge of Probate of wills &c. Jan. 26, 1701/2.

Thomas Fuller Tertius & Jonathan Fuller both personally appeared & made oath that they were present and did see Bray Wilkins sign & seal and heard him publish and declare the above & what is written on the other two sides to be his last will & testament & that when he so did he was of disposing mind to their best discerning & that [they] then subscribed as witness in his presence and that Thomas Putnam signed as a witness together with themselves at the same time.

Sworn attest John Higginson, Reg.

The testimony of William Ireland, of full age, testifies & says that Bray Wilkins dec'ed. did deliver this paper to me to keep which is here delivered as his last will & he declared it to me to be his last will and desired me to witness to it, and I said that there was three witnesses already and needed no more, so I did not sign as a witness. And according to his desire I have kept this will for him till after his death & delivered it to the executors. And several times in his life he declared it to me to be his last will, and in particular not above a month before his death he declared it to me again that this was his last will and would not have it brought to be altered.

William Ireland

Essex Ss before the Hon. Jonathan Corwin, Esq., Judge of Probate &c. Jan. 26, 1701/2 William Ireland made oath to the truth of the above written evidence.

Attest John Higginson, Reg.

Upon which this will is proved, approved and allowed being presented by Bnj. Wilkins, one of the executors therein named.

Attest John Higginson, Reg.

William Towne and Margaret (Willard) Towne Appointed Administrators of John Willard's Estate (1711)

Essex Ss. Ipswich, May 28, 1711

Letter of Administration on all and singular [of] the goods and estate of John Willard, late of Salem, yeoman, died intestate, was granted to Wm. Towne and Margaret, his wife, former widow of the said deceased, they having given bond to admini[strate] according to law. To exhibit an inventory and render an account at or before the first Monday in December next ensuing.

John Appleton

Chapter Fourteen

George Burroughs

[In addition to the following documents, much material concerning George Burroughs' earlier career in Salem Village is included in Part Four. (See especially "The Village and Its Ministers" and the Village Book of Record for the years 1680-83.)]

Jeremiah Watts Admonished for Writing Offensive Letters to Ministers (May 1682)

Summons

Summons, dated Salem, May 3, 1682, to Jeremiah Watts, for speaking scandalously of the ministry, and writing offensively against and concerning the leaders of churches in this place, and to Thomas Heines and Daniell Ray as witnesses.

Signed by Bartho. Gedney, Assistant

Jeremiah Watts to the Reverend Mr. George Burroughs, April 11, 1682

This for Mr. Burrows, living in Salem Village.

Mr. Burrows:
Sir, when I came unto you with our neighbors the last week, I was disappointed of my intention in the main thing I aimed at, because of your friends and my judge Mr. Gerrish.

The thing I aimed at was and is this: this village is aiming to make it a town, which is all very necessary work and beneficial unto us. But how can this be accomplished in a way of God when brother is against brother and neighbors against neighbors, all quarreling and smiting one another? Will this encourage neighbors to join with us to the work?

Secondly, you aim to erect a church in this place, which also is a good work, done in God's way. But how is it provable [i.e., possible] this posture we are in?

Therefore, I did intend to propound this thing unto you with the rest with us: that you would consider a way to prepare for such a work by setting forward private Christian meeting[s] amongst us, that we may come together for to know one another's spirits, and that differences may be healed and so united together. Will a righteous and holy God own contention and strife? Will the form of godliness serve only, without the power? This will serve [in] turn to set up some usurping lords to smite and trample upon their fellow brethren, but such foundations will not stand before a just and holy God. But, again, these private Christian meetings is our Christian privilege, wherein Christians are to exhort and edify one another by speaking often one to another, to declare our grievances one to another, and help one another.

The minister should be the leading man in this work, but I do perceive that ministers do aim to bring all to pulpit preaching, and there they may deliver what they please and none must object. And this we must pay largely for. Our bread must be taken out of our mouths to maintain the beast's mark and be wholly deprived of our Christian privilege. These practices the scripture doth everywhere condemn. This is the time of Antichrist's reign, and he must reign his time. And now are the witnesses slain, and the leaders in churches are their slayers, which I shall sufficiently prove. For I do intend to draw up the marks of the beast, Antichrist, which prevail in our times.

But I see plainly it's a vain thing to debate about these things with our fellow brethren, for they are all for lording of it and trampling under foot. Therefore I shall apply myself to our honoured fathers, for if fellow brethren have that privilege to judge their own case and reign as lords over one another, then we need not to choose magistrates to rule.

You asked me this question when I was with you, why I was so slighted of the societies I have been with. Now I shall give a true answer which none of my adversaries can deny. The answer is this: because I am singled out alone to give my testimony for Christ, discovering Antichrist's marks which appear in the land privately amongst those I have had society with. It's certain true when Antichrist reigns, if any will be faithful for Christ they must witness against Antichrist, which is self-love and lovers of pleasure more than lovers of God. These must be hated by Diotrephes, who loveth preeminence. The witnesses are now slain, but shortly they rise again.

April 11, [1682]

Jere: Watts

Disposition of the Case

Jeremiah Watts, complained of for matter of great moment, tending to the scandalizing of many, both ministers and others of good credit, by his papers and letters, yet considering that they were in private to the persons, was admonished.

Salem Village Versus George Burroughs (1683)

Petition of Salem Village to the County Court (April 1683)

To the Honoured Court held at Ipswich, 10th of April, 1683.

The humble petition of the inhabitants of Salem Village to this honoured Court showeth that your petitioners have been at great charge and cost in providing and settling of Mr. George Burroughs in the work of the ministry among us, and mutual engagements have passed between us, as will be plainly demonstrated, wherein he is engaged to continue with us in that work. And we engaged to pay him a yearly maintenance according to agreement, wherewith he declared himself satisfied, and we have accordingly complied with the agreement and our parts hitherto.

Yet notwithstanding, the said Mr. Burroughs, without any just reason that we know of, hath withdrawn himself from us, and there hath been no public worship amongst us for four Sabbaths past. And, that which is more suprising to us, we are certainly informed that he is going out of the colony speedily and that he will be gone this week, and we cannot prevail with him to come to an account with us, or yield unto a council, that there may be a right understanding of the case between us.

Considering that the law doth direct in [such] case to inquire into and inspect the matter of ministers' maintenance, and we think practice, too, your petitioners do humbly pray the favor of this honoured Court that they will be pleased to peruse the engagements that are mutually passed between us and our minister, and, finding them such as above intimated, that you will be pleased to write to Mr. Burroughs to require him to attend an orderly hearing and clearing up of the case between your petitioners and himself, according to our agreement, and that speedily, or any other way that this Court shall think fit for the relief of your poor petitioners, who think themselves greatly wronged at present by such a sudden breaking away from us and not giving us a reason. Things not being cleared up may greatly [illegible] us and hinder us of a future supply, and a [illegible] order hearing we believe will be acceptable to God and will greatly oblige your poor petitioners to pray.

In the name and by the order of the inhabitants of Salem Village.

Thomas Putnam, senior
Nathaniel Putnam
Thomas Fuller, senior
John Putnam, senior
Daniel Andrew

[The following documents were entered as evidence in connection with the case of Salem Village against the Reverend Mr. Burroughs.]

George Burroughs' Account of His Negotiations with Salem Village in 1681

Lieut. Thomas Putnam, Sarg. Fuller, Goodman Wilkins, senior, according to the vote of the inhabitants, August 26th, 1681, came to me to receive my answer relating to a settlement among them, December the first, 1681.

My answer is as followeth:

Whereas I have expressed myself in answer to the call and desire of the people of Salem farms, that I give up myself to the work of the ministry among them, my answer is:

1. That I settle among them with a true intention and a true affection to live and die in the work of the ministry among them.
2. That in case any difference should arise in time to come, that we engage on both sides to submit to counsel for a peaceable issue.

Lieut. John Putnam
present at this meeting.

George Burroughs

All is to be understood so long as I have gospel encouragement.

When the three years are out (mentioned at a public meeting February the 16th, 1680/81), I expect but the just sum of sixty pounds to be paid, as expressed in their vote. Excepting the place increasing, they will of themselves do more. They are to give me the firewood.

December the first, 1681.

George Burroughs

This abovewritten is a true copy taken out of the book, by me, Jonathan Putnam, by order of the Committee.

Salem Village Chooses a Committee to
Handle Its Complaint Against George Burroughs (1683)

At a meeting of the inhabitants of Salem Village, March the 30th, 1683: voted, the men chosen to manage the case in council concerning the difference between Mr. Burroughs and ourselves are: Lieut. Thomas Putnam, Nathaniel Putnam, Thomas Fuller Senr., and Lieut. John Putnam and Daniel Andrew—or the major part of them; and to appoint the time and to choose our men. And these men are further empowered to act with Mr. Burroughs, as they shall for cause concerning our aggrievances if he refuses to submit to council.

A true copy, taken out of the Records

by me: Jonathan Putnam, by order of the Committee

Salem Village Hires George Burroughs (1681)

At a meeting of the inhabitants of the Farms, the 16th of February 1680/81: voted that Mr. Burroughs shall have for the next three years [illegible], for his encouragement and settlement in the work of the ministry amongst us, ninety-three pounds, six shillings per year; one-third part in money, the other two-thirds to be in or as money. And after the three years are expired: sixty pounds per year, according to our former vote.

A true copy, taken out of the Records by me:

Jonathan Putnam, by order of the Committee.

[A fourth entry from the Salem Village Records, dated November 25, 1680, was offered as evidence also. Unlike the previous three entries, this fourth entry may be found in the Village Book of Record later in this book.]

Lieutenant John Putnam Versus George
Burroughs, in an Action for Debt
(May-June 1683)

Testimony of Nathaniel Ingersoll
and Samuel Sibley

We, whose names are underwritten, testify and say, that at a public meeting of the people of Salem Farms, April 24, 1683, we heard a letter read, which letter was sent from the Court. After the said letter was read, Mr. Burroughs came in. After the said Burroughs had been a while in, he asked whether they took up with the advice of the Court, given in the letter, or whether they rejected it. The moderator made answer, "Yes, we take up with it"; and not a man contradicted it to any of our hearing. After this was passed, was a discourse of settling accounts between the said Burroughs and the inhabitants, and issuing things in peace, and parting in love, as they came together in love. Further, we say that the second, third, and fourth days of the following week were agreed upon by Mr. Burroughs and the people to be the days for every man to come in and to reckon with the said Burroughs; and so they adjourned the meeting to the last of the aforesaid three days, in the afternoon, then to make up the whole account in public.

We further testify and say, that, May the second, 1683, Mr. Burroughs and the inhabitants met at the meeting-house to make up accounts in public, according to their agreement the meeting before; and, just as the said Burroughs began to give in his accounts, the marshal came in, and, after a while, went up to John Putnam, Sr., and whispered to him, and said Putnam said to him, "You know what you have to do: do your office." Then the marshal came to Mr. Burroughs, and said, "Sir, I have a writing to read to you." Then he read the attachment, and demanded goods. Mr. Burroughs answered, that he had no goods to show, and that he was now reckoning with the inhabitants, for we know not yet who is in debt, but there was his body. As we were ready to go out of the meeting-house, Mr. Burroughs said, "Well, what will you do with me?" Then the marshal went to John Putnam, Sr., and said to him, "What shall I do?" The said Putnam replied, "You know your business." And then the said Putnam went to his brother, Thomas Putnam, and pulled him by the coat; and they went out of the house together, and presently came in again. Then said John Putnam, "Marshal, take your prisoner, and have him up to the ordinary and secure him till the morning."

> Nathaniel Ingersoll, aged about fifty.
> Samuel Sibley, aged about twenty-four.

To the first of these, I, John Putnam, Jr., testify, being at the meeting.

Warrant for the Arrest of George Burroughs

To the Marshall of Salem, or his deputy:

You are required in his majesty's name to attach the goods and, for want thereof, the body, of Mr. George Burroughs of Salem Farms in the County of Essex, and take bond of him to the value of sixty-six pounds, ten shillings money, with sufficient security or surety, for his appearance at the next county court held at Salem, then and there to answer the complaint of Lieut. John Putnam of the said Salem farms, in an action of debt to the value of thirty-three pounds and six shillings and eight pence in money, it being for so much received by him, the said Burroughs, of Jno. Putnam, as may appear by a receipt under his hand, dated 27 January, 1681, with all just damages, and [illegible].

Dated this first of May, 1683.

> Hilliard Veren [illegible]
> for the Court of Salem

[Reverse] I attached the body of George Burroughs. He tendered to me because he said he had no pay, and read this attachment to him, the 2nd May, 1683. And holden bound to the value of sixty-six pounds, five shillings money.

By me, Henry Skerry, Marshall.

Bail Posted for George Burroughs

We whose names are underwritten do bind ourselves jointly and severally to Henry Skerry, Marshall of Salem, in the sum of fourteen pounds money, that George Burroughs shall appear at the next County Court at Salem, [to answer?] Thomas Putnam, according to the form of this attachment, and to abide the order of the Court therein, and not depart without, as witness our hands, this 2nd May, 1683.

> George Burroughs
> Nathaniel Ingersoll
> John Buxton
> Thomas Haynes
> Samuel Sibloe [Sibley]
> The mark of William X Siblye
> William Ireland, junior.

Summary of the Case

County Court, June 1683—Lieutenant John Putnam *versus* Mr. George Burroughs. Action of debt for two gallons of canary wine, and cloth, etc. bought of Mr. Gedney on John Putnam's account, for the funeral of Mrs. Burroughs.

[The following testimony and documents were introduced in the case.]

Testimony of Thomas Haines

The testimony of Thomas Haines, aged 32 years or thereabouts, testifieth and saith, that at a meeting of the inhabitants of Salem farms, May the second, 1683, after the marshall had read John Putnam's attachment to Mr. Burroughs, then Mr. Burroughs asked John Putnam what money it was he attached him for. John Putnam answered: for five pounds and odd money at Shippen's at Boston, and for thirteen shillings at his father Gedney's, and for twenty-four shillings at Mrs. Darby's.

Then Nath. Ingersoll stood up and said: Lieut., I wonder you attach Mr. Burroughs for that money at Darby's, and your father Gedney's, when to my knowledge you and Mr. Burroughs have reckoned and balanced accounts two or three times since, as you say, this money was due, and you never made any mention of it when you reckoned with Mr. Burroughs.

John Putnam answered: it is true, I own it.

Samuel Siblee, aged 24 years or thereabouts, testifieth to all abovewritten.

Statement of John Putnam's Claim
Against George Burroughs

John Putnam's account.
Mr. George Burroughs, debtor.

		£	s.	d.
1:6:82	by a bill to Mr. Shippen	05	17	00
	by 2 gallons canary wine	00	12	00
	by 2 yards ½ serge & [illegible]	00	10	00
	by one yard fustian	00	01	10
	by two yards [illegible]			
	of the [illegible]	00	01	00
		£ 07	01	10

All above [illegible] money.

Affirmed by the [illegible] to the truth of the above account in court at Salem, 26:4:83.

attest, Hilliard Veren, Clerk.

Testimony of Sarah [illegible]

Sarah [illegible], aged 18 years, testifieth that I boarded with Mr. Borrous about two years since, and then my mistress Burroughs did tell me that she had some serge of John Putnam's wife to make [illegible] out of, and also some fustian of his wife to make my mistress a yard of [illegible].

Sworn, 26 June, 1683.

Before me, Barth. Gedney.

Testimony of Susanna Gedney

The testimony of Susanna Gedney, aged 39 years, saith, that there was two gallons of wine [bought?] at my father Gedney's on John Putnam's account for

Mrs. Burroughs's funeral, and John Putnam hath paid for the wine.
wine.

Sworn, 26 June, 1683.

Before Barth. Gedney, Assistant

Testimony of Alexander Osborn

Testimony of Alexander Osborn, aged 35 years, testifieth that some time in September '81, Mr. Burroughs desired me to fetch some wine at Salem for his wife's funeral, and then John Putnam did send me to Mr. Gedney's for two gallons of wine on his account for [illegible]. And I did fetch two gallons [illegible] for Mr. Burroughs on John Putnam's account, and I did bring the wine to Mr. Burroughs's house, and further saith not.

Sworn in court at Salem, 26:4:83

Testimony of Nathaniel Ingersoll

The testimony of Nath. Ingersoll, aged 50 years or thereabouts, testifieth and saith, that I heard Mr. Burroughs ask Lieut. John Putnam to give him a bill to Mr. Shippen's. The said Putnam asked the said Burroughs how much he would take up at Mr. Shippen's. Mr. Burroughs said, it might be five pounds. But after the said Burroughs had considered a little, he said to the said Putnam, it may be it might come to more, therefore he would have him give him bill to the value of five or six pounds. John Putnam answered it was as one to him.

Then the said Putnam went and wrote it, and read it to Mr. Burroughs, and said to him that it should go for part of the thirty-three pounds, six shillings, and eight pence, which he had given bill to him in the behalf of the inhabitants.

I, Hannah Ingersoll, aged 46 years or thereabouts, testify the same.

Record of Salem Village's Remaining Indebtedness to
George Burroughs for the Year 1682

A bill committed to Constable Thomas Haines of 33 pounds, eight shillings, and four pence, being part of Mr. Burroughs's salary for the year 1682, and ordered by Mr. Burroughs to John Putnam, senior, to require of the Constable.

This is a true copy taken out of the book.

Jonathan Putnam, by order.

John Putnam Withdraws His Suit

At a County Court held at Salem the 26 of June, 1683.

Lieut. John Putnam, plaintiff, against Mr. George Burroughs, defendant, in an action of debt, et. [?] answer to attachment dated 1 May, 1683.

Withdrawn.

George Burroughs and Other Residents
of Wells, Maine, Address the General Court (1691)

Wells: Sept. 28th, 1691

To the honored Governor and Council:

Whereas it hath pleased God (both formerly and now) to let loose the heathen upon us, who have been a sore scourge to us and still distress us by holding us off from our improvements, cooping us in close garrison, and daily lying in wait to take any that go forth; whereby we are brought very low: not all the corn raised in the town is judged enough to keep the inhabitants themselves one-half year, and our stocks both of cattle and swine are much diminished;

We therefore humbly request your Honors to continue soldiers among us, and appoint a commander over them; and what number shall be judged meet to remain with us for the winter, that provisions—corn, and clothing suitable for them—may be seasonably sent; also one hogshead of salt, all ours being spent; also a present supply, in that what was sent before is almost gone. We had a youth of 17 years of age last Saturday carried away, who went (not above gun-shot) from Lieut. Storer's garrison to fetch a little wood in his arms. We have desired our loving friends, Capt. John Littlefield and Ensign John Hill, to present this to your Honors; who can give a further account of our condition. We subscribe,

Your Honors' most humble servants,

George Burroughs
Joseph Storer
Jona: Glamond
John Wheelwright
John Cloyes
Nath: Cloyes

Part Three

The Accusers

Chapter Fifteen

Samuel Parris

Deposition by Samuel Parris (1697?)

[This deposition presumably was made in 1697 in connection with the countersuits between Samuel Parris and Salem Village. The following abstract was published by Charles W. Upham in his book Salem Witchcraft *(1867). Parris's own language is enclosed in quotation marks; the connecting narrative is Upham's.]*

It appears from his [Parris's] statement that a committee, consisting of "Captain John Putnam, Mr. Joshua Rea, Sr., and Francis Nurse," was appointed, on the 15th of November, 1688, to treat with him "about taking ministerial office." On the 25th of November, "after the services in the afternoon, the audience was stayed, and, by a general vote, requested Mr. Parris to take office."

He withheld response to the call.

On the 10th of December, another committee was raised, consisting of Lieutenant Nathaniel Putnam, Sergeant Fuller, Mr. Joshua Rea, Sr., and Sergeant Ingersoll, as "messengers, to know whether Mr. Parris would accept of office." His answer was, "the work was weighty; they should know in due time."

On the 29th of April, 1689, "Deacons Nathaniel Ingersoll and Edward Putnam, Daniel Rea, Thomas Fuller, Jr., and John Tarbell, came to Mr. Parris from the meeting-house," where there had been a general meeting of the inhabitants, and said, "Being the aged men had had the matter of Mr. Parris's settlement so long in hand, and effected nothing, they were desirous to try what the younger could do."

The younger men were determined to go ahead. They said they were desirous of a speedy answer. Finding them in a temper to "finish the thing up," and

183

seeing that they were ambitious to get the credit of "effecting something," and, for that end, predisposed to come to his terms, he disclosed them. They had offered him a salary of sixty pounds per annum,—one third in money, the rest in provisions, at certin specified rates. He agreed to accept the call on the foregoing terms, with certin additional conditions thus described by himself:

"First, when money shall be more plenteous, the money part to be paid me shall accordingly be increased.

"Second, though corn or like provisions should arise to a higher price than you have set, yet, for my own family use, I shall have what is needful at the price now stated, and so if it fall lower.

"Third, the whole sixty pounds to be only from our inhabitants that are dwelling in our bounds, proportionable to what lands they have within the same.

"Fourth, no provision to be brought in without first asking whether needed, and myself to make choice of what, unless the person is unable to pay in any sort but one.

"Fifth, firewood to be given in yearly, freely.

"Sixth, two men to be chosen yearly to see that due payments be made.

"Seventh, contributions each sabbath in papers; and only such as are in papers, and dwelling within our bounds, to be accounted a part of the sixty pounds.

"Eighth, as God shall please to bless the place so as to be able to rise higher than the sixty pounds, that then a proportionable increase be made. If God shall please, for our sins, to diminish the substance of said place, I will endeaver accordingly to bear such losses, by proportionable abatements of such as shall reasonably desire it."

He says that the committee accepted these terms, and agreed to them, expressing their belief that the people also would.

Three Sermons (1689-1692)

Ordination Sermon at Salem Village, November 19, 1689

My poor and weak ordination sermon at the embodying of a Church in Salem Village on the 19th November 1689. The Rev. Mr. Nicholas Noyes embodying of us, who ordained my most unworthy self Pastor, and together with the Rev. Mr. Sam: Phillips and the Rev. Mr. John Hale imposed hands, the same Mr. Phillips giving me the right hand of fellowship with beautiful loveliness and humility.

. . .

Joshua 5:9 (first part): "And the Lord said unto Joshua, this day have I rolled away the reproach of Egypt from off you."

Doctrine: It is an Egyptian-like disgrace and reproach to any people to be out of visible and sacramental communion with God in his ordinances, which ordinances, when God doth graciously bring a people to the enjoyment of, then and thereby God doth not only take away their former disgrace and reproach, but also most highly exalt, promote and dignify them.

[The Biblical text on which Samuel Parris bases this sermon (Joshua 5:9) deals with the circumcision of the Jews after they had escaped from Egypt and struggled for forty years in the desert before returning to the promised land. In the first part of the sermon, Parris suggests that the circumcision of the Jews is a symbol of all divine ordinances and especially of the requirement that God's saints must organize churches and partake of communion together. Roughly the last third of the sermon follows.]

I aim at a word or two of use, and so shall shut up with great brevity because of the shortness and somewhat sharpness of the season, and the considerableness of time that the remaining work [i.e., the service] calls for.

Use 1: Information.

1. Hence learn we to adore, and in our very souls to magnify, the free grace of God in our Lord Jesus for the gracious distinction he is pleased to make between us in New England and millions of others. We are all one by nature with Egyptians, Turks, Pagans, Indians, Ethiopeans, etc., but we differ vastly in his privileges. If we ask ourselves, as Paul does the Corinthians (I Cor. 4:7), who makes the difference? There is a vast difference indeed. But how comes it? Why, [the answer is:] not from any merit in us, but from the mercy of God to us as to Israel of old (Deut. 7:6-8). It is God who hath rolled away our disgrace and reproach, and brought this honor and dignity upon us. And seeing it is the Lord's gracious doing, let it be marvellous in our eyes. Says David, when Zadock brought after him (in his flight from Absalom) the ark of the covenant of God: "Carry it back. If I shall find favor in the eyes of the Lord, he will bring me again, and show me both it and his habitation" (II Sam. 15:24-25). So I say we have found favor in God's eyes: let us thankfully own it and admire at it, and say, Not unto us, not unto us or our merits, but unto God's name is due the glory of these distinguishing privileges.

2. Hence learn, you of this place (this Village), that God hath graciously brought you to a good day this day. This is the day wherein God is giving you hopes that he will roll away the reproach of Egypt from off you. It is true, indeed, some of you (and yet, alas, but a few of you) were partakers of visible and sacramental communion with God in his ordinances by virtue of your membership with other Churches of our Lord Jesus. Aye, but still you had no such settled, sacred, and royal dignities and distinguishing privileges among yourselves. The reproach of Egypt continued in the place, though some few persons were exempted from it. Now, what an Egyptian-like disgrace and reproach was it for such a number of people (so well able to maintain the Lord's ordinances), in such a land as New England, so long to continue, unlike their

professing neighbors, without the signs and seals of the blessed covenant of grace? In the eyes of God, and in the eyes of Godly persons, this was your reproach. But this day God gives you hopes of rolling away this reproach from off you.

3 and last (to say no more): This doctrine serves to vindicate and justify the holy and spiritual disquietness of such who were groaning in spirit under the want of the seals of the covenant to be brought home to their own doors. If there are any grieved at the restlessness of such [who are] in that condition, let them but remember the reproach such were under, and that is enough to vindicate their labor after the rolling of it away. Therefore:

Use 2 may be of caution and admonition. Let none be offended at the work of this day. Do not reproach the goodness of God when he is about [the] rolling away of your reproach. Let none say in their hearts [that] they were in as good a case before. They see not that they were under any reproach, or the like. I may say to such [just] as Moses did to Korah (Numb. 16:9): "Seemeth it a small thing to you that the God of Israel hath brought you near to himself, etc."

1. Consider [that] by so thinking or speaking, you contradict God himself. He calls it a rolling away of your reproach, etc.

2. Consider [that] by so thinking or speaking, you will be found in God's eyes—whatever you are in men's—guilty of a profane Pagan-like spirit.

Use 3: Exhortation.

1. To all who belong to this small congregation: Oh! be exhorted to meet God in the gracious work that he is this day about, of rolling away your reproach from off you, by getting into the covenant of grace, and so coming under the seals of the covenant. And to that end attend heedfully and constantly to the preaching of the word, by which the spirit of God is wont first to move the soul to entertain Christ, before it sets his seal upon the soul of its interest in Christ in the sacrament. And remember, whilst you keep off from the seals of the covenant, you are maintainers of your own reproach. The very seals of the covenant whereby we are initiated into and confirmed in an interest in Christ, is (as holy Calvin says) worth an hundred lives. And remember, it is not the bare privation, but the *contempt* of sacraments (as Bernard says truly) [which] is damnable and destructive. Therefore you cannot hereafter live without partaking of the ordinances, but [i.e., or else] you will of necessity heighten your sins by such neglects or omissions. But I must not insist.

2. To all of us who are more especially concerned in the work of this good day, from off whom God is rolling away our reproach, and upon whom God is about conferring honor and dignity: Oh! let us be exhorted in our places most heedfully to beware of reproaching and disgracing the work of this day. And for prevention thereof, there is no better way in all the world than to take direction from the word of God, how we are each of us from this day forward to behave ourselves. In a word:

(1) I will begin with myself. Much work is laid, or like to be laid, upon my weak shoulders. I will labor to sum it up in a word.

I am to carry it not as a Lord but as a servant, yet not as man's but the Lord's servant. Now, the greater the master, the greater the service.

I am to be zealous in my master's service: to give myself wholly to these things. I am in all godliness to labor to be exemplary.

I am to labor that my doctrine may burn, and my conversation may shine.

I am to make differences between the clean and unclean, so as to labor to change and purge the one, and confirm and strengthen the other.

As I am to give cordials to some, so I must be sure to administer corrosives to others. And what I do this way, without partial respect to persons, you must not, you cannot, you ought not to be angry: for so I am commanded.

Here is some (and but some) of my work, and yet here is work enough, and work hard enough. Yet this must be attended, or I shall reproach the work of this day. And therefore for my help herein I crave, and humbly challenge an interest in, all your fervent prayers who would not have your God reproached.

(2) I will now come to you, my Brethren and usual hearers: something you are to do, and not a little, neither.

You are to pay me that reverence which is due to an ambassador of Christ Jesus.

You are to bear me a great deal of love (I Thess. 5:13). You are, indeed, highly to love every minister of Christ Jesus; but, if you can (notwithstanding the vast disproportion between myself and others) you are to love me best. You are to obey me (at least) so far as I watch your souls (Heb. 13:17).

You are to communicate to me of your carnal good things, both that which is stable, sufficient, and (according to your capacity) honorable—and that not as a piece of alms or charity, but of justice and duty (Rom. 15:27, 1 Cor. 9:11, Gal. 6:6, 1 Tim. 5:17-18).

You are to pray for me, and to pray much and fervently always for me, but especially when you expect to hear from God by me.

You are to endeavor by all lawful means to make my heavy work, as much as in you lies, light and cheerful (Heb. 13:17). And not by Unchristian-like behavior to myself, or one another, or other Churches of God, or any whether within or without [a Church], or to God, or man, to add to my burden and to make my life among you grievous and my labor among you unprofitable.

So that you see, here is work enough for you also. And therefore by your leave, and in your name, what I just now requested for myself, I will also desire for you: of all praying persons, that they would pray for a sufficiency of grace, that both you and I may give up a good account in the season thereof. And as every lover of God's honor will, so let them, say: Amen.

"Cursed Be He . . ."*

Post Meridian, 24 November, 1689

Jer. 48:10 (first part). "Cursed be he that doeth the work of the Lord deceitfully."

[*Sermon preached at Salem Village, November 24, 1689.]

My brethren and ,beloved, friends and neighbors, we have lately, you know—even but this last week past—been doing a great work of the Lord: *viz.* building him an house and habitation. Now, it most highly behooves us (you and me) to be very wary lest we should be found deceitful, and so pull down a curse instead of a blessing upon ourselves and the heads of our poor children. And therefore I have thought good, for prevention hereof, to spend some time upon meditating on this text, now read in your audience.

In these words, two things may be taken notice of:

1. Here is a curse denounced. "Cursed be he, etc."

2. The object of this curse, or a description of the person or persons this curse shall light upon: namely, they who do the work of the Lord deceitfully. What may need explication I propose to take notice of in handling the doctrinal point, which is this:

Doctrine: *It is a cursed thing to do the work of the Lord deceitfully.*

1 Q.   What is meant by the work of the Lord?

2 Q.   When is the Lord's work done deceitfully?

3 Q.   What is meant by being cursed? ("Cursed be he, etc.")

4 Q.   Why is such a one as does the Lord's work deceitfully so cursed?

5 Q.   How may it appear that such are so cursed?

Question 1. What is meant by the work of the Lord?

Answer: By *the work of the Lord* in Scripture, many things sometimes and in some places are intended which I shall now pass by, and speak only of the meaning of this phrase according to the sense and import of our text and doctrine. As:

1. By *the work of the Lord* is intended the execution of the judgments of God according to his divine commandment. And in this sense is our text especially to be understood. "Cursed be he that doeth the work of the Lord deceitfully": i.e., the work of the Lord in destroying the Moabites, and doing execution upon them: which God hath now given in charge to the Chaldeans, by a secret instinct concerning the Moabites—as by an express word to Saul concerning the Amalekites (I Sam. 15:3). So the meaning is: Cursed be those Chaldeans to whom I have given a charge to destroy Moab, who shall be deceitful in doing this work that I have cut out for them and appointed to them. (As is plain by the other part of the verse: "And cursed be he that keepeth his sword back from blood." A curse there is on such as shed not blood when they have commission from God, as well as on those who do the like without such divine commission—so Jer. 50:25.) The destruction of Babylon is called the work of the Lord: though man be made use of in it, yet it is God's work whose providence, justice and power appears in it.

2. By *the work of the Lord* is intended church-work, temple-work and sanctuary-work which is undertaken by and from God's command and authority. So, speaking of Jerusalem (Neh. 3:5) says the text, "Next unto them the Tekoites repaired; but their nobles put not their necks to the work of the

Lord": i.e., to the repairing the mines of Jerusalem, which God by a special providence called them with others to be the repairers of. But to their shame and dishonor, says the holy ghost, they would not meddle in this matter: the meaner sort would and did, but their nobles and chief would not; and so all the service relating to the building of the Temple David calls it the work of the Lord (I Chron. 28:20).

3. By *the work of the Lord* is intended the work of preaching the Gospel, or the performance of the ministerial office (I Cor. 16:10): "Now if Timotheus come, see that he may be with you without fear: for he worketh the work of the Lord, as I also do." Hence ministers of Christ Jesus are said to be called to that work of the holy ghost (Acts 13:2).

4. By *the work of the Lord* is intended the divine service or worship which is exercised in the Lord's house (Neh. 10:33)—"for all the work of the house of our God." This is a general and comprehensive expression, wherein they engage and tie themselves to the upholding of all God's service in his house.

5. By *the work of the Lord* is intended sometimes more generally all good works, whatsoever they are, by which God and Christ may be glorified, and the kingdom of grace more and more advanced—and that both in our own souls and the souls of others (I Cor. 15:58). "Therefore, my beloved brethren, be ye steadfast, unmovable, always abounding in the work of the Lord," etc.—i.e., doing daily more and more for God and his service, as God puts opportunity into your hands. And all these senses are imported in our text and intended in our doctrine.

Question 2. When is the Lord's work done deceitfully?

Answer: In general, then the Lord's work is done deceitfully when it is not done as the Lord's work: i.e., when due respect is not had to the dignity and other excellencies of the person for whom the work is—as is plain from Mal. 1:14. "But cursed be the deceiver, which hath in his flock a male, and voweth and sacriceth to the Lord a corrupt thing: for I am a great king, saith the Lord of hosts, and my name is dreadful among the heathen." Whereby is plainly intimated that the slighty apprehensions of the great God is the cause of men's slighty and deceitful performance of his holy work and service.

But yet a little more, particularly in a few things:

1. Then the work of the Lord is done deceitfully when it is done for another end than God designs and prescribes. As for instance:

(1) When a man undertakes that great and dreadful work (which I have so lately undertaken among you) of ministerial office, merely as a trade—to pick a living out of it—quite contrary to the design of God in this most holy service (I Pet. 5:2): "Feed the flock of God which is among you, taking the oversight thereof not by constraint but willingly; not for filthy lucre, but of a ready mind." So a Popish writer says, we preach the Gospel amongst us (says he) *tantum ut nos pascat et vestiat:* merely for food and raiment. Ministerial employment (as has been hinted) is the Lord's work. Aye, but now when a man aims principally at himself in it, then he does it deceitfully: for he converts

God's service to his own service; and that which God hath designed for his own glory, to his own private profit. Everyone will readily acknowledge such a one to be—as indeed he is—a deceitful worker: for he works for himself, and yet pretends he works for God. As if an ambassador, entrusted by his prince to do him special service, should under pretence of serving his master do indeed somewhat for him, but yet chiefly and principally aim at himself. And so it is here. It is very true, as one wittily says, the ministry is a most noble calling; aye, but it is a bad trade—a pernicious trade indeed.

(2) Again, when a man undertakes civil government and disposing justice to the wicked, out of a pretence of zeal for God's service and honor, but yet in truth aims at himself and his own private interest: such a one is deceitful in the Lord's work. As you see in Jehu, who did cut off the house of wicked Ahab, and slew that cursed woman Jezebel, and Jehoram the king of Israel, and Ahaziah the king of Judah, and the seventy sons of Ahab, and the brethren of Ahaziah, and also all the worshippers of Baal, and utterly destroyed the house of Baal—and all this according to the commandment and appointment of God: this was the zeal for the Lord that you find him boasting of (II Kings 10:16). Aye, but still poor Jehu did not forsake the sins of Jeraboam: his fire was false fire; he was rotten-hearted (as the text tells us, v. 29-31). So that though Jehu did the work of the Lord, yet because he did it for another end than God designed, he did it deceitfully.

(3) Again, when persons attend any duty, any service or ordinance—suppose baptism, the Lord's supper—hearing, praying, fasting or the like (which are the Lord's work), but yet aim at some private or carnal interest, some by-end of their own; if that be the principal weight that moves them, not the honor, service and glory of God, the getting of grace and increasing in grace, then these also are to be ranked among such as do the work of the Lord deceitfully. And God may say—yea, God will say—to such as to those deceivers of old (Zech. 7:4-6): "Did ye at all fast unto me, even to me, etc.?" God does not deny that they did fast; nor will he deny what duties you have performed: aye, but he will remember them with such cutting interrogatories that it would be better for you that they were forgotten than that they were remembered. God will speak (as it were) after this manner: I know you heard my word preached at such a time and such a time, and you fasted and prayed at such a time and such a time. Aye, but did you fast to me, even to me? Did you hear to me, even to me? Did you get any good by hearing my word? Are you a whit better now than you were before? Have you broken off from any sin that before you were addicted unto, etc.? Have ye not done all these things for yourselves—for your own repute, credit, etc.?

"All True Believers Are Urgently Desirous of Sensible Manifestations of Christ's Love"*

Canticles [Song of Solomon], 1st chap.

[*Sermon preached at Salem Village, October 23, 1692.]

I Canc. 2: "Let him kiss me with the kisses of his mouth: for thy love is better than wine." In these words, two things are observable, *viz.*: (1) a request; (2) the reason of it, or the motive to press it.

1. Here is a request, desire, or petition. "Let him kiss me with the kisses of his mouth."

2. The reason of this request, or the motive to urge the grant of this petition: "For thy love is better than wine." We shall begin with the first, *viz.*

   1. Then, here is an option, wish, desire, or petition in the former part of the words. "Let him kiss me with the kisses of his mouth." Where we may note:

      1. The matter wished or desired, *viz.*, kisses.

      2. The person wishing or desiring these kisses, *viz.*, the spouse, or church, the Bride, the Lamb's wife, (Rev. 21:9). And so in her every true believer (II Cor. 4:13).

      3. The manner how she would be kissed, *viz.*, "with the kisses of his mouth."

      4. Last, the person she desires these kisses of or from, *viz.*, her Bridegroom, her Beloved, the Lord Jesus Christ. Let him (that is Christ) kiss me. Let him kiss me, i.e., Let me see him manifested in the flesh, say some. Let him kiss me, i.e., Let me have friendly, familiar feeling, and sensible manifestations of his love, say others. For kisses were, and are, used amongst friends, for manifestation of love. Hence we may take up this doctrine, *viz.*

Doctrine: *All true believers are very urgently and fervently desirous of sensible and feeling manifestations of the love of Christ, their Lord, Bridegroom, and Husband.* This is imported in this earnest wish of the church here for kisses of Christ. Now, it is evident that kisses are mentioned on sundry occasions, used for divers ends, and signified several things.

1. We read of a kiss of true affection. As the father kisses his son. Jacob kissed Isaac (Gen. 27:26-27). David kissed Absolom (II Sam. 34: *ult*), the father kissed the prodigal (Luke 15:20). And a brother kissed his brethren, as Joseph kissed his brethren (Gen. 45:15). And Aaron kissed his brother Moses (Exodus 4:27). And the son kissed his father, as Joseph kissed his father Jacob (Gen. 50:1). And Moses kissed his father-in-law (Exodus 18:7). And one friend kisseth another, as David and Jonathan (I Sam. 20:41). And the like.

2. We read of a kiss of valediction. As Naomi kissed her daughter-in-law upon parting with them (Ruth 1:9).

3. We read of a kiss of subjection (Psalm 2:12). Kiss the son, i.e., readily and willingly, and lovingly and gladly submit unto, and obey the commandments of Christ Jesus, the Son of God.

4. We read of a kiss of treachery. Thus Joab kissed Amasa (II Sam. 20:9). And Judas kissed his Master, Christ (Matt. 25:49). These are the kisses of enemies, which are deceitful, says the Holy Ghost (Prov. 27:6). Such was Absolom's flattering kisses (II Sam. 15:5).

5. We read of kisses of idolators, or idolatrous kisses (Hosea 13:2): "Let the men that sacrifice kiss the calves." Idolators in token of their adoration of their idol, were wont to kiss their [blotted] (I Kings 19:13, and Job 31:26-27).

6. We read of whorish, lustful, and carnal kisses, as of the whore in the Proverbs, 7th chap, 13.

7. We read of a kiss of reconciliation. Thus Esau kissed his brother Jacob (Gen. 33:4). Joseph his brethren (Gen. 45:15). David his son Absalom (II Sam. 14: *ult*). The father his prodigal son (Luke 15:20).

8. We read of a spiritual kiss. Text. "Let him kiss me," etc. 8 ch., 1.

9. We read of a holy kiss (Romans 16:16). "Salute one another with an holy kiss." With a sincere, chaste, honest, [illegible], brotherly, religious kiss, proceeding from a heart wherein was not a little, but abundance, of holy love, and as a token of it. In those times they had a custom to kiss one another, and that not only among the Jews, but even among the Christians also, who (as history says) after prayers, were wont to express their love to each other, by wishing grace and love of God to one another, and so parted with a kiss. To this purpose is that I Cor. 15:20, II Cor. *ult*: 12, I Thess. 5:26, I Pet. 5:14.

10. Last, we read of a kiss of approbation (Prov. 24:26).

Question. But now it may be asked, what are meant by the kisses mentioned in the text. (1st Ans.) More generally, in two or three words; (2nd Ans.) More particularly, by opening the allegory, for the text is purely allegorical.

1st. Ans. These in general: Since the Church desires kisses in the plural number, kisses of Christ's mouth, it may refer:

1. To a kiss of reconciliation. Absalom, after he had highly incensed his father, why, his father was reconciled to him again, and in token thereof, kisseth him (II Sam. 54: *ult*). And so in the parable, the father was reconciled to his prodigal son, and confirms his reconciliation with a kiss (Luke 15:20). Why, so the church here desires a kiss, a symbol, a seal of her Beloved's reconciliation. *Q. D.* Oh, with Absalom, I have offended my Heavenly Father. As the Prodigal, I have run away from my Father, I have lived too long upon the husks of this world. Oh, I fall down, and confess mine iniquities. Oh, be reconciled to me, and give me a kiss of reconciliation.

2. To a kiss of affection. Jacob showed his affection to his son Isaac by a kiss. And Joseph to his brethren. Oh, let Christ manifest his affection, his love to me.

3. Last, to a kiss of approbation. Oh, let me see and feel that Christ accepteth my person and my services. As, Eccles. 9:7: "Go thy way, eat thy bread with joy, and drink thy wine with a merry heart, for God now accepteth thy works."

2nd Ans. More particularly, we may see what is intended by this allegory, or metaphor, by running the parallel, and so:

1. We may consider, what is meant by kisses?

2. What by kisses of his mouth?

1. Then what may be meant by kisses?
   Ans.   In these following particulars:

1. Kisses betoken love and good will to the party kissed. Why, so then, when the church desires kisses of Christ, she means tokens and manifestations of his love and goodwill to her.

Q. D. Thou dost love me, as a testimony of it thou hast died for me. Oh, let me sense and feel thy love. Kiss me, i.e., evidence to me feelingly thy love and goodwill to me. Let me see, let me feel, let me sense thy love. As Cant. 2:14: "Let me see thy countenance, let me hear thy voice; for sweet is thy voice, and thy countenance is comely."

2. Kisses betoken a hearty conjunction and cordial union between two parties. Why, so when the church desires kisses of Christ, she means farther tokens and assurances of the blessed conjunction and union that is between herself and the Lord Jesus Christ. John 17:21: "That they may be one in us."

3. Kisses betoken such a friendship as allows a liberty of access and communication at all times. Why, so when the church desires kisses of Christ, she means more spiritual intimacy and communion with Christ. "When wilt thou come unto me?" says the soul (Psalm 101:2). She desires to dwell in the house of the Lord, and there to behold his beauty (Psalm 27:4): "With my soul have I desired thee in the night; yea, with my spirit within me will I seek thee early" (Isa. 26:9).

4. Kisses leave such impressions as engage the affections to a future remembrance of the object. Why, so when the church desires kisses of Christ, she means such favor and manifestations of Christ's love and grace that she may never forget his love. Cant. 1:4: "We will remember thy love more than wine." I desire to see thee, "as I have seen thee in the sanctuary" (Psalm 63:1-2).

5. Kisses oblige the giver to show farther favors and acts of love and goodness to the party he bestows them on. Why, so when the church desires kisses of Christ, she means that Christ would lay himself under such obligations of love and friendship to her, as that he may never forget her (Psalm 37:28; Romans 11:1-2). "Can a woman forget her sucking child? Yet will I not forget thee" (Isa. 49:15-16).

6. Kisses are a confirmation of love. Why, so when the church desires kisses of Christ, she means strongest and sweetest confirmation of his love (Psalm 35:3): "Say unto my soul, I am thy salvation."

7. Kisses are the especial privileges of covenant relations, as husband and wife, etc. Why, so the church when she desires kisses of Christ, she means those special manifestations of his love which are peculiar to his church and elect. *Q. D.*, by virtue of covenant relations, I may sue for kisses.

8. Kisses are very sweet among true friends after some jars and differences, whereby they testify true reconciliation. Why, so manifestations of Christ's love are exceeding sweet after there hath been a seeming breach and estrangement, especially since they know the fault is wholly on their side.

9. Kisses are high favours when they come from great persons, and beget in others longing after the like favour. Why so the expressions of Christ's favour to the [illegible] makes the daughters of Jerusalem long after the like. Cant. 6:1:

"Whither is thy Beloved gone, O thou fairest among women—that we may seek him with thee." Compared with the last verse of the 5th chapter: "His mouth is most sweet."

10. Kisses are exceeding sweet among friends that have been long absent. Why, so Christ's manifestation of his love after a long-seeming absence is exceeding sweet (Cant. 3:1-5).

11. Kisses are wont to be used as an initiatory ceremony in courteous entertainment, as in the case of the [illegible] and extravagant prodigal (Luke 15:20). Why, so the kisses of Christ are the first beginnings of blessed entertainment with God and Christ.

12. Last: Kisses, tho' but of the hand, of a great personage, a prince, or princess, is a very grand honour, but to kiss the mouth is extraordinary. Why, so the kisses of Christ's mouth are an infinite and exceeding great honour.

Salem-Village Land Transactions, 1690-1700

Date of Sale	Grantor (Seller)	Grantee (Buyer)	Acreage	Price
Jan. 2, 1690	Nathaniel and Hannah Ingersoll	Samuel Parris	4½	Gift
Feb. 15, 1692	John and Hannah Shepard	Samuel Parris	2	£10
Aug. 13, 1693	John Bullock (of Salem Town)	Samuel Parris, Jonathan Putnam and John Putnam III	10	?
Dec. 5, 1693	Thomas and Sarah Haines	Samuel Parris	3	£12
July 3, 1696	Samuel and Elizabeth Parris	William Russell (of Reading)	3	£12
Feb. 16, 1697	Samuel Parris	Jonathan Putnam and John Putnam III	*	?
Aug. –, 1697	Samuel Parris	Nathaniel Ingersoll	4½	£18
July 2, 1700	Samuel and Dorothy Parris	John Giles	2	£17

*"...one-third part of a piece of meadow which I bought in partnership with Jonathan Putnam and John Putnam..."

The Will of Samuel Parris (1720)

In the Name of the Ever Blessed God, I Samuel Parris of the Town of Sudbury in the County of Middlesex, in his Majesty's Province of the Massachusetts in New England, clerk, being of a perfect and sound disposing mind and memory, but perceiving the approach of the King of Terrors drawing near, therefore make and declare (after many other wills made) do declare this to be my last will and testament, viz.,

Imprimis, I humbly commit my precious soul into the hands of the Living God as my merciful Father of Christ Jesus, his carnal son and my only Savior and Redeemer, through whose merit only I look for mercy from the Lord at that

Day. And this vile body to the dust here to be buried by my Executors in trust herein named, without any pomp and as little expense as decency will admit, and as to that little which God hath mercifully left me of once a fair worldly estate, I will and bequeath thereof as follows:

(Namely) that all my just debts and levies be duly paid.

Item, I give unto my loving daughter Elizabeth Barron and my son-in-law her husband Benjamin, to each of them, ten shillings to buy them rings, besides all the household stuff, silver and money and plate and other things which I have formerly given unto them, except what hereafter is excepted, and is now in full of her whole portion from me her father.

Item, I will and bequeath unto my loving sons Noyce Parris and Samuel Parris, their heirs, executors, and assigns forever, one certain tract of land or plantation near Spick Town [i.e., Speights Town], being part of a plantation sometimes called Cotton Boll, upon which tract of land, near the common road leading from the town called Bridgetown to the aforesaid Spick Town, hath stood for many years a large, fair Quaker meeting house and yard for burial, with other edifices, with all the benefits and profits thereof or pertaining [?] thereunto or anywise belonging, situate, lying, and being in the parish of Saint Peter in the Island of Barbados, and was let out the 27th of February, 1656, for the term of 82 years from the date aforesaid by my honored uncle, John Parris, of the aforesaid island, Esquire, as attorney to my honored father, Thomas Parris, at that time of the city of London, merchant, unto Richard Hall, carpenter, and Thomas Clark, cooper, both of said Island of Barbados, containing twenty acres, be the same more or less, as by lease recorded in the Secretary's office in the Island aforesaid the 20th of August, 1657, may more fully appear, which said tract of land descended to myself and heirs forever by virtue of my aforesaid father Thomas Parris's last will and testament in the island aforesaid and recorded in the aforesaid Secretary's office September the 4th, 1673, by which will he appointed and nominated myself to be his sole heir and executor of all his whole estate, both real and personal, in the island aforesaid.

Item, my will is that if either my aforesaid sons should depart this life without lawful issue, or be lawfully seized of the aforesaid premises, then the same shall descend to either of my surviving sons and their lawful heirs, executors, or assigns forever, and if it should please God that both of my aforesaid sons should die before they be seized of the aforesaid premises, leaving no lawful heirs, in such a case my will is that, and I hereby bequeath, that all the premises abovesaid to my loving daughters Dorothy Brown and Mary Parris in equal proportion, and to their lawful heirs, executors or assigns, forever.

Item, I give to my aforesaid son Noyce Parris, who hath dedicated himself to learning, my whole library of books of learning, saving such books as are in English shall be divided among my three other children, namely Dorothy Brown, Samuel Parris, and Mary Parris.

Item, I give unto my aforesaid sons my father's picture and my own picture and my maps of the world at large and my iron candlestick, a standing one, all which are at present in the hands of my aforesaid daughter Barron, which I hereby will to be divided to them or the survivor of them.

Item, I give unto my said son Noyce Parris my escrittoir, my coat of arms, and my best saddle.

Item, I give unto my son Samuel Parris my silver seal and my agate case of knives.

Item, I give unto my loving daughter Mary Parris my whole [illegible] looking-glass now in the hand of my aforesaid daughter Barron.

Item, I give unto my son Samuel Parris my riding beast and a colt of three years old.

Item, I do hereby freely and absolutely give and bequeath unto my sons aforesaid, Noyce and Samuel Parris, all the residue of my undisposed estate, both royal and personal, in whatsoever part of the world to me belonging, they paying to my daughter Mary Parris on some convenient time one hundred and ten pounds in the current money of this province.

Item, I will and bequeath unto my son Samuel Parris my Indian woman Violet and to his heirs forever.

Item, I give unto my daughter Mary Parris the linen that her mother gave her and the silver that her mother gave her and the cup with one handle. I give her two of the cows.

Furthermore, I do hereby request and desire that worshipful Francis Fullam, Esquire, of Sudbury and Mr. John Rice of Sudbury, yeoman, to be my executors in trust to see this my last will fulfilled and executed, unto whom I give full power to sell and alienate forever my lands and building in Boston if occasion call for it to defray charges, and furthermore I intreat my aforesaid executors to give their assistance to my aforesaid sons not only during their minority but thereafter, also, as the occasion shall require. To each of which, my executors in trust in my sons' minority, I do give each of them forty shillings apiece to buy them rings.

Item, I give unto my daughter Dorothy Brown a silver [illegible] and one silver spoon.

Sam^{ll} Parris

Signed and sealed and publicly declared in presence of us:

> Phillip Thompson
> Zechariah Heard
> Richard Heard
> Johanna Moundjoy

[Will probated March 28, 1719/20]

Inventory of the Estate of Mr. Samuel Parris, Late of Sudbury, Deceased [illegible] , 1719/20, and was taken by us the Subscribers, March the 25th, 1720, [illegible] was Shown to Us to be Mr. Samuel Parris's Estate.

	£	s.	d.
His wearing apparel	20	0	0
His Library	58	19	1
His Coat of Arms	5	0	0
[canopied bed & furnishings]	13	0	0
a bed in the chamber with bedding & green curtains	7	10	0
a bed in the porch chamber & bedding with white curtains	7	0	0
Linen and sheets	7	10	0
Plate and [illegible] glass	7	10	0
Pewter and a pewter still [?]	11	10	0
2 brass kettels, 2 brass pans and other brass things	9	0	0
2 iron pots, 1 kettel, 2 pair of andirons and other iron things	5	0	0
2 Scridders	8	0	0
a chest of drawers	1	0	0
2 trunks	0	10	0
a looking glass	00	8	0
2 tables	0	6	0
chairs	1	5	0
a seal's skin chest and 3 other chests	1	4	0
a cupboard	0	9	0
[?] barrels whole dry culks [?] and other things	1	10	0
Corn, Indian & English, 10 bushels	10	10	0
Agate case of knives and forks and silver seal	1	10	0
2 horsekind	9	0	0
2 oxen	13	0	0
5 cows	22	10	0
5 young cattle 2 years old	9	0	0
2 steers, 1 year old	3	0	0
7 sheep & 3 lambs with the hay	3	10	0
3 swine 1 year old and four pigs	4	16	0
cart with cop & pin	4	0	0
plow irons	0	10	0
harrow & a stand	0	11	0
3 axes	0	12	0
2 hoes	0	8	0
wedges and betel [?] rings	0	3	0
a grindstone and iron winch	0	4	0
scythe & scythe tackling	0	6	0
2 yokes & irons belonging	0	8	0
a plow chain	0	10	0
2 forks	0	2	0
2 hand saws & hammer & pinters [?] & shane [?]	0	9	0
2 pair of halyards	0	14	0
2 saddles & bridles	3	0	0
a side saddle & pillion	3	0	0
a gun	1	0	0
a burning glass	1	0	0
meat, beef & pork	3	10	0
an Indian girl	30	0	0
a house and land in Boston	[no sum entered]		

Sudbury, June the 20th, 1720. Ephraim Curtis & John Noyes & Jonathan Wilk then appeared before me the subscriber, one of his Majesties' justices of the peace, and made oath to this inventory that the several particulars contained therein were valued by them accordingly to their best skill and judgment as they stand therein appraised.

[signatures]

An Account of What Has been Received Into and Paid out of the Estate of Reverend Mr. Sam^ll Parris, Late of Sudbury in the County of Middlesex, Clerk, Deceased, by the Executors Named in His Last Will and Testament.

	£	s.	d.
[Receipts]			
a house and land sold at Boston pursuant to the Testator's Will to pay his debts	120	00	00
Cash received of Danl Walker due to the deceased	2	00	00
Rent received of the tenants at Boston at sundry times *viz.*, of Mrs. Hannah Bedford.	6	07	06
also of Mrs. Mary James at sundry times & payments	6	15	00
2 cows sold at nine pounds four shillings & six	9	04	06
4 more received in corn & sheep	4	17	00
Total	141	04	00

Debts of the said Deceased paid out as followeth

[Here follows an itemization of debts to 30 persons ranging from 44 pounds down to 5 shillings.]

Total   129   13   05

Chapter Sixteen

The Wilkins Family

[The Wilkins family was one of many in Salem Village whose accusations helped convict one or more witches. We have included the family here for its representativeness rather than to suggest that it played an unusually active role. Other documentation on the Wilkinses, including genealogies, deeds, and the will of Bray Wilkins are found in Chapter Thirteen (pages 163ff), which deals with the executed wizard John Willard, a Wilkins in-law.]

Governor Richard Bellingham versus
Bray Wilkins and John Gingell (1666)

[Richard Bellingham, a lawyer, emigrated to Massachusetts in 1634 and settled in Boston. In 1638 he received from the General Court a grant of 700 acres of meadow and woodland in the western part of what would become Salem Village. In 1659, having in the interim served two terms as governor of the colony, Bellingham sold the land to Bray Wilkins and John Gingell, then of Lynn. Wilkins and Gingell paid Bellingham £ 25 in cash and received from him a mortgage for the balance of the £ 250 purchase price, with interest at 8 percent. In June 1666, having the year before again been elected governor, Bellingham brought two actions against Wilkins and Gingell: The first action was for illegally retaining possession of the land after they had (according to Bellingham) forfeited it by defaulting on their mortgage payments; the second, for continuing to conduct logging operations on the disputed land.

The following documents pertain to the case. In some instances the documents were summarized when the record of the case was published in 1913.]

Testimony of Richard Way

Richard Way, aged forth-two years, deposed that the last of January 1664 he was with Wilkins, Gengall, and Nathaniell Putnam at Mr. Richard Bellingham's house, and he heard the latter say that he would mortgage it for two thirds, that the land which they had improved should be in their third part, [and] that they should go on with their building, etc. *[The meaning seems to be that Bellingham agreed to negotiate a new mortgage for one-third the original sum, with Wilkins and Way, of course, receiving title to only one-third the land upon payment of the sums due.]*

When they went to the Governor the next summer to demand their third part, and showed several receipts from him, also their accounts for the farm, he looked at the papers, and upon their demanding their return he said: "No, now I have them I will keep them"—and so did; which action was so grievous to the spirit of this deponent that after the said Wilkins and Gengell were gone out of the room this deponent stayed back again and desired the Governor to consider how dishonorable a thing this action of retaining their receipts would be unto him. Whereupon he replied: "Here is one of the receipts which was not written by myself; take that if you will." And he took it to me, but owned that he had received the sum in that specified, and the rest he would keep, and so did.

Testimony of Bellingham's Attorneys

John Smith, aged about forty-two years, and William Howard, aged about fifty-seven years, deposed that on June 20 [1666], they demanded possession of the farm in behalf of Mr. Bellingham, and Bray Wilkins owned then that the past winter he had felled and made from off the said farm six thousand barrel staves for Mr. Curwin, etc.

Testimony of Nathaniel Putnam

Nathaniel Putnam, aged about forty-six years, deposed that the latter end of January 1664, Bray Wilkins having "by Providence his house burned, and by that means being brought to a mean and low condition, I myself and some other neighbors taking the sad condition of the said Bray Wilkins and his family into our consideration, we were willing to contribute something to the help and assistance of the said Bray Wilkins in his sad and deplorable condition provided that the said Wilkins might have the benefit of it himself. And then understanding that the farm he then lived on, where his house was burned, was entangled to Mr. Richard Bellingham, our new Honored Governor," he went to treat with him, Lieut. Richard Way being also present, etc. The Governor promised that the division of the farm should be left to indifferent men, and said that there was much due for interest. To which Lieut. Way replied that he hoped he would not take interest *and* have the benefit of the improvements which had been made. Finally the Governor agreed to leave that matter also to arbitration.

Writ

Writ, dated 19 June, 1666, signed by Jonath. Negus for the court, and served by Willm. Howard, marshal general's deputy, by attachment of three parcels of cedar shingles lying near Wilkins' house, and two parcels near Gingell's house. Defendants had made bolts, clapboards, and other vendable commodities.

Testimony of Phillip and Jonathan Knight

Phillip Knight, aged about fifty-two years, and Jonathan Knight, aged about twenty-four years, both of Salem, deposed that Samuel Wilkins, of Bray Wilkins' family, informed deponents that they had cut twenty thousand white oak barrel staves the past year, and had cut about eleven hundred feet of boards.

[In both cases the jury returned a verdict in favor of the defendants, Wilkins and Gingell, but in each instance the court refused to accept the verdict. In 1673, however, Bellingham's executors (Bellingham had died the year before) negotiated a new mortgage with Wilkins and Gingell, joined by William Ireland and Aaron Way, under which the four were able by 1681 to take title to at least a part of the original land.]

Chapter Seventeen

The Putnam Family

Putnam Genealogies

First Generation

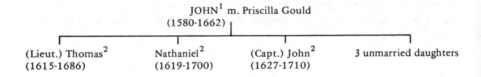

JOHN[1] m. Priscilla Gould
(1580-1662)

(Lieut.) Thomas[2]	Nathaniel[2]	(Capt.) John[2]	3 unmarried daughters
(1615-1686)	(1619-1700)	(1627-1710)	

Second Generation

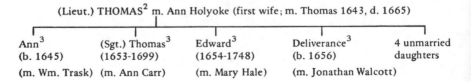

(Lieut.) THOMAS[2] m. Ann Holyoke (first wife; m. Thomas 1643, d. 1665)

Ann[3]	(Sgt.) Thomas[3]	Edward[3]	Deliverance[3]	4 unmarried
(b. 1645)	(1653-1699)	(1654-1748)	(b. 1656)	daughters
(m. Wm. Trask)	(m. Ann Carr)	(m. Mary Hale)	(m. Jonathan Walcott)	

(Lieut.) THOMAS[2] m. Mary Veren (second wife; widow of Nathaniel Veren; m. Thomas 1666)

Joseph[3] (1669-1725)
(m. Eliz. Porter, daughter of Israel Porter, 1690)

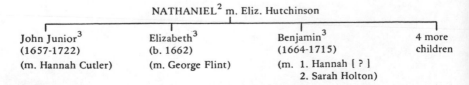

NATHANIEL[2] m. Eliz. Hutchinson

John Junior[3]	Elizabeth[3]	Benjamin[3]	4 more
(1657-1722)	(b. 1662)	(1664-1715)	children
(m. Hannah Cutler)	(m. George Flint)	(m. 1. Hannah [?]	
		2. Sarah Holton)	

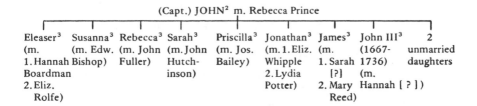

(Capt.) JOHN² m. Rebecca Prince

Eleaser³	Susanna³	Rebecca³	Sarah³	Priscilla³	Jonathan³	James³	John III³	2
(m.	(m. Edw.	(m. John	(m. John	(m. Jos.	(m. 1. Eliz.	(m.	(1667-	unmarried
1. Hannah	Bishop)	Fuller)	Hutch-	Bailey)	Whipple	1. Sarah	1736)	daughters
Boardman			inson)		2. Lydia	[?]	(m.	
2. Eliz.					Potter)	2. Mary	Hannah [?])	
Rolfe)						Reed)		

The Property of Lieutenant Thomas Putnam, Senior: A Documentary History

Walter Price and Thomas Cole to Thomas and Nathaniel Putnam (1652)

Walter Price and Thomas Cole of Salem have sold unto Thomas Putnam [Senior] and Nathaniel Putnam 140 acres of upland and 14 acres of meadow.

This entry is only by way of *caveat* [i.e., warning], their writing being not yet acknowledged before a magistrate.

Their writing bears date the first month [i.e., March], the 3rd day thereof, 1652.

John Putnam "The Elder" to Thomas Putnam, Senior, and Nathaniel Putnam (1653)

Be it known to all men by these presents that I, John Putnam the elder, of Salem in the County of Essex, yeoman, do alien, give and grant unto my son Thomas Putnam of the same, the one moetie, or half, of all my lands, meadows and pasture, except what I have formerly granted to my son Nathaniel Putnam and his heirs, all lying and being within the bounds of Salem, in the County of Essex abovesaid. . . . And by these presents granted unto my said son Tho. Putnam full power and authority to make equal division of such lands and meadows as are yet undivided, and where division is already made and bounds set, that these bounds shall stand for landmarks between him and his brother.

In witness whereof I have hereunto put my hand and seal, this 3rd day of the first month [i.e., March] , 1653.

The mark of John Putnam and his seal.

Signed, sealed and delivered in the presence of us,

Emman. Downing
Will. Norton

John Putnam came before me and acknowledged this to be his act and deed, 13, May, 1661.

Per me, Will. Hathorne

Recorded per me, Hilliard Veren, Recorder

Thomas Putnam, Senior and Nathaniel
Putnam Divide Their Property (1669)

Whereas there is about 500 acres of ground, more or less, lying together in one parcel, and also several other parcels of meadow, which have been held in partnership between Lieut. Thomas Putnam and his brother Nathaniell Putnam, both of Salem, which now by mutual consent they have made division of between them [as follows] . . .

Imprimis, to say: the said 500 acres of land, be it more or less, containing meadow and upland, the whole parcel being bounded as followeth: *viz.,* with Ipswich River so-called on the north, with the land formerly called Jeffery Massey's northeasterly, with the land of John Ruck and the land of the said Thomas Putnam east-southerly, with the land of the said Nathaniell Putnam southerly, and the land of Jonathan Walcott on the west. . . . [A dividing-line running through the property is then described.] The land to the northeast of the said divisional line to belong to the said Tho. Putnam, and the land to the southwest to belong to the said Nathaniell Putnam. . . .

The meadows in partnership lying on the north side of the River are also divided as followeth, *viz.:*

2. To Thomas Putnam, the meadow adjoining to the north side of the said River, lying from the bridge to the lower end of a parcel of upland of the said Tho. Putnam's—of about 15 acres.

3. To Nathaniell Putnam, the meadow commonly called Price's Meadow . . . beginning where the former parcel of meadow ends . . .

4. To Nathaniel Putnam also, a pond called Massey's Pond, lying within the upland of Robert Prince.

5. The parcel of meadow formerly called Cromwell's Meadow also is divided as followeth: *viz.,* the brook that runs through the said meadow to be the bounds between them, and the southwest side to belong to Tho. Putnam and the northeast side to belong to Nathaniell Putnam.

6. And to Tho. Putnam, a small parcel of meadow about 3/4 of an acre . . . about 30 or 40 rods distant from the upper end of the aforesaid parcel last mentioned.

. . .

In witness hereof [they] have put their hands and seals, this 20th day of December, in the year of our Lord God 1669.

Thomas Putnam [with a seal]
Nathaniel Putnam [with a seal]

Signed, sealed and delivered in the presence of us,

Hilliard Veren, Sen.
Tho. Maule
Edmund Batter

Entered by me, Hilliard Veren, Recorder.   21 December 1669

Thomas Putnam, Senior to
Thomas Putnam, Junior (1686)

To all Christian people to whom this present writing shall come: Know ye that I, Thomas Putnam Sr., of the town of Salem, in the county of Essex, in New England, for diverse good and lawful causes and reasons me thereunto moving, but more especially for that true love and natural affection which I bear to my son Thomas Putnam Jr., I say in consideration hereof, I, the above Thomas Putnam Sr., do by these presents give, grant, pass over and freely confirm unto my son Thomas Putnam Jr. certain parcels of land, house, barn, orchard and fences, swamp and meadow as is hereafter expressed by the bounds thereof, be it more or less, the land on which is his housing and fencing, being part in the bounds of Salem and part in the bounds of Topsfield, bounded on the west with Ipswich river with a hornbeam tree and a maple tree marked on the end of an island on the east side of Ipswich river, which is also John Putnam Jr. bounds; from thence to run easterly to a black oak tree marked where now three fences meet, which is also John Putnam Jr. bounds; from that to run southerly by the land of John Putnam Jr. to a great black oak tree marked, which tree is commonly called Cromwell's bound tree, which is John Putnam Jr. bounds, and also now brother Edward's bounds; from thence to run easterly to a heap of stones lying at the east end of the little hill which is Joshua Rea's bounds, and also his brother Edward's bounds; from thence to run northerly by the land of Joshua Rea, to a great red oak marked, which is also Joshua Rea's bounds; from thence to run still northerly to a heap of stones, and so to a great white oak tree marked, and standing near the southerly corner of the meadow, commonly called Hathorn's great meadow; and from thence to run along as the fence of my meadow now runneth to Joshua Rea's meadow and so to run along by Joshua Rea's meadow till he come over the brook which runneth out of Hathorn's great meadow, to a red oak tree marked, standing on the north side of the abovesaid brook; from thence to run across the sponge of Hathorne's great meadow to a dead poplar on the bounds of Mr. Ruck's farm; from thence to run northerly by the line of Mr. Ruck's farm to a red oak tree marked, and [i.e., which] stands near the west corner of Jonathan Knight's field; which was from thence to run westerly across the swamp to the lower end of a little flag meadow; and so to run along by the east side of that meadow to the end of the swamp above it, till he come against a black oak tree marked and standing on the south end or corner of Bare Hill being on the north side of Andover highway, which tree is also his brother Edward's bounds; from thence to run southwest cross a swamp to a little ridge, on which stand two white oak trees marked, which are also his brother Edward's bounds; and from thence to run southeast to a great rock lying on the north side of the brook which runneth out Hathorn's great meadow; from that to run over the abovesaid brook by the bridge which is now made, and so all the upland, housing, orchard, fences, swamp and meadow on the easterly side of the abovesaid brook, till the abovesaid brook runneth into Ipswich river, which is near to the hornbeam tree and maple tree where he began.

Also a parcel of upland, swamp and meadow lying in the bounds of Topsfield, be it more or less, bounded on the east corner with the black oak tree which standeth on the south end or corner of Bare Hill, on the north side of Andover highway; from thence to run northerly to three white ash's marked and standing near Ipswich river, which is Lt. Pebodie's bounds, also his brother Edward's bounds; from thence to run over Ipswich river to the meadow commonly called Scuder's meadow; from thence to run up the river by the upland of Jno. Putnam Sr. till he come to the spring which runneth into the river of the south side of the bridge or causeway, which was made for Andover men; from thence to run easterly as Andover highway was laid out, till he come to the black oak tree on the north side of Andover highway where he begun.

Also five acres of meadow more or less, as it is bounded, now lying and being in the meadow commonly called Blind hole, or Rea's meadow, lying in Salem bounds, bounded on the south side with the meadow of Daniell Andrew, and on the west end with a island to a white oak tree marked, which is Daniell Andrew's bounds; from thence to run northerly to a little red oak tree marked, on the said island, which also is his brother Edward's bounds; from thence to run easterly to a stake standing near the upland of Joseph Porter, which upland is his easterly bounds, which stake is also his brother Edward's bounds . . .

. . .

In witness whereof I have set to my hand and seal, this second day of January, Anno Domino: 1685 [1685/86]. Memorandum, that it is to be understood that notwithstanding the abovementioned deed of gift, the grantor has reserved to himself the liberty of cutting what wood and timber he shall need for his own use, during the term of his natural life: this before the ensealing hereof. . . .

Thomas Putnam Sen.

Signed, sealed and delivered
in presence of us

Deodat Lawson
Nathaniel Putnam
Jonathon Putnam

Lieut. Thomas Putnam acknowledged the abovewritten instrument to be his act and deed. Salem. January second: 1685 [1685/86] before me Jno. Hathorne Asst.

The Estate of Thomas Putnam, Senior (1686)

The Will of Thomas Putnam, Senior

Know all men by these presents, that I Thomas Putnam, Sen., of Salem, being ancient and sensible of the declining of old age, and weakness and symptoms of mortality daily attending upon me, but being of sound mind and memory, blessed by God, do make this my last will and testament, this eighth day of February A.D. 1682/83 as follows:

I give my soul into [the] hands of Jesus Christ in whom I hope to live forever, and my body to the earth, in hope of a Glorious resurrection with him when this vile body shall be made like unto his Glorious body. And for the estate God has given me in this world (my debts being paid), I dispose of as follows:

I give and bequeath to my son Thomas Putnam and to his heirs and assignes the dwelling house he now lives in, with the barn and orchards, with all the land belonging there, to contain by estimation, 150 acres, be it more or less, according as it lies bounded, as is hereafter expressed: From Hathorne meadow as the water runs out of the meadow, till it comes into the Ipswich River, then from the bound by the river to the end of the island, to the great black oak between my cousin John Putnam's land and mine. From there to Cromwell's bound tree, and from there to a walnut tree and a little red oak where lies a heap of stones, the trees having fallen down, which is also the bounds between Joshua Rea's land and this land. From there to another heap of stones, and from there to the fence at Hathorn's meadow where is a tree marked by the fence, and from there with or along the fence all the upland and swamp, till it comes to the place where the water comes out of the meadow. From there [to] my sponge of meadow on the other side of the brook, and the upland on Jonathan Knight's side, till it comes to a marked tree, near said Knight's corner of his field next to Bear Hill, and then across the swamp to the cart-way that is at the lower end of the flaggy meadow, and to take in all the meadow, and to run by the swamp, not over the Andover Way, till it comes to the tree where there are three rocks, and the tree marked and the tree on the westward of the rocks, on the north side where the Andover Highway turns. And from there to the bound where I join to Topsfield men, and so to the River, till I meet Mr. Bayle's meadow at the spring, that runs into the River, a little above the bridge. And from the bridge, the Andover Road to be bounds to the tree, where there are tree stones, at the turn of the way, and from there to two trees marked on the ridge or top of the hill, that lies on the right hand of the path as we come from the bridge to Thomas Putnam's house. And from the two trees to a giant rock that is near Hathorn's Brook, where Thomas and Edward are to make a bridge over the brook against the corner of Thomas's field by his barn: within which bounds is included a piece of land, containing about 50 acres lying by the river. Said 50 acres also I give and bequeath to my said son Thomas, his heirs and assignes, together with the aforesaid house, barn and orchards and about 150 upland and meadow, all which my said son Thomas and his heirs and assignes shall have and enjoy forever, after my decease.

I give and bequeath to my son Edward Putnam and to his heirs and assignes a certain tract of land, upland and meadow, containing about 80 acres be it more or less, with the house he now dwells in, and the barn and orchard upon the said land. Said piece of land is bounded by the land before specified given to my son Thomas aforesaid, easterly, and the Ipswich River westerly. Also I give unto him, my son Edward, one piece more of land, lying upon the little hill, so called,

containing about 60 acres more or less, being bounded as follows: from a forked
walnut, that is also Joshua Rea's and Nathaniel Putnam's bounds, from there to
a stake and heap of stones near the cartway, from there to Cromwell's bound
tree so called, from there to a walnut and red oak blown down where there lies a
heap of stones, from there to the forked walnut. Also I give unto my said son
Edward one piece of land more, lying upon Bear Hill, containing about 60 acres
more or less, being bounded by the three rocks and a tree standing by them
marked, from there to Phillip Knight's bounds behind Bear Hill and from there
along Knight's line till it comes to a marked tree, and from the said marked tree,
across the land to a red oak tree standing by a great rock on the northeasterly
side of the Andover Road. Also I give to my said son Edward, a piece of meadow
containing four acres more or less, lying on the west side of the river, near his
house, and the upland against his said meadow, from the upper end of the said
meadow across my upland, to the top of the high hill, and so straight to my
brother Nathaniel's line, and then to run along the line, to his bounds, at the
lower end of the meadow, which is a heap of stones upon the top of a hill about
twenty pole from the meadow: containing eight acres more or less, of upland.
Also I give my said son Edward all that my part of meadow that lies in Hathorn's
so called, lying bounded by Joshua Rea's meadow on the west, Ezekiell
Cheever's meadow on the south, Jonathan Knight's upland on the east and
Thomas Putnam's sponge of meadow on the north, I give and bequeath to my
said son Edward and to his heirs and assignes forever, after my decease.

I give and bequeath to Mary, my beloved wife, and to my son Joseph Putnam,
borne by her, my said wife, all that my farm I now live upon, with all the
buildings and housing there upon with all the appurtenances there to belonging,
both upland and meadow, orchards, fences, and privileges there to belonging for
them to have, hold and enjoy the same, to them and their assignes to enjoy the
same, to them and assignes after my decease, for the term of my said wife's
natural life (they making no strip nor waste). Either of them or their assignes to
enjoy the one half part thereof, who are to maintain and keep in good repair
either of them their said part the said term. And after my said wife's decease,
then my will is, and I do by these presents bequeath the whole of all the said
farm buildings and appurtenances to my said son Joseph and to his heirs and
assignes from the time of my wife's said decease and forever after. Which said
farm contains about 120 acres be it more or less, that is to say the upland and
meadow or mowing ground that is adjoining to the house which is bounded as
follows: On the west with the land formerly Richard Hutchinson's, a red oak
marked near the house where Bragg dwelt, from there to a heap of stones and a
stake standing near my orchards, from there to another heap of stones, which
was the said Hutchinson's Corner toward the meadow, from there to a heap of
stones, which is Rea's bounds also, and Hutchinson's and mine, from there to
another heap of stones that is also the bounds of Joshua Rea's and Thomas
Putnam's and mine. From there across the upland down to the marked tree by
the meadow, which is my share of meadow in Hathorn's meadow, so-called
(which meadow is to be understood as part of the farm, as it now lies fenced),

and from there upland on the east to a tree fallen where is a heap of stones that is the bounds of Peeter Prescott's and Mr. Cheever's land. From there to Hammer-beam, so called, where lies a heap of stones on the stump. From there to a white oak on the top of the hill that is the bound also of Henry Kenny and Mr. Cheever's, and from there along by the land of Robert Prince's to a great white oak at Beaver Dam, and from there to the red oak marked by Hutchinson's land by Bragg's house. Also as belonging to the farm a piece of upland and meadow sixteen acres more or less lying on the west side of the great river, from the log bridge down the river to the place where the water runs from Thomas Putnam's and Edward Putnam's meadow into the river. From there to the top of the hill and straight to my brother Nathaniell Putnam's bound or line, from there to Prince's bounds by the pond, and so to a great rock lying near the highway where we go into the meadow, and so along the way to the bridge. Also one parcel of meadow more containing two acres more or less, lying in Hathorn's Little Meadow, so called, with the fences as it now lies, John Darling lying on the west, Joseph Hutchinson on the east, the brook on the south. Darling's upland on the north. Also five acres lying in Peeter's meadow, so called, be it more or less. Also my meadow at Bishop's, so called, containing two acres more or less. Also my meadow by John Nichol's upland, about two acres. Also my old orchard with all the land fences and timber with the share of Hathorn's farm as it now lies bounded by my brother Nathaniell Putnam's land and my brother John Putnam's land and with the land that was Robert Prince's. All, which said parcels of land and meadow with all the privileges and appurtenances thereof is a part and so by me accounted (as a part of my said farm) as belonging there unto, and is to be understood intended by me as so, and given to my said wife and son Joseph during the term of her life, and afterwards the whole to Joseph, his heirs and assignes forever, after the decease of his mother.

I give and bequeath to my beloved wife Mary and my son Joseph all that my house and ground in the town with all its appurtenances and privileges according as is mentioned and bounded in my said wife's bill of sale (which said house and ground my said wife bought of Phillip Veren before her marriage), to possess and enjoy the same the term of my said wife's natural life (after my decease); and after my wife's decease I give and bequeath all the said house and land as aforesaid to my son Thomas and my son Joseph, to have and to hold to them their heirs and assignes, forever after my said wife's decease. And my will is that when my said sons shall (them or either of them), divide the same between them in two distinct parts, they shall divide it equally and at the front next the street: to divide it there, an equal breadth each part.

I give and bequeath to my son Edward my half acre of land that I bought of Robert Temple and John Simond (deceased) and Job Swinerton, jr., as by their deeds of sales appears, to him and his heirs forever after my decease.

I give to my daughter Ann, deceased, late the wife of William Trask, to her four children: Ann, William, Sarah, and Susanna, ten pounds to each of them, to be paid as they come of age, the sons and daughters, as they come to the age of 21 years, in current pay.

I give to my daughter Deliverance 100 pounds to be paid her within one year after my decease, in part in household goods in proportions as her sisters have had, and the rest in current pay.

I give to my daughter Elizabeth, 43 pounds to be paid her in current pay, within one year after my decease.

I give to my daughter Prudence, 50 pounds to be paid her within two years, next after my decease, in current pay.

I give to my three sons: Thomas, Edward, and Joseph, ten acres of meadow more or less lying in the place called Blind Hole, joining to Joseph Porter's upland, to be equally divided between them, to enjoy to them and their heirs forever next after my wife's decease.

I give to Mary, my beloved wife, 50 pounds out of my estate after my decease, the plate to be a part (as inventoried), and the rest out of my other goods as she pleases (except any coined money which is to be excepted), and the said 50 pounds, with what shall remain of it or other of the estate undisposed of, by this my will as she is executor at her decease to dispose of it to and amongst my children as she shall think fit.

I give to my son Joseph after my decease all my plow gear and cart and tacking of all sorts, with all my tools, implements of all sorts and kinds and quality whatsoever, my mill stone and cider mill and appurtenances, and his mother to have half the use of them while she lives, provided she maintains the half of them, to keep them in repair and make them good at her decease.

I give to my servant Joseph Stacy if he shall live to serve out his time and be diligent, a piece of land containing about 11 acres of upland and swamp as it lies and bounded from the tree marked by Jonathan Knight's field, near his corner next to Bare Hill, and so by Thomas Cane's land, to a tree marked, on the hill called Bare Hill, so across, down to a rock and red oak tree marked, on the north side of Andover Road, and from there along by the swamp, along by the flaggy meadow side to the place where the carts have lately gone over, and so across to the said Knight's marked tree.

I do appoint and ordain my beloved wife Mary to be my executor and my son Joseph executor jointly together with his mother of this my last will and testament. It is to be understood and it is my will that in case I depart this life before my son Joseph becomes of age and my said wife see cause to marry another man (also before he comes of age), that then before she marries, the estate shall be divided between them and either to pay proportions of what legacies shall be unpaid. My said son Joseph may then choose his guardian to assist him and take care of his part. And my will is that my said son Joseph shall have the possession and improvement of his part at the age of 18 years. I do desire my loving friends and appoint them: Ensign Isreal Porter and Sargt. John Leach to be overseers to see this will performed, to whom I give twenty shillings each of them. In witness that this is my last will and testament, I have set to my hand and seal, the day and year first abovewritten, being the 8th day of February A.D. 1682/83.

Signed, sealed and declared to be the last will and testament of the said
Thomas Putnam by him, in the presence of us. With further additions; that in
case my son Joseph depart this life before he comes to power to make his will
(which I conceive to be when he comes to the age of eighteen years, when he is
to inpossess his estate, as by my will). I say if he dies before then, his estate (*viz.*
the land) to fall to his brothers, Thomas and Edward (only out of the land to his
brother Nathaniell Veren, the value of twenty pounds in pay), and the rest of his
estate to be divided among his three sisters, my daughters. It is to be understood
the housing is meant as the land, to the brothers.

Thomas Putnam, Sen. [and seal]

Witnesses:

Hilliard Veren
Thomas Field

Codicil to the Will of Thomas Putnam, Senior

This 4th day of January 1685

Whereas my will being made some considerable time past and therefore [I]
do see cause to alter some particulars in my said will, and it being the pleasure of
God to visit me sickness and weakness, yet through his goodness of sound mind
and memory (Blessed be God for it);

And whereas it is expressed in my will that I have given to my three sons,
namely Thomas, Edward, and Joseph, my meadow, being ten acres more or less,
lying in Blind Hole so called, adjoining the land of Joseph Porter, I do give and
bequeath it to my two sons Thomas and Edward as also part of the land that I
have purchased and given to my sons Thomas and Edward lying in Topsfield
Township at this time; and they [i.e., men from Topsfield] threatening as if they
would deprive them [i.e., Thomas and Edward] of it, the which if it should be,
then my will is that my land and orchard belonging to my old house, as also my
land that was my brother John Hathern's share of the Danforth's farm, all which
contains about eighty acres more or less, I do give to my three sons Thomas,
Edward, and Joseph, equally to be divided between them after my wife's
decease.

And whereas I have given my wife 50 pounds to be taken out of my estate
after appraisal, I do also give and bequeath to my son Joseph out of my estate
after appraisal his liberty of choice to take two oxen and two cows and six sheep
and a horse and a mare.

And whereas I have given to my daughter Deliverance a hundred pounds upon
my will [of which] there remains but 43 pounds to pay (the rest being already
paid), and as also my daughter Elizabeth having already received 68 pounds,

seven shillings and six pence, there remains to make her one hundred pounds, 31 pounds, twelve shillings and six pence.

My daughter Prudence also having received 59 pounds, five shillings, there remains to make up to her an hundred pounds, 40 pounds and fifteen shillings.

Signed and sealed as with some alterations and with some considerations in this my last will and testament, as witness my hand.

Thomas Putnam, Sen. [seal]

Witness to the whole will:

Israell Porter
John Leach

Petition of Thomas Putnam, Junior

Boston, June 17, 1686

To the Honorable Joseph Dudley Esq., President of His Majesty's Council and Territory of New England in America. The humble petition of Thomas Putnam, eldest son of Lt. Thomas Putnam of Salem Village, lately deceased, humbly shows:

That whereas my late honored father Lt. Thomas Putnam, deceased, made an instrument in form of will for the disposal of his estate, which instrument or will is now in the hands of Mrs. Mary Putnam, relict and executor of my late and honored father, these are to enter caution against the said will, humbly entreating your Honor that there may not be any procedure in the probation of said will until I be heard what I have to allege concerning it, your petitioner shall evermore be bound to pray, etc.

Thomas Putnam

Testimony of Israel Porter, John Leach,
and Thomas Field

Mr. Israel Porter and Mr. John Leach having renounced their legacies of 20 shillings per man given in this will, and Thomas Field, all three sworn, say that they were present (Field on the eighth of February 1682/83 and Mr. Porter and Leach upon the 4th day of January, 1685) and saw Thomas Putnam sign, seal, and publish this will to which this is annexed as his last will and testament, and that when he did so he was of sound memory and understanding to the best of their judgment, and Field further adds that he saw Mr. Veren sign with him as a witness.

Boston, 8 July 1686.   Jurat Curiam, J. Dudley, President
                                                      Attest, Daniel Allin, Clerk

Request of Mary Putnam

Mrs. Mary Putnam prays the allowance of Daniel Wicum for her attorney to answer the plea of Thomas Putnam, which is adjourned to July 22, 1686.

Petition of Edward Putnam, William Trask, and Jonathan Walcott

Boston, this 8th of July 1686

To the Honorable Joseph Dudley, Esq., President of His Majesty's Council and Territory of New England in America. The humble petition of the several persons underwritten, son and sons-in-law of the late Lt. Thomas Putnam of Salem, deceased, humbly shows:

That whereas there is an instrument called a will left by our late honored father Lt. Thomas Putnam late of Salem in the hands of our mother-in-law, which instrument as we humbly conceive was occasioned to be made as it is by our mother-in-law: by which instrument as we humbly conceive we shall be extremely wronged if it must stand in force against us; and whereas our brother Thomas Putnam with good advice as we humbly conceive hath entered caution against said instrument:

Our humble petition to your Honor is that he may have liberty and time to make his plea, by which means your Honor may come to understand how much we are all wronged. And so your Honor will be pleased to hear the cry of the fatherless and motherless and not suffer such an injustice to stand in force against us, to deprive us of that portion which by the law of God and man belongs to us, but that the power of administration of our deceased father's estate may be granted to our eldest brother Thomas Putnam, that he may bring in a true inventory of the same unto your Honor, that so each of us may have that proportion of our deceased father's estate which by the law of God and man humbly belongs unto us. In which request if your Honor shall be pleased to favor us, your humble petitioners shall evermore be bound to pray etc.

Edward Putnam
William Traske
Jonathan Walcott

The Estate of Mary Putnam (Widow of Thomas Putnam, Senior)

The Will of Mary Putnam (1695)

In the name of God, Amen. I, Mary Putnam, widow, of Salem in the County of Essex in New England, relict to Lieutenant Thomas Putnam of the town and county aforesaid, deceased, and Executrix to his last will and testament, being sick in body but of good and perfect memory, thanks be to almighty God, do declare and make this my last will and testament, in manner and form following:

Imprimis. My immortal soul I do desire humbly and believingly to commit unto the everlasting mercies of God, Father, Son and Holy Ghost.

My body I commit to the earth to be decently buried at the direction of my Christian friends and relations.

And my outward estate that I have left me to dispose of, I do dispose of it as followeth, *viz.*:

To my husband Putnam's children: *Item*, I give unto Thomas Putnam five shillings, and unto Edward Putnam five shillings, and Deliverance Walcot five shillings, and unto Elizabeth Bayle ten shillings, and unto Prudence Wayman ten shillings. Unto all which I have done something already according to my ability and might, and would have done more but that some of my husband's children and relations have brought upon me inconvenient and unnecessary charges and disbursements at several times.

And all the rest or remaining part of my estate, without doors or within doors, of what kind and nature so ever, I give and bequeath unto my son Joseph Putnam and to his heirs forever, whom also I do constitute and ordain sole executor of this my last will and testament, in witness whereof I have hereunto set my hand and seal this twentieth and eighth day of January in the year of our Lord, One Thousand Six Hundred Ninety and Five.

Witnesses			The mark of
George Jacob	Jurat by all three. May 20, '95.	Mary /\/\\) Putnam [seal]	
The mark of Sarah Cave			
The mark of Deborah Knight			

Essex Ss. By the Honourable Bartho. Gedney, Esq., Judge of the Probate of Wills, etc., for said county.

May 20th, 1695.

George Jacob, Sarah Cave, and Deborah Knight made oath that they were present and saw Mrs. Mary Putnam sign and seal this instrument, and heard her publish and declare it to be her last will and testament, and that she was then of a disposing mind to their best discerning.

Sworn, attest Steph. Sewall,
Reg.

Thomas Putnam's Caveat, May 6, 1695

Thomas Putnam enters caviat against the probate of his mother's will and prays that it may be stayed till he has opportunity to declare and plead against the same.

Salem, May the 6th, 1695.

Petition of Thomas Putnam, Edward Putnam, and Jonathan Walcott, June 3, 1695

Salem, this third of June, 1695.

To the Honourable Bartholomew Gedney, Esq., Judge of the Probate of Wills, etc., for the County of Essex.

The humble complaint and petition of us whose names are underwritten most humbly showeth that whereas our honoured father, Lieut. Thomas Putnam, late of Salem, deceased, did by his last will and testament appoint our brother Joseph Putnam his executor, together with his mother, in which said will our father doth several times make mention of an inventory or an appraisal of his estate that should be made before executrix or executor did meddle to dispose of his estate, yet contrary to our father's will they have for these several years used and disposed of our father's estate of their own will and pleasure, without exhibiting a just and true inventory of the same into any court of record, as we can find, though they also have been commanded by authority so to do.

And now also our mother-in-law [i.e., stepmother] Mistress Mary Putnam being deceased, our brother Joseph Putnam has exhibited an instrument into your Honour's office which is called his mother's will. Which instrument, as we humbly conceive, is not according to the intention of our father's last will and testament, for if she had any power to make any will she must derive it from his, and not having fulfilled his will, we humbly conceive, make her seeming power void.

Therefore, our most humble petition to your Honour is that before the aforesaid instrument pass the seal of your office, that your Honour would be pleased to command our brother Joseph Putnam, executor to our father's last will and testament, to exhibit a just and true inventory of the goods, estate, and credits our father died possessed of, into your registry of wills, and also a just and true inventory of the goods and estate of our father which was left at our mother's decease which was undisposed of by our father's last will and testament. For, though he be executor, his portion is therein stated as well as ours, and that both we and others that are concerned may have the liberty and opportunity to contest the aforesaid instrument before it pass the seal of your office.

So praying the all-wise God to give your Honour abundant wisdom that the cause which you yet know not you may search out, and to do that which is well pleasing in his sight, desiring nothing but that truth and righteousness may take place, we remain your most humble petitioners, always praying for you.

Thomas Putnam
Edward Putnam
Jonathan Walcott

Petition of Thomas Putnam, Edward Putnam, and Jonathan Walcott, June 10, 1695

To the Honourable Bartholomew Gedney, Esq., Judge of the Probate of Wills, etc., for the County of Essex.

The humble petition of Thomas Putnam of Salem Village, most humbly showeth that whereas I came this morning providentially to the Town of Salem and accidentally heard that my brother Joseph Putnam doth intend this day to prosecute a confirmation of that instrument which is called his mother's last will, against which there is caution entered in your Honour's office, and several of us that are concerned therein have also petitioned your Honour that we may have liberty and opportunity to contest the aforesaid instrument before it pass the seal of your Honour's office, which petition I do again most humbly pray your Honour would be pleased to hear and grant, though I am now here alone accidentally, for neither I nor either of my brothers concerned had any notice when we should have a hearing, as ever I heard of, and there being none of them here.

My most humble petition to your Honour is that your Honour would be pleased to appoint a time when we may have a hearing, and also to grant that a citation may be sent to Sarah Cave and Deborah Knight, who are two of the witnesses to the aforesaid instrument, to appear before your Honour at the same time to answer to what shall be alleged against them about their evidence, and that your Honour would be pleased to examine them apart about that matter, by which means your Honour, it may be, may find out great iniquity. For it is evident that our mother Putnam was not of a sound mind and memory for near three months before she last died, and that she had been looked upon by standers-by for dead several times before the date of the aforesaid instrument. For it seemeth very hard for flesh and blood to bear, that those which know not what an oath means in a word to swear away three or four hundred pounds from the right owners thereof, when the law also requires credible witness in so weighty [an] affair. Therefore, I also pray we may have liberty for summonses for witnesses.

So, praying that God, that has made your Honour a father to the fatherless, to give you wisdom to do that which is well pleasing in His sight, I remain your most humble petitioner.

Dated in Salem, 10th June, 1695

Thomas Putnam
Edward Putnam
Jonathan Walcott

Testimony of Nathaniel and Hannah Ingersoll

The deposition of Nathaniel Ingersoll and Hannah his wife, who testifieth and saith that we being discoursing with Sarah Cave some time about Mistress Mary Putnam's death, about the said Mistress Mary Putnam's making a will, and she told us she knew of no will she had made.

And Nathaniel Ingersoll further saith that Sarah Cave said further she did not believe she was capable of making any, and they add that this was some few days before she died.

Nathaniel Ingersoll

mark of
Hannah Ingersoll

Summons to Sarah Cave and Deborah Knight

Essex Ss. Bartholomew Gedney, Esq., Judge of the Probate of Wills, etc., for said County.

To Sarah Cave and Deborah Knight, Greeting:

Whereas complaint hath been made to the said Bartholomew Gedney, Esq., by Thomas Putnam, that the last will and testament of Mrs. Mary Putnam, deceased, was made by her when she was not of sound mind and memory, or at least that she was not before and after the making thereof sound in memory, unto which will you were witnesses—

You are in his Majesty's name required, both and every of you, to make your personal appearance before the said Bartholomew Gedney, Esq., on Monday next, being the 17th instant, at the house of Mr. Francis Ellis in Salem at two of the clock in the afternoon, in order to your being examined relating to said evidence. Hereof fail not, at your peril.

Dated in Salem, June the 19th, 1695, and in the seventh year of his Majesty's reign.

Steph. Sewall, Register

[The testimony of Sarah Cave and Deborah Knight has not been found.]

Testimony of William Griggs

The deposition of William Griggs, Senior, physician, who testifieth and saith that about the beginning of last winter, Mistress Mary Putnam, widow, late of Salem, deceased, sent for me in the beginning of her last sickness. And when I came to her first I found her in a good disposition of mind and spirit, and her discourse was very understanding. But, according to my understanding, I thought she was not a woman long for this world, by the disease that was upon her. However, I gave or left with her something that I thought might comfort her.

After a while I went to visit her again before her dying fits took hold on her, and then I found by her discourse that her memory and understanding was much decayed. And after her dying fits took her, they sent for me to come to her again, and I gave her something which I hoped might mitigate them. And then I found that her dying fits had so stupefied her understanding and memory that though she spoke sometimes seemingly rationally, yet presently she would say she knew not what. And I went several times to visit her after her dying fits took her, and according [to] that understanding which God has given me in diseases and in the constitutions of persons, and of what I saw in her before and after those dying fits took her, that she could not *possibly** be said to be of a perfect and good memory from the first time her dying fits took her to the day of her death, but much the contrary.

Mark of William Griggs

Testimony of George Ingersoll, Senior

The deposition of George Ingersoll, Senior, who testifieth and saith that this last winter I went often to visit my sister, Mistress Mary Putnam, widow, late of Salem, deceased, in the time of her last sickness, for she being my wife's only sister, and my wife not being able herself to go often to see her, I having little to do, went the oftener. And I perceived by her discourse that I had with her, before her dying fits took her, *that she failed much in her*** memory and understanding. But after her dying fits came upon her, her understanding and memory was so stupefied that when I came to visit her sometimes she would know me and sometimes she did not. And sometimes she would speak seemingly

*[In the original, a line is drawn through this word.]
**[In the original, the italicized words are marked out, and the words "she was of good" substituted.]

rational and presently would say I knew not what.*   And I must say that according to that understanding which God has given me in what I saw by her and heard her say in the times that I went to visit her after her dying fits took her, that she could not *possibly*** be said to be of good and perfect memory from the first time her dying fits took to the day of her death, but much the contrary, so far as I observed her.

George Ingersoll

Testimony of Timothy Lindall

The testimony of Timothy Lindall, aged about 53 years, saith that I was to see my mother-in-law Mrs. Putnam some time after she had her fits, and she spoke to me much of many things, but especially about her spiritual condition, as decently and rationally as ever I heard her speak. And from time to time when my wife went to see her, some did say they thought she did not know them that were there, but after they were gone she would speak rationally to her and speak of the persons and discourse that had been in the room, as my wife informed me.

Timo. Lindall

Testimony of Mary (Veren) Lindall

The testimony of Mary Lindall, aged about 45 years, saith that I was often with my mother Putman after she had her fits. From first to last, I apprehended her to be as rational as ever she was, between the time of her fits. But the nearer she grew to her end, the time of her having her reason was shorter than before.

And after people were gone that thought she had lost her reason, she would speak to me sensibly. And some told her that her husband's children would trouble her son, but she said she could not believe it. And when she desired advice about making her will, was advised to give them something. And she answered that there was nothing due to them. For, she said, she had given considerably already [?] among them, which she had not told any of it but to myself, and often said she desired to do the thing that was right.

Testimony of Thomas Preston

The testimony of Thomas Preston, aged 52 years or thereabouts, testifieth that some time in February last, Thomas Putnam being asked by one how his

---

*[The phrase "because she spoke so low" is here inserted in the original.]
**[This word is crossed out in the original.]

mother Putnam did, he answered and said she was a very weak woman. I question whether she will recover this sickness: her fits have brought her very low. But yet she retains her sense and reason, I think, as well as ever she had.

Testimony of Abigail Darling

The deposition of Abigail Darling, aged 20 years, who testifieth and saith that I was spinning at the house of Mrs. Mary Putnam, widow, late of Salem, deceased, about the beginning of January last past and then my aforesaid mistress had been sick for a considerable while, and about the eighth day of the month, as I remember, though I am not so certain of the day of the month as of the day of the week, for I remember it was upon a Tuesday that my aforesaid mistress, being in her chamber, fell down and we concluded she was dead, and we being all grievously frightened, some run one way and some another to tell our neighbors that she was dead. But after a considerable while she began to revive, and at last she seemed to mind what we did, but continued very sick, so that we thought she would quickly draw her last breath, and continued very bad all night.

The next day, being Wednesday, she died away again, and was gone for I know not how long, I not being always in the chamber with her that day. At night, she being somewhat rational, I perceived by the discourse of those that were there that they were exceedingly troubled that she had not made a will *and feared that she would die quite before she did make any. But at last she was urged by some that were there to make a will, which she seemed to be unwilling to do, but at last consented* [?] *

The next day, being Thursday, Deborah Knight and I were sent into the malt house to work, and all of a sudden we were called to go into the chamber to our mistress. And when we came into her chamber to her, there was Mr. Israel Porter with a paper written, and asked her to set her hand to it. And, Mr. Israel Porter steadying her hand, she made a mark on the paper and took off the seal and delivered to Mr. Porter. And then Deborah Knight and I signed for witnesses, and then Mr. Israel Porter told us that we must take notice that our mistress was sensible, or to that effect, but I thought presently with[in] myself that I would not testify so for all the world, for I could not testify that she was sensible, nor I could not testify she was not. For sometimes I thought she did speak sensible and sometimes I thought she did not. And I don't know but that I might tell Deborah Knight so. I know I told so at my father's house.

So I tarried there the Friday and Saturday following, in which she was very sick and weak. And Saturday night I went home to father's house, leaving her very sick. And the Monday following I called at the house as I went to

---

*[*In the original, a line is drawn through the italicized words.]*

Mr. Cheever's to spinning, and they told me she was much as I left her, but then I saw her not.

Mark of

Abigail  Darling

Ezekiel Cheever and Abigail Cheever testifieth and saith that Abigail Darling came to the house of these deponents to spin on the 14th day of January last, according to these deponents' best remembrance.

Ezekiel Cheever
Abigail Cheever

Testimony of Ann Douglass

The deposition of Ann Duglis, widow, who testifieth and saith that that very Monday that my sister Abigail Darling went to Mr. Cheever's to spinning, I was sent for to nurse my old mistress Mary Putnam, widow, late of Salem, deceased, and accordingly I went to her house that Monday night, and when I came to her she seemed to be sensible, for she knew me, though she was very sick and weak. And she continued pretty sensible for the first week I tended her, though on the Friday and Saturday she seemed to stare with her eyes. On the Saturday night I went home to my father Darling's house. On Sabbath Day night next, Joseph Putnam's wife sent for me again, fearing she would have a fit on the Monday or Tuesday next. While we was assisting her up, she died away and was gone for I don't know how long, but at last revived again for a while. And the same day she died away again, but at last revived again. So I tarried there the Tuesday and Wednesday and part of the Thursday following, in which time she had two or three fits every day. And not being well myself, and being frightened with her fits, I desired to go home. And Thomas Putnam coming there on Thursday, being the last day I was there, they desired him and I desired him to go get Sarah Cave to come to tend her, and accordingly she came the same day and I went home.

Mark of

Ann ✗ Duglass

Testimony of Israel Porter

The testimony of Israel Porter, aged 52 years or thereabouts, testifieth and saith that Mrs. Mary Putnam being about to make her will, I was desired to write it for her. Therefore, in order to [do] it, I did discourse with her about how she did intend to dispose of what she had to dispose of and what she would give to her sons and daughters-in-law. Truly, said she, I have done for them already according to my abilities, and if I should give them a small matter it will but give offense, and to give them a great deal I don't know how Joseph can pay it, for there is a great deal to pay yet.

Then I asked her whether she would not be willing to give ten pounds equally between them. She said, aye, it is easy to write down a thousand, but where will it be had. I asked her whether I should speak with her son to see what he thought of it, he being not well able to come to her. She said, you may if you will. Accordingly I did, and he said what his mother should do he would be satisfied with. And I made return to her, but she showed her dislike of it. But while I was waiting I was informed that I should set down five shillings apiece for three of them and ten for two of them. And her son should be Executor to her will.

And I do judge, according to my best understanding, she was of disposing mind, and because it did agree with all her discourse as far as ever I did discern, having heard her what she said at several times about settling her estate.

Israel Porter

Thomas Putnam, Junior to the Topsfield Men (1696)

Know all men by these presents that I Thomas Putnam [Junior] and Ann Putnam my wife, of Salem Village in the County of Essex in his Majesty's Province of the Massachusetts Bay in New England, yeoman, for and in consideration of 15 pounds in money to me in hand already paid, and security given me at the signing of these presents of [i.e., for] what shall hereafter be paid me, by Samll. Symonds, Senior, of the town of Boxford (of the one part), and John Towne and Jacob Towne, Junior, of the town of Topsfield (of another part), and John, Nathaniell and Job Averill of the town of Topsfield (of the other part), being all of the same County and Province aforesaid, being all owners and proprietors of the new mill that is now set up upon the Great River commonly called Ipswich River, . . . do by these presents . . . sell unto the aforementioned parties . . . about eight acres of upland, swamp and meadow-land, be the same more or less, as is hereafter expressed by the bounds, situated and lying on both sides of the aforesaid river, above the aforesaid mill. . . .

And in witness hereof we have hereunto set our hands and seals, this 4th day of June, A. D. 1696, and in the eighth year of the reign of our sovereign Lord William the Third, by the grace of God King of England, etc.

Thomas Putnam [and a seal]
Ann Putnam [and a seal]

Signed, sealed and delivered in presence of [us],

John Gould, Mary Pabody, Banja. Stacy [his mark]

Thomas Putnam and Ann Putnam personally appeared this 25th June 1696 and acknowledged the abovewritten instrument to be their act and deed.

Before me, Jonathan Curwin, Just. Peace

[Thomas Putnam, Jr. also sold two other pieces of real estate in these years: a lot to his cousin Eleazar Putnam in 1696 and a small lot (which included his house) to Samuel Braybrook in 1697.]

Report by the Administrators of the Estate of Thomas Putnam, Junior (1699)

An Inventory of the Estate of Lieut. Thomas Putnam, Late of Salem, Taken by us whose names are underwritten, the 22nd of June, 1699.

	£	s.	d.
Imprimis. The dwelling house and barn with about 160 acres of [torn] and meadow, with all the improvements upon it.	370	00	00
A piece of land at Amesbury	15	00	00
Two horses and one mare, all	8	00	00
Four oxen and three cows; one three year old heifer	20	00	00
One two year old heifer, two of one year old, three young calves	3	00	00
Three sheep and eleven swine and ten pigs	4	18	00
A cane with a silver head and ferule	1	15	00
One long table, four stools, a bedstead, two pine chests, an old cupboard	2	14	00
Four chairs, two [torn], a trundle bedstead with another high bedstead		18	00
Beds and bedding, brass and iron pots and pewter ironware within doors	7	04	00
A saddle and pillion and other small things in the house	1	00	00
For a cart and wheels and other tackling [?] without doors	3	00	00
	£ 437	09	—

Nathaniel Ingersoll
John Putnam, Jun.
Jonathan Putnam

Essex Ss. Before the Hon. Jonathan Corwin, Esq., Judge of the Court of Wills, etc., Mr. Edward Putnam and Mr. Joseph Putnam, Administrators, exhibited the abovesaid inventory, and made oath that the same is a true and perfect inventory of the estate of their brother, Lieut. Thomas Putnam, so far as hath come to their knowledge, and if more come to their knowledge, they will give account of the same into the Registrar's office.

Sworn. Attest, John Higginson

The above estate is credited per advance on the cattle sold per so much due from Salem Village £ 8 74 s.

Further Report by the Administrators of the Estate of Thomas Putnam, Junior (1704)

Account on the Estate of Lt. Thomas Putnam, Deceased

Essex Ss.

Edward Putnam and Joseph Putnam, administrators for the estate of Lt. Thomas Putnam, late of Salem, deceased, exhibited their additional account of their administration on said estate since the account allowed by the Hon. Jonathan Corwin, Esq., late Judge of Probate, etc., at Ipswich, Oct. 27, 1704, before the Hon. John Appleton, Esq., Judge of Probates of Wills, etc. in said County.

The Said Estate Credited

	£	s.	d.
Per real estate as per inventory in the former account	385	00	0
Per sundries of the personal estate as in the former account particularly examined	54	10	5
Per sundries of the personal estate in Edward Putnam's hands	23	17	0
Per rent of the farm	12	00	0
Per sundry in Joseph Putnam's hands	3	15	0
Per debts due to the said estate	10	00	0
	£ 489	2	5

The Said Estate Debted

	£	s.	d.
As per sundries on file as per account given in to the Hon. Judge Corwin, Esq.	£ 162	17	2
To further disbursements since said account was exhibited as per particulars appears:			
To sundry payments to sundry persons more than before allowed . . .	£	s.	d.
To Deac. Nath. Ingersoll	00	2	3
To Dan. Bacon, Jun.	00	15	1
To Col. Jno. Wainwright	3	04	6
To Capt. James Fry	1	01	0
To Benj. Stevens	1	00	0
To Capt. Walcott		3	6
To Henry West		5	6
To funeral charges		3	4
To Henry Wilkins		5	6
To Lt. Peabody	2	15	0
To Richd. Wheeler		8	0
To William Good		4	0
To Joseph Porter		6	0
To Jona. Fuller		1	9
To Sam. Shaddock		7	0
To Sam. Lane		1	11
To Josh. Brown & Josh. Bailey	5	06	0
To Ezekial Cheever		2	0
To Joshua Rea		10	0
To Tho. Fuller		9	9
To Benj Wilkins		6	8

	£	s.	d.
Per mistake: twice giving credits per Jno. Deale	00	08	8
Per debts not received per Sam. Rea		3	0
Per debts not received per John Darling		8	0
Per charges on the committee in laying out the farm, and expenses therein	2	14	0
To writing 3 bills of sale		6	6
To my trouble since I made up my account at Salem about said administration	3	13	0
To time and fees per registering and stating the account and administration		15	0
	£ 25	2	11

The land sold by the administrators for the payment of debts as to particular persons:

	£	s.	d.
To John Putnam, Tertius [i.e., 3rd]	15	00	0
To Charles Sergeant	6	00	0
To Joseph Hale	47	00	0
To Joshua Baily (land at [A] m[e] sbury)	8	00	0
	£ 76	00	0

To sundry old things which the administrator takes to himself, appraised at £13 16 6, part of which the said deceased's children have taken and the creditors not accepting of them. The said administrator Edward Putnam alloweth for the remainder—£6 16 07.

	£	s.	d.
Cr. per the personal estate and the land sold being	£ 180	2	5
Cr. goods sold Lt. Putnam	6	16	7
	£ 186	19	0

Edward Putnam } Administrators
Joseph Putnam }

Part Four

The Community: Salem Village

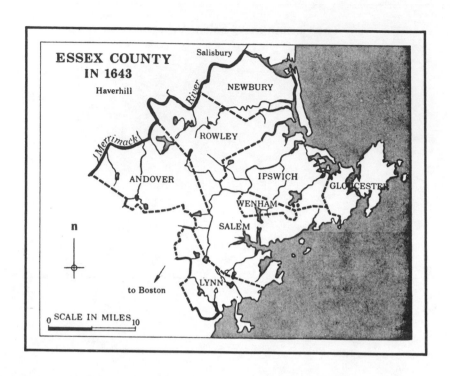

ESSEX COUNTY
IN 1643

Salisbury

Haverhill

NEWBURY

Merrimack River

ROWLEY

ANDOVER

IPSWICH

GLOUCESTER

WENHAM

SALEM

n

to Boston

LYNN

0 SCALE IN MILES 10

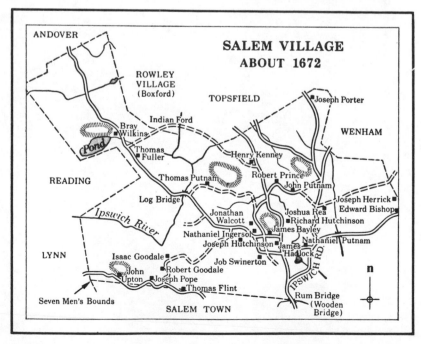

ANDOVER

SALEM VILLAGE
ABOUT 1672

ROWLEY
VILLAGE
(Boxford)

TOPSFIELD

Joseph Porter

WENHAM

Indian Ford

Bray
Wilkins

Pond

Thomas
Fuller

Henry Kenney

Thomas Putnam

Robert Prince

READING

John Putnam

Joseph Herrick
Edward Bishop

Log Bridge

Ipswich River

Jonathan
Walcott

Joshua Rea
Richard Hutchinson

Nathaniel Ingersol
Joseph Hutchinson

James Bayley

Nathaniel Putnam

James
Hadlock

LYNN

Isaac Goodale

Job Swinerton

John
Upton

Robert Goodale

Joseph Pope

IPSWICH RD.

n

Thomas Flint

Rum Bridge
(Wooden
Bridge)

Seven Men's Bounds

SALEM TOWN

Chapter Eighteen

The Village Forms

Petition of the Salem Farmers about the
Military Watch (1667)

To the honored General Court at Boston

The humble petition of the Inhabitants of the Farms belonging to Salem most humbly showeth:

Whereas your petitioners have been required by our Commanders to attend the military watch at Salem Town, which (considering how remote our dwellings are from the Town) we did and do still conceive law doth not require it of us.

But because we are men, subject to be partial in our own case, and might not be acquainted with all the laws, we did present or request to the County Court at Salem last June to give us their judgment therein: namely, whether it were our duty by law to attend the said watch or not. And the judgment of the said Court, as far as we perceived, was that we were neither bound by law nor reason to attend the said watch, except in case of an exigency (which we do fully consent to—[as we would] if our dwellings were many miles further from the Town than they are, in case they wanted help, and ourselves in safety).

Yet notwithstanding the judgment of the Court, they did again require us (by express warrant in his Majesty's name and per order of the Militia) to attend the watch. And most of us did obey rather to avoid any occasion of trouble (because the spirits of [the] men seemed to be very high) than that we thought it our duty by law.

Since [then] we presented our case to Major Denison, who, being the Major of this regiment, we thought was the next person to seek to for help, [and] who did write in our behalf to dissuade them from any further troubling of us. But all took no effect, but still they warned us to [attend the] watch, by the authority aforesaid, until the watch was ended.

Your petitioners did also request the last County Court at Ipswich to relieve us, but the Court was pleased not to determine the matter, but willing us rather to present it to this honored Court, which we do: as briefly as we can, humbly beseeching this honored Court to consider of our reasons, which are as followeth:

Imprimis: The remoteness of our habitations from the Town. Some of us live ten miles; some, eight or nine; the nearest are at least five miles from Salem meeting-house (upon the road)—and then 'tis nearly a mile farther to the sentry-place, and both horse- and foot-[men] required to go with arms and ammunition, every way fixed according to law, so that some of us must travel armed 11 miles to watch—which is more than a soldier's march that is under pay. And yet [we are] not excused from paying our part to all charges, both ecclesiastical and civil, besides the maintenance of our families [in] these hard times when the hand of God is heavy upon the husbandman.

2. The distance of our houses, one from another—some a mile, some further—that it is difficult sending one neighbor to another in dark nights in a wilderness that is so little cleared and [by] ways so unpassable.

3. The weakness of many of our families: when one man is taken away, the rest are some young, some sickly and weak—not able to help themselves, much less to make resistance if violence be offered. [So] that the news that we are to watch strikes like darts to the hearts of some of our wives, that are weak—[so] that one man was forced to go four or five miles to get a man to stay with his family, whilst himself went to Salem Town to watch.

4. The opportunity and advantage that Indians and other ill-affected persons have by knowledge-before, that such and such families are such nights left destitute of help for two or three miles about: for warning of the watch and watching is no private thing. For example, there was 29 warned for one night, as will plainly appear by warrants under the Captain's own hand and by testimony. Had they all gone, it would have cleared the strength of two or three miles about. If it be pleaded the number is altered [now] , and but four warned for a night, for answer [we say that] as sometimes it falls, four will clear two miles about. It may also be questioned, whether it be not a profanation of the Lord's Day for persons to travel so far armed (as is before expressed), to watch a populous town in times of peace—consisting of near 300 able persons within the limits of the watch (and ourselves left out).

Whereas the Captain pleaded an exigency at Salem Court, because a Jersey or Guernsy ship came in (as they said) in the night undiscovered—to which we answer, there were several of us in company with our Captain at the Fort, and we saw the ship some hours before night; and [it] was discovered before night in the Town to be a stranger. For how can it be thought possible that a ship could come in in a clear day, and none see her, considering how many boats are daily out a-fishing, and [considering that] Cape Ann and Marblehead lie before the harbor, and many men at work at the Fort that day, besides [the proximity of] a populous town.

They further pleaded, these were dangerous times, and they were not able to keep a watch without us. For answer, if we should grant that these times are more dangerous than former, yet not so much to Salem Town as to ourselves, and other places in this Colony. For we know no obligation upon the enemy first to assault Salem Town, when they may come ashore at diverse places and come upon us (and other places also, by land) and meet neither with fort nor 400 men under the warning of an alarm to oppose hem. 'Tis probable, if the French or Dutch should come, they will have a convoy of Indians from east or west, and come first upon remote dwellers. The consideration whereof is able to strike terror into the hearts of women and weak ones, especially considering what dreadful examples former times hath afforded in that respect, in this country, from Indians (and from others also), in the night season, when their husbands have been absent.

If what hath been said may be granted (as it may in every part be proved), then whether Salem Town hath not more cause to send us help to watch among ourselves, than we have to go to them—we consisting of not 50 persons able to watch; they a compact town, we so scattered [that] six or eight watches will not secure us. Our dwellings are so scattered and remote one from another, and so far from the Town, that Cambridge Village or Milton may as easy go to Boston to watch as we may go to Salem Town—and leave their families in a great deal more safety, because they have towns near to help them.

Your petitioners' humble request to this honored Court is that you would be pleased to release and ease us from this burden of watching, which is too heavy for us or our children to bear. Your petitioners shall always pray for you.

[October 15, 1667]	Job Swinnerton, Sen.	John Porter
	Robert Goodell	Richard Hutchinson
	Philip Knight	Iacob Barnet, Sen.
	Jonathan Knight	Richard Leach
	Isaach Goodell	Nathaniel Putnam
	Zachary Goodell	Iacob Barnet, Jun.
	Robert Prince	Joseph Hutchinson
	Joseph Houlton	Henrie Keine [Kenny]
	Jonathan Walcutt	Joseph Porter
	Nathaniel Ingersoll	John Putnam
	Robert Moulton	Giles Cory
	John Smith	Thomas Small
	Nath. Carrill	Benjamin Woodroe
	Job Swinnerton, Juner	John Leach
	Thomas Flint	Joshua Rea
		James Hadlock

[The General Court held a hearing about this petition on October 21, 1667 at which time it ordered that "henceforth all Farmers dwelling above four miles from the meeting-house shall be exempt from constable-watches, any law or custom notwithstanding." However, in January 1669 Nathaniel Putnam and

Henry Kenny were brought to court for refusing to participate in the watch and for "highly affronting and abusing" the officers and the Salem militia committee. For his actions Putnam was ordered to issue a public apology or pay a fine of £ 20.]

Votes of the Salem Town Meeting (1670)

At a general Town Meeting held April the 5th, '70: It's ordered that there shall be a new meeting-house built for the worship and holy service of God in public, and that it be about 60 foot long, 50 foot wide and 20 foot high in the stud, and to be set at the west end of the old meeting-house, toward the prison. And Mr. Wm. Browne Sen., Capt. George Corwin, Edmond Batter and Mr. Bartholmew are empowered to agree with carpenters and other workmen for to build the said house and finish it, not exceeding the sum of £1,000 price.

At a general Town Meeting held the 18th day, 5th month [i.e., July] 1670: It's ordered that the payment for the building [of] the meeting-house shall be raised by a rate [i.e., tax]. The Selectmen are empowered to make and raise the rate for payment of some for building a new meeting-house.

Petition of the Salem Farmers to the Salem Town Selectmen (1670)

We whose names are here subscribed, taking into consideration the motion that is now on foot concerning the building of a new meeting-house now at Salem, have with one consent agreed not to contribute to the same at all (not knowing how long it may be beneficial to us), unless you likewise of the Town will share with us when we shall build one for ourselves.

John Porter, Sen.	Henery Kenney
Thomas Putnam [Senior]	John Leach
Richard Leach	Thomas Small
Nathaniel Putnam	Bray Wilkins
Thomas Fuller	John Gingell
John Putnam [Senior]	Thomas Wilkins
Joshua Rea	Philip Knight
Robert Prince	Richard Hutchenson
Joseph Hutchinson	John Buxton
Joseph Holton	Jonathan Walcot
Nathaniell Ingersoll	Jobe Swinerton, Jun.
James Hadlock	Edward Bishop
John Wilkins	Joseph Herick
Zerobabel Endecott	Jeremiah Watts

March 1669/70

Testimony of John Putnam and
Joseph Hutchinson (1674)

[John Putnam, Senior, and Joseph Hutchinson testify] that being at a Town Meeting at Salem in the year '70, wherein the matter was to be decided whether the old meeting-house should be repaired or a new house built—there being several of the Farmers [present, they] sent in a writing wherein there was the subscription of several persons, [to the effect that] they would not contribute to the building of a new meeting-house without the Town would contribute to us in the building one ourselves. Lieutenant [Thomas] Putnam and John Putnam were desired by us to give this writing to be read in the Town Meeting. Capt. Corwin was moderator for that day and received a paper of Lieut. Putnam, which was that paper (as we do conceive) which we did subscribe to. And he [Corwin], being often desired to read that writing, would not read it till the vote was passed. And there being no negative vote, we had no opportunity to show our minds.

Petition of the Salem Farmers to the
General Court (1670)

To the honored General Court Assembled at Boston

The humble petition of the inhabitants of the Farms belonging to Salem, whose names are hereunto subscribed, most humbly showeth that whereas our habitations are so remote from our public meeting-house at Salem Town (as four miles the nearest, and the furthest eight or nine miles upon the road), that besides many other inconveniences and distractions in leaving our families, we judge it too far (if it may be lawfully remedied) to travel on the Lord's Day. This our condition many of us have several times presented to Salem Town by way of petition some years ago, in which we did request the Town [either] that we might have a minister amongst ourselves to maintain in common with them, or that we might have such a number of families allotted to us as dwell at such a distance from Salem as is before expressed, [i.e.,] from Beverly to Lynn bounds: that so we may maintain a minister ourselves. To which petition the Town have given us no answer, although we have used all the means we could.

This our condition we humbly present to the wise and Christian consideration of this honored Court, hoping if our bodies were in such an afflicted state, you would (according to equity) relieve us: how much more the condition of souls! Humbly entreating you to relieve us herein, as being our last means under God, from whom we hope to have relief. Your petitioners shall always pray for you.

October 6th [1670]

Thomas Small	Jonathan Knight	[illegible]	Thomas Fuller, Sen.
Lott Kellum	Philip Knight	Richd. Hutchison	John Putnam

John Smith	[illegible] Hutchison	Job Swinnerton, Sen.	Bray Wilkins
John Buxton	John Hutchison	[illegible] Putnam?	John Gingell
John [Wilkins?]	[illegible]	Robert Goodell	Nathl. Ingerson
Thomas [Flint?]	[illegible]	Nathl. Putnam	

[On October 26, 1670, the lower House of the colonial legislature—the Deputies—consented to the Farmers' request, but the upper House—the Assistants—refused to go along.]

Vote of the Salem Town Meeting
(March 22, 1672)

At a general town meeting held at Salem the 22nd of March 1671/72.

Voted that all farmers that now are, or hereafter shall be, willing to join together for providing a minister among themselves, whose habitations are above Ipswich Highway, from the horse bridge to the wooden bridge at the hither end of Mr. Endicot's plain, and from thence upon a west line, shall have liberty to have a minister by themselves, and when they shall have provided one, and pay him maintenance, that then they shall be discharged from their part of Salem minister's maintenance, and this to continue so long as the ministers abide with them and is maintained by them.

Provided always, that they shall bear all other charges whatsoever among themselves, both with respect to their meeting-house, and minister's house, or otherways whatsoever in carrying on this work, and also bear their proportion of all other public charges in the town.

Order of the General Court (October 8, 1672)

In answer to the petition of the Farmers of Salem, Richard Hutchinson, Thomas Fuller, etc., the Court judgeth it meet that all persons living within the tract of land mentioned in the Town's grant to the petitioners, together with all lands and estates lying within the said bounds, shall contribute to all charges referring to the maintenance of a ministry or erecting of a meeting-house there, and that they shall have liberty to nominate and appoint persons amongst themselves or [the] Town of Salem, not exceeding the number of five, who are hereby empowered (from time to time) for the making and gathering of all rates and levies [i.e., taxes] for the ends above expressed, and that in case of refusal or non-payment of the same by any person or persons amongst them, that then the Constables of Salem [Town] shall and hereby are empowered to make distress upon the goods of any that shall so neglect or refuse to afford their help in that case; and the same [Constables are] to deliver [these goods] to the persons aforesaid, to be improved [i.e., used] accordingly; and that when a ministry shall be so settled amongst them, they shall be freed from contributing to the maintenance of the ministry of Salem.

Chapter Nineteen

The Village Defines Itself

The Boundary Dispute with Topsfield
(1682-1683)

[The town of Salem was settled as early as 1626, four years before the founding of the Massachusetts Bay Colony. But the actual boundaries of the town remained vague until 1636, when the General Court drew a line six miles north of the Salem town meetinghouse as the northern boundary of the town's jurisdiction. But in 1639 the same body gave the town permission to "plant a village" beyond the six-mile limit, "near the river which runs to Ipswich." This area included much, if not all, of what would later become both Topsfield and Salem Village. In the next few years the Salem selectmen granted land in the region to a number of men; at the same time the town of Ipswich permitted several of its inhabitants to settle in the northern section of the same land. The settlers from Ipswich even hired their own minister. Apparently for this reason the General Court in 1643 modified its earlier order and granted the northern section of the area to Ipswich. Fifteen years latter these settlers organized as the separate town of Topsfield. In accepting this action the General Court added the proviso that Salem Town would retain jurisdiction over all the lands Salem had granted in the northern section. Thus, within the town of Topsfield were pockets of land which for tax purposes still belonged to Salem. Furthermore, for several reasons Salem had never made fully clear, in a legal manner, just which of these pockets it had actually granted to Topsfield.

For over thirty years Topsfield regularly attempted to tax the contested land, and just as regularly the owners of the land (who were already being taxed by Salem) refused to pay. With the formation of the Salem Village parish in 1672, this dispute became of major concern to the new Village, since the disputed lands lay within its bounds and in the hands of its inhabitants.

The largest owner of lands in the disputed territory was John Putnam, Senior, who therefore became the central figure on the Salem Village side of the controversy. Putnam took the "Topsfield men" to court—and in turn they took him to court—on a number of occasions. The boundary issue was not finally resolved until well after 1700.

In the particular case from which the following depositions have been selected, Putnam brought suit for trespass against one Thomas Baker (a Topsfield official) at the June 1682 session of the County Court.

For further information on the Topsfield dispute, see the Salem Village Book of Record.]

Action of the General Court (1639)

Whereas the inhabitants of Salem have agreed to plant a village near the river which runs to Ipswich, it is ordered that all the land near their bounds, between Salem and the said river, not belonging to any other town or person by any former grant, shall belong to the said village.

Order of the Selectmen of Topsfield (May 1682)

At a lawful meeting of the selectmen the 4th day of May 1682. We do hereby give full power to Mr. Thomas Baker, Corp. Jacob Townes and John How to demand of any or all the men of Salem or Wenham that [claim] some land or meadow in our town bounds, to show their rights and titles to those lands claimed by them and also their several bounds to those lands claimed by them. And if any or all of them shall refuse, or do not make it legally appear how they came by these lands they claim, to the satisfaction of the abovesaid Baker, Townes and How, we do hereby give them full power in the name of the town to make trespass on those lands, or sue the claimers thereof and prosecute the law against them or any of them, or to compound and agree with any of them as they shall see meet. And whatsoever they shall do therein, we will own and stand by and confirm, as witness our hands: John Gould Senior, Francis Pebody, Thomas Perkins, John Redington.

Testimony of Jacob Town and John How (1682)

Jacob Town and John How testify that Mr. Thomas Baker went with them to Goodman Niquall's house, where they met John Putnam, Senior, and showed them an order from Topsfield to demand of any of Salem men that claimed land within Topsfield bounds to show them their bounds and grants, and if they were not satisfied, they had liberty to fell timber on their claimed land and stand suit with them. Lieut. John Putnam told them that his land there was never laid out by any lot-layers and that he had no bounds except what his grant gave him. So deponents, before his face, felled one timber tree within Topsfield line a considerable way. John Putnam further told them that he had a hundred acres or more adjoining that [which] they felled the tree on [which was] within Salem line. Deponents told him he had more than his due there, and he had no reason to claim theirs.

Sworn in Court.

Order of the General Court (1683)

In answer to the petition of Thomas Baker, Jacob Town and John How, in behalf of the town of Topsfield, for explanation of an order of Court made the 19th of October 1658, referring to lands granted by Salem within Topsfield bounds, upon a full hearing of the case, and what hath been alleged both by Salem and Topsfield, the Court do judge that the aforesaid order refers only to such lands as were granted by Salem before the 10th of May 1643.

Salem Village and Salem Town (1690-1691)

Petition of Some Salem Villagers
(February 20, 1690)

We who are hereunto subscribed, understanding there is a motion of the Village for a Township, unto the Town of Salem, which motion we do comply with, provided we may have an enlargement, that is to say from Rum Bridge [i.e., "Wooden Bridge" on the map] down the [Endicott] River, so as the river runs, all the properties and the common lying on the north side of the said river, until we come to Beverly bounds. Now in case the Town of Salem do not see cause to grant our desires, we desire still to remain to Salem as we are, provided our just grievances may be removed.

> Joseph Houlton, Jr.; Joseph Hutchinson; Job Swinnerton;
> Daniel Andrew; Joseph Putnam; Nethanell Putnam;
> John Putnam [Junior?] ; Benjamin Porter; Israel Porter;
> Thomas Flint.

Petition of Salem Village to the General Court
(December 1690)

To the honored General Court now sitting at Boston

The humble petition of us whose names are underwritten, by the order and in the behalf of the inhabitants of Salem Village, most humbly showeth that whereas this honored Court in October 1672 was pleased to grant us an order in which they did empower us for the erecting a meeting-house and maintaining a minister amongst ourselves, and therein also declaring that when we so did we should be freed from the maintaining of the ministers of Salem;

Therefore our most humble petition to this honored Court is to give us an explanation of that Court order: whether or not this honored Court did intend that we should be freed from building and repairing and tending the meeting-house at Salem, as well as maintaining their ministers; which we have been forced to do, and also to build and repair our own without any help from the town of Salem—which has cost us near four hundred pounds besides yearly salary. Which burden we feel heavy for us to bear. And we have several times made our application to the town of Salem, but can get no relief.

Therefore we most humbly petition that we may be freed from building and repairing their meeting-house at Salem Town, or else that our public charges relating to the building and repairing our meeting-house may be equally borne by the town of Salem.

So hoping your Honors will be pleased to grant us our petition, we leave your Honors to the direction of the Most High in all weighty affairs that come before you; praying always for you.

Salem Village, this 9th December 1690

John Putnam
Thomas Fuller, Sen.
Francis Nurse
Daniell Andrew
Thomas Putnam

Action of the General Court on this Petition

Upon hearing this petition, it is ordered that the petitioners shall be free from any charge towards the meeting-house in Salem Town, or the maintenance of the ministry there, from the date hereof: Feb. 10, 1690/91.

Passed in the affirmative,
Per the said [Court],

Joseph Lynde, [Secretary]

Petition of Salem Town to the General Court (1691)

To the honored General Court assembled in Boston

We, the Selectmen of Salem [Town], having lately had a sight of a petition signed by Jno. [Putnam], Francis [Nurse], etc., and in the name of others of Salem Village, do present this briefly as our answer:

1. The terms which Salem Town holds our neighbors of the Village to are no other than what they gladly accepted of and were dismissed upon, as may appear by the Town record relating to that affair.

2. The whole township of Salem, of which the Village is part, was granted by the General Court for the bearing of public charges amongst us, and therefore we humbly conceive that no part thereof can be justly taken away without the Town's consent.

3. The Village contains the best part of the land belonging to our township, so that should the inhabitants thereof be dismissed from bearing public charge with us, we should be greatly disenabled for defraying those charges that necessarily come upon us.

4. Notwithstanding all this, to demonstrate to all mankind how favorably we will deal with them, we will on the next town-meeting-day propound to the town that if our neighbors of the Farms will at their cost and charge maintain their minister and meeting-house and charges thereunto belonging, and maintain the highways within their limits, and half the highway that parts between them and us, then we will maintain our ministers and defray the charges of our meeting-house and repair our highways and half the highway that parts between them and us.

Lastly. We are grieved to see the restless frame of spirit that prevails in some to trouble this honored Court with such trifles as this, the burden that they groan under so—not amounting to above the weight of six pence apiece per annum: which is inconsiderable to what goes before you during this calamitous and dangerous war. And we cannot but think it hard that the House of Deputies should pass a vote concerning what hath been before mentioned before we had the least knowledge of it—much less any notification to answer for ourselves.

We pray God direct and counsel you in all the weighty affairs before you.

Your humble servants,

By order, etc., in the name of
the Selectmen of Salem,

Samuel Gardner, Recorder

[For the final separation of Salem Village and Salem Town, in 1752, see the Epilogue.]

Chapter Twenty

The Village and Its Ministers

[Salem Village had troubles with each of its first four ministers: James Bayley, George Burroughs, Deodat Lawson, and Samuel Parris. In fact, divisions within the Village prevented any of the first three of these men from being officially ordained. Only in 1689, under Parris, did Salem Village actually organize a real "Church," in the official sense of the word (that is, a body of believers who had by covenant attested to their faith in God and their fellowship with each other and who were entitled to take communion together). Until 1689 the Village was merely a "parish"—a geographical unit whose only official function was the construction of a meetinghouse, the hiring of a minister (who could preach but not administer communion), and the choice of local men (the Village "Committee") to raise money for the minister's salary.

We have already presented documents conveying Burroughs' relationship with the Village. The following documents record the process by which Bayley and Parris ended their tenure in the Village pulpit.]

Salem Village and the Reverend
Mr. James Bayley

Deed of Property to Reverend James Bayley (1674)

We whose names are underwritten do upon consideration of Mr. James Bailey coming amongst us to the ministry, give unto him a certain parcel of up-land and meadow—to him, his heirs and assignees forever—the said up-land containing thirty acres, the meadow containing ten acres: *viz.*, Lieut. Thomas Putnam giving three acres of meadow lying in a parcel of meadow commonly called Cromwill's Meadow; Nathaniell Putnam giving eleven acres of up-land and two acres of meadow, the up-land lying and being upon the hill commonly called Hadlock Hill, his meadow lying in the abovesaid meadow commonly called Cromwell's Meadow; Capt. John Putnam giving ten acres of up-land and four acres of meadow (be it more or less), the upland lying upon the hill called Misty Hill butting upon a parcel of meadow, his meadow lying on the northwest side of a river called Ipswich River at the bridge called the Indian Bridge; Joshua Ray giving him six acres of up-land lying by and adjoining to the land of John Putnam upon the north side and the said Ray's upon the south side thereof; Joseph Hutchinson giving three acres of up-land and one acre of meadow, the upland lying upon the hill called Hadlock's Hill, the meadow lying in the meadow called Cromwell's meadow: this land and this meadow being laid out and bounded.

For the true performance of this we do oblige ourselves, our heirs and assignees, to the said Bayley, his heirs or assignees; as witness our hands to every parcel wherein we are concerned.

This 21 of February, 1673/74. And we promise each of us to assign deed of gift of all and every parcel.

Thomas Putnam
Nathl. Putnam
John Putnam
Joseph Hutchison
Joshua Ray

This is a true copy as attest.

Thomas Putnam, Jun.

Salem Village Votes to Retain Reverend James Bayley (1673)

[The following entry in the Village Book of Record was submitted as evidence by Bayley's defenders in the Village when they argued their case before the General Court in 1679. It was later omitted—deliberately, it seems—when the Book of Record was recopied some years later.]

23 June 1673. At public meeting it was voted that Mr. Bayley should continue in the work of the ministry amongst us still. . . .

[This omission is in the copy submitted to the General Court.]

Thirdly, it was also voted that Mr. Baylie should have 40 pounds in [illegible] and in drink and in [two or three lines illegible] amongst us in the work of the ministry.

This is a true copy taken out of our Book of Records and written by me.

Thomas Putnam, Sen.

Reverend James Bayley to the Inhabitants
of Salem Village (February 1679)

To the Inhabitants of the Farms now Convened Together

Beloved friends:

There hath (as yourselves well know) some uncomfortable divisions and contentions fallen out amongst us here, which I cannot express without much grief, fearing what effects there may be of it. And these divisions being about myself, my request and desire is, that as you have called me amongst you to the work of the ministry (which hath occasioned me, in order to a settlement, to expend some considerable estate amongst you), that so you will consider well how I was called, and in what condition I now stand amongst you: that so I may come to know what the will of God is, and what to do in this case.

And whereas Nathaniel Putnam and Bray Wilkins (as I have been informed) have publicly charged me, at a meeting here, as being not qualified for the work of the ministry, and (one of them) also for being offensive in practice, my desire is that you will be pleased to let me understand whether you are of the same mind. The great thing that I desire and pray for is that we may know and do the will of God; therefore, I pray, be serious about those things of so great weight.

So beseeching the God of peace to be with you and guide you in his way, I rest,

Yours in what God calls me to,

James Bayley

Febr. 11th, 1678/79

Some Inhabitants of Salem Village to
Reverend James Bayley (February 1679)

Answer to Mr. Bayley's Letter which [he] sent to the Inhabitants 11 February 1678/79. To consider his case amongst us and his present standing.

1. Upon our serious consideration, we cannot find that Mr. Bayley was called at all by those that were capacitated so to do. Therefore we think it will not [be] upon Mr. Bayley to prove his call amongst us.
2. If upon invitation of a few—and that but for one year—if Mr. Bayley should have carved out a considerable estate, we think he might have been better advised.

3. That which concerns the inhabitants in general, let that be so considered; if anything be of [a] mere private nature, let that be considered by persons concerned.

4. Mr. Bayley's present standing amongst us is upon suffrance. Therefore we think God calls Mr. Bayley and us seriously to consider what to do. We neither desire Mr. Bayley's damage nor dishonor, but [only] that we might have peace in order.

5. Mr. Bayley names two persons that are unsatisfied with his qualifications as to the work of the ministry: there be several others that be unsatisfied as well as they.

To the fifth particular we sign:

Aron Way	Henry Wilkins	Nathanl. Putnam
Benjamin Wilkins	Job Swinerton	Jeremy Watts
John Putnam	William Way	John Gingell
John Kenny	Thomas Fuller, Jun.	Henry Kenny
Thomas Wilkins	Bray Wilkins	

This being compared with their writing which Bray Wilkins and Joshua Rea brought to Mr. Bayley: by us being compared, we find it a true copy.
Daniel Andrew.   James Smith.   Nathl. Ingersoll.

Three Salem Villagers in Defense of the Reverend James Bayley (1679)

The abovewritten [petition] coming to our hands, and having noted the premises, we underwritten thought it necessary so far to take notice of it as to bear our testimony against it; [it] being, as we conceive, very unsuitable for so small a number of the inhabitants to presume to give such answer to Mr. Bayley's letter, which was directed unto—and an answer expected from—the body of the people by whom he was called. Also considering that some of the chiefest of the subscribers of the abovewritten acted zealously in his call to the work of the ministry amongst them.

Answer to their first article: We must needs say it doth not agree with the truth, for Mr. Baily was called by a general consent and vote of the inhabitants, who by order of the General Court had power and liberty so to do.

Answer to their second article: There being little in it but evidence of their slighting and flouting Mr. Bayley, we conceive it deserves not an answer.

Answer to their third article: We consider this matter of calling a minister concerns the inhabitants in general, being warranted thereunto by order of General Court.

In their fourth article they strangely express that Mr. Baylie's standing amongst us is upon suffrance, whereas it is evident that his continuance in the work of the ministry is desired by the inhabitants generally except the above subscribers, and Mr. Baily so engaged to them by his promise that he cannot leave us unless we release him—and, as an inhabitant, [he] hath his freedom and right amongst us as well as any other.

And in answer to their fifth, to which only they say they sign, as [being] unsatisfied with Mr. Bailie's qualifications for the work of the ministry, we say that it is strange that those of the above subscribers who think themselves the only persons capacitated to act about a minister, should so contradict themselves as to admit of Tho. Wilkins, Henry Wilkins, Jno. Keny, etc., as competent judges of a minister's abilities, in order of expelling of him. All which considered, we are sorry that our neighbors have proceeded in such an undue and immodest way, to the grief of Mr. Baily, with reflections on the rest of their neighbors, who do hereby manifest their desire of Mr. Bailie's continuance amongst us in the work of the ministry.

> Thomas Putnam, Sen.
> John Putnam [Senior]
> Joseph Portor

Some Salem Villagers Covenant
to Support a Minister (February 1679)

Voted: 16 February 1678/79

We whose names are underwritten, being sensible of the evil consequences of living without the public preaching of the word of God amongst us, do hereby engage ourselves one to another that we with our persons and estates (according to our proportion) will join for the getting of and maintaining of an able, pious and powerful ministry amongst us. Provided our neighbors and brethren mentioned in the Court order will join with us according to the proportion. We keeping in God's way for the attaining of such: amen.

Bray Wilkins	Job Swinerton	William Way	Thomas Keny
Nathanell Putnam	Henary Keny	Benjimin Wilkins	Thomas Fuller, Jun:
John Gingell	Joseph Hutchinson	John Putnam, Jun.	Thomas Wilkins
Jeremiah Watts	Aaron Way	John Keny	Henry Wilkins

Bayley's Opponents Agree to Request
Outside Help (February 1679)

Voted the 16 February 1678/79

We whose names are underwritten, being unsatisfied with Mr. Bayley's ministry, and with his call to that ministry among us, and his standing here, do hereby agree to desire the church of Salem [Town] for their help and advice in our case.

Bray Wilkins
Nathaniel Putnam
Jeremiah Watts
John Gingell
Henry Kenny
Job Swinnerton
Joseph Hutchinson
Aaron Way

William Way
Benjamin Wilkins
John Putnam
John Keny
Thomas Keny
Thomas Fuller, Jun.
Thomas Wilkins
Henry Wilkins

Some Nonresidents of Salem Village
Come to Bayley's Defense (March 1679)

We whose names are underwritten, having heard Mr. Baly several times teach, and upon the Sabbath days open and apply the Scriptures, we have been much edified by him, and do testify that what he delivered (to our understanding) was both orthodox and according to the mind of God speaking in the Scriptures; and do earnestly desire that the Lord would be pleased to continue him amongst us, and bear up his spirit in the midst of such discouragement as he may meet withal.

Moreover, concerning his conversation, as far as we can learn he is blameless and is generally known to be one of a very self-denying frame of spirit.

March 3rd, 1678/79

Zerubbabel Endecot
Isaiah Cooke
Willyam Osburne
Anthony Needham
Nathaniel Holton, Jun.

Samuel Aburne, Sen.
Nathaniel Holton, Sen.
John Pease, Sen.
Anthony Buxton
John Holton

Henry Kenny Brought to Court For Slandering
Reverend James Bayley (1679): Abstract of Depositions

Complaint of Thomas Putnam Senior, John Putnam Senior, Daniel Andrew and Nathaniel Ingersoll: that Henery Keeny [Kenny] had greatly slandered their minister, Mr. Bayeley, by reporting that he neglected family duties [i.e., family prayers], at several places, i.e., to John Collins, to the wife of Nathaniel Ingersoll, to the wife of Jonathan Knight, to Edw. Putnam, and to the wife of Joseph Holtone, Senior.

Warrant, dated April 4, 1679, for the appearance of Henry Kenny, for slandering Mr. Baily, minister, by reporting that he did not perform family duties. Also summonses to the wife of Nathaniel Ingersoll, the wife of Jonathan Knight, Edward Putnam, and the wife of Joseph Holton, as witnesses.

Ann King, aged about 50 years, deposed that being at Mr. Baly's house for three weeks together, she never heard him read a chapter, not expound any part of the Scripture, which was a great grief to her.

Edward Putnam, aged about 23 years, deposed that he heard Kenny make the charges. The wife of Nathaniel Ingersoll and the wife of Joseph Holten testified the same.

James Smith, Frances Geferd, John Shepard and Mary Woodrow deposed that they had lived in Mr. Bayly's family at different times, and he always performed family duties, morning and evening, unless sickness or some other unavoidable providence prevented.

Sworn March 2, 1678/79

Francis Geffards and Mary Woodrow deposed that during the time they lived at Mr. Bayley's house (one being a boarder there at times for the space of two or three years, and the other having lived there for about a year and a quarter) he read the Scriptures and other profitable books, and also repeated his own sermons in his family, as well as family prayers. He always endeavored to keep good order in his family, carrying himself exemplarily therein.

Advice of the Salem Town Church
(April 21, 1679)

Whereas the inhabitants at the Farms, being in difference amongst themselves in relation to Mr. Baily, have desired the advice of the church of Salem, and for that end they have given in their papers on both sides (which have been read); having also heard their discourses upon the matter, we find:

1. That the liberty granted to them by the town of Salem, whereby the Court order (to have a minister amongst themselves within such bounds) was not granted to any of them under the notion of church members, but to the whole number of inhabitants there—for their present ease, being so far from the meeting-house here.
2. By the records of the votes amongst themselves in relation to Mr. Baily in the year '73, whereby the people's general attendance on his ministry for above six years past, we find that he hath been their settled minister hitherto.

3. Setting aside human frailties, we find not any just exception against Mr. Baily—why he may not continue in preaching to them still as formerly.
4. We find that (notwithstanding the dissent of a smaller number yet) Mr. Baily's continuance in preaching amongst them is approved and desired by the generality of the people there, and by a considerable number of such as belong to Salem [Town] still, who do hear him sometimes for their ease.

Therefore our Advice is:

1. That the lesser number would submit to the desires of the generality of the people there for Mr. Baily's peaceable continuance, without any further trouble.
2. Whereas the continuance of a preacher amongst them is granted to them in this present state, it is to be understood only until there be a church amongst themselves; and then it is their liberty to choose and call either him or any other unto [ministerial] office, as God shall direct them. We do therefore advise that such as at first would seriously apply themselves to join the church here, that when by mutual consent there shall be a competent number to be a church there of themselves, that then they do make use of that liberty according to the order of the Gospel and law of the General Court.
3 That in their present state, all and only the householders amongst them do choose the five men to make the rate for the minister's maintenance.
4. We also advise and desire that what defects may be on the people's part in their minister's maintenance, may be reformed as much as may be, that Mr. Baily may give such a diligent attendance to his studying and preaching work, without distraction, that his profiting may appear unto all (II Tim. 2:4, I Tim. 4:15-16, II Tim. 2:15).

These things we propound and advise as agreeable to the general rule of the Apostle (Rom. 14:19): "Let us follow the things that make for peace, and things wherewith we may edify one another."

After the reading and considering of these fore-mentioned propositions, they were consented unto (for the substance of them) as the advice of the church: signified by their vote in the church meeting at Salem [Town].

April 21, 1679. Until things further appear.

John Higginson

Statement of Support for the Reverend James Bayley

We whose names are here underwritten, having had experience of Mr. Bayley's ministry amongst us, and desirous for his continuance amongst us in the ministry, do hereto set our hands.

Thomas Putnam, Sen.

John Putnam, Sen.

Richard Hutchinson

Joseph Mazary

Thomas Ferman [?]

Joseph Porter

Henery Renols [?]

Peter Prescott

Thomas Flint

Lott Killam

William Rayment [?]

Abraham Wallkot

Joseph Holltoun, Senior

Joseph Holltoun, Jun.

John Adams

Jonathan Knight

Isaac Goodell

Alexander Osburn

Jonathan Walcott

Daniel Andrew

Nathanial Ingersoll

Edward Bishop

John Buxton

Joseph Harrick

James Smith

William Sibly

John Shepard

James Hadlock, Sen.

Thomas Putnam, Jun.

Frances Geford

Thomas Haynes

Zachery Goodale

John Burrowes

John Gustin

Samuel Wilken

Samuell Brabrook

John Brown

James Hadlouck, Jun.

Letter from the Reverend James Bayley
to the Inhabitants of Salem Village
(July 31, 1679)

To the Committee and the Rest of the Inhabitants of the Farms:

After seven years' experience, having also waited nigh four months and finding the church's advice not attended in relation to me—nor like to be—I see no further grounds of hope for my future comfortable living amongst you in that work of the ministry in this place, and therefore am seriously thinking of my removal from you in time convenient. Though for the present, during my continuance among you, my purpose is to preach unto you as often as I can conveniently do. Beseeching the Lord to bless you, and provide a minister for you that may be more to your edification, I rest,

Yours unfeignedly,

James Bayley

From my house; 31 July 1679

Votes of a Salem-Village Meeting
(September 11, 1679)

[The following votes, copies of which were submitted to the General Court, were omitted from the Village Record Book when that book was recopied several years later.]

At a public meeting of the inhabitants of the Farms the 11th day of September, 1679. It was voted, first, that we agree to raise Mr. Bayley's maintenance, for this year ensuing, to fifty-five pounds, and that Mr. Bayley shall be at liberty at the year's end—or before, if he have a call to another place. Secondly, that the inhabitants shall have their liberty to get a minister in this year's time, and by this means we shall take the [Salem] church's advice if we raise our minister's maintenance.

Secondly, it was voted in way of answer[ing] terms by us [to] those which he sent to us the last meeting, whereas he said the church's advice was not attended in relation to him, and that he saw little hope of his comfortable subsistence among [us]. Therefore we do agree to give him the year ensuing fifty-five pounds for his encouragement among us.

Petition of a Salem-Village Committee to
The Governor and General Court (October 1679)

To the honorable Simon Bradstreet, Esq., Governor, the honored Deputy Governor and Magistrates, with the Deputies now Assembled in General Court at Boston, 15 October 1679.

Whereas it pleased the honored General Court held at Boston, 8th October 1672, to grant unto the Farmers of Salem liberty to have a minister amongst them, and that all persons living within that tract should contribute to his maintenance, and also to all other charges referring to the ministery; there being since many uncomfortable divisions amongst us about voting for choosing a Committee, and other things referring to the ministry:

We, your humble petitioners whose names are subscribed (being chosen by our inhabitants to that end) do earnestly request of this honored Court, that you would please to grant us an explanation of the former Court's order concerning our liberty about voting: who they are that may vote for calling a minister, and for the choice of a Committee: which we hope may be a means for settling of peace and unity among us. Also that you would be pleased to determine whether it be not the duty of our Constable, as well [here] as in other places, to collect the rates for our minister's maintenance. And if this honored Court see meet to inquire anything more particularly concerning this matter, we are ready waiting to give your Honors further information.

Your humble petitioners,

Thomas Fuller, Sen.
Daniel Andrew

Response of the General Court to this Petition

For answer to the questions above, the Deputies declare that the Farmers of the Village and other [of] their inhabitants are to attend [i.e., observe] the law regulating voters in this and all other cases, as other towns are enjoined to do. The second question is answered in the former grant—to which they are referred. The Deputies have passed this, with reference to the Council. Sent before honored Magistrates,

October 17, 1679   John Richards, per order

Consented by the Magistrates.

J. Dudly

Petition of Some Salem Villagers
to the General Court (October 20, 1679)

To the honored General Court now sitting in Boston, this 20th October, 1679:

The humble motion and petition of the Farmers of Salem showeth to this honored Court that whereas we have presented a petition to this honored Court for an exposition of the Court order to us, and the Court's clemency to us was such as to give us an answer by referring us to the law to be our guide; which we heartily submit unto as being welcome and good. But we would humbly present our condition to this honored Court, which is this:

1. We have neither township nor church, but belong to Salem, both town and church.
2. We conceive the law directs only to church-members to call a minister.
3. There are but about 11 or 12 church-members amongst us and about 50 freeholders with the church-members, living on their own land, all Englishmen and most of them town-born children.
4. There being a difference amongst us about our minister, and most principally between some of the church-members and him, insomuch that some of them

who had the choicest hand in calling of him and settling him amongst us, did charge him with something (which they were not able in any wise to make out against him). We then desired them that they would agree with us to go to the church of Salem, to whom some of them and us belong, and that the church might hear and determine the differences betwixt us. To this proposition they would not consent: that the church should determine the case. But in the issue [they] consented that they would have the church's advice: which advice of the church (which we have presented to your Honors with this petition) they would not attend. And nothing will satisfy them but the removal of our minister, without giving any sufficient cause or reason for it unto the church or us. Which [removal] if they obtain, we have cause to fear that we shall be left destitute of any [minister], there being such differences betwixt the church-members that have liberty to call another. Not that we are so engaged to our wills, but that truth might appear and the ministry [be] continued amongst us.

Therefore the [above] considered, our humble request is that this honored Court will be pleased to give liberty to all our freeholders that aren't scandalous to vote about the calling, settling or maintaining of a minister amongst us, with the approbation of the church at Salem, and their direction and advice to be attended by us till we come to be a town, or have a church amongst us.

Further, our request is that this honored Court will be pleased to inquire of our Deputies (the gentlemen of Salem) for the further satisfaction concerning our lives and conversations and practices on both sides; who we doubt not are in capacity to give information concerning us.

Thus we humbly leave our case to your Honors' wise consideration, desiring the Lord to direct you what to do in this and all cases that may come before you.

These are church-members and freemen	Thomas Putnam, Sen.	Jonathan Walcott	Thomas Rayment
	John Putnam, Sen.	Daniel Andrew	Zachery Goodale
	Peter Cloyse	Thomas Flint	Peter Prescott
	Thomas Putnam, Jun.	Nath. Ingersoll	William Sibley
	Joseph Portor	Edward Bishop	John Shepard
	Richard Hutchinson	Jonathan Knight	James Hadlock, Sen
		Thomas Haines	James Hadlock, Jnr.
		Joseph Holton, Jun.	John [illegible]
		John Buxton	James Smith

Petition of Some Salem Villagers
to the General Court (October 25, 1679)

To the Honored General Court Now Sitting in Boston, the 25th of October, 1679:

We whose names are underwritten, being part of the inhabitants amongst the Salem Farms, being informed that since there was a request by other inhabitants preferred to this honored Court for an interpretation of this Court's order formerly granted to us by this Court and an answer returned to us from yourselves; that some of our neighbors have presented another paper to this honored Court, wherein they (as it is hinted to us) do render some or most of us to be persons not willing to have a minister amongst us; which if so, we do and can truly say their charges upon us therein is not true. But on the contrary, as our duty is, so we most heartily desire a godly, pious, orthodox minister amongst us: that so both we and our families may be instructed according to the word of God, and such a one as by doctrine and conversation may be an example for us all to follow. And therefore, with submission and that we may not be accounted a number of self-willed persons, [we] do humbly offer to this honored Court that some suitable persons, unconcerned, may be appointed by yourselves to consider of our condition and of such or such a person who may be nominated, and if by them judged qualified for the work, and the person be willing to accept thereof, that then with their approbation we may engage him with whom we shall be well satisfied, and communicate to him to the utmost of our ability for his comfortable subsistence. So hoping that this honored Court, upon serious consideration, will choose to grant our request and prevent all clamors and following distresses, we rest your humble servants:

	Bray Wilkins
	Nath Putnam
	Thomas Fuller, Sen.
	Joshua Rea
	John Gingill
Thomas Fuller, Jun.	Joséph Hutchinson
Henary Keny	Aaron Way
Henary Wilkins	William Way
John Putnam, Jun.	Thomas Keny
Thomas Wilkins	John Keny
William Iorland	Bena. Wilkins

Order of the General Court (October 28, 1679)

Upon the motion and request of sundry of the inhabitants of Salem Village, called the Farmers of Salem, touching the continuance and maintenance of their present minister:

Whereas the inhabitants of this place (being thereunto authorized by this Court, with the consent of the town and church of Salem) to call a minister to preach the word of God to them; and for as much as they have called Mr. Bayly to be their preacher, who hath for about six years been among them, and hath the testimony of the church of Salem—and several others testified under their hands—that he is orthodox and competently able and of a blameless and self-denying conversation; and it also appears under the hand of about thirty householders of that place, who are the greater number of the inhabitants there, are very desirous of his continuance and settlement among them as their minister, and that a comfortable maintenance be allowed him for the support of himself, wife and children, that so he may the better attend his ministry without distraction:

In answer to this motion, this Court do order that Mr. Bayly be continued and settled the minister of that place, and that he be allowed sixty pounds per annum for his maintenance: one-third part whereof to be paid in money, the other two-thirds in provisions of all sorts, such as a family needs, at equal prices, and fuel for his family occasions. This sum to be paid by the inhabitants of that place, and the said inhabitants are to choose three or five men among themselves to proportion every man's share according to equity. And if they cannot agree to choose men to make the said rate, then the Court do hereby appoint Mr. Batter, Capt. John Corwin and Capt. Price of Salem to make the said rate upon the said inhabitants in the most equal way, and if any person shall neglect or refuse to pay their proportion according to the rate determined, the Constable of the place or Marshal of that county are hereby empowered to levy the same by distress. And all the rate is to be paid in, for the use of the minister, unto two persons chosen by the householders to supply the place of Deacons for the time, who are to reckon with the people and to deliver the same to the said minister or to his order. And this settlement to continue until this Court take further order, or that there be a church of Christ orderly gathered and approved in that place. Then the choice of the minister and officers doth resolve upon them according to law.

Voted in the affirmative by the Magistrates: desire the consent of our brethren the Deputies.

J. Dudley

The Deputies consent hereto, provided this order shall continue for one year only from the last of September last past, and in the meanwhile all parties endeavor an agreement in him or some other meet person for a minister among them; provided also that the said Farmers pay but five pounds for hearing the case: the whole number of Villagers equally to bear their proportion thereof. The honored Magistrates hereto consenting.

William Torrey

28th October 1679: Consented to by the Magistrates, Edw. Rawson, Secretary

Thomas Putnam Senior, Nathaniel Putnam, Thomas Fuller Senior, John Putnam Senior, and Joseph Hutchinson Senior Deed to the Reverend James Bayley (1680)

To all Christian people, Thomas Putnam Sen., Nathaniel Putnam, Thomas Fuller Sen., John Putnam Sen. and Joseph Hutchinson Sen. send greeting. Know ye that whereas Mr. James Bayley, minister of the gospel now resident of Salem Village, hath been in the exercise of his gifts by preaching amongst us several years, having had a call thereunto by the inhabitants of the place; and at the said Mr. Bayley's first coming amongst us, we the above named put the said Mr. Bayley in possession of a suitable accommodation of land and meadow, for his more comfortable subsistence among us; but the providence of God having so ordered it that the said Mr. Bayley doth not continue amongst us in the work of the ministry, yet considering the premises, and as a true testimony of our good affection to the said Mr. Bayley, and as full satisfaction of all demands [made] of us (or any of us) of land relating to the premises, [we] do by these presents . . . give . . . unto the said Mr. Bayley . . . the several quantities or parcels of meadow and upland as is underneath expressed, *viz.*:

Lieut. Thomas Putnam Sen. for his part doth hereby as is above expressed make conveyance of three acres of meadow, lying and being in that which is called Cromwell's Meadow. . . .

Nathaniel Putnam abovesaid doth hereby make conveyance as is above expressed of ten acres of upland, wherein the said Mr. Bayley's new dwelling house now standeth. . . .

Thomas Fuller Sen. doth for his part hereby make conveyance as is above expressed of five acres of upland, lying and being situated on the side of a hill near John Phelps's land, within Redding bounds butting on [the] Salem line . . . and two acres of meadow, lying at the upper end of the Great Meadow. . . .

John Putnam Sen. doth for his part make conveyance as is above expressed of ten acres of upland, be it more or less, lying and being situated on the northeast side of Misty Hill. . . .

Joseph Hutchinson doth hereby make conveyance as is above expressed of three acres of upland . . . and an acre of meadow lying in Cromwell's Meadow. . . .

And for the true performance of the premises, each party for himself hath hereunto set their hands and seals, this 10th day of May in the year of our Lord 1680.

> Thomas Putnam Sen. [and a seal]
> Nathaniel Putnam Sen. [and a seal]
> Thomas Fuller [and a seal]
> John Putnam [and a seal]
> Joseph Hutchinson [and a seal]

Signed, sealed and delivered in the presence of us,

Bartho: Gedney
Israel Porter

Recorded May 18th, 1686

[In addition to this property Bayley received two separate grants of property from Joseph Hutchinson, Senior. In 1700 the former minister (Bayley became a physician after he left the Village) sold his Salem property for one hundred pounds.]

Salem Village and the Reverend Mr. Samuel Parris

Petitions (1692-1695)

Petition of Salem-Village Church to the Court of Common Pleas (December 26, 1692)

To the Honored Court of Common Pleas to be held at Salem, 27 Dec. 1692

The humble petition of the church abovesaid humbly showeth, that whereas among the other laws passed by the Great and General Court of their Majesty's Province of the Massachusetts Bay in New England, some of them bear particular respects to the maintenance of religion; and whereas our village, as to some of its inhabitants in special, hath indispensible need of support by such wholesome acts, several among us for several years having made no payment to our Reverend Pastor, and other some as little as they pleased; and some have been chosen to the service of making rates, who have refused (though urged by this church) to make any, insomuch that the first of January next, one year and half is passed, and no rate made.

Besides the former rates in great part uncollected: Nay, no reparation of the very meeting-house has for a great while been regarded, so that by reason of broken windows, stopped-up, some of them, by boards or otherwise, and others wide open, it is sometimes so cold that it makes it uncomfortable, and sometimes so dark that it is almost unuseful. Besides the neglect of our Ministry-land fences, and the great and long disquietments of a few, who in this hour of sore tribulation and temptation have drawn away others who heretofore could not by an means join with them; by reason whereof we have no meetings to relieve our minister; or, if any, several well-affected persons absent themselves because they cannot bear the jars amongst us, by which means others to our great disquietment and injury obtain casting vote; besides many other things too tedious to trouble your Honors with at present.

All which considered, we pray your command of Mr. Joseph Porter, Joseph Hutchinson Senr., Joseph Putnam, Daniel Andrews, and Francis Nurse to appear personally before your Honors (or rather with submission before a committee appointed and fully empowered to settle all differences by your Honors, which we conceive most suitable to this tedious affair) and to give in their reason, if they have any, why the last year which expired the 1st July, last, was suffered to elapse, and their committee-ship to die totally without making any just rate, in such manifest contempt of that Law entitled *An Act for Collecting the Arrears of Town and County Rates* passed at the session 8 June.

The grant of this our necessitous petition, as it will be exceeding joyful to our small church, and many other [of] our religious neighbors, so particularly to your Honors' deputed and humble petitioners,

Nath: Putnam
John Putnam
Jonathan Walcot

The aforesaid petition was voted the day aforesaid by the church abovesaid to be presented as abovesaid by Lt. Nathaniel Putnam, Capt. John Putnam, and Capt. Jonath: Walcot.

Witness us,

Nathaniel Ingersol ⎫
                   ⎬ Deacons
Edward Putnam   ⎭

Action of the Court on the Petition of the
Salem-Village Church (January 17, 1693)

At a General Sessions of the Peace holden at Salem for the County of Essex, by adjournment, 17 Jan. 1692/93.

Essex Ss. In answer to the Petition of the Church at Salem Village relating to the Ministry: This Court having fully examined the case and heard the pleas and allegations of the parties concerned, do find that the Committee for the year 1691 hath wholly neglected their duty, in not raising their Minister's maintenance for that year, which was settled upon him by the inhabitants of said Village; and the Committee for this present year 1692 have also neglected their duty relating thereunto; and also to this Court utterly refused to attend their duty in that respect, and several of the principal inhabitants having prayed this Court to appoint a meeting requiring the inhabitants to make a choice of a Committee that will attend that service, alleging that otherwise they cannot lawfully be convened together.

This Court do order that Constable John Putnam of Salem, do warn and give notice unto the inhabitants of said Village that they convene together at the usual place of meeting on Wednesday next, being the 25th of this instant January, at ten of the clock in the morning, to make choice of a Committee according to the power given them by the General Court at their first Settlement.

The Salem-Village Church Enters Complaint
Against the Salem-Village Committee (March 1693)

At a General Sessions of the Peace holden at Ipswich, March the 28th, 1693.

Mr^S Nathaniel Puttman and John Puttman of Salem Village, in the name and by the order of the Church of Christ in Salem Village, entered complaint against Thomas Preston, John Tarbell, Joseph Pope, James Smith, and Joseph Holton, Junior, the present Committee of Salem Village, for not raising their minister's maintenance, etc. according to complaint filed with this court record, according to law.

Action of the Court in the Case
(May and December 1693)

The pleas and allegations of both sides being read and heard in open court, matters of fact committed to the jury, who find Thomas Preston, Joseph Pope, Joseph Holton, and John Tarbell as guilty according to said complaint.

James Smith, making [?] it appear that he refused office and published the same, is dismissed, having never acted therein. Joseph Holton, being lame, not present.

The court's judgment is that Thomas Preston, for neglect of his duty for not raising the minister's maintenance as one of the Committee of Salem Village, according to complaint filed with this Court record, being found guilty by a jury, shall pay the sum of forty shillings money, fine and costs, bill of costs allowed: 12s./6d., and stand committed till this judgment be performed.

Received in full.

[The same judgment was entered against John Tarbell and Joseph Pope, both of whom also paid the fine in full.]

The Court do order and appoint that the present Committee for Salem Village do assess the inhabitants of said village for what arrears of money or provision or else is yet due to Mr. Samuel Parris, their minister, for the two years last past, which hitherto no rate hath been made for, together with the present year's salary, according to agreement entered in the said Village Book, and to collect, or cause the same to be collected and paid to the said Parris accordingly.

At a General Sessions of the Peace holden at Salem, December 26th, 1693.

Whereas it is made manifest to this Court that there remains a great part of the salary due to Mr. Samuel Parris, minister of Salem Village, (*viz.*), for the years 1691 and 1692, uncollected, the Committee of said Village setting forth and alleging that many persons have not paid, though demand was made, of their respective rates,

Therefore, this Court doth order and direct the Constables that live within the said Village to make distress on such persons as neglect or refuse to pay their respective rates according to the assessment of the committee, pursuant to the order of the General Court relating thereunto.

Petition to the Governor (July 7, 1693)

[Marginal note: "Read July 7, 1693"]

To his Excellency, Sir William Phips, Knight, Captain, General and Governor-in-Chief of their Majesties' Province of the Massachusetts Bay; and to the much honored the General Court of the same Province, now sitting in Boston.

The humble address of us whose names are subscribed, inhabitants of Salem Village and others necessarily concerned in that Plantation:

There being very uncomfortable differences at this time, chiefly relating to our present minister in our plantation; whereby the name of God, the good of his church, and the peace of their Majesties' good subjects is not a little disadvantaged; and inasmuch as we have tried and do despair of a desirable issue upon the use of all other methods of bringing matters to a good composure;

We do humbly petition that your Excellency and the much honored General Court would, out of compassion unto this distressed plantation, appoint a sufficient number of prudent and impartial persons to take cognizance of our miserable condition and give us what advice they shall in their wisdom think fit, for the speedy and happy composure of our lamentable differences, [so] that peace and truth (which are now so much wanting) may prevail among us; and your petitioners shall ever pray,

Israel Porter	Benjamin Bridges	Joseph Portor [Senior]
John [illegible]	Benjamin Nurse	Franses Nurs
James Kettle	Isaac Nedham	Joseph Hutchinson
Alexander Osburn	Joseph Flint	Thomas Preston
Joseph Holten	Peter Cloayse, Sen.	Joseph Holton, Sen.
Joseph Swinerton	Daniel Ealoatt [Eliot]	Job Swinnerton
Joseph Pope	Beniamin Porter	Daniel Andrew
Samuel Nurse	John Wilkens	Joseph Herrick, Sen.
Joseph Putnam	Joseph Portor [Junior]	John Tarbell

Richard William [?]
John [illegible]
William Upton
Samuell Upton
Frances Eloatt [Eliot]
Thomas Wilkins, Sen.
Samuell Lane
William Portor
Edward Bishop, Sen.

Samuel Portor

John Buxton
John Houlton
Henry Houlton
Joseph Hutchinson, Jun.
Thomas Fuller [Senior]
Samuell [illegible]
Jasper Swinerton
Thomas Rayment
Joseph Trumball
Thomas Wilkins, Jun.
Samuel [illegible]
John Hutchinson
Edward Bishop

Petition of the Salem-Village Committee
to the General Court (February 1695)

To the honored General Court or Assembly of their Majesties' Province of the Massachusetts-Bay in New England, Convened and Held at Boston this 26th day of February, 1694/95.

The humble petition of we whose names are underwritten, being at this present the Committee or Assessors of the inhabitants of Salem Village in the County of Essex in the Province aforesaid, in behalf of ourselves and also of the inhabitants of Salem Village, for whose good we are concerned; most humbly showeth:

That whereas at a General Court held at Boston, the 8th of October, 1672, the said honored Court did give unto our inhabitants liberty to nominate and appoint persons amongst themselves or [the] Town of Salem from time to time for the making and gathering of all rates and levies for the maintenance of a minister or erecting of a meeting-house amongst us, and in case of refusal or non-payment by any person or persons amongst us, that then the Constables of Salem were empowered to make distress upon the goods of such as did neglect or refuse to afford their help in that case: which order, as we conceive, makes our Committee [into] collectors as well as assessors—and yet all of them together [have] not so much power as one Constable; which we have found troublesome to us: for the Constables of Salem would never yet go to make distress upon the goods of any person that did neglect or refuse to pay their proportions to the rates or assessments that have been made amongst us, unless the Committee, or the major part of the assessors that made the rate would go along with them and immediately receive the goods which they distressed.

And not only so: but some also that have been chosen for a Committee or Assessors amongst us have wholly neglected their duty upon that account, and also others, that have made rates or bills of assessments and have raised great sums of money on our inhabitants, do neither take care to collect and gather it themselves nor employ the Constables of Salem to do it. Neither will they so much as enter the rates or bills of assessments which they have made in our Village Book of Records, though we have several votes in our Book of Records that enjoin them so to do.

Therefore our most humble petition to this honorable Court is that the Constables which are annually chosen by the Town of Salem in Salem Village for the collecting and gathering of the Town and Country rates may be ordered and appointed to collect and gather all rates or bills of assessments that shall be made amongst us, till we come to be a Township; and pay the same according to the direction that shall be given them, orderly, as the law directs; and also that those that are annually chosen in Salem Village for Committees or Assessors may be ordered and required to make the bills of assessments which they do make as the law directs, and to enter the same in our Village Book of Records together with the warrants which they make out to the Constables, that so our inhabitants may know what sums of money is raised on us, and of whom to demand arrearages.

So praying your Honors to release us, we remain your Honors' most humble servants in what we may always [be] praying for you.

Nathaniel Putnam

Thomas Putnam   Thomas Flint
Thomas Fuller, Jun.   Henry Wilkins

Response of the General Court (March 1695)

Voted upon the petition of Salem Village, that what they petition for is granted them, [the] said petitioners.

Passed in the affirmative by the House of Representatives and sent up to the honorable Lieutenant Governor and Council for [their] consent.

Nehemiah Jewet, Speaker

March 4th, 1694/95

Anti-Parris Petition (1695)

To the Revd. Elders of the Churches at Boston, with other [of] the Elders and Brethren of other Churches late of a Council at Salem Village:

We whose names are under-subscribed are bold once more to trouble you with our humble proposals. That whereas there have been long and uncomfortable differences among us, chiefly relating to Mr. Parris; and we have, as we apprehend, attended all probable means for a composure of our troubles; and whereas we had hopes of an happy issue, by your endeavors among us, but now are utterly frustrated of our expectations; and that instead of uniting, our rent is made worse and our breach made wider. We humbly query, whether yourselves being straitened of time might not admit such satisfactory liberty of debating the whole case of our controversy, whereby yourselves had not so long an opportunity of understanding the case, nor the offended so much reason to be satisfied in your advice. We therefore humbly propose:

1. That if yourselves please to take the trouble with patience once more to hear the whole case, and give full liberty of proving and defending what may be charged on either hand, leaving it to yourselves to appoint both time and place;

2. Or that you will more plainly advise Mr. Parris, the case being so circumstanced that he cannot with comfort or profit to himself or others abide in the work of the Ministry among us, to cease his labors and seek to dispose of himself elsewhere, as God in his providence may direct; and yourselves would please to help us in advising such a choice wherein we may be more unanimous—which we hope would tend to a composure of our differences;

3. Or that we may without offence take the liberty of calling some other approved Minister of the Gospel to preach the word of God to us and ours, and that we may not be denied our proportionable privilege in our public disbursements in the place.

So leaving the whole case with the Lord and yourselves, we subscribe our names.

Young men--16 years old	Householders	Members	Non-Members
Joseph Porter	Jos: Holton	Josh: Rea	Rebecca Preston
Sam: Porter	Job Swinnerton	Jno: Tarbell	Sarah Andrew
Jno: Preston	Francis Nurse	Tho: Wilkins	Ruth Osborn
Nath: Porter	Jos: Porter	Tho: Fuller	Eliz: Rea
Ben: Swinnerton	Jos: Hutchinson	Sam: Nurse	Mary Braybrook
Jno: Buxton	Dan: Andrew	Joseph Herrick	Bethia Martin
Jos: Buxton	Jos: Swinnerton		Mary Smith
Will: Porter	Tho: Preston	6	Joanna Nickols
Dan: Andrew	Jno: Buxton		Eliz: Putnam
Jno: Ingersoll	Alex: Osburn	Sarah Holton	Sarah Needom
Ely Porter	Jos: Holton	Lydia Hutchinson	Abigail Flint
Sam: Nurse	Josh: Rea	Sarah Buckley	Mary Holton
Sam: Byshop	Henry Kenney	Esther Swinnerton	Eliz: Flint
Jonath: Byshop	Tho: Wilkins	Mary Swinnerton	Eliz: Kettel
David Byshop	Jno: Martin	Hanah Wilkins	
	Jos: Hutchinson	Mary Herrick	
	Sam: Braybrook	Mary Tarbell	

Young men—16 years old	Householders	Members	Non-Members
Will: Buckley	Abr. Smith	Mary Nurse	Eliz: Porter
Will: Byshop	Joseph Pope	Mary Raiment	Eliz: Swinnerton
17	Tho: Raiment	Widow Holt	16
29	Edw: Byshop	11	
6	Jos: Putnam		
11	Isaac Needom		*Free-holders*
16	Jos: Flint		
5	Sam: Upton		Ben: Porter
—	Will: Upton		Will: Small
84	Jno: Holtin		James Kittel
	Jno: Flint		Israel Porter
	Will: Buckley		Jasper Swinnerton
	29		5

Pro-Parris Petition (May 20, 1695)

Salem Village May 20, 1695

To the Reverend Mr. Increase Mather and other [of] the Reverend Elders which lately met at Cambridge:

Whereas by a letter from yourselves dated May 6, 1695, wherein you put us upon consideration how to maintain the religion of our Lord Jesus Christ threatened to be taken from us: we are not insensible of such threatenings; and for prevention hereof, we whose names are hereunto-subscribed are sensible that the removing of Mr. Parris from his present station will not unite us in calling another Minister. For we are sensible that the removing of Mr. Parris will not [in] any way be for the upholding of the kingdom of God amongst us. For we have had three Ministers removed already, and by every removal our differences have been rather aggravated. Therefore we justly fear that the removing of the fourth may rather prove the ruining of the interests of Christ amongst us, and leave us as sheep without a shepherd. Therefore we desire that Mr. Parris may continue in his present station.

Householders	Householders	Church-Members	Church-Members
Jane Wilkins	Jonath: Walcot	Bray Wilkins	Anna Wilkins
Sarah Wilkins	Thomas Flint	Nath: Putnam	Rebek: Putnam
Mary Fuller	Jno: Walcot	Jno: Putnam, Sen.	Rachel Griggs
Ruth Wilkins	Benj: Hutchinson	Wm: Griggs	Han: Ingersoll

Householders	Householders	Church-Members	Church-Members
Eliz: Wilkins	Jno: Dale	Nath: Ingersoll	Han: Putnam
Mary Richards	Wm: Allin	Hen: Wilkins	Priscilla Wilkins
Sarah Morall	Jno: Putnam [III]	Tho: Putnam	Ruth Fuller
Hannah Stacy	Jno: Wheldon	Benj: Wilkins	Mary Putnam
Susan: Fuller	Jonath: Walcot, Jun.	Tho: Fuller, Jun.	Mary Way
Sarah Goodale	Isaac Goodale [Jun.]	Edw: Putnam	Lidia Putnam
Mary Walcot	Tho: Haines	Aaron Way	Abagail Walcot
Mary Goodale	Geo: Ingersoll	Jonath: Putnam	Mary Sibly
Eliz: Goodale	Benj: Stacy	Abraham Walcot	Eliz: Flint
Mary Hutchinson	Sam: Wilkins [Junior]	Zech: Goodale,	Sarah Putnam
Priscilla Walcot	Rob't. Morall	Sen.	Percis Way
Eliz: Allin	Jonath: Fuller	Sam: Abby	Sarah Putnam
Mary Goodale	Zech: Goodale, Jun.	Geo: Flint	Abagail Cheever
Hannah Putnam	Jno: Hutchinson	Sam: Sibly	Eliz: Prescot
Abagail Lain	Henry Holton	Benj: Putnam	Han: Putnam
Eliz: Dale	Francis Eliott	Wm: Way	Mary Wheldon
Susan: Byshop	Jos: Goodale	James Putnam	Deliverance Walcot
Ruth Ray [Rea]	Jno: Hadlock	Ezek: Cheever	Sarah Fuller
Abagail Eliot	Henry Brown	Peter Prescot	Abagail Holton
Jane Hutchinson	Eliazar Putnam	Jno: Putnam, Jun.	Mary Darlin
24	Jno: Rea	Jos: Whipple	Sarah Hadlock
29	Sam: Lane	Jno: Wilkins	Sarah Prince
25	Jos: Prince		Han: Brown
27	James Prince	25	
——	Edward Byshop [III?]		27
105	29		

Paper Said to Have Been "Handed About"
by Parris's Opponents Some Time
During the Period 1693-1696

As to the contest between Mr. Parris and his hearers, etc., it may be composed by a satisfactory answer to Lev. 20:6: "And the soul that turneth after such as have familiar spirits, and after wizards, to go a-whoring after them, I will set my face against that soul, and will cut him off from among his people." I Chron. 10:13-14: "So Saul died for his transgressions which he committed against the Lord—even against the word of the Lord, which he kept not—and also for asking counsel of one who had a familiar to inquire of it, and inquired not of the Lord: therefore he slew him."

Countersuits Between Samuel Parris and the Salem-Village Committee (1697)

Salem Village Versus Parris: Judgment of the Court

Inferior Court at Salem by Adjournment, April 13th, 1697

Joseph Hutchinson Sen., Daniel Andrews, Thomas Flint Sen., Joseph Herrick, Joseph Putnam, Agents or Attorneys for and in behalf of the inhabitants of Salem Village, plaintiffs, v. Mr. Samuel Parris, Defendant.

The plaintiffs are non-suited, and to pay costs to the defendant.

	£	s.	d.
Bill cost	3	16	8

Parris Versus Salem Village: The Verdict of the Jury

Mr. Samuel Parris, plaintiff, v. the Inhabitants of Salem Village, defendants, in an action of the case [?] and according to writ of cause, being heard and committed to the jury, who returned their verdict as followeth:

The jury find for the plaintiff one hundred twenty-five pounds in specie according to agreement in said Village record, and costs of court.
Which, being considered by this Court, their judgment is that the plaintiff recover of the defendants one hundred twenty-five pounds in specie, according to contract, and costs.
The defendants appeal. Nathaniel Putnam, Joseph Herrick Sen., Thomas Putnam, Joseph Putnam, Daniel Andrew, attorneys to the inhabitants of Salem Village. Israel Porter and Joseph Porter [illegible] recognized in 300 pounds bond. The condition is that the said appellants shall prosecute this appeal with effect at the next Superior Court to be holden for this County.

Testimony of John Tarbell, Samuel Nurse, Joseph Putnam, and Daniel Andrew

Ipswich Court, 1697.—Parris Versus Inhabitants of Salem Village.

We the undersigned testify and say that, a considerable time after Mr. Parris's ordination, there was a meeting of the inhabitants of Salem

Village at the usual place of meeting; and the occasion of the meeting was concerning Mr. Parris, and several persons were at that meeting, that had not, before this meeting, joined with the people in calling or agreeing with Mr. Parris; and the said persons desired that those things that concerned Mr. Parris and the people might be read, and accordingly it was. And the entry, that some call a salary, being read, there arose a difference among the people, the occasion of which was finding an entry in the book of the Village records, relating to Mr. Parris's maintenance, which was dated the 18th of June, 1689; and, the entry being read to the people, some replied that they believed that Mr. Parris would not comply with that entry; whereupon one said it was best to send for Mr. Parris to resolve the question. Accordingly, he was sent for.

He coming to the people, this entry of the 18th of June, 1689, was read to Mr. Parris. His answer was as follows: He never heard or knew any thing of it, neither could or would he take up with it, or any part of it; and further he said, They were knaves and cheaters that entered it.

And Lieutenant Nathaniel Putnam, being moderator of that meeting, replied to Mr. Parris, and said, Sir, then there is only proposals on both sides, and no agreement between you and the people.

And Mr. Parris answered and said, No more, there is not; for I am free from the people, and the people free from me: and so the meeting broke up. And we further testify that there hath not been any agreement made with Mr. Parris, that we knew of or ever heard of,—never since.

Joseph Porter
Daniel Andrew
Joseph Putnam

Sworn in Court, at Ipswich, April 13, 1697, by all three.

Attest, Stephen Sewall, Clerk.

Arbitration

[In the summer of 1697, three prominent Bostonians—Wait Winthrop, Elisha Cooke, and Samuel Sewall—agreed to arbitrate the dispute between Parris and the Salem Villagers. The following documents relate to this arbitration.]

Petition of John Tarbell, Samuel Nurse, Joseph Putnam, and Daniel Andrew (July 1697)

To the Honorable Wait Winthrop, Elisha Cook, and Samuel Sewall, Esquires, Arbitrators, indifferently chosen, between Mr. Samuel Parris and the Inhabitants of Salem Village.

The Remonstrances of several Aggrieved Persons in the said Village, with further Reasons why they conceive they ought not to hear Mr. Parris, nor to own him as a Minister of the Gospel, nor to contribute any Support to him as such for several years past, humbly offered as fit for consideration.

We humbly conceive that, having, in April, 1693, given our reasons why we could not join with Mr. Parris in prayer, preaching, or sacrament, if these reasons are found sufficient for our withdrawing (and we cannot yet find but they are), then we conceive ourselves virtually discharged, not only in conscience, but also in law, which requires maintenance to be given to such as are orthodox and blameless; and said Mr. Parris having been teaching such dangerous errors, and preached such scandalous immoralities, as ought to discharge any (though ever so gifted otherways) from the work of the ministry, particularly in his oath against the lives of several, wherein he swears that the prisoners with their looks knock down those pretended sufferers. We humbly conceive that he that swears to more than he is certain of, is equally guilty of perjury with him that swears to what is false. And though they did fall at such a time, yet it could not be known that they did it, much less could they be certain of it; yet did swear positively against the lives of such as he could not have any knowledge but they might be innocent.

His believing the Devil's accusations, and readily departing from all charity to persons, though of blameless and godly lives, upon such suggestions; his promoting such accusations; as also his partiality therein in stifling the accusations of some, and, at the same time, vigilantly promoting others,—as we conceive, are just causes for our refusal, &c.

That Mr. Parris's going to Mary Walcot or Abigail Williams, and directing others to them, to know who afflicted the people in their illnesses,—we understand this to be a dealing with them that have a familiar spirit, and an implicit denying the providence of God, who alone, as we believe, can send afflictions, or cause devils to afflict any: this we also conceive sufficient to justify such refusal.

That Mr. Parris, by these practices and principles, has been the beginner and procurer of the sorest afflictions, not to this village only, but to this whole country, that did ever befall them.

We, the subscribers, in behalf of ourselves, and of several others of the same mind with us (touching these things), having some of us had our relations by these practices taken off by an untimely death; others have been imprisoned and suffered in our persons, reputations, and estates,—submit the whole to your honors' decision, to determine whether we are or ought to be any ways obliged to honor, respect, and support such an instrument of our miseries; praying God to guide your honors to act herein as may be for his glory, and the future settlement of our village in amity and unity.

John Tarbell,
Samuel Nurse,

Joseph Putnam,
Daniel Andrew,
Attorneys for the people of the Village

Boston, July 21, 1697

Vote of Salem-Village Inhabitants,
September 14, 1697

At a general meeting of the inhabitants of Salem Village the 14th of September, 1697, it was agreed and voted that the committee in being shall raise a rate of seventy nine pounds, nine shillings and six pence money upon the whole inhabitants of this Village, and shall also gather the same and pay it to Lieut. Nathaniel Putnam; Daniel Andrew, Senior; Joseph Herrick, Senior; Thomas Putnam; and Joseph Putnam, or either of them, that so they or either of them may pay the same to Mr. Samuel Parris, his heirs or assigns, according to the award, decree, and determination of the honourable Wait Winthrop, Elisha Cooke, and Samuel Sewall, Esqrs., arbitrators between Mr. Samuel Parris and the inhabitants of this village.

At a general meeting of the inhabitants of Salem Village, the 14th of September, 1697, it was agreed and voted that Lieut. Nathaniel Putnam; Daniel Andrew; Joseph Herrick, Senior; Thomas Putnam; and Joseph Putnam, or the major part of them, are hereby chosen and empowered to be collectors, with as full power as ever any of our committees have, to collect and gather in all the averages of Mr. Parris's rates, and to pay the same to Mr. Samuel Parris, his heirs or assigns, according to the award, decree, and determination of the honourable Wait Winthrop, Elisha Cooke, and Samuel Sewall, Esqrs., arbitrators between Mr. Samuel Parris and the inhabitants of this Village.

Deed: Samuel Parris to the Salem-Village Trustees*

Know all men by these presents, that I, Samuel Parris, late of Salem in the County of Essex in the Province of Massachusetts Bay in New England, clerk,

For divers good causes and considerations me thereunto moving, but more especially for and in consideration that, whereas Nathaniel Putnam, Daniel Andrew, Joseph Herrick, Thomas Putnam, and Joseph Putnam, all of Salem aforesaid, for and in behalf of the inhabitants of Salem Village, did agree with myself to leave all controversies, matters, and things whatsoever depending betwixt said Village and myself unto the final determination of Wait Winthrop,

*[*Dated September 24, 1697; recorded January 16, 1699]*

Elisha Cooke, and Samuel Sewall, Esqrs. of Boston, being arbitrators mutually chosen betwixt the said inhabitants and myself,

And whereas, also, among other things contained in the award of the said arbitrators, given under their hands and seals the thirtieth day of August, 1697, they did award and determine that I, the said Parris, should give unto the said Nathaniel Putnam, Daniel Andrew, Joseph Herrick, Thomas Putnam, and Joseph Putnam, for and in behalf of the inhabitants of said Village, a deed or instrument of release, in writing under my hand and seal, duly executed and acknowledged, of all right, interest, title, pretention, claim and demand of, in, or unto the messuage [?] or tenement known by the name of the ministry house and land in said Village, and dependencies thereof, or to any part or parcel of the same, and to the copper in the lean-to of said house,

Know ye therefore, that for the consideration aforesaid, I, the said Samuel Parris, do for myself, my heirs, executors, and administrators remiss, release, and surrender and forever quit claim to the said tenement situated in Salem Village, as also unto all of the land purchased by said Village of Joseph Holton of Salem, with all the dependencies thereto belonging, called or known by the name of the ministry house and land, as also to the copper hung or set up in the lean-to of said house. . . .

Samuel Parris [seal]

[Signed, sealed, witnessed, and acknowledged September 24, 1697, before Bartholomew Gedney. Recorded January 16, 1699, before Stephen Sewall, Recorder.]

Records of the Salem-Village Church from November 1689 to October 1696, as Kept by the Reverend Samuel Parris

The Covenant agreed upon and consented unto [torn] the Church of Christ at Salem Village, at [torn] first embodying, on the 19th November, 1689.

We whose names (tho' unworthy of a name in this [Church]) are hereunto subscribed, lamenting our own great unfitness [for such] an awful and solemn approach unto the Holy God and [deploring] all the miscarriages committed by us, either in the days [of] our unregeneracy or since we have been brought into acquaintance with God in the communion of his churches [which we] have heretofore been related unto: And yet apprehending ourselves called by the Most High to embody [ourselves] into a different society, with a sacred covenant to [serve] the Lord Jesus Christ and edify one another according [to the] rules of his holy word, being persuaded in matters [of faith] according to the Confession of Faith owned and [consented] unto by the Elders and Messengers of the churches [assembled] at Boston in New-England, May 12, 1680, [which] for the substance of it, we now own and profess.

We do, in some measure of sincerity, this day give up ourselves one unto another in the Lord, engaging (with divine aid) as a church of God, to submit to the order, discipline and government of Christ in this his church, and to the ministerial teaching, guidance, and over sight of the Elder (or Elders) thereof, as to such as watch for our souls; and also to a mutual brotherly watchfulness according to Gospel rules, so long as by such rules we shall continue in this relation to each other; and promise also to walk with all regular and due communion with other churches of our Lord Jesus, and in all cheerful endeavor to support and observe the pure Gospel institutions of our Lord Redeemer, so far as He shall graciously reveal unto us his will concerning them.

In order hereunto: We resolve uprightly to study what is our duty, and to make it our grief, and reckon it our shame, whereinsoever we find ourselves to come short in the discharge of it, and for pardon thereof humbly to betake ourselves to the blood of the Everlasting Covenant.

And that we may keep this covenant, and all the branches of it inviolable forever, being sensible that we can do nothing of ourselves,

We humbly implore [that] the help and grace of our Mediator may be sufficient for us, beseeching that whilst we are working out our own salvation, with fear and trembling, He would graciously work in us both to will and to do. And that he being the Great Shepherd of our souls would lead us into the paths of righteousness, for His own Name's sake. And at length receive us all into the inheritance of the Saints in Light.

1.	Samuel Parris, Pastor	The women which embodied with us are by their several names as followeth, *Viz.*
2.	Nathanall Putnam	
3.	John Putnam	
4.	Bray Wilkins 79	1. Eliz (wife to Sam) Parris
5.	Joshua Rea	2. Rebek. (wife to John) Putman
6.	Nathanail Ingersoll	3. Anna (wife to Bray) Wilkins
7.	Peter Cloyes	4. Sarah (wife to Joshua) Rea
8.	Thomas Putnam	5. Hannah (wife to Jn⁰ Junʳ) Putman
9.	John Putnam Junʳ	6. Sarah (wife to Benjᵃ) Putman
10.	Edward Putnam	7. Sarah Putman
11.	Jonathan Putnam	8. Deliverance Walcott
12.	Benjamin Putnam	9. Peircy [Persis] (wife to William) Way
13.	Ezekiel Cheever	10. Mary (wife to Sam.) Abbie
14.	Henry Wilkins	
15.	Benjᵃ Wilkins	
16.	William Way	
17.	Peter Prescott	
18.	[left blank by Parris]	

Illi quoni nominibus hoc signum praefigitur
+ e vivis cesserunt.

24 November, 1689, Sabbath Day.

Brother Nathanael Ingersoll chosen by a general vote of the brethren to officiate in the place of a Deacon for a time.

[23 December 1689]

At a church meeting (appointed the Sabbath last) at Brother Edward Putnam's house, 23 December 1689, these following particulars were consented to and voted:

That our attendance on the Lord's Supper be once in about six weeks space. A universal vote.

That such as offered to join in church membership shall be admitted before, and in presence of, the whole congregation [torn] else at a church-meeting warned for the purpose [torn] other well-disposed persons may have liberty to [torn] unless we shall find it needful to be more private. When such meetings are to be warned, the time and the place where shall be as the pastor shall desire.

That persons (that is of the male-kind) can hold forth [torn] of faith and repentance wrought in their souls, with their own tongues and mouths, we account of that way [torn] of all eligible. But where natural impediments hinder, we would not lay too much stress upon [a verbal confession] but admit of a written confession and profession, taken from the person or persons by our Pastor.

Persons shall not be admitted by a mere negative: that is to say, without some testimony for them from the Brethren.

9 January 1689/90

Admitted into the church at a public meeting forewarned:

19. Abraham Walcott, aged about 54.
20. Zechariah Goodale, aged about 50.

12 January 1689/90 Sabbath-day

Admitted into the church in the forenoon, being Sacrament day:

11. Sarah (wife to Brother Peter) Cloyes, aged about 48

9 Feb. Sab: day 1689/90

Admitted into the church:

12. Eliz. (wife to Sam.) Cuttler, *An. Aetat* 60

16 Feb. Sab: day 1689/90

Admitted into the church:

13. Priscilla (wife to Bro. Benjamin) Wilkins, *Anno Aetat* 36, who was then baptized

21. Aaron Way. *Anno Aetat 39*

    14. Mary (wife to Aaron) Way, *An. Aetat 37*
    15. Mary (wife to Brother Edward) Putnam, *Anno Aetat*
    16. Mary Flint, *Anno Aetat 35*

22. James Putnam, *Anno Aetat 27*

At a church-meeting (appointed the last Sabbath) at Brother John Putnam's house, 20 Feb. 1689/90. The question being put by the Pastor to his Brethren: Who are the proper subjects of baptism?

Answer: Covenant professing believers and their infant seed. To this (I think) all voted: none in the least opposed.

Question (again): How far may we account such seed infant seed? And so to be baptized?

Answer (After some debating): When one of the parents is in full communion and the child religiously educated and free from open vices, and not exceeding the age of twelve years (which I understand and mean ordinarily, and not always; for as I told my Brethren, there is difference in men, and so in children, so that some are mature before others). To this there was a major vote but [for] two or three (I think not four) which dissented.

At the same time I told them there were two ways by which persons might come to baptism: *viz.,* by their own profession and by their parents'. When therefore (if God gave grace) they were capable of profession ordinarily, at such time of age they are not to be baptized but upon their own profession; and (as I conceive) to be baptized till such time as children.

Sab: day 2 March 1689/90

Admitted into the church:

23. Samuel Nurse and baptized, *An. Aetat 37*
24. John Tarbell, *An. Aetat 36*

    17. Lydia (wife to Brother Jonath:) Putnam, *An. Aetat*
    18. Mary (wife to Brother John) Tarbell and baptized, *An. 35*

Sab: day 16 March 1689/90

25. Thomas Wilkins, *An. Aetat 44* ⎫
26. Samuel Sibley, *An. Aetat 33* ⎬   Admitted into the church

Sab: day 23 March 1689/90

Admitted into the church:

    19. Mary (wife to Brother Samuel) Nurse and baptized, *An. Aetat 36*
    20. Hannah Holton, *An. Aetat 31*

Sab: 30 March 1690

Admitted into the church:

27. Geo: Flint and baptized, *An. Aetat* 37

21. Eliz: (wife to Brother Geo:) Flint, *An.* 27
22. Ruth Fuller, *An. Aetat* 41

The same Sab: Brother Cheevers who having, in distress for a horse upon his wife's approaching travail about five or six weeks past, taken his neighbor Joseph Putnam's horse out of his stable and without leave or asking of it, was called forth to give satisfaction to the offended Church, as also the last Sabbath he was called forth for the same purpose, but then he failed in giving satisfaction, by reason of his somewhat mincing in the latter part of his confession, which in the former he had more ingenuously acknowledged. But this day the Church received satisfaction, as was testified by their holding up of their hands. And upon the whole a word of caution by the Pastor was dropped upon the offender in particular, and upon us all in general.

Admitted into the church 27 April Sab: 1690:

23. Lydia Hutchinson, *An.*
24. Martha Korey, *An. Aetat* [torn]
25. Mary (wife to Bro: Samuel) Sibly, *An. Aetat* 30

Received into our church 25 May 1690:

26. Sarah Byshop, dismissed [from the] church at Topsfield

[8 June, 1690]

Received into the church 8 June, 1690:

27. Abigail (wife to Brother Ezekiel) Cheever, and baptized. *An. Aetat* 33

10 August, 1690

28. Elizabeth Goold, widow, *An Aetat* 58

Sabbath, 30 November, 1690

This evening, after the public service was over, the church was, by the pastor, desired to stay, and then by him Brother Edward Putnam was propounded as a meet person for to be chosen as another deacon. The issue whereof was, that it now being an excessive cold day, some did propose that another season might be pitched upon for discourse thereof. Whereof the pastor mentioned the next fourth day, at two of the clock, at the pastor's house, for farther discourse thereof, to which the church agreed by not dissenting.

3 December 1690

This afternoon, at a church meeting appointed the last Sabbath, Brother Edward Putnam was again propounded to the church for choice to office in the place of a deacon to join with, and be assistant to, Brother Ingersoll in the service, and in order to said Putnam's ordination in the office, upon his well approving himself therein. Some proposed that two might be nominated to the church, out of which the church to choose one. But arguments satisfactory were produced against that way. Some also moved for a choice of papers; but that way also was disapproved by the arguments of the pastor and some others. In fine, the pastor put it to vote (there appearing not the least exception from any, unless a modest and humble exception of the person himself, once and again), and it was carried in the affirmative by a universal vote, *nemine non suffragante.*

Afterwards, the pastor addressed himself to the elected brother, and, in the name of the church, desired his answer, who replied to this purpose: —

Seeing, sir, you say the voice of God's people is the voice of God, desiring your prayers and the prayers of the church for divine assistance therein, I do accept of the call.

Sab. day, 7 December 1690

After the evening public service was over, several things needful were transacted; *viz.* : —

1. The pastor acquainted those of the church that were ignorant of it, that Brother Edward Putnam was chosen deacon the last church meeting.
2. He also generally admonished those of the brethren that were absent at that time, of their disorderliness therein, telling them that such, the apostle bids, should be noted or marked (2 Thess. iii. 6-16); that is, with a church mark,—a mark in a disciplinary way; and therefore begged amendment for the future in that point and to that purpose.
3. He propounded whether they were so far satisfied in Brother Ingersoll's service as to call him to settlement in the deaconship by ordination, or had aught against it. But no brother made personal exception. Therefore, it being put to vote, it was carried in the affirmative by a plurality, if not universality.
4. The Lord's Table, not being provided for with aught else but two pewter tankards, the pastor propounded and desired that the next sacrament-day, which is to be the 21st instant, there be a more open and liberal contribution by the communicants, that so the deacons may have wherewith to furnish the said table decently; which was consented to.

Sabbath day, May 31, 1691

Admitted into the church:

29. Hannah (wife to Brother Thomas) Wilkins and baptised, *An. Aetat* 44

30.   Sarah (wife to Benj.) Fuller and baptized, *An. Aetat* 27

The pastor spoke to the brethren to this purpose, *viz.*: —

BRETHREN,—The ordination of Brother Ingersoll has already been voted a good while since, and I thought to have consummated the affair a good time since, but have been put by, by diversity of occurrents; and, seeing it is so long since, I think it needless to make two works of one, and therefore intend the ordination of Brother Putnam together with Brother Ingersoll in the deaconship, if you continue in the same mind as when you elected him; therefore, if you are so, let a vote manifest it. Voted by all, or at least the most. I observed none that voted out.

At a church-meeting, 4 June 1691

Admitted into the church:

31.   Ann (wife to Brother Thomas) Putnam, *An. Aetat* 27

Sab: 28 June 1691

After the afternoon sermon upon I Tim. 3:8-13, as the brethren had renewed their call of Brother Ingersoll to the office of a deacon, and he himself had declared his acceptance, the pastor proceeded to ordain him, using the form following:

BELOVED BROTHER, God having called you to the office of a deacon by the choice of the brethren and your own acceptance, and that call being now to be consummated according to the primitive pattern, 6 Acts 6, by prayer and imposition of hands,—

We do, therefore, by this solemnity, declare your investiture into that office, solemnly charging you in the name of our Lord Jesus Christ, the King of his Church, who walks in the midst of his golden candlesticks, with eyes as of a flame of fire, exactly observing the demeanor of all in his house, both officers and members, that you labor so to carry it, as to evidence you are sanctified by grace, qualified for this work, and to grow in those qualifications; behaving of yourself gravely, sincerely, temperately, with due care for the government of your own house, holding the mystery of the faith in a pure conscience; that as they in this office are called "helps," so you be helpful in your place and capacity, doing what is your part for the promoting of the work of Christ here. We do charge you, that, whatever you do in this office, you do it faithfully, giving with simplicity, showing mercy with cheerfulness. Look on it, brother, as [a] matter of care, and likewise of encouragement, that both the office itself and also your being set up in it is of God, who, being waited upon, will be with you, and accept you therein, assisting you to use the office of a deacon well, so as that you may be blameless, purchasing to yourself a good degree and great boldness in the faith.

NOTE. — That Brother Putnam was not yet willing to be ordained, but desired further considering time, between him and I and Brother Ingersoll, in private discourse the week before the ordination above said.

Sab:, 12 July 1691

Admitted into the church:

32. Abigail (wife to Brother Abr:) Walcott, member of the church of Reading, upon recommendation
33. Eliz: (wife to John) Buxton, *An. Aetat* 32
34. Abigail (wife to Jun. Henry) Holton, *An. Aetat* 23, and baptized

Sab:, 9 Aug. 1691

After all public worship was over, and the church stayed on purpose, I proposed to the church whether they were free to admit to baptism, upon occasion, such as were not at present free to come up to full communion. I told them there was a young woman, by name Han: Wilkins, the daughter of our Brother Thomas Wilkins, who much desired to be baptized, but yet did not dare to come to the Lord's Supper. If they had nothing against it, I should take their silence for consent, and in due time acquaint them with what she had offered me to my satisfaction, and proceed accordingly.

No answer was made pro or con, so the church was dismissed.

Sab:, 23 Aug. 1691

Hannah Wilkins, aged about twenty-one years, was called forth, and her relation read in the full assembly, and then it was propounded to the church, that, if they had just exceptions, or, on the other hand, had any thing farther to encourage, they had opportunity and liberty to speak. None said any thing but Brother Bray Wilkins (Han: grandfather), who said, that, for all he knew, such a relation as had been given and a conversation suitable (as he judged hers to be) was enough to enjoy full communion. None else saying any thing, it was put to vote whether they were so well satisfied as to receive this young woman into membership, and therefore initiate her therein by baptism. It was voted fully. Whereupon the covenant was given to her as if she had entered into full communion. And the pastor told her, in the name of the church, that we would expect and wait for her rising higher, and therefore advised her to attend all means conscientiously for that end.

After all, I pronounced her a member of this church, and then baptized her.

28 August, 1691

This day, Sister Hannah Wilkins aforesaid came to see me, and spake to this like effect, following: —

Before I was baptized (you know, sir) I was desirous of communion at the Lord's Table, but not yet; I was afraid of going so far: but since my baptism I find my desires growing to the Lord's Table, and I am afraid to turn my back upon that ordinance, or to refuse to partake thereof. And that which moves me now to desire full communion, which I was afraid of before, is that of Thomas 20, John 26, &c., where he, being absent from the disciples, though but once, lost sight of Christ, and got more hardness of heart, or increase of unbelief. And also those words of Ananias to Paul after his conversion, 22 Acts 16, 'And now why tarriest thou? Arise,' &c. So I am afraid of tarrying. The present time is only mine. And God having, beyond my deserts, graciously opened a door, I look upon it my duty to make present improvement of it.

Sab: and Sacrament Day, 30 Aug. 1691

Sister Han: Wilkins's motion (before the celebration of the Lord's Supper was begun) was mentioned or propounded to the church, and what she said to me (Before hinted) read to them, and then their vote was called for, to answer her desire if they saw good; whereupon the church voted in the affirmative plentifully.

35.   Hannah Wilkins, daughter to Brother Tho: Wilkins. *An Aetat*: 21

8 October, 1691

Being my lecture day, after public service was ended I was so bare of fire-wood that I was forced publicly to desire the inhabitants to take care that I might be provided for, telling them that had it not been for Mr. Corwin (who had brought wood, being then at my house) I should hardly have any to burn.

1 Nov. 1691

The pastor desired the brethren to meet at my house, on to-morrow, an hour and half before sundown.

2 Nov. 1691

After sunset, about seventeen of the brethren met; to whom, after prayer, I spoke to this effect: Brethren, I have not much to trouble you with now; but you know what committee, the last town-meeting here, were chosen; and what they have done, or intend to do; it may be, better than I. But, you see, I have hardly any wood to burn. I need say no more, but leave the matter to your serious and godly consideration.

In fine, after some discourse to and fro, the church voted that Captain Putnam and the two deacons should go, as messengers from the church, to the committee, to desire them to make a rate for the minister, and to take care of necessary supplies for him; and that said messengers should make their return to the church the next tenth day, an hour before sunset, at the minister's house, where they would expect it.*

10 Nov. 1691

The messengers abovesaid came with their return, as appointed; which was, that the committee did not see good to take notice of their message, without they had some letter to show under the church's and pastor's hand. But, at this last church meeting, besides the three messengers, but three other brethren did appear,—namely, Brother Thomas Putnam, Thomas Wilkins, and Peter Prescot,—which slight and neglect of other brethren did not a little trouble me, as I expressed myself. But I told these brethren I expected the church should be more mindful of me than other people, and their way was plain before them, &c.

Sab:, 15 Nov. 1691

The church were desired to meet at Brother Nathaniel Putnam's, the next 18th instant, at twelve o'clock, to spend some time in prayer, and seeking God's presence with us, the next Lord's Day, at his table, as has been usual with us, some time before the sacrament.

18 Nov. 1691

After some time spent, as above said, at this church meeting, the pastor desired the brethren to stay, for as much as he had somewhat to offer to them, which was to this purpose; *viz.*: Brethren, several church meetings have been occasionally warned, and sometimes the appearance of the brethren is but small to what it might be expected, and particularly the case mentioned 10th instant. I told them I did not desire to warn meetings unnecessarily, and, therefore, when I did, I prayed them they would regularly attend them.

Furthermore, I told them I had scarce wood enough to burn till tomorrow, and prayed that some care might be taken. In fine, after discourses passed, these following votes were made unanimously, namely:—

1. That it was needful that complaint should be made to the next honoured County Court, to sit at Salem, the next third day of the week, against the neglects of the present committee.

[*Marginal note in Mr. Parris's hand: "The town-meeting about or at 16 October last (elected):
Jos: Porter
Jos: Hutchinson
Jos: Putnam
Dan: Andrew
Francis Nurse"]

2. That the said complaint should be drawn up, which was immediately done by one of the brethren, and consented to.

3. That our brethren, Nathaniel Putnam, Thomas Putnam, and Thomas Wilkins, should sign said complaint in behalf of the church.

4. Last, That our brethren, Captain John Putnam and the two deacons, should be improved to present the said complaint to the said Court.

In the meantime, the pastor desired the brethren that care might be taken that he might not be destitute of wood.

27 March, Sab. 1691/92, Sacrament day.

After the common auditory was dismissed, and before the church communion at the Lord's Table, the following testimony against the error of our sister, Mary Sibly, who had given direction to my Indian man in an unwarrantable way to find out witches, was read by the Pastor.

[Samual Parris's Statement on the Witchcraft Outbreak]

It is altogether undeniable, that our great and blessed God, for wise and holy ends, hath suffered many persons in several families of this little village, to be grievously vexed, and tortured in body, and to be deeply tempted, to the endangering of the destruction of their souls; and all these amazing feats (well known to many of us) to be done by witchcraft and diabolical operations.

It is also well known, that when these calamities first began, which was in my own family, the affliction was several weeks before such hellish operations, as witchcraft, was suspected. Nay, it never brake forth to any considerable light, until diabolical means were used, by the making of a cake by my Indian man, who had his direction from this our sister, Mary Sibly; since which apparitions have been plenty, and exceeding much mischief hath followed. But by this means (it seems) the Devil hath been raised amongst us, and his rage is vehement and terrible, and when he shall be silenced, the Lord only knows.

But now that this our sister should be instrumental to such distress, is a great grief to myself, and our godly, honored, and reverend neighbours, who have had the knowledge of it. Nevertheless, I do truly hope, and believe, that this our sister doth truly fear the Lord, and am well satisfied from her, that what she did, she did it ignorantly, from what she had heard of this nature from other ignorant, or worse, persons. Yet we are in duty bound to protest against such actions, as being indeed a going to the Devil for help against the Devil; we having no such directions from nature, or God's word, it must, therefore be, and is, accounted by godly Protestants, who write or speak of such matters, as diabolical, and therefore, call this our sister to deep humiliation for what she has done; and all of us to be watchful against Satan's wiles and devices.

Therefore, as we in duty, as a church of Christ, are deeply bound to protest against it, as most directly contrary to the Gospel, yet inasmuch, as this our sister did it in ignorance, as she professeth, and we believe, we can continue in our holy fellowship, upon her serious promise of future better advisedness and caution, and acknowledging, that she is indeed sorrowful for her rashness herein.

Brethren, if this be your mind, that this iniquity be thus borne witness against, manifest it by your usual sign of lifting up your hands.

The brethren voted generally, or universally: None made any exceptions.

Sister Sibley, if you are convinced that you herein did sinfully, and are sorry for it; let us hear it from your own mouth. She did manifest to satisfaction her error and grief for it.

Brethren, if herein you have received satisfaction, testify it by lifting up of your hands.

A general vote passed: No exception made.

Note. 25 March, 1691/92. I discoursed said sister in my study about the grand error above said, and also, then read to her what I had written as above to read to the church, and said sister Sibley assented to the same with tears and sorrowful confession.

Sabbath-day, 14 Aug. 1692.

The church was stayed after the congregation was dismissed, and the Pastor spoke to the church after this manner:

Brethren, you may all have taken notice that several Sacrament days past, our brother Peter Cloyes, and Sam: Nurse and his wife, and John Tarbell and his wife have absented from Communion with us at the Lord's Table, yea have very rarely (except our brother Sam: Nurse) have been with us in common public worship. Now it is needful that the church send some persons to them to know the reason of their absence. Therefore if you be so minded, express yourselves.

None objected: but a general or universal vote after some discourse passed that Brother Nathaniel Putman and the two Deacons should join with the Pastor to discourse with the said absenters about it.

31st August [1692]

Brother Tarbell proves sick, unmeet for discourse. Bro. Cloyes hard to be found at home, being often with his wife in prison at Ipswich for witchcraft, and Brother Nurse and sometimes his wife attends our public meeting, and he the Sacrament.

11 Sept. 1692

Upon all which, we choose to wait further.

11 September, Lord's day

Sister Martha Kory, taken into the church 27th April 1690, was after examination upon suspicion of witchcraft, 21 March, 1691/92, committed to prison for that fact, and was condemned to the gallows for the same yesterday: and was this day in public by a general consent voted to be excommunicated out of the Church; and Lieut. Nathaniel Putman, and the two Deacons chosen to signify to her with the Pastor the mind of the church herein. Accordingly this 14 September 1692 the aforesaid Brethren went with the Pastor to her in Salem prison, whom we found very obdurate, justifying herself and condemning all that had done any thing to her just discovery or condemnation. Whereupon after a little discourse (for her imperiousness would not suffer much) and after prayer (which she was willing to decline) the dreadful sentence of excommunication was pronounced against her.

The Church's Petition to the Court for the maintenance of the Ministry here, *viz.*:

At a church-meeting at Salem Village 26 Dec. 1692 warned the Lord's day before, the following humble petition was unanimously voted, *viz.*:

[This petition, dated December 26, 1692, in which the Salem Village Church requests the Court of Common Pleas to intercede in the matter of neglect on the part of the Village to provide for Mr. Parris's salary, is presented on pages 255-56.]

Note: The petition abovesaid was granted and the honored Court of Quarter Sessions adjourned to this Village to sit 17 Jan. next ensuing to hear and determine the matter.

12 Jan: 1692/93

At a church meeting regularly warned the last Sab. was chosen by a unanimous vote of the present Brethren: Lt. Nath.: Putnam, Capt. John Putnam, the two Deacons, Capt. Jonath: Walcot, and Ensigne Tho: Flint as principal agents in behalf of the Church to negotiate in the affairs respecting the abovesaid Petition, before the honoured Court, adjourned as aforesaid.

15 Jan. Sab: 1692/93

After the Sacrament it was fully if not unanimously voted that hereafter, our Sacraments shall be the first Lord's Day in each month, partly for better remembrance of such as may not always be warned of it, and partly and more especially for the more easy of getting of Bread which then at Salem is provided on purpose for sundry other Churches, and we are to begin the 1st March next, if God please.

[At this point Parris inserts a verbatim copy of the Court's response (dated January 17, 1693) to the Church's petition. This response is presented on pages 256-57.]

25 Jan. [1692/93]

At a meeting of the inhabitants by the order of the Court abovesaid, Jos: Pope, Jos: Holten, jun'r, John Tarbell, Thomas Preston, and James Smith, were chosen Committee-men.

Sabbath, 5 February 1692/93

In the evening the church was stayed; and upon discourse the Pastor and the two deacons and Bro. Nathaniel Putman, and Bro. John Putman sen., and Bro. Bray Wilkins's were chosen by a general vote of the Brotherhood to discourse with Bro. Sam: Nurse, and Bro. John Tarbell about their withdrawing of late from the Lord's Table and public worship of God among us.

7 Feb. 1692/93

The abovesaid brethren, chosen for debate with the abovementioned brethren, met about one a'clock at the Pastor's house; and after prayer the Pastor applied himself to the said three dissenting brethren, telling them that we were appointed by the church to inquire into the grounds of their declining religious communion with us of late. After some pause they each one, one after another, desired further time to consider of our demands. The Pastor replied, You know, brethren, of your dissent and doubtless you cannot be to seek of the reasons of it. But after some words more, some of us looking upon such pleas needless, others being willing to concede to them, it was concluded, that they should meet us again the 16 instant and then give in their reasons; and also if they saw good to bring their dissenting wives with them, or to leave them to another season, as they pleased: with this proviso, that they may acquaint the Pastor timely of it, that he may acquaint the church therewith, that so we may be commissioned to treat with them also, for as yet we were only sent to the brethren, and not to the sisters.

16 Feb. 1692/93

According to the aforesaid concession we, the abovesaid, met again at the Pastor's house to receive answer from the dissenting brethren abovesaid as to the reasons of their dissent; when they gave in a paper containing the matter following, *viz.*:

"Whereas we, Tho. Wilkins, and John Tarbell, and Samuel Nurse, having a long time gone under the burden of great grievances by reason of some unwarrantable actings of Mr. Parris, as we esteem them, and were proceeding in an orderly way to obtain satisfaction from him, and had taken some steps thereunto, according to the advice of some neighbouring elders. But obstructive to our proceeding therein, Mr. Parris and some brethren of the church are appointed by the church to demand a reason of us of our withdrawing from communion. The regularity of which, the proceeding, we do not understand, because in this case we esteem ourselves to be the plaintiffs, and parties offended, and in an orderly way seeking satisfaction, tho' hitherto denied.

"Our answer to the church is that we esteem ourselves hereby prevented in our duty, which we account a grievance, seeing we were first in prosecution of the rule of our Lord Jesus Christ laid down in Matth. 18, 15-16.* Wherefore, if the church please to give us the liberty and freedom of attending our duty, as according to rule bound, possibly then further trouble may be prevented; or otherwise the case will unnecessarily and regularly come before them. But if they deny us this request, we shall as in duty bound give the reasons of our proceeding to the church, or any others, when orderly demanded."

The paper abovesaid was read to us by Sam: Nurse, but they were altogether unwilling to leave it with us; but at length [they were] prevailed with to let us take a copy of it. I gave it to Dea. Putman who desired a copy of it, and from his copy I wrote as abovesaid. These displeased brethren were told that they did ill to reflect upon the church, who, as also the Pastor, was ignorant of their methods; and also that they should first have spoken with the Pastor himself before they went to consult with neighbouring Elders. But to this last, they pleaded ignorance. So we gave way to their request of proceeding orderly.

The 7 Feb. last before the brethren appointed by the church came, the abovesaid three brethren, Jno. Tarbell, Sam: Nurse, and Thom: Wilkins came to my house desiring speech with me; so I took them singly into my study except Tho: Wilkins, for the other two each of them, taken up so much time, *viz.* one an hour at least, and the other more, that before time could be allowed for the other, the appointed brethren came.

Jno: Tarbell said he thought I was guilty of Idolatry, in asking the afflicted persons who they saw upon other afflicted persons. He thought it was agoing to the God of Ekron. Nor did he understand how my oath was safe in court that such and such, by such and such, were knocked down by their looks, and raised up by their touches. And had it not been for me his mother Nurse might have been still living, and so freed from execution; that I had been the great

[*St. Matthew 18:15-17:

'15.   Moreover if thy brother shall trespass against thee, go and tell him his fault between thee and him alone: if he shall hear thee, thou hast gained thy brother.

16.   But if he will not hear thee, then take with thee one or two more, that in the mouth of two or three witnesses every word may be established.

17.   And if he shall neglect to hear them, tell it unto the church: but if he neglect to hear the church, let him be unto thee as an heathen man and a publican.'

Much of the jockeying between Parris and his opponents in these months becomes clearer if one understands that this Biblical passage was being used by each side in the effort to gain an advantage over the other.]

prosecutor, and that others wise and learned who had been as forward as myself were sorry for what they had done, and saw their error, and 'til I did so too, he could not join. His brother Sam: Nurse, for about an hour's time has the same objections.

I answered them that I did not see yet sufficient grounds to vary my opinion, which was confirmed by known and ancient experience frequent in such cases &c. But however in matters of debate, they must give me my opinion, as I would not now quarrel them for theirs &c.

The 8 Feb: Bro. Peter Cloyes came from Boston to me with the very same objections, whom I answered after the like manner.

Some short time after this the abovesaid four displeased brethren came again desiring to speak with me, and Brother William Way along with them.

I told them I would go up to my study, asking which would go first: so Brother Cloyes came up first, bringing Bro: Way and Tho: Wilkins with him, as witness to his demand of satisfaction to what he lately objected. I told him there was but one Brother, there should be two, Tho: Wilkins was in this case Peter Cloyes, and Peter Cloyes [was] Tho: Wilkins; and so I told the rest, when I saw what they aimed at, and advised them to take (according to rule) some other brother or brethren besides brother Way, or else I could not hear them, in the way they aimed at. But they would urge that this was enough, and one was sufficient; I answered that Christ's rule was for two or three: so they departed.

27 March 1692/93

At night Bro: Cloyes, and Brother Tarbell abovesaid came to my house together with Mr. Joseph Hutchinson, Sen., and Mr. Joseph Putman and a little after William Osburne of Salem (which three last, it seems, came for witnesses, as Bro: Cloyes owned the 20 Apr. following) and they gave me a paper not subscribed by any person, but a cut in the place of subscription, where two or three names might be written. The contents of which paper was as followeth, *viz.*:

"To our pastor and minister, Mr. Sam: Parris of Salem Village, and to some others of the plantation.

"We whose names are underwritten, being deeply sensible that those uncomfortable differences that are amongst us, are very dishonourable to God and a scandal to religion, and very uncomfortable to ourselves, and an ill example to those that may come after us. And by our maintaining and upholding differences amongst us, we do but gratify the Devil, that grand adversary of our Souls. For the removal of which we have thought meet to proffer our present thoughts to your serious consideration, hoping that there may be such methods propounded as may be for the settling and confirming peace and unity amongst us both at the present and for the future. And our desires are that such a foundation may be laid for peace and truth that the gates of Hell may not prevail against it. And in order thereunto Solomon adviseth to counsel. And our desires are that a council of Elders may be mutually chosen to hear all our grievances between Mr. Parris and us, and to determine where the blameable cause is. And we hope that their wisdom and prudence may direct us to such a method, as may be for our comfort, for both present and future."

When I had read it, I asked them who this paper came from. They answered, all the Plantation, or a great many of them at least. I demanded why, then, did none subscribe it: They said, all in good time. So I put it in my pocket. They demanded an answer to it: I told them I would consider of it.

28 March 1693

The abovesaid brethren, together with said Hutchinson, came again at night for an answer to the abovesaid Paper: I told them I had not considered of it yet.

14 April 1693

Our displeased Brethren, Jno: Tarbell, Sam: Nurse, and Tho: Wilkins came again, bringing with them said Hutchinson and Francis Nurse. After a little while I went down from my study to them: asking them if they would speak with me. They said yes, they came to discourse about the paper (abovesaid) they had brought to me. I told them I had no time to talk. I was this day to preach to a private meeting. Nor was I willing to discourse with them alone: but appoint time and place I would meet with them. So we agreed after our next lecture to meet at Bro. Nathaniel Putman's.

20 April 1693

After Lecture, my self, Capt. Putnam, Ensign Flint, and the two Deacons, met the four displeased brethren abovesaid at Lt. Nath. Putnam's abovesaid, where we found together with them, and for them, said Mr. Hutchinson and Mr. Israel Porter. After a little while, I told them, to gratify them, I was come to hear what they had to offer. They demanded an answer to the paper abovesaid. Whereupon I plucked it out of my pocket, and read it openly. They owned that to be the paper. I asked them what they called it: they being to seek of a name for it. I told them I looked upon it as a libel. Then they produced a like paper subscribed by said brethren, and divers more to the number of forty and two names, but all seemed to be one and the same hand. I desired the original paper. They said they knew not where it was. Then it was asked whether those men wrote their own names. It was answered, yes, or they were written by their order. Then I desired them to subscribe this paper with the hands to it, testifying that no name was there, but such as had consulted thereto. But none would yield to this. Then I told them we must know what we do: had I to do with displeased people, or displeased brethren? They answered, they came as brethren. Then I told them, none but brethren should have been present. They said they had been with me already; and I refused to give them satisfaction. I answered, I did not understand their drift, and therefore did not discourse them, as I would have done had I apprehended they came to reason as such as had taken offence. And when they came the second time, they brought but one brother, *viz.* William Way, and took others of themselves.

Lt. Putman told them it was not too late yet; now there were several of the brethren [present], and they might take any two of them, and discourse with the Pastor. No, they said they had done it already. Thus much time was spent till just night; and myself and other Brethren upon going home, the four displeased brethren agreed to meet me tomorrow morning about an hour after sunrise, with the two Deacons and Bro. William Way and Brother Aaron Way, to discourse the matter; to which I readily assented.

21 April 1693

This morning we met as abovesaid at Deacon Ingersoll's. After a little while, I began with prayer. Then brother Nurse read a large scroll of about fifteen articles, as reasons why they withdrew communion from us. Seven of them I think, were reasons of absenting from public worship with us, and the other eight, I think, causes of separation from my ministry. I desired to see them, but was denied for a great while; at length I had liberty to read them myself, upon the promise of returning them to them. After all, I demanded them, or a copy of them. But they would not consent thereto: nor to the desire of the other four indifferent brethren, tho' we urged it by argument. But the Dissenters said, no: They had told me, and that was enough; and they desired me to call the church, and then I should have it.

Sab: 30 Apr. 1693

After public worship was ended, the Church was stayed, to whom the Pastor spoke to this effect: Brethren, you know some of our Brethren have for a time withdrawn from us. I do not understand their methods. They desire to speak with the Church: if you gratify them herein, I recommend their motion to you. After a little discourse it was voted that the Church meet 18 May next, after Lecture, at the Pastor's house, and in the meantime Brother Benj. Putman and Bro. Sam Sibly to acquaint Bro: Nurse and Bro. Tarbell tomorrow (Bro. Cloyes being at Boston, where he has lived these many months; so that we sent not to him, supposing the abovesaid his kinsmen would); and Bro. Benj. Wilkins and Bro. Aaron Wey to acquaint their neighbor Tho: Wilkins tomorrow also; so that all of them may have timely notice.

18 May 1693

At a church-meeting appointed as abovesaid at the Pastor's, twenty Brethren (besides the Pastor and the abovesaid displeased Brethren, *viz.* three of them, *viz.* Jno. Tarbell, Tho: Wilkins and Sam: Nurse) being present. After prayer the Pastor applied himself to the three abovesaid Brethren, saying to this effect:

Brethren, you desired the Church to give you a meeting, now they are here and I have you to acquaint them with your reason for desiring of it.

They answered it was to tell their charge against Mr. Parris, and now they had witnesses to prove it. After much agitation Brother Nath: Putnam was by vote of the Church chosen to put to vote which was needful. And it being put to vote whether they apprehended the said Brethren had proceeded regularly according to 18 Matth.,* and so whether the Church could now hear it, it was passed negatively by a general or universal vote, excepting the said three dissenting Brethren. Also by a like vote it passed in the affirmative that the Church would hear the said dissatisfied Brethren upon their bringing the case to them according to Christ's Rules.

Note: that the general deportment of the said three displeased Brethren was at this meeting exceeding unchristian, both to Minister and the other Brethren; very inreverent towards him, and as rough towards them to the great grief of many, if not the whole Church. Nor did they stick to affirm that the Church could not judge the case, was not capable of it. Being asked, why then did they desire the Church to come together? they replied that they might tell the Church, and so bring it to council; which was the point they aimed at and abundantly insisted upon. The Church made return, that they would be ready for a council in a regular way. The said three Brethren being asked whether they were offended with any of the Brethren besides the Pastor? they replied, they did not come to tell that now; that was not their present business. Being asked by the Pastor himself, whether they there were all one and equal in their offence with him? they answered, yes. The Pastor then replied that he would not then have them hereafter meet with him together, but each of them singly; for when they came the very first time he did not understand this drift, and therefore did not debate with them, and the case required arguing. Sam: Nurse replied he did not care to come to the house, nor to discourse me alone.

Sab: 23 July, 1693

Admitted into the Church:

28.   Joseph Whipple, *An. Aetat.* 27, 1st Nov. next.

Sab: 17 Sept. 1693

Admitted unto full communion:

36.   Sarah (wife to James) Prince, *Anno Aetat.* 29

Sab: 24 Sept. 1693

Received into full communion:

37.   Hannah (wife to Deacon) Ingersoll., *An. Aetat.* 56

[*See note, page 282.]

13 Octob. 1693

I received a letter from the Rev. Mr. Jno. Higginson directed to myself and brethren of this Church. The sum whereof was to advise us to join with the complainants in calling a Council of neighbouring churches, not excepting against any [one] on either side. Which letter, he writes, was occasioned from another letter from Mr. Willard in the name of the Elders of Boston, directed to himself, Mr. Noyes, and Mr. Hale, to desire him to persuade us so to do. Communicated the same letter this day to sundry of the Brethren at a private meeting at Deacon Ingersoll's.

14 October, 1693

I received a letter from the Rev. Mr. Hale and Mr. Noyes, directed to myself and church, of the same tenor, for substance, with the abovesaid of Mr. Higginson's, only herein were several conditions upon which a council should be chosen, omitted in that.

Sab: 15 Octob. 1693

I stayed the Church at night, telling them of the 2 abovesaid letters; we appointed a Meeting the 10th instant at the Pastor's house to read and debate upon them, at three a'clock afternoon.

19 Octob. 1693

A very stormy day, wind and rain, so that but 12 Brethren besides myself were present. After prayer, we read and debated the abovesaid 2 letters, and some of the petitions of the complainants to the General Court and several remote Churches.

We voted unanimously that we concurred with the advice abovesaid to call a Council in an orderly way, and therefore chose Broth. Bray Wilkins and Brother Peter Prescot to go to Bro. Tho: Wilkins with our desire that he would meet the Church the 23d instant at 2 a'clock afternoon at Deacon Ingersol's house in order to join with them in calling a Council, according to our late advice from some neighboring Elders: And Bro. Nath: Putnam and Bro. Joshua Rea and Bro. Nath: Ingersol to go likewise tomorrow with the like message to Bro: Jno. Tarbel, Bro. Sam: Nurse and Bro. Peter Cloyes (if in the Village). And also voted that we the concording Brethren meet at the same place at the hour of eleven, and that the Brethren have notice of the same the next Lord's day.

Sab: 22 Ditto 1693

The Church was stayed in the afternoon and the Brethren told by the Pastor that the last sixth day we wanted several of them, and supposed that the great storm hindered some of them. But those of us present had consulted the abovesaid letters from neighboring Elders sent to us with advice: upon which we

had gone to the dissenting Brethren to meet us tomorrow, and desired all come
that possibly then could, as agreed 19 instant.

At Deacon Ingersoll's. 23 Ditto 1693

The Church (i.e., Brethren) met as above agreed, and again there being about
20 Brethren the abovesaid letters from Mr. Higginson, Mr. Hale and Mr. Noyes
were read, and the counsel therein given us by all approved, *viz.*: to join in
calling a Council with our dissenting Brethren upon these orderly conditions (as
abovesaid given) *viz.*: 1. That the case be stated which we go to Council for, as
15 Acts 2.* 2. That the dissenting Brethren give in their charge under their
hands and have known which persons they are dissatisfied with, according to 15
Acts 2 and 25-27. 3. That we will likewise give in our charge against them
which we would bring to Council against them, as we expect of them, under our
hands. 4. That as they shall have from us, so we will have from them the
particular witnesses to each particular charge. 5. That we agree how the charges
of the Council shall be borne.

Almost 3 a'clock the dissenting Brethren came, and after much debate (they
desiring to bring up others which we had not sent for and they had brought with
them) we gave way that they should bring up such of them as were in full
communion with other Churches. So they brought up Mr. Israel Porter. Then I
told them we were met in order to call a Council, and we desired to know what
we should call a Council about.

They said their offence was against Mr. Parris and not the Church, and
offered to read a paper as matter for the Council. But we answered that we
would not hear it unless they would leave it with us after it was read, or a copy
of it, that we might consider of it: And we would deal the like by them, give
them our charge under our hands. They replied they would never do so: each of
them expressing their unwillingness to this: and withal said they would have a
Council whether we would or not; and thus they parted, after we had much
urged as abovesaid.

[Samuel Parris to the Ministers of Salem and Beverly]

"To the Revd. Mr. John $\begin{cases} \text{Higginson} \\ \text{Hale} \end{cases}$ and Mr. Nicholas Noyes, Ministers of the
Churches in Salem and Beverly

[*Acts. 15:1-2:

'1. And certain men which came down from Judaea taught the brethren, and said,
Except ye be circumcised after the manner of Moses, ye cannot be saved.

2. When therefore Paul and Barnabas had no small disputation with them, they
determined that Paul and Barnabas, and certain other of them, should go up to Jerusalem
unto the apostles and elders about this question.'

*This passage provided the Biblical justification and procedure for carrying the dispute
beyond the confines of the local church to a Council of Churches.]*

"Revd. and much honored Sirs:

"This day and 19th instant also (at Church meetings purposely warned) we deliberately read your advice to us, and debated upon it, concluding with a universal concurrence the scheme following, *viz.*: We do in the first place very acceptably receive your counsel. And as we conceive, we have not hitherto been obstructive to the orderly calling of a Council, for help in, and if it might be, healing of our ill-circumstanced case; so we hope we shall not for the future. We are glad to hear our dissenters have promised the Bay Worthies a compliance with the motion of mutual and orderly choosing of a Council. If they do so, we shall be in a fair way (by the merciful smiles of God) to some needful issue. We are conscious to ourselves of standing upon nothing but what is exceeding requisite, *viz.* matter and order; in which, had we been conceded to before, we presume a union (if possible) had been attained, or a Council called in to our help thereto, long ago. It is not a little our frequent and daily grief to consider what amazing confused noises (by the by) we hear go of us. The reports, reporters, and upon what grounds received, we are to seek of. We might groan out some things before men, but we will content ourselves (at present) to sigh them out before the Lord. Our troubles (particularly our Minister's) right and left, as far as we know in the circumstances of them, have hitherto been unparalleled; and for Zion's sake we pray they ever may.

"Since the abovesaid the dissenting Brethren met us (upon appointment the 19 instant, being sent for by us to meet in order to counsel) but refused (as soon as [they] came, and long afterwards) to discourse with the Church unless they might be permitted to intrude others not of the Church upon us; which we for a time argued against. At length we gave place (still declaring against its irregularity) that they should be suffered to bring up, of such as they had brought with them, such as stood in full communion with other Churches. After this they would bring in no charge or accusation against any, otherwise than by reading of what they had prepared, unless we would first consent to the actual choosing of a Council: which we, quoting 15 Acts 2 and 25, could not consent unto; unless besides reading of their paper (whatever it was) they would leave it with us, or a copy of it. On the other hand, we offering them the like, to give in our charges against them under our hands, which we would have a hearing of by the said Council. But all was rejected, and so near sunset broke up to no purpose. Thus in haste, leaving you to the all-good God, to whom we desire you earnestly and constantly to recommend our persons and bewildered case, we remain, Worthy Sirs, yours truly in him who is love and truth,

Sam: Parris $\left\{ \begin{array}{l} \text{with consent of the} \\ \text{Brethren of the Church} \end{array} \right.$

Salem Village, 23 Octo. 1693"

Sab: 5 Nov. 1693

At night, by vote of the Church, Bro. Ingersoll and Bro. Benj. Putnam were chosen to go tomorrow to Bro. Nurse and Bro. Tarbell with this message: that they meet us the 13 instant at 10 a'clock at the Pastor's house, farther to discourse of, and also to have communicated to them, the late advice we spoke of last time from our neighboring Elders, in order to calling in of Council, if we cannot issue amongst ourselves; and to leave with said Tarbell and Nurse the said message to be communicated to Bro. Cloyes if he be not too remote. And by same vote the like message was sent to Bro. Tho: Wilkins by his father and Bro. Aaron Wey.

13 Nov. 1693

Almost 1 a'clock at noon after the Church had been long together 3 of the abovesaid dissenting Brethren came, *viz.*: Peter Cloyes, Sam: Nurse and John Tarbell, to whom after prayer, and caution from the Pastor of observing order and meetness, he read the advice of the Revd. Mr. Higginson and of the Revd. Mr. Hale and Mr. Noyes to the Church, with the places of Scripture quoted by them; and then desired and long urged an account of their accusations, subscribed by them, according to said advice. But after all we could obtain none, they saying the Church had refused it already, and ([illegible] to their old irregular proceedings) they would read them now before the Church (but not leave them) in case they might be suffered to bring in with them some members of other Churches as witnesses, whom they had brought near at hand for that purpose. To which the Church answered that it would not give way to such innovations. The upshot was a paper they brought in, signed by said Cloys, Nurse and Tarbell, dated this day, in way of petition for themselves and neighbors, as follows:

[Petition of Peter Cloyce, Samuel Nurse, and John Tarbell]

The humble petition and request of us under-named, though unworthy for ourselves and the rest of our neighbors, who being greatly grieved and much oppressed (unto our Revd. Pastor and the rest of our Brethren in the Church of Salem Village) humbly showeth, that whereas you have been pleased to give us some encouragement of a discourse this day in order to an accommodation of supposed but unhappy differences; and praying that it may be effectual, we offer if you please that a Council of indifferent persons be indifferently chosen: Or that we agree together for a Council chosen by the General Court; who may have full power to hear and determine all differences, real and imaginable, which hath arisen amongst us; which if obtained, then we do promise to give unto you our Pastor the particulars of our grievances, in writing, thirty days before the said Council shall meet, to consider thereof. Provided that you our said Pastor and the rest of our Brethren will give us an answer in writing six days before said meeting.

This 13 Nov. 1693

Peter Cloyes
Sam: Nurse
John Tarbell

When we had this paper, we asked them whether this was all that they would now come to. They said yes. Then Bro. Cloyes being in haste to be gone, we told them we would consider of it, and give them some answer hereafter to it; and desired them to stay a little and hear what the Church had to say against them. So the Pastor read a charge against them containing above thirty articles, and so dismissed them.

[Parris inserts this document, listing his more than thirty grievances against the dissenters, later in the record, under the entry for February 7, 1695.]

Sab: 26 Nov. 1693

To our Beloved Brethren, Peter Cloyes, Sam: Nurse and Jno. Tarbell. When you were with us last, *viz.* 13 instant, at our sending for, to hear and pursue the advice from the Revd. Mr. Higginson, Mr. Hale and Mr. Noyes, sent to us at the request of the Revd. Elders at Boston, you knew that the utmost which you would come up to then was at last to leave a paper with us, subscribed with each of your names. To which upon consideration of it (as we then promised) we now return answer, *viz.*:

That we find said paper far other than we hoped for, and altogether alien (or strange) from the said advice, which no sooner came to our hands but had acceptance with us; and since that, we are informed, is well approved by the Revd. Elders at Boston, who on your behalf, and as your sureties, occasioned it. So that to say no more (though we might enlarge upon it) we cannot at all take up with your offer therein; but hereby manifest to you that we still stand to said advice. So exhorting you to study the things which made for peace (Romans 14: 19). And therefore that you seriously weigh those texts: II Sam. 2: 26, Pro. 16: 32, Matth. 6: 12 and 18: 21-22, [illegible] 4: 26-27, Gal. 5: 9, James 3: 13 to the end. And that you have a care of destroying the Church of God, II Corinth. [illegible]. Always praying for your best good, we subscribe your [illegible] and affectionate Brethren:

Salem Village, 26 Nov. 1693	Sam. Parris	{ with consent { of the Brethren

The same day the abovesaid answer was voted by the Brethren: Deacon Ingersol and Broth. Jonathan Putnam [were] voted to carry it. But the 27th day Bro. Joshua Rea came to me with Deacon Ingersoll, telling me bro. Jonathan could not go this day, so I made said Bro. Rea join with said Deacon in the message, both which two-mentioned Brethren carried it.

Sab: 4 March 1693/94

Received into full communion with the Church:

29. John Wilkins, and baptized: *Anno Aetat 28*

[Seven Massachusetts Ministers Advise
the Salem-Village Church]

Salem, June 14, 1694

We whose names are underwritten, being desired by some persons of Salem
Village to meet together and try if we could give any direction how the said
differences there may be healed, and having heard the particulars which the
dissatisfied Brethren and neighbors have drawn up on matters they would
present to a Council, and also signifying their averseness to apply themselves to
the Church there for an accommodation, and considering the sad effects likely
to follow on the continuance of this fire of contention, would suggest to the
Revd. and beloved the Pastor and Brethren of the Church at the Village that
they join with their dissatisfied Brethren and neighbors in calling of a Council of
six Churches, indifferently chosen by your and their consent, mutually agreed
on. Provided that they and you consent that the said Council be acknowledged
to hear and determine according to the mind of Christ upon matters in
difference which they shall fairly represent to you and you to them, in writing
before the Council be called, of all matters proper for an Ecclesiastical Council;
and that you agree how the charges of said Council shall be borne before the
Council be called. We beseech you to study those things which make for peace
and edification, Eph. 4: 1-3.

John Higginson	Sam: Cheever
James Allen	Nich: Noyes (consents to this
John Hale	advice with this proviso:
Sam: Willard	that he be not chosen
	one of the Council)
	Jos: Gerrish

Sab: 17 June 1694

The above advice was in the evening communicated by the Pastor to the
Church, and the 21 instant a Church meeting at 2 a'clock appointed farther to
discourse of it.

21 June 1694

At the meeting before appointed, several things were discoursed of and left
unto farther consideration. As: (1) The Church's compliance with the abovesaid
advice; (2) That the charges be borne by such as are so eager for a Council;
(3) That the Brethren following, viz.: Lft. and Capt. Putnam, Bray Wilkins, with
the two Deacons assist the Pastor at meetings, when and where he shall appoint,
to negotiate in affairs appertaining to matters abovesaid, that the whole Church
may not be oppressed otherwise with multitudes of meetings, nor called together
but as necessity requires. And at such private meetings any Brother may come
(he by inquiry knowing when and where they are) and all are desired at such
times times to meet who can give any personal help for greater expedition. These
things were discoursed and left to farther consideration, but not voted.

Ditto 29

At a usual Church-meeting (before the Sacrament) towards evening, we again discoursed of the 7 Ministers' advice abovesaid, but concluded upon nothing—most if not all of the Brethren present—being rather farther off from approbation of said advice than before: Nor indeed were some of us willing to come to determination till we had first by solemn fasting and prayer sought unto God for his guidance. And therefore the 4 July next was appointed for that purpose.

July 5, 1694

At a Church fast at Lft. Putnam's (the text being on Ps. 5: 8, last part) where were 20 Brethren present, in the evening it was voted (after as much reasonings to and fro as time would allow) that the seven Ministers' advice dated June 14 last (as abovesaid) should be read publicly before all the congregation the next Lord's day, and then that the thirteenth instant July should be published as a day, wherein at two a'clock in the afternoon, we would meet at the meeting-house, openly to hear all dissatisfactions that should be brought by any of the inhabitants of this Village, in order to a Council, according to said advice: And that our Brethren William and Aaron Way be desired and are hereby appointed to acquaint our dissatisfied Bro. Tho: Wilkins with this our agreement, both for himself the said Tho: Wilkins, and also the Brethren dissatisfied with him. And that the Church (and such neighbors as are in amity with them, if they please) meet the same thirteenth instant at 12 a'clock at noon at Deacon Ingersoll's.

Note: That this vote abovesaid was not approved by all; several could not concur with it. I also propounded that some messengers should be sent with notice of said vote to some of the dissatisfied neighbors in behalf of all of them. But this could not be assented to: one and all (I think) did dislike it and gave reasons for their dislike of it.

Sab: July 8, 1694

The above agreement was published by the Pastor.

July 13, 1694

We met in public as above appointed but came to no agreement: the dissenters refusing to give in any charge unless we would first engage to choose a Council.

Sept. 20, 1694. Received the following letter:

"To the Revd. and Beloved the Elders and Brethren of the Church at Salem Village:

"Being informed that the advice offered to yourselves and signed by us with one other Elder is not accepted by you for calling of a Council in your case; and that you interpret the meaning of some general and ambiguous expressions in that writing contrary to our unanimous declared sense at the time of our subscribing. We whose names are underwritten find it to be our duty to express our minds more plainly and particularly, that we may be the more clearly understood without mistake, *viz*.: Our advice is that you join with your unsatisfied Brethren and neighbors for calling a Council of six Churches, not excepting against any that are chosen on either side; and that after you have agreed on the place and time of the Council's meeting, and how the charges shall be borne, we say after this is done, we advise that the unsatisfied Brethren and neighbors do give into Mr. Parris a true copy of those two papers of grievance which were showed to us, at least 20 days before the time of the Council's meeting. And because we fear that longer delays will be of dangerous consequences to you in diverse respects, we pray you so to agree, that you may have a Council before winter. Consider what we have said, and the Lord give you understanding in all things.

Sept. 10, '94

"Subscribed to the Reverend Mr. Parris, the Pastor, and the Brethren of the Church at Salem Village

John Higginson
James Allen
Sam. Willard
Sam: Cheever
Joseph Gerrish"

The same day at a public and general meeting the following offers were given to our dissenters, being before prepared:

"We have long discoursed of a Council, and look upon yourselves as the only bar to it, because you refuse to give in to us the matters you would bring to a Council. But that we may not contend forever, we rather concede that a Council shall be chosen this moment, we choosing four Churches and you three; and that you give us immediately your dissatisfactions signed under your hands; and only such things be brought in as are proper for an Ecclesiastical Council; and if we find among your matters such as are improper for such a Council, you shall withdraw the same before the session of said Council: otherwise the said Council to fall [illegible].

"Voted this 29 Sept. 1694 by twenty Brethren present besides the Pastor, Sam: Parris.

"To our dissenting Brethren and neighbors."

2 Nov. At a Church meeting at Deacon Ingersoll's—15 Brethren besides the Pastor being present. It was debated whether it was not high time to call our 3 dissenting Brethren to give us in the grounds of their withdrawing from us. And after some discourse it was concluded and voted by a universal vote that the next Lord's day in public it should be put to vote of all the Brethren whether they thought meet that the next Lord's Day after, Bro. Jno. Tarbell should be desired and required in public to bring in his reasons etc.

Sab: 4 Nov. 1694

After sermon in the afternoon, it was propounded to the Brethren, whether the Church ought not to inquire again of our dissenting brethren after the reason of their dissent. Nothing appearing from any against it, it was put to vote, and carried in the affirmative (by all, as far as I know, except Brother Josh: Rea), that Brother Jno: Tarbell should the next Lord's Day, appear and give in his reasons in public; the contrary being propounded, if any had aught to object against it. But no dissent was manifested; and so Bro. Nathaniel Putnam and Deacon Ingersoll were desired to give this message from the Church to said Bro. Tarbell.

Sab: 11 Nov. 1694

Before the evening blessing was pronounced, Bro. Tarbell was openly called again and again; but, he not appearing, application was made to the abovesaid Church's messengers for his answer: whereupon said Brother Putnam reported that said Brother Tarbell told him he did not know how to come to us on a Lord's Day, but desired rather that he might make his appearance some week-day. Whereupon the congregation was dismissed with the blessing; and the Church stayed, and, by a full vote renewed their call of said Brother Tarbell to appear the next Lord's Day for the ends abovesaid; and Deacon Putnam and Bro. Jonathan Putnam were desired to be its messengers to said dissenting Brother.

Sab: 18 Nov. 1694

The said Bro. came in the afternoon; and after sermon, he was asked the reasons for his withdrawing. Whereupon he produced a paper which he was urged to deliver to the Pastor to communicate to the Church; but he refused it, asking who was the church's mouth. To which when he was answered, "The Pastor," he replied, Not in this case, because his offence was with him. The Pastor demanded whether he had offence against any of the Church besides the pastor. He answered, "No." So at length we suffered a non-member, Mr. Jos: Hutchinson, to read it. After which the Pastor read openly before the whole congregation his Overtures for peace and reconciliation. After which said Tarbell, seemingly (at least) much affected, said that if half so much had been said formerly, it had never come to this. But he added that others also were dissatisfied besides himself: and therefore he desired opportunity that they might come also, which was immediately granted; viz., the 26 instant, at 2 a'clock.

26 Nov. 1694

At the public meeting above appointed at the meeting-house, after the Pastor had first sought the grace of God with us in prayer, he then summed up to the church and congregation (among which were several strangers) the occasion of

our present assembling, as is hinted the last meeting. Then seeing, together with
Bro: Tarbell, two more of our dissenting brethren, *viz.*, Sam: Nurse and Thomas
Wilkins (who had, to suit their designs, placed themselves in a seat conveniently
together), the Church immediately, to save farther sending for them, voted that
said Bro. Wilkins and Bro. Nurse should now, together with Bro. Tarbell give
their reasons of withdrawing from the Church. Then the Pastor applied himself
to all these three dissenters, pressing the Church's desire upon them. So they
produced a paper, which they much opposed the coming into the Pastor's hands
and his reading of, but at length they yielded to it. Whilst the paper was reading,
Bro. Nurse looked upon another (which he said was the original): and after it
was read throughout, he said it was the same with what he had. Their paper was
as followeth:—

[John Tarbell, Thomas Wilkins, and Samuel Nurse
Summarize Their Grievances, November 26, 1694]

"The reasons why we withdraw from communion with the Church of Salem
Village, both as to hearing the word preached, and from partaking with them at
the Lord's Table, are as followeth:—

1. Why we attend not on public prayer and preaching the word, these are,
   (1) The distracting and disturbing tumults and noises made by the persons
   under diabolical power and delusions, preventing sometimes our hearing
   and understanding and profiting of the word preached; we having, after
   many trials and experiences, found no redress in this case, accounted
   ourselves under a necessity to go where we might hear the word in quiet.
   (2) The apprehensions of danger of ourselves being accused as the Devil's
   instruments to molest and afflict the persons complaining, we seeing
   those whom we had reason to esteem better than ourselves thus accused,
   blemished, and of their lives bereaved, forseeing this evil, thought it our
   prudence to withdraw. (3) We found so frequent and positive preaching
   up some principles and practices by Mr. Parris, referring to the trouble
   then among us and upon us; therefore thought it our most safe and
   peaceable way to withdraw.
2. The reasons why we hold not communion with them at the Lord's Table
   are, first, we esteem ourselves justly aggrieved and offended with the
   officer who doth administer, for the reasons following:
   (1) From his declared and published principles, referring to our
       molestation from the invisible world, differing from the opinion of
       the generality of the Orthodox Ministers of the whole country.
   (2) His easy and strong faith and belief of the affirmations and accusa-
       tions made by those they call the afflicted.
   (3) His laying aside that grace which above all, we are required to put
       on; namely, charity towards his neighbors, and especially towards
       those of his Church, when there is no apparent reason for the
       contrary.
   (4) His approving and practising unwarrantable and ungrounded methods
       for discovering what he was desirous to know referring to the

Bewitched or possessed persons, as in bringing some to others, and by and from them pretending to inform himself and others who were the Devil's instruments to afflict the sick and pained.

(5) His unsafe and unaccountable oath, given by him against sundry of the accused.

(6) His not rendering to the world so fair, if true, an account of what he wrote on examination of the afflicted.

(7) Sundry unsafe, if sound, points of doctrine delivered in his preaching, which we esteem not warrantable, if Christian.

(8) His persisting in these principles and justifying his practices, not rendering any satisfaction to us when regularly desired, but rather farther offending and dissatisfying ourselves.

John Tarbell
Tho: Wilkins
Sam: Nurse"

When the Pastor had read these charges, he asked the dissenters above mentioned whether they were offended with none in the Church besides himself. They replied that they articled against none else. Then the officer asked them if they withdrew from communion upon account of none in the Church besides himself. They answered that they withdrew only on my account. Then I read them my "Meditations for Peace," mentioned 18 instant; *viz.*: —

[Samuel Parris, "Meditations for Peace," November 1694]

"For as much as it is the undoubted duty of all Christians to pursue peace (Ps. 24: 14) even unto a reaching of it, if it be possible (Rom. 12: 18, 19); and whereas, through the righteous, sovereign and awful Providence of God, the Grand Enemy of all Christian peace has of late, been most tremendously let loose in divers places hereabouts, and more especially amongst our sinful selves, not only to interrupt that partial peace which we did sometimes enjoy, but also, through his wiles and temptations and our weaknesses and corruptions, to make wider breaches, and raise more bitter animosities between too many of us, of one mind for a time, and afterwards of differing apprehensions, and, at last are but in the dark, — upon serious thoughts of all or most of all, and after many prayers, I have been moved to present to you (my beloved flock) the following particulars, in way of contribution towards regaining of Christian concord (if so be we are not altogether unappeasable, irreconcilable, and so destitute of that good spirit which is first pure, then peaceable, gentle, easy to be entreated, James 3: 17); *viz.*,

(1) In that the Lord ordered the late horrid calamity (which afterwards, plague-like, spread in many other places) to break out first in my family, I cannot but look upon as a very sore rebuke, and humbling providence, both to myself and mine, and desire so we may improve it.

(2) In that also in my family were some of both parties, *viz.*, accusers and accused, I look also as an aggravation of the rebuke, as an addition of wormwood to the gall.

(3) In that means were used in my family (though totally unknown to me or mine, excepts servants, till afterwards) to raise spirits and create apparitions in a no better than diabolical way, I do also look upon as a farther rebuke of Divine Providence. And by all, I do humbly own this day before the Lord and his people, that God has been righteously spitting in my face (Num. 12: 14). And I desire to lie low under all this reproach, and to lay my hand upon my mouth.

(4) As to the management of those mysteries, as far as concerns myself, I am very desirous (upon farther light) to own any errors I have therein fallen into and can come to a discerning of.

In the meanwhile, I do acknowledge, upon after-considerations, that, were the same troubles again (which the Lord of his rich mercy forever prevent), I should not agree with my former apprehensions in all points; as, for instance,

(1) I question not but God sometimes suffers the Devil (as of late) to afflict in the shape of not only innocent but pious persons, or so to delude the senses of the afflicted that they strongly conceive their hurt is from such persons, when indeed it is not.

(2) The improving [i.e., use] of one afflicted to inquire by who afflicts the others, I fear may be and has been unlawfully used, to Satan's great advantage.

(3) As to my writing, it was put upon me by authority; and therein have I been very careful to avoid the wronging of any.*

(4) As to my oath, I never meant it, nor do I know how it can be otherwise construed, than as vulgarly and [by] everyone understood; yea and upon inquiry it may be found so worded also.

(5) As to any passage in preaching or prayer, in that sore hour of distress and darkness, I always intended but due justice on each hand and that not according to man, but God (who knows all things most perfectly), however, through weakness or sore exercise, I might sometimes, yea and possibly sundry times, unadvisedly expressed myself.

(6) As to several that have confessed against themselves, they being wholly strangers to me but yet of good account with better men than myself, to whom also they are well known, I do not pass so much as a secret condemnation upon them; but rather, seeing God has so amazingly lengthened out Satan's chain in this most formidable outrage, I much more incline to side with the opinion of those that have grounds to hope better of them.

(7) As to all that have unduly suffered in these matters (either in their persons or relations) through the clouds of human weakness, and Satan's wiles and

[*Here occurs a marginal note in Mr. Parris's handwriting: "(a) Added by the desire of the Council, this following paragraph; viz., Nevertheless, I fear that in and through the throng of many things written by me, in the late confusions, there has not been a due exactness always used; and, as I now see the inconveniency of my writing so much on those difficult occasions, so I would lament every error of such writings.— Apr. 3, 1695. Idem. S.P."]

sophistry, I do truly sympathise with them; taking it for granted that such as drew themselves clear of this great transgression, or that have sufficient grounds so to look upon their dear friends, have hereby been under those sore trials and temptations, that not an ordinary measure of true grace would be sufficient to prevent a bewraying of remaining corruption.

(8) I am very much in the mind and abundantly persuaded that God (for holy ends, though for what in particular, is best known to himself) has suffered the evil angels to delude us on both hands, but how far on the one side or the other is much above me to say. And, if we cannot reconcile till we come to a full discerning of these things, I fear we shall never come to agreement, or, at soonest not in this world. Therefore:

(9) In fine, the matter being so dark and perplexed as that there is no present appearance that all God's servants should be altogether of one mind, in all circumstances touching the same, I do most heartily, fervently, and humbly beseech pardon of the merciful God through the blood of Christ, of all my mistakes and trespasses in so weighty a matter; and also all your forgiveness of every offence in this or other affairs, wherein you see or conceive I have erred and offended; professing, in the presence of the Almighty God that what I have done has been, as for substance, as I apprehended was duty,—however through weakness, ignorance, &c., I may have been mistaken; I also, through grace, promising each of you the like of me. And so again, I beg, entreat, and beseech you, that Satan, the devil, the roaring lion, the old dragon, the enemy of all righteousness, may no longer be served by us, by our envy and strifes (where every evil work prevails whilst these bear sway, Isa. 3: 14-16); but that all from this day forward, may be covered with the mantel of love, and we may on all hands forgive each other heartily, sincerely, and thoroughly, as we do hope and pray that God, for Christ's sake, would forgive each of ourselves (Matt. 28: 21 *ad. fine*; Col. 3: 12, 13). Put on therefore, as the elect of God, holy and beloved, bowels of mercies, kindness, humbleness of mind, meekness, long-suffering, forbearing one another, and forgiving one another. If any man have a quarrel against any, even as Christ forgave you so also do ye (Eph. 4: 31, 32). Let all bitterness and wrath and anger and clamor and evil-speaking be put away from you, with all malice; and be ye kind to one another, tenderhearted, forgiving one another, even as God, for Christ's sake, hath forgiven you.

Amen. Amen.   Sam: Parris.

29.9 [Nov.], 1694."

After I had read these overtures abovesaid, I desired the Brethren to declare themselves whether they remained still dissatisfied. Bro: Tarbell answered that they desired to consider of it, and to have a copy of what I had read. I replied that then they must subscribe their reasons (abovementioned) for as yet they were anonymous: so at length, with no little difficulty, I purchased the subscription of their charges by my abovesaid overtures, which I gave, subscribed with my name, to them to consider of; and so the meeting broke up.

Note that, during this agitation with our dissenting Brethren, they entertained frequent whisperings with comers and goers to them and from them; particularly Dan: Andrews, and Tho: Preston from Mr. Israel Porter, and Jos: Hutchinson, &c.

Nov. 30, 1694

Bro: Nurse and Bro: Tarbell (bringing with them Joseph Putnam and Tho: Preston) towards night came to my house, where they found the two Deacons and several other Brethren; *viz.*, Tho: Putnam, Jno: Putnam, Jr., Benj: Wilkins, and Ezek: Cheever, besides Lft. Jno Walcot. And Bro. Tarbell said they came to answer my paper which they had now considered of, and their answer was this; *viz.*, that they remained dissatisfied, and desired that the Church would call a Council, according to the advice we had lately from the Ministers.

Sab: Dec. 2, 1694

I publicly reported the abovesaid answer of the dissenting Brethren, and then desired the Church to stay after the dismission of the congregation; and then we appointed a Church meeting at Deacon Putnam's for farther agitation the 6 instant.

Dec. 6, 1694

At the meeting above concluded upon, we agreed that the Church (excepting the Pastor, who was even quite tired out, and also because he thought they might be more free in his absence) would meet the 20 instant with the dissenting Brethren at Deacon Ingersoll's to discourse with them about their reasons of withdrawing.

Jan. 21, 1694/95

At a meeting at Capt. Putnam's of several of the principal of the Church, we concluded that at our next Church meeting we would propound a fresh tender both to our dissenting Brethren and neighbors for a Council.

Sab: 27 Jan. 1694/95

Received into full communion with the Church:

38. Mary (wife to John) Wheldon, and baptized. *An. Aetat* 37
The Church was stayed after the congregation was dismissed, and desired to meet the 31st instant at the Pastor's house in order to prepare another offer of a Council to our dissenters, both Brethren and neighbors.

Jan. 31, 1694/95

At a full meeting of the Church as above appointed, it was universally voted that the next Lord's Day public notice should be given for a public meeting at the meeting house the 7 Feb. next, at 2 of the clock, to prosecute the Ministers' advice for a Council, dated 14 June last. And our Brethren Wm. Way and Jno. Wilkins be desired this evening to declare this our purpose to Bro. Tho: Wilkins in behalf of the rest of the dissenting Brethren. We also concluded that the third Tuesday in March next would be as convenient a time as we could pitch upon for the meeting of said Council.

Sab: 3 Feb. 1694/95

After the afternoon sermon was ended the Pastor published the above-mentioned agreement of the Church, and desired that all would bring in at that day the matter which they had to offer to a Council.

Feb. 7 [1695]

The Church met as above appointed in public, when after prayer, and the occasion of this meeting being hinted, the Ministers' advice to us dated 14 June last was again publicly read. And the dissenting neighbors then present were desired to bring in such matters as they desired a Council for. This was much urged, but to no purpose. They pleading that the explanation of said advice dated 10 September last and sent to us, was that a Council should be first chosen, and then the matters for calling a Council should be given in. We answered that we would stand to the advice of 14 June which they themselves had been the procurers of. And therefore desired them only to give in the things they would offer to a Council—let them be what they would—and we would join with them, they nominating any 3 Churches (excepting Ipswich and those six Churches whose Elders had already been concerned so as to give advice as before hinted, [i.e.,] only upon hearing of the dissenters, without our Church's privity records [?]) and we would immediately before the half-hour was out vote then for them, and then ourselves elect 3 other Churches. But none would take up with this notion. Then we told our dissenting Brethren, seeing the neighbors had nothing they would offer to us for calling a Council, [that] inasmuch as we had lately received their reasons for withdrawing from us, we would also give in to them the charges we had against them, to tender unto a Council; which accordingly we did after we had first read them openly and publicly—*viz.*, as followeth:

[Samuel Parris and the Salem-Village Church Summarize Their Grievances Against the Dissenting Brethren, Originally Composed in November 1693]

"Sundry Objections which we have against our Dissenting Brethren, and were read to them (at least the Heads) 13 Nov., 1693, as matters we would offer to a Council, *viz.*:

1. Their precipitant, schismatical and total withdrawing from the Church
   (yea, and congregation) so as at once to renounce all religious
   communion, without giving the least reason for their so doing. See
   Dan. 2: 15, Pro. 25: 8. By which means (1) the Church suffers:
   (a) defamation abroad; (b) reproach and grief at home; (2) the Sepa-
   ratists become guilty: (a) of general breach of covenant; Neh. 10: all,
   Jude 19, Heb. 10: 25; (b) of evil example.
2. Their refusing to give the Church messengers (sent to them on purpose
   7 Feb. 1692/93) any reason for their withdrawing; most absurdly
   desiring time for answer, directly contrary to the laws of Christ: I Pet.
   3: 15. And to this end (as we then suspected, and now has proved too
   true), *viz*.: that they might consult with such others amongst us as
   have frequently evidenced themselves to be obstructive to Church-
   settlement, as these Brethren themselves have heretofore abundantly
   professed, and yet now are their only companions: see II Cor. 6: 14
   etc., I Cor. 9: 6.
3. When they came to the Church members the next time, *viz*. 16 Feb.
   1692/93 (which time was at their desire granted to them for their
   answer), instead of lovingly speaking their minds, they read a dateless
   paper reflecting upon Church and Elders, for calling them to account;
   and yet refused to leave said paper, and were exceeding hardly
   prevailed with to let us take a copy of it.
4. Their bringing 27 March following, together with 3 other men not in
   full communion, and one of them a stranger to our Village, a factious
   and seditious libel to the Pastor, consisting of confused calumnies or
   reflections on said Minister and others of the Plantation (we know not
   whom, because not particularly named therein).
5. Their impetuous pursuit of the Minister at his house the night
   following for an answer to said libel, to his great disquietment.
6. Their (with 2 others not in full communion) restless pursuit of the
   Minister again 14 Apr. 1693 for answer to said libel.
7. Their reading a general and ambiguous charge 21 Apr. 1693 against the
   Minister (if not others of the Church) before 4 more Brethren
   mutually agreed on by them; and the Minister to hear their difference
   in order to bring it to the Church, and yet refusing to leave said
   charge, or to suffer any of us (though much urged thereto by us) to
   take a copy, and so to debate of them—though this meeting was
   appointed for that end. See Eph. 5: 21, Phil. 2: 3.
8. Their peremptory withstanding the whole Brotherhood's council (met
   on purpose at their desire 18 May 1693) to bring the matter orderly
   before them; only insisting on it with great heat that immediately their
   charge might be read, and witnesses heard, before the Church had any
   knowledge of the matter, contrary to I Tim. 5: 19. Yea, loudly and
   fiercely before the whole Brotherhood clamoring against the Church
   that she would not hear them, whereas the Church had, both in their
   presence and audience, but just before passed a vote that she would
   hear them in case they brought the matter before them according to
   Christ's rules.

9. Their publishing under their own hands, in diverse places of the country, sundry obloquies against Church and Elders, whilst still the persons so besmeared are denied cognizance of the surmised crimes, either wholly or too much. See Pro. 25: 9 and 10: 12-18.

10. Their ensnaring several themselves (or joining with such as did so) to subscribe a petition to his Excellency and General Court, scandalizing the Church and Minister as unpeaceable with their neighbors. Whereas several whose names are there and who subscribed do utterly disown any such speech or intention. See II Sam. 15: 6-11, Rom. 16: 17-18, Ps. 101: 5.

11. Their gross dissimulation in their letter to the Church at Malden dated 11 Sept. 1693 (and, as we supposed, to other Churches they then sent to for a Council) wherein they do fallaciously disown the abovesaid petition to his Excellency, notwithstanding all their own 11 names are subscribed thereunto: see Ps. 12: 2, Jer. 9: 4-5.

12. Their sending abroad petitions to highest Court and Churches with names subscribed, unknown to some of the persons whose names they bear, as some of us have been informed by said pretended subscribers.

13. Their frequent soliciting others themselves (or confederating with such as did so) to subscribe such like petitioners. See Acts 14: 2, Pro. 16: 28-30.

14. Their gross mistake in their letter to the Church at Malden 11 Sept. '93, wherein they profess so much dissatisfaction with the doctrine, practice and ministerial administration of their Pastor, for above a year before the date of said letter; as that they were forced to withdraw from all public worship for more than 12 months before said letter. Whereas it is most notorious that they were in no wise wanting as to a profession of much respects to their said Pastor, all along before—yea, and a considerable while after—the breaking forth of the late horrid witchcraft. And some of them did communicate in Sept. 1692 and after; and one of them had a child baptized 30 October 1692.

15. Their withdrawing their purses (as well as their persons) from upholding the Lord's Table and Ministry.

16. Their great contempt of the Church, as oft as hitherto (viz. 13 Nov. '93) they have been with them: (1) In unchristian fastness to such as have treated them mildly, though officers and aged; (2) In constant refusing lovingly and brotherly to debate matters unless a Council were first chosen, or in some irregular way; (3) In frequent threatening us with a Council whether we would or not; (4) In imposing upon the Church others not of our Church society, as witnesses (they said) of what was spoken on both hands. Whereby (1) They openly charged the whole Church as a nest of deceivers; (2) They bring unheard-of innovations into the house of God; (3) They scandalize the Church to all that hear of such a protest: I Cor. 6: 5; (4) They declare themselves void of all charity to the whole Church, etc.

17. In fine, to add no more: by all that has been said, their extremely disturbing the peace of this Church and many other good people amongst us, sadly exposing all unto ruin. Gal 5: 15, Matth. 12: 25.

> Sam: Parris, Pastor
>
> In the name of the Church, it being
> first voted by them this day at
> Deacon Ingersol's."

As soon as the public reading of these articles was ended, Bro. Tho:
Wilkins in a scoffing and contemptuous way said openly: This is a large
epistle. Yet our Brethren accepted not neither of this offer. So that seeing
[that] though there had been by some a loud and long cry for a Council,
and yet now a declining of it when in so fair a way (as we conceive)
tendered, we were forced to break up, it being even sunset; only first we
told them, if they saw not good to join with us in a Council, we intended
to call one ourselves—to be held the third Tuesday in the next month.
After we were withdrawn to Deacon Ingersol's, the Brethren Sam: Nurse,
and a while after Tho: Wilkins, came to us, desiring time to consider of our
offer. We replied that we were even spent and tired out with the multitude
of meetings which they had occasioned us; nevertheless we were willing to
gratify them in anything we might; and so appointed another Church
meeting for their sakes at Lft. Putnam's house at 1 a'clock the 12 instant.

Feb. 12 [1695]

The Church met again, as last agreed upon, and, after a while, our
dissenting brethren, Tho. Wilkins, Sam. Nurse, and Jno. Tarbell, came also.

After our constant way of begging the presence of God with us, we desired
our dissenting brethren to acquaint us whether they would accept of our last
proposals, which they desired this day to consider of. They answered that they
were willing to drop the six Churches from whose Elders we had had the advice
abovesaid, dated 14 June last, but they were not free to exclude Ipswich. This
they stuck unto long, and then desired that they might withdraw a little to
confer among themselves about it, which was granted.

But they quickly returned, as resolved for Ipswich as before. We desired them
to nominate the three Churches they would have sent to, and, after much
debate, they did, *viz.*, Rowley, Salisbury, and Ipswich. Whereupon we voted, by
a full consent, Rowley and Salisbury Churches for a part of the Council, and
desired them to nominate a third Church. But still they insisted on Ipswich,
which we told them they were openly informed [at] the last meeting that we
had excepted against. Then they were told that we would immediately choose
three other Churches to join with the two before nominated and voted, if they
saw not good to nominate any more, or else we would choose two other
Churches to join with the aforesaid two, if they pleased.

They answered they would be willing to that, if Ipswich might be one of
them. Then it was asked them if a dismission to some other Orthodox Church,
where they might better please themselves, would content them. Brother Tarbell
answered, Aye, if we could find a way to remove their livings, too.

Then it was propounded whether we could not unite amongst ourselves. The particular answer hereunto I remember not, but (I think) such hints were given by them as if it were impossible.

Thus much time being gone, it being well towards sunset, and we concluding that it was necessary that we should do something ourselves, if they would not (as the Elders had heretofore desired) accept of our joining with them, we dismissed them and, by a general agreement amongst ourselves, read and voted letters to the Churches at North Boston, Weymouth, Malden, and Rowley, for their help in a Council, as followeth:

"To the Revd. Elders of the Church in North Boston, to be communicated to the Church.

Salem Village, 12 Feb. '94/95

"Revd., Hon'd., and Beloved:

"Grace, mercy and peace from God our Father, through our Lord Jesus Christ to you be multiplied. It hath justly pleased the Lord, in his awful and holy providence, for many months past, sorely to exercise us, his poor and unworthy people, with the fires of strife, division, etc. We have not been wholly wanting, according to our poor ability, as to the use of means for the quenching of the same. But by all obtaining no prospect thereof, we have in the next place, and for a long time together, done what we could to work at making an orderly way for the calling-in of more fit and meet help than our own. Upon [illegible] whereof, our earnest and humble request unto yourselves is, that you would please to send your Elders and Messengers to meet here, at the Minister's house (with other Churches now sent to for the same cause) in way of Council, the 19 day of the next month, at ten of the clock. So praying for all fulness of spiritual blessing upon you, and most affectionately entreating the like of you for ourselves, we rest, Sirs, your unworthy Brethren,

Sam: Parris, Pastor

In the name of the Church."

Letters of the like tenor were also wrote to the Churches at Rowley and Malden and Weymouth.

Mar. 1 [1695]

At a usual Church-meeting (at Bro. Cheever's house) before the sacrament, after the praying, preaching, etc. was ended, our Brethren the Messengers to the Churches before-mentioned made report to us of the answers thereto made by the several Reverend Elders thereof. By which we understood that the Reverend Elders in the Bay accounted it advisable that we should add to the 4 Churches which we had already sent unto, the other two Churches in Boston, *viz*.: the old Church and the third Church; and also that the said Council might be deferred till the first Wednesday in April next. The thing being somewhat debated of, we quickly assented to that advice or motion. And accordingly shortly after dispatched letters and a messenger to said Churches, for that end. And deferred the time as above desired for a fortnight longer.

Sab: March 31, 1695

Received unto full communion:

30. Tho: Fuller, Jun. *Anno Aetat* 51.

April 3 and 4, 1695

Five of the Six Churches before mentioned sent Messengers and Elders: The Church of Malden only was absent, occasioned by sickness of the wife of the Revd. Elder thereof, who it's said had death very near approaching to her. The third day in public they examined matters, having in the first place had this Church's question propounded to them, *viz.*:

"To the Revd. and Hon'd. Elders and Messengers of the Several Churches now Sitting in Council at Salem Village, Apr. 3, 1695

Our gracious God having inclined your hearts to undertake a difficult service for his interest here, which we take thankful notice of; the great request which we have now to lay before you is, that you would by the help and from the word of our common Lord endeavor to rescue us out of the distresses now upon us, with an answer to the ensuing question, which is the case upon which we have desired counsel, *viz.*:
"Inasmuch as the Church in this place hath labored under much difficulty, through the dissatisfactions of certain Brethren upon the late grievous troubles among us, by which others also have been influenced; and our Pastor hath made public offers toward the satisfaction of all concerned: hence our question is, *viz.*:
"What advice is to be given, or what may there yet remain, for the comfortable composure of our unhappy differences?"

The 4th Apr. in public they read and gave in the following advice, as the result of the said Council:

[Conclusions of a Council of the Churches Convened at Salem Village, April 3, 1695]

"The Elders and Messengers of the Churches—met in council at Salem Village, April 3, 1695, to consider and determine what is to be done for the composure of the present unhappy differences in that place—after solemn invocation of God in Christ for his direction, do unanimously declare and advise as followeth:

I. We judge that, albeit in the late and the dark time of the confusions, wherein Satan had obtained a more than ordinary liberty to be sifting of this plantation, there were sundry unwarrantable and uncomfortable steps taken by Mr. Samuel Parris, the Pastor of the church in Salem Village, then under the hurrying distractions of amazing afflictions, yet the said Mr. Parris, by the good hand of God brought unto a better sense of things, hath so fully expressed it, that a Christian charity may and should receive satisfaction therewith.

II. Inasmuch as divers Christian brethren in the church of Salem Village have been offended at Mr. Parris for his conduct in the time of the difficulties and calamities which have distressed them, we now advise them charitably to accept the satisfaction which he hath tendered in his Christian acknowledgments of the errors therein committed; yea, to endeavor, as far as 'tis possible, the fullest reconciliation of their minds unto communion with him, in the whole exercise of his ministry, and with the rest of the church (Matt. 6:12-14; Luke 17:3, Jam. 5:16).

III. Considering the extreme trials and troubles which the dissatisfied Brethren in the church of Salem Village have undergone in the day of sore temptation which hath been upon them, we cannot but advise the Church to treat them with bowels of much compassion, instead of all more critical or rigorous proceedings against them, for the infirmities discovered by them in such an heart-breaking day. And if, after a patient waiting for it, the said Brethren cannot so far overcome the uneasiness of their spirits, in the remembrance of the disasters that have happened, as to sit under his ministry, we advise the Church, with all tenderness, to grant them a dismission unto any other society of the faithful whereunto they may desire to be dismissed (Gal. 6:1, 2; Ps. 103:13, 14; Job 19:21).

IV. Mr. Parris having, as we understand, with much fidelity and integrity acquitted himself in the main course of his ministry since he hath been Pastor to the Church in Salem Village, about his first call whereunto, we look upon all contestations now to be both unreasonable and unseasonable; and our Lord having made him a blessing unto the souls of not a few, both old and young, in this place, we advise that he be accordingly respected, honored, and supported, with all the regards that are due to a faithful minister of the gospel (I Thess. 5:12, 13; I Tim. 5:17).

V. Having observed that there is in Salem Village a spirit full of contentions and animosities, too sadly verifying the blemish which hath heretofore lain upon them, and that some complaints brought against Mr. Parris have been either causeless and groundless, or unduly aggravated, we do, in the name and fear of the Lord, solemnly warn them to consider, whether, if they continue to devour one another, it will not be bitterness in the latter end; and beware lest the Lord be provoked thereby, utterly to deprive them of those which they should account their precious and pleasant things, and abandon them to all the desolations of a people that sin away the mercies of the gospel (James 3:16; Gal. 5:15; II Sam. 2:26; Isa. 5:4-6; Matt. 21:43).

VI. If the distempers in Salem Village should be (which God forbid!) so incurable, that Mr. Parris, after all, find that he cannot, with any comfort and service, continue in his present station, his removal from thence will not expose him unto any hard character with us, nor we hope, with the rest of the people of God among whom we live (Matt. 10:14; Acts 22:18).

"All which advice we follow with our prayers that the God of peace would bruise Satan under our feet. Now, the Lord of peace himself give you peace always by all means.

Increase Mather, Moderator

Joseph Bridgham*	Ephraim Hunt*
Samuel Checkley*	Nath'l Williams*
William Torrey*	Samuel Phillips
Joseph Boynton*	James Allen
Rich'd Middlecot*	Samuel Torrey
John Walley*	Samuel Willard
Jer. Dummer*	Edward Payson
Nehemiah Jewet*	Cotton Mather

"To Mr. Sam. Parris, Pastor, and the Brethren of the Church in Salem Village."

[Letter of Increase Mather and Other Elders to the Salem-Village Church, May 6, 1695]

"Much Respected:

"Since that some of us did, in Council with other worthy persons met at your desire to consider your difficult affairs, offer you such advice as we judged most according to the mind of God and for the good of your whole plantation: we have had that represented unto us which very much confirms the apprehensions wherewith the last article of that advice was given. We have received an instrument, signed by several score of persons concerned in your Village. Of which there seem to be six men and eleven women, communicants in the Church; twenty-nine men householders, five men freeholders, seventeen young men, and sixteen other women—more than four score in all—wherein they express their despair of Mr. Parris's continuing with comfort or profit in the work of the Ministry among you. And it is our own just fear, that such implacable offences be arisen, as do render Mr. Parris's removal necessary.

"We cannot but think that so considerable a number of souls, as by the invincible temptations and prejudices which have happened among you, will probably be otherwise driven from joining with you in supporting the means of common edification, does call for you to consider what course may be most likely to maintain the kingdom of the Lord Jesus Christ, now threatened through your divisions to be taken from you.

"But we think your best friends can't put you into any such course without your consenting that Mr. Parris do come away from his present station. And

[*Lay members of the Council.]

then your uniting, as far as you can, in calling another Minister, and forgiving and forgetting all former grievances.

"As for Mr. Parris, you know what care hath been taken to preserve his capacity of being futher serviceable in other Churches of Christ; and we have now particularly before us a probability of an opportunity, if he please to accept it, of doing elsewhere that service for which we do, with grief, see the door so far shut up among yourselves. 'Tis with all tenderness and affection, and not without utmost concern for his and your prosperity, that we lay these things before you; and recommending you to the mercy of the Lord, subscribe ourselves

Cambridge, May 6, 1695   Your servants in him,

"To the Reverend Mr. Sam: Parris, Pastor   Increase Mather
of the Church in Salem Village. To be   Charles Morton
communicated unto the Church.   Michael Wigglesworth
                                                  Sam: Willard
                                                  Jabez Fox
                                                  James Sherman
                                                  Cotton Mather
                                                  Nehemiah Walter
                                                  Jonathan Pierpont"

The instrument mentioned by the abovesaid Elders is as follows, *viz.*:

[At this point Parris includes a transcript of his opponents' 1695 petition, which is presented on pages 260-62.]

The following paper (in answer to the aforesaid instrument, and [to the] classical letter from Cambridge) was brought by Deacon Putnam and several other of our Brethren to the Elders assembled at Boston at Mr. Willard's, May 29, 1695, being the day of Election, after dinner—where was present the body of Elders belonging to this Province. *Viz.*:

[Here Parris has copied out his supporters' petition, dated May 20, 1695, which is found on pages 262-63.]

Sab:, June 2, 1695

After public worship was ended, the Pastor desired the Brethren to stay, and then desired them to meet at his house the next morning at eight a'clock.

June 3, 1695

The Brethren being met as abovesaid appointed, the Pastor acquainted them that here were two Messengers from Suffield who were looking out for a Minister, and by the direction of some Elders in Boston made application to myself, who was willing to go with them if the Brethren pleased; and in my absence for a few months, they might try if they could (with others who now dissented) to unite in some other Minister. But after several hours debate, both with the Brethren and some other Christian neighbors, they all declared an averseness to my motion. Whereupon thanking them for their professed love to me, I told them I was not free to go without their consent; and seeing they would not let me go, I pressed them to keep me, and make much of me.

"Salem Village, June 3, 1695

"Revd. Sirs:

"We cannot fault the intendment of our Brethren, Searg. David Winchill and Corpl. Victory Sikes, Messengers from Suffield, sent by yourselves to obtain the Ministry of our Pastor, if we were so minded as to part with him. But upon a meeting together this day both of the Church and others (warned yesterday, being Lord's Day) to concert that affair, do hereby signify, at the desire of abovesaid Suffield Messengers, that with unanimous agreement—not one excepted (save the four known dissenters)—we are resolved, God helping, against such a separation during our ability to prevent it; and our Pastor, though otherwise inclined, [is] yet as unwilling to leave so many of his flock as testify so strong affection toward him. So earnestly requesting the constant help of your prayers, and as much otherwise as you can, we rest, Worthy and much-esteemed Sirs,

"To the Reverend Mr. Increase   Your needy Brethren,
Mather and Mr. Cotton
Mather, in Boston   Sam: Parris, Pastor

                                       In the name of the Church
                                       and other Christian
                                       neighbors."

Oct. 5, 1695

Brother Cloyes came to me desiring a letter of dismission of himself and wife from our Church to the Church of Marlborough.

Lord's Day—Oct. 6, 1695

After the sacrament the abovesaid Bro: Cloyes's request was propounded to the Brethren, and his dismission together with his wife as desired was voted by the major part.

"Salem Village, Oct. 8, 1695

"To the Revd. and much-esteemed the Pastor and beloved Brethren of the Church at Marlborough in New England:

"Whereas our Brother Peter Cloyes, for himself and wife (our Sister) Sarah Cloyes, hath desired dismission unto yourselves, unto whom by divine providence they are (as we are informed) now become near neighbors: the same request being the last Lord's Day propounded to the Church here was readily consented unto. So begging all fullness of blessings upon yourselves through our Lord Jesus, and most earnestly requesting the help of your constant and fervent prayers for us,

"To the Revd. Mr.——Brinsmeed, Your needy Brethren,
Pastor to the Church at
Marlborough   Sam: Parris, Pastor

            In the name of the Church."

Oct. 9 [1695]

I sealed and left the abovesaid letter for Bro. Cloyes at his cousin Tarbell's, as he desired.

Oct. 10 [1695]

Bro. Cloyes brought me back the letter abovesaid, saying it was a letter of recommendation and not of dismission that he desired.

April 9, 1696

At a Church-meeting at Brother Thomas Putnam's house, warned at the last sacrament, voted that our Brethren John Putnam Sen. and Nathaneal Putnam and Deacon Putnam and John Putnam Jun. be appointed to meet as many of the dissenters when Col: Gidney of Salem shall appoint himself being Moderator, to treat in order to an amicable issue. And I acquainted the Church that I intended to hold my station not after my year was up, etc.

"Salem Village, Apr. 13, 1696

"Col: Gidney:

"Sir, upon a motion from yourself sent [by] Capt. Putnam and Deacon Putnam to this Church, that we would chose and send some Brethren to treat with as many of our dissenters (yourself being Moderator) in order to an amicable issue for the future, upon condition that I would surcease my Ministerial station here. The same being agitated at a Church-meeting the ninth instant, the abovesaid Captain and Deacon, together with Lft. Putnam and his son John, were accordingly made choice of to meet—when and where you shall appoint for that purpose: Myself, then and now, promising full purpose to attend the same, if I possibly can and have timely notice. I am unwilling to hinder the good of the place, and if my remove may be beneficial, let the Church be provided for, and myself be fairly dealt with in payment of all my dues, [and] I shall readily gratify those who are so earnest for my giving way.

"To the Honored Bartholomew Your servant,
Gidney, Esq. in Salem. These
per Deacon Putnam.   Sam: Parris"

April 20th, 1696

At a Church-meeting at Deacon Ingersol's (warned yesterday, being Lord's Day): Voted (upon a motion sent to us from the Honored Col: Gidney of Salem, who was willing to advocate between the two parties in this Village) that our brethren Lieut. Nathaneal Putnam, Capt. John Putman, Jonathan Putman, and Benj. Putman, together with our Pastor, be fully empowered to discourse, conclude, and agree with as many of our dissenting brethren and neighbors, who likewise shall be fully empowered by the rest of their party, in writing under their hands, to agree and conclude on their part according to the tenor of the following propositions. (All of whom so chosen on both parts are to choose artibrators to determine, if need be, the second proposition.) *Viz.*:

1. That the Pastor's disbursements on the ministry-land and buildings shall be duly re-paid by the inhabitants,   each his proportion.
2. That as to said Pastor's arrears for maintenance, we do engage to pay the whole thereof to him, or what shall be awarded by four men, each party choosing two to hear and determine what thereof shall be paid. And if those four so chosen agree not among themselves, then the same four to choose a fifth. And what shall be awarded by any three of those five so elected, shall be made good and paid by all the inhabitants, each his proportion, according as he shall be found to have fallen short of paying his part thereof.
3. That all persons, both of church and other inhabitants, shall attend the directions of our law in calling and settling some able, pious, and orthodox minister in the place, and procuring him to enter and engage himself therein.
4. That upon the fair and full performance of all the abovesaid propositions, our pastor then to attend the Providence of God in removing, or to acquit his ministerial station amongst us.

An extract of the abovesaid premises was the same day sent to Col. Gidney, per Benj. Putnam.

Oct. 11, 1696. Lord's Day.

The dismission of our brethren and sisters Wm. Way and Persis his wife, and Aaron Way with Mary his wife, together with their children, to the Church of Christ lately gathered at Dorchester in New England and now planted in South Carlina, whereof the Reverend Mr. Joseph Lord is pastor, was consented to by a full or universal vote at the motion and desire of the brethren and sisters, and accordingly letters dismissive were written, 17th instant.

[This is the last entry in the Church Book in the handwriting of Samuel Parris.]

Chapter Twenty-One

The Salem-Village Book of Record: 1672-1697

[The Book of Record actually begins with copies of two documents we have included earlier and hence omitted here: the vote of the Salem Town Meeting of March 22, 1672, and the Order of the General Court of October 8, 1672.

In February 1687 the Village appointed a committee to review the Book of Record for the years up to 1683, expunging certain actions and votes. Accordingly, the following record, through the meeting of May 24, 1683, is the version approved in 1687. From June 1683 on, the record is presumably complete.

Any transcription of a written record to print inevitably involves a certain loss, and this Book of Record is no exception. For example, in the original, most of the entries that we have included are in the careful and legible hand and the grammatical style of a single clerk (Thomas Putnam, Jr.), but the entries from May 21, 1688, to March 20, 1694, are in a variety of hands, often hastily scrawled, and more erratic in spelling and grammar.]

A Book of Record of the Several Public Transactions of the Inhabitants of Salem Village, Vulgarly Called The Farms

Beginning at the time when they first sat up the ministry among them by order from the General Court, October the 8th, *Anno Domini* 1672

The company being met together the 11th of November, 1672, there was a Committee chosen to carry along the affairs according to the Court order, *viz.*, Lieut. Thomas Putnam, Thomas Fuller, Senior, Joseph Porter, Thomas Flint, and Joshua Rea.

The instructions for the Committee chosen to raise our public charges for the year ensuing were:

1. All vacant land at one-half penny per acre.
2. All improved land, both meadow and upland, at one penny per acre.
3. All heads and other estate at country price.
4. It was also voted that they were to make a rate of forty pounds for this present year for Mr. Baily.

26th of the 10th month [*i.e.*, December], 1672

1. At another meeting it was voted that we will build a meetinghouse of 34 foot in length, 28 foot broad, and 16 foot between joints.
2. It was voted that we have chosen to join with the Selectmen, for to agree with a carpenter to build the meetinghouse and setting men to work, Nathl Putnam, Henry Kenney, Joseph Hutchinson, and John Putnam.
3. Voted that the Selectmen shall make a rate according to the Court order equally for the paying for the building the meetinghouse.

[It was voted that the fifth part of the rate for the building of the meetinghouse and finishing of the same shall be paid in money or butter or wheat at money price, and the rest of the pay in such pay as shall carry the work along. This money and butter and wheat is to provide glass and nails for the meetinghouse.*]

4. Voted that it shall be accounted a lawful warning to warn a public meeting with a paper written under the Committee's hands and set upon the meetinghouse post.

The 6th of March, 1672/73

At a meeting of the Farmers it was voted that the 5 part [i.e., one-fifth?] of the rate for building of the meetinghouse and finishing the same shall be paid in money or butter at 5 d. per pound, or wheat at money price, and the rest of the pay in such pay as shall carry it along. This money and butter and wheat is to provide glass and nails for the meetinghouse.

The 6th of May, 1673

It was voted that Lieut. Putnam and John Putnam should to go B[oston?] Court to make answer to any petition that may come from Salem against the Court order.

[*The bracketed sentence was dropped when the Book of Record was recopied in 1687. It was, however, introduced into a court case in 1675 (Salem-Village Committee v. John Upton, in an action for debt) and may be found in Records and Files of the Quarterly Courts of Essex County, Massachusetts, VI, 46.]

The 23rd of June, 1673

1. At a public meeting it was voted that Mr. Bayley should continue in the work of the ministry among us still.
2. It was voted that Henry Kenny should gather Mr. Bayley's [rate?].
3. Voted that we will have plain windows made to our meetinghouse.

The 2nd of October, 1673

At a meeting of the Farmers it was voted that Lieut. Putnam, Nathl Putnam, Joseph Houlton, Joseph Hutchinson, Nathl Ingersoll, John Hutchinson, Jonathan Walcutt, these were chosen by a vote to meet with the gentlemen of Salem for to go with them to see the running of the west line between Salem and ourselves.

The 7th of November, 1673

1. At a meeting of the Farmers, it was voted that the Committee for the time being which is chosen to make rates for the ministry or other public charge among the Farmers, that they [also?] shall gather those rates which they make.
2. There was a Committee chosen for the year ensuing, which [was?] [Bray?] Wilkins, [illegible, Jona] than Walcut, Thos. Small and [Joseph? illegible].
3. It was voted that Mr. Bayley should have forty-seven pounds for the year ensuing, and he is to find himself firewood, or else the Committee to take the seven pounds, and they to find Mr. Bayley's wood.
4. It was also voted that Mr. Bayley shall have his maintenance at every half year's end.

The 14th of November, 1673

At a meeting of the Farmers it was voted that Nath^{ll} Putnam and Lieut. Putnam are employed to treat with the town about laying out of highways and mending of them amongst us.

[9th] month, 1673. The persons formerly chosen to run the west line between the town and us are now desired to perfect it by themselves or otherwise.

[Jos] eph Hutchinson's [deed of] gift [to the] Farmers [in the] year 1673.

"These presents testify that I, Joseph Hutchinson of Salem, do give up all my right, title, [and] interest that I have in that acre of land that the meeting-house now stands upon, and as the land stands now bounded, to the inhabitants of the Farms for them to make use of for the meeting-house and ministry among them, peaceably to enjoy without any molestation from the abovesaid Joseph Hutchinson, his heirs or assigns, to them, their heirs and assigns, forever, so long as they do make use of it for that end."

[9th] month, 1673. Voted that there should be a house built for the ministry, 28 foot in length, 13 foot between joints, 20 foot in breadth, and a lean-to of 11 foot at the end of the house.

It was voted that 5 should be added to the Committee for the carrying on the work of the house for the ministry, *viz.*, John Putnam, John Buxton, Henry Kenny, Nathaniel Ingersoll, and Robert Prince.

The 21st of November, 1673

At a meeting of the inhabitants it was voted that so many of the inhabitants here that have a mind to set up a house for their horses have their liberty to build as they see cause, and that if any afterwards have a mind to build, they have the same liberty, provided they do build together on that side [of] the meeting-house next [to] the swamp.

It was voted that the public charge should be defrayed in the same way as it was the last year.

The 15th of January, 1673/74

At a meeting of the inhabitants it was voted that the Committee now in being, together with John Putnam, shall seat the meeting-house according to the rates to the m[inister in this?] respect.

"Received forty pounds of Lt. Thomas [Putnam] and Goodman Rea, which was the rate made by [them], 8 October, 1672, and continued to October 8th, 1673. I say rece[ived,]

James Bayley

24 December, 1674

"Received thirty-four pounds, ten shillings, and seven pence, which was part of the rate made for my maintenance for the second year of my being at the village of Salem, which began October 8th [1673] and ended October 8th, 1674.

I say received so much as abovementioned from those who were the selectmen that year, by me,

James Bayley.

"Received since the writing of the abovewritten receipt so much as makes the abovementioned sum amount to forty pounds, which was so much as was voted for my maintenance for that year. I say received by me,

James Bayley

The 10th January, 1675

"Received forty-seven pounds, which was the rate made for my maintenance for the year beginning the eighth of October, 1674, and ending the eighth of October, 1675. I say received of the Committee for that year, b[y me]

[James Bayley]

"Received forty-seven pounds, which was the rate made for my maintenance for the year beginning the 8th October, [1675], and ending the 8th October, 1676. I say received of the [Committee] for that year. By me,

James Bayley

"Received 47 pounds of the inhabitants of the Farms for the year beginning October 8th, 1676, and ending the 8th October, 1677. I say received by me,

James Bayley

January 14, 1679

"Received of the account of my rate beginning October 8th, 1677, and ending October the 8th, 1678, I say received forty-four pounds, four shillings, and eight pence, by me,

James Bayley

"Received afterwards of those whose names were entered in Constable Joshua Rea's bill, two pounds, sixteen shillings, and eight pence, by me,

James Bayley

"The inhabitants of the Farms discharged from their two last years' rates made for my maintenance, for the two last years of my being in the ministry among them.
The 25th 8th [month], 1681, by me,

James Bayley"

All the abovewritten receipts are true copies taken out [of] the originals written with Mr. Bayley's own hand, as [attest] Thomas Putnam, Recorder to the Committee of Salem Village.

[These receipts are the only entries from January 1674 to November 1678 which were preserved in the revised Book of Record. However, in the afore-mentioned court case (Salem-Village Committee v. John Upton, action for debt—EQC, VI, 46), the following entries from the original Book of Record were introduced as evidence:

"At a meeting of the farmers the 6th of November, 1674, there was a Committee chosen for the year ensuing, which are John Putnam, John Gingell, John Buxton, Nathaniel Ingersoll and Henry Kennye."

"At a meeting of the farmers the 22nd, 7th month, 1674, it was voted that the former Committees are desired to give an account of the rates that they have made to the Committee in being, and the Committee in being are to receive the account."]

The 18th of the 9th month, 1678

The inhabitants of the Farms are desired to meet at their ordinary place of meeting on the 23rd of this instant month of November at ten of the clock in the morning for the choice of a new committee and to agree about Mr. Bayley's maintenance this year, and what other things may fall in, for these are great things of concernment. Therefore we desire that all the inhabitants may be there.

By order of the Committee.

John Putnam

At a meeting of the Farmers, 23 November, 1678

1. There was a Committee chosen for the year ensuing: *viz.*, Lt. Thomas Putnam, John Buxton, Daniell Andrew, Allex Osborn, William [Sibley].
2. Voted that Mr. Bayley shall have forty-seven pounds for this year's maintenance, to be raised as it was last year upon the inhabitants.
3. Voted that the forty-seven pounds shall be paid in the s[ame] specie as before, in provision, the half at the half year's end.

At a public meeting of the inhabitants of the Farms, 11th September, [1679]

1. Voted that we agree to raise Mr. Bayley's maintenance for this year ensuing to fifty-five pounds, and that Mr. Bayley shall be [at liberty] at the year's end, or before, if he have a call to any other place, and
2. That the inhabitants shall have their liberty to get a minister in this year's time, and by this means we shall take the Church's advice if we raise our minister's maintenance.

Rates made in the year 1678 and 1679 for the minister con[illegible] to fifty-two pounds, six shillings, and ten pence.
Abated to her that was the wife of Isaac Goodell, 00:2s:6.
Paid James Hadlock for sweeping the meetinghouse: 0:10:0.
Abated to John Brown for Nurse's farm: 0:4:0.
A bill committed to Constable Job Swinerton by warrant of [illegible]
Bearing date the twenty fourth of November, 1679: 05:12:09.

The 9th of December, 1679

At a meeting of the Farmers, chosen for a Committee for the year ensuing: Joshua Rea, Jonathan Walcott, Joseph Herrick, Thomas Fu[ller, illegible]

Thomas Putnam.

2. Chosen to [supply the] place of deacons for this year [ensuing]
To D[illegible] Lt. John Putnam, Nathaniel [illegible] Mr. Bayley if he would take 5 [illegible].
[illegible Ba]yle's answer to the proposition was [illegible provi]sion he would accept and [illegible] be paid [illegible].

The sixth of April, 1680

At a public meeting of the inhabitants of the Farms, it was voted that we will choose men to reckon with those to whom the inhabitants are in debt, and also to call the Constables to an account for the several sums committed to them by several Committees. The persons chosen and empowered are Lt. John Putnam, Sergeant Thomas Fuller, and Joseph Hutchinson. We leave it to their discretion to act as they see cause, only they shall do it, and the inhabitants to bear their charges and make return, within a year.

At the same meeting abovesaid, it was voted that we would have a minister among us to preach the word of God to us, and that Nathaniel Putnam, Sergeant Thomas Fuller, Bray Wilknes, and Joshua Rea are desired to look out for a minister and to take advice of Mr. Higginson or the Church of Salem about that matter, and bring one hither, that we may hear him and to approve of him.

The minister's rate for this year, beginning October 1679 and ending October 1680, amounts to sixty-six pounds, four shillings, and four pence.

Abated out of the rate to M[is] Davenport 11 pence money, 2 shilling provision.

A bill committed to Constable John Buxton, by warrant, containing the sum of six pounds, seven shillings, and two pence, bearing date the fourth of November, 1680.

Also there are some of Beverly men as have not paid the rate the year.

William Dodge, 8 pence money; s:6[4] in pay.

John Giles, 8 pence money; s:6 pay.

Petter Woodbery: 3 pence money; 7 pence pay.

> Jonathan Walcott
> Joseph Herrick
> Thomas Putnam, Junior
>
> The Committee

[9th] November, 1680

[At a meeting] of the inhabitants of the Farms the year and day abovewritten,

These was chosen for a Committee for the year ensuing: Bray Wilkens, Nath[1] Ingersol, John Putnam, Daniel Rea, Joseph Hutchinson.

Voted that all our householders for the future time shall have liberty to choose, and to be chosen on, the Committee, and to act in all other matters that concern us, until there be a Church gathered among us.

The 25th of November, 1680

Voted at a meeting of the inhabitants of the Farms that it was agreed that Mr. Burroughs for his maintenance amongst us is to have, for the year ensuing, sixty pounds in and as money. One-third part in money certain, the other two-thirds in provision at money price as follows: rye and barley and malt at three shilling per bushel, Indian corn at two shillings a bushel, beef at three half pence a pound, and pork at 2 pence a pound, butter at 6 pence a pound, and this to be paid at each half-year's end.

It is to be understood that it shall be at the inhabitant's liberty to discharge the whole sixty pounds in all money, if they see cause, and his firewood.

Voted that Lt. Thomas Putnam and Jonathan Walcott are chosen to supply the place of Deacons for the year ensuing.

The 31st day of December, 1680

At a meeting of the inhabitants of the Farms, it was voted that the rate that is made for the maintenance of Mr. Burroughs for this year ensuing is to be raised as formerly.

The 16th of February, 1680/81

At a meeting of the inhabitants of the Farms, it was voted that we will build a house for the ministry and provide convenient land for that end. The dimensions of the house are as followeth: 42 foot long, twenty foot broad, thirteen foot stud, four chimneys, no gable ends.

Also, what is expended about the house shall be allowed for by the inhabitants.

The rate made for the ministry house and land amounts to two hundred and twenty one pounds, nine shillings, and six pence.

"Received of the Committee the full and just sum of sixty pounds for the year beginning in 'eighty, in the month of November, and ending in the same month, 'eighty-one, which sum was the rate made by them, and firewood for the year abovementioned. I say received by me,

George Burroughs."

The 27th of December, 1681

At a meeting of the inhabitants of the Farms, there was a Committee chosen for the year ensuing, *viz.*: Lt. John Putnam, Nathal Ingersoll, Sergeant Thomas Fuller, John Buxton, and Daniel Rea.

Also chosen to supply the place of deacons for the year ensuing, Lieutenant Thomas Putnam and Sergeant Jonathan Walcott.

At the same meeting abovesaid, it was agreed upon and voted for the future by the inhabitants of Salem Village, that the rate made for the defraying of all our charges in the year 1681, both for houses and lands, with all other concerns belonging to the ministry among us, shall be entered in our Book of Records, with the names and particular sums. And that it shall not be lawful for the inhabitants of this village to convey the houses or lands, or any other concerns belonging to the ministry, to any particular persons or person, not for any cause, by vote or other ways. But this estate to stand good to the inhabitants of this place and to their successors forever, for the ministry.

	£	s.	d.
Luet: Tho: Putnam	10	6	3
Richard: Hutchinson	2	9	6
Natha¹ putnam	9	10	—
Lt John putnam	8	—	—
Joseph porter	6	3	—
Henry Kenny	2	5	—
Jonathan Walcott	3	6	—
Isarell porter	1	10	—
John Buxton	3	15	—
Lott Kellom	1	4	—
Joseph Holton senʳ	3	6	—
Isaac Goodell's widdow		10	—
Thomas Flint	5	2	—
Gilles Gory	—	4	—
Joseph pope	3	—	—
Elisha Cuby	—	3	3
William Nickols	—	10	—
Isaac Cooks	—	4	3
William Sibley	4	16	—
	66	5	3
Joseph Roots	—	4	5
John Giles	—	6	[3(?)]
Andrew Eliot	—	5	—
William Dodge	—	6	6
Joseph Boys	—	3	3
Samuel Sibley	1	18	—
Job Swinaton Senʳ	3	—	—
Job Swinaton jur	4	10	—
Peter prescott	1	4	6
James Smith	1	4	6
John Burroughs	1	5	6
Thomas Keny	1	10	—
William Way	1	10	—
Tho: putnam jur	2	14	—
John putnam jur	2	14	—
George Flint	1	7	—
John Flint	1	7	—
William Osborn	—	3	—
Nath¹ Aires	1	4	—
Tho: Bayly	—	13	—
Daniel Rea	3	—	—
Thomas Cave	—	3	—
petter Cloys	1	8	6
Abraham Walcott	—	9	—
peter Woodbery	—	2	6
Frances Nurs	—	18	—
Sam¹ Nurs	1	4	—
John Tarbill	1	4	—
Thomas preston	1	10	—
William Buckly	1	4	—
Benj: Holton	1	1	—
Joseph Woodrow	—	15	—
Thomas Clark	—	13	—
John Nockols	—	10	—
John Darling	—	10	—

	£	s.	d.
Joseph Holton jur	1	12	—
Edward putnam	1	17	—
Jona^t putnam	1	16	—
Thomas Haile	—	7	6
Daniel Andrew	5	19	3
Sam: Brabrook	—	16	—
Zacca Herrick	—	12	—
Nath felton junr	—	5	—
Tho: Fuller sen^r	8	6	—
Henry Renols	—	2	3
Jerimy Watts	1	5	—
Joseph Hutchinson	6	12	3
Natha: Ingersoll	3	12	—
Joshua Rea	7	7	—
John Brown	3	1	6
James Hadlock senr	1	9	3
James Hadlock junr	1	4	—
Frances Gefords & farm	1	7	6
Thomas Haines	2	2	6
Jonathan Knight	1	10	—
John Kenny	1	10	—
Aron Way	1	19	—
William Ierland	2	5	—
Thomas Fuller junr	2	8	—
John Sheepard	1	10	—
Zaccary Goodell	2	14	—
John Gingill	3	10	6
Bray Wilknes	2	12	6
Samuell Wilknes	1	16	—
Thomas Wilknes	2	16	9
Henry Wilknes	1	10	—
Benjamin Wilknes	1	16	—
Edward Bishop	2	8	—
Joseph Herrick	3	—	—
Thomas Rament	2	14	—
Ezekill Chever	—	13	—
Joseph Mazary	2	—	—
Allexander Osborn	2	2	—
John Adams	1	2	6
William Rament	—	9	9

This is a true copy of the rate entered according to the vote, per me,

Daniel Rea

At a meeting of the inhabitants the 26th of January, 1681/82

Voted that Lt. Thomas Putnam, Joseph Hutchinson and Henry Kenney are hereby empowered to go fence the ministry land according to their best understanding, and the inhabitants to pay the charge.

2. Voted that it is left to the Committee to finish the ministry house and the inhabitant to pay the charge.

The 21st of December, 1682

At a meeting of the inhabitants of Salem Farms there was chosen for to supply the place of deacons for year ensuing, Lt. Thomas Putnam and Sargeant Jonathan Walcott.

2. Voted that the instructions given to the Committee in November, 1672, shall be the instructions for the year ensuing for the raising our public charge.

The 11th of January, 1682/83

At a meeting of the inhabitants of the Farms there was a Committee chosen for the year ensuing, *viz.*: Daniell Andrew, Thomas Fuller, Jun., Jonathan Putnam, William Way, and Samuel Sibley.

2. Voted that John Putnam, Jun., and John Sheepard and Benjamin Wilknes are chosen to take an account of men's estate in our inhabitants and bring it in to the Committee in order to making of rates.
3. It was agreed that for the future time all vacant land shall be rated at but four shillings per hundred to a sixty pound rate, and that to be the rule for greater or lesser sums for the time to come after this year after November, 1683. Voted the 11th December, 1682.

The 25th of January, 1682/83

At a meeting of the inhabitants of the Farms it was voted that all the debts of the inhabitants are to be brought in to the Committees the which were the Committees the two last years or the major part of them,

Which shall take an account of them the first of February next ensuing at nine a'clock in the morning at the meetinghouse.

Nextly voted that all those of our inhabitants that do not give in an account of their estates, or that give in a false account of their estate, the Committee then in being shall have liberty to rate them by will and doom from time to time.

The 15th day of March, 1682/83

At a meeting of the inhabitants of Salem Village it was voted that for the time to come that the Committee then in being shall warn all lawful meetings for the inhabitants to come together to act all public business, either by warrant on the meetinghouse post on a public day, or by going from house to house, or by warning given at the head of the foot company, or any of these three ways shall be accounted lawful warning.

The 24th day of May, 1683

At a meeting of the inhabitants of Salem Village it was voted that Sargeant Fuller is desired to write to Mr. Lawson to come to preach with us on the next sabbath day come[illegible].

Nextly voted that the Committee shall make a rate of fifteen pounds for Mr. Burroughs for the last quarter of a year he preached with us.

The fifth day of June, 1683

At a meeting of the inhabitants of this Village it was voted that those things shall be inserted in the warrant for a public meeting of the inhabitants that are to be acted that day and no other thing shall be acted but what is inserted in the warrant.

The 16th day of August, 1683

At a meeting of the inhabitants of Salem Village it was voted that Mr. Lawson shall have an invitation to come to preach among us, in order to a further trial among us if himself and the people can agree.

2. Voted that Lt. Nathaniel Putnam, Thomas Fuller, Senr., Goodman Wilknes, Senr., Mr. Joseph Porter, and Daniel Andrew or any two or three of them are desired to go to Mr. Lawson to treat with him according to the vote abovewritten.

The 19th day of October, 1683

At a meeting of the inhabitants of this Village it was noted that Lt. Thomas Putnam, Lt. Nathaniell Putnam, Lt. Jno. Putnam, Lt. Thomas Fuller, Joshua Rea, Senr., and Joseph Hutchinson are chosen to treat [with] Mr. Lawson and to make return to the inhabitants.

2. Voted that Lt. Thomas Fuller and Henry Kenny are chosen to go to Boston to desire Mr. Lawson to come to preach with us and that we may treat with him.

3. Voted that for the time to come all necessary charge either for fetching or entertaining a minister shall be borne upon public charge.

The 9th day of November, 1683

At a meeting of the inhabitants of this Village there was chosen and empowered to treat with Mr. Lawson and to make a full agreement with him relating to his salary, and to come to a result with him in the behalf of the inhabitants, *viz.*: Lt. Thomas Putnam, Lt. Nath. Putnam, Lt. Jno. Putnam, Sargeant Fuller, Joseph Hutchinson, Job Swinaton, Joseph Porter, Daniell Andrew, and Henry Keny, or the major part of them.

The inhabitants of this Village are desired to meet together at their ordinary place of meeting on the sixth day of this instant month, December, at ten of the clock in the morning to receive answer of those men that were chosen to treat with Mr. Lawson, and to consider what to do about a minister, and to consider about the disbursements: Daniell Andrew, Jonathan Putnam, Samuel Sibley.

The sixth day of December, 1683

At a meeting of the inhabitants of Salem Village, agreed that we will desire our elders of Salem Town to be helpful to us in procuring a meet person for us to preach the word of God to us. And if our elders do advise to any in Cambridge, then our messengers are desired to take advice with the magistrates there and president and pastor of the church there, and if our elders do advise to any other place than Cambridge our messengers are to attend their advice.

Voted the persons chosen and empowered for the work abovewritten were Ensign Daniell Andrew and Corporal Nathaniell Ingersull.

The 25th day of December, 1683

At a meeting of the inhabitants of this Village upon some objection it was voted to be a legal meeting.
2. Voted that we will give Mr. Epps for the time he doth preach with us twenty shillings per day, one half in money and the other half in provision at the current price.
3. Voted that Lieut. Thomas Putnam and Corporal Nathaniell Ingersull is to receive the contribution for Mr. Epps.
4. Voted that the Committee shall make a rate to discharge all the righteous debts of the plantation that are already due.

There was a rate made to pay the debts of the plantation. The whole rate was fifty-two pounds, one shilling, and a penny, and the whole rate was committed to Constable Joseph Pope the 12 of January, 1683, with an order to pay to the several persons that the plantation was indebted unto.

Daniell Andrew
Jonathan Putnam
Samuell Sibley

The 17th day of January, 1683/84

At a meeting of the inhabitants of Salem Village there was chosen for a Committee for the year ensuing Joseph Herrick, Job Swinaton, Frances Nurs, Thomas Wilknes, Ezekill Chever.
2. Chosen to take an invoice of men's estates: Edward Putnam, Thomas Preston, and Jacob Fuller.
3. Voted that the Committee now chosen shall make a rate of fifteen pounds for Mr. Epps.
4. Voted that the deacons shall take men's words for what money they have contributed to Mr. Epps for the time past.
5. Voted that all they that contribute for time to come shall put their money in papers and write their names in them.

6. Voted that we will send to Mr. Lawson to treat with him to see whether he will come to us upon Mr. Burroughs's salary of sixty pounds, only Indian corn at 2:6 per bushel.
7. Voted that we will send to Mr. Samuell Andrew, fellow of the college, to desire him to come to preach with us. The men chosen for that end are Lt. Nathaniell Putnam and Lt. Thomas Fuller, and Corporal Thomas Flint.

The 22nd day of January, 1683/84

At a meeting of the inhabitants of Salem Village: first voted that the Committee shall have the book and the papers.
2. Voted that the Committee shall raise our public charges as formerly, only to observe that order in vacant land.

The 22nd day of February, 1683/84

At a meeting of the inhabitants of Salem Village: first voted that the Committee shall make, instead of the fifteen pounds formerly voted to be made for Mr. Epps, a rate of twenty pounds to pay Mr. Epps and to repair the ministry house and pasture, and what this wanteth to discharge the whole as above, the inhabitants are to pay and Mr. Epps to have seven pound: one-half in money, and the other part of the rate to be one-half money and the other half part in pay.
2. Voted that this Committee now in being shall make a quarter rate for Mr. Burroughs.
3. Voted that Sargeant Walcott and John Buxton are desired to take care to get the ministry house and pasture repaired and the Committee are to pay them.
4. Voted that Joseph Herrick and Jonathan Putnam and Goodman Cloys are desired to take care for to get a boat for the removing of Mr. Lawson's goods.

The inhabitants of this Village are desired to meet at their ordinary place of meeting on the 17th day of this instant April, there to consider how the contribution shall be carried on, and how the salary to Mr. Lawson shall be paid: whether every quarter or other ways; and also how the wood shall be provided for Mr. Lawson, and how the bounds of the ministry land shall be settled; and to whom the quarter rate shall be paid that is to be made for Mr. Burroughs.
Dated the 11th April, 1684. Frances Nurs, Joseph Herrick, Tho. Wilknes.

The 17th day of April, 1684

At a meeting of the inhabitants of this Village: firstly, voted that this is a legal meeting.
2. Voted that the inhabitants must come to the deacons every quarter of a year to reckon about their contribution of money, and that the last Sabbath of the quarter they shall put in a paper into the box of what money they have contributed the quarter before.

3. Voted that we will each man pay his proportion of this rate each quarter of the year to Mr. Lawson or his order, and all other former votes that have passed concerning Mr. Lawson's salary are hereby confirmed and the specie thereof, provided that no man pay more than a quarter part of his part of the forty pounds in Indian corn, which forty pounds is to be paid in pay.

4. Voted that Mr. Lawson shall have thirty cords of wood for this ensuing year and that each man's proportion of wood shall be set in the margin of his rate; the wood to be brought in at four shillings a cord, and all those that do not bring in their proportion of wood by the last of November are to pay their proportion in money.

5. Voted that we make choice of Thomas Putnam, Senr., Nathaniell Putnam, Jonathan Walcott, Nathaniell Ingersoll, Tho. Flint, Tho. Haines, Saml. Nurs, and John Putnam, Junr., or the major part of them, to renew the bounds of the ministry land and the bounds of the acre of land about the meetinghouse some time this month.

6. Voted that the Committee are ordered to pay the quarter rate to Mr. Burroughs or his order.

"Lieut. Thomas Putnam.

Sir: Receive this as an order from me to you to receive of the Committee what is due to me from the inhabitants of Salem Farms. February 16th, 1683.

George Burroughs"

The first of September, 1684

The inhabitants of Salem Farms are desired to meet at the usual place of meeting on the eleventh day of this instant month, September, at eleven of the clock in the forenoon, to consider and take order about the maintenance of the minister after the expiration of this present year, the repairing of the ministry house and carrying in of wood for the minister, the discharge of the removal of Mr. Lawson hither, the providing of further accommodations of seats in the meetinghouse, and what means may be used suitable [to] rectify the defects in the inhabitants' book. Francis Nurs, Job Swinaton, Joseph Herrick.

The 11th day of September, 1684

At a meeting of the inhabitants of this Village: firstly, it was voted that we make choice of Lt. Thomas Putnam, Bray Wilknes, Lieut. Nathaniell Putnam, Frances Nurs, and Lt. John Putnam to treat with Mr. Lawson to know his mind about his settling with us in the work of the ministry.

2. Voted that the meetinghouse shall be filled and daubed all where it wants below the beams and plates, and that six casements shall be hanged in the meetinghouse; and that there be a canopy set over the pulpit. All which is to be on the inhabitants' charge, and that the desk be made flatter.

3. Voted that Corporal Kenny is chosen to fill the meetinghouse, lath it and plaster it, and he shall be paid for it by the inhabitants.
4. Voted that Lt. Nathaniell Putnam, Lt. Thomas Putnam, Sarg. Jonathan Walcott, and Sarg. Nathaniel Ingersoll are chosen to be joined to the Committee now in being to peruse the book and to have inspection into the defects thereof to see what should not be there, and to see what should be there that is not there, and copy it out; and to make their return to the inhabitants or the major part of these men joined to the Committee.
5. Voted that this meeting is adjourned to the 24th day of this instant month, September.

At an adjournment of the meeting from the eleventh day of this instant month, September, in the year 1684, to the 24th day of the same month and the same year, it was voted that after this year is out we will give to Mr. Lawson for his encouragement sixty pounds in money for his yearly salary, to be paid every quarter fifteen pounds, and two men shall be appointed to look after it and see that it be done. And he is to find himself wood out of this sixty pounds. And this to continue so long as he continue in the work of the ministry amongst us as now he doth.

2. Voted that the deacons shall for time to come declare the Sabbath before the quarter is out that the next sabbath the quarter is out, so the inhabitants may do their duty.

The 17th day of December, 1684

The inhabitants of this Village are desired to meet at their ordinary place of meeting upon the 18th day of this instant month, December, to complete the works that the last meeting was warned for, and also to receive the return of the men that were chosen to look into the defects of the book; and also those that are concerned about the book are desired to meet after lecture to complete their work. It is desired that the inhabitants would all attend this meeting and be at place appointed by ten a'clock in the morning, there being a great deal of work to be done. Frences Nurs, Thomas Wilknes, Ezekill Chever.

The 18th day of December 1684

At a meeting of the inhabitants of this Village

1. It was voted that Nathaniell Ingersoll shall have 20 shillings for entertaining Mr. Epps.
2. Voted that we make choice of Lt. Nathaniell Putnam, Sargeant Walcott, and Samuell Nurs to treat with Joseph Hutchinson about the acre of land that he hath given to the plantation to set the meetinghouse upon.
3. Voted that this bill of disbursements shall be entered into the book and that this bill shall be paid to the particular persons within named, and this is the whole debt that is due to the persons within named for the ministry house and land and for work done there, and for work done at the meetinghouse,

and for work carried to Mr. Burroughs; and that Constable Pope shall forthwith gather his rate committed to him and pay the same according to his order. And this vote to take place from the date of the bill, February the fifth, 1682.

Debts due from the inhabitants to the persons under named:

	£	s.	d.
Lt. Tho: putnam	6	2	3
Nathaniell putnam	1	3	10
Jonathan Walcott	1	13	3
Jno putnam senr	3	12	6
Joseph Hutchinson	1	3	4
Daniell Rea	1	9	9
John Flint	1	11	9
Nath: Ingersoll	1	17	3
sarjant Fuller	2	4	6
Thomas Fuller junr	1	5	10
Joshua Rea	1	16	6
Thomas Flint	1	1	—
Thomas Haines	1	5	—
John Gingill	—	3	
Benj Wilknes	—	16	—
Samuel Wilknes	—	5	—
Henry Wilknes	—	17	—
Allex: osborn	—	3	—
Jona: putnam	—	12	6
Benj Holton	—	6	—
Joseph Herrick	—	2	—
James Hadlock sen[r]	—	2	6
Zaccary Goodell	—	2	8
William Sibley	—	2	—
John Sheepard	—	5	6
Aron Way	1	12	5
William Way	—	7	4
Thomas Fuller	—	8	—
	—	—	—
	37	14	9

We whose names are underwritten, being empowered by the plantation for to examine the accounts both of debt and credit of their disbursements, do give in this account to the best of our understanding to be the debts due from the inhabitants. John Putnam, Joseph Hutchinson, Nathaniell Ingersoll, Tho. Fuller.

A bill of disbursements:

	£	s.	d.
Lt. Thomas putnam	1	3	3
Lt. John putnam	1	14	3
Edward putnam	—	5	—
Thomas Wilknes	—	3	4
Joseph Hutchinson	1	1	—
Zaccary Goodell	—	8	9

	£	s.	d.
Jonathan putnam	–	4	6
Thomas Haines	–	10	6
Allexander osborn	–	9	–
Daniell Rea	–	15	1
Nathaniell Ingersoll	–	10	–
John Buxton	–	13	–
Job Swinaton	–	6	–
Tho: putnam jur	–	3	4
Henry Kenny	–	4	6
Thomas Kenny	–	3	–
William Sibley	–	6	6
Sarjant Fuller	1	12	–
Tho: Fuller junr	–	6	–
Samuell Brabrook	–	2	6
Henry Holton	–	2	6
James Stimson	–	2	–
Joseph porter	–	12	6
Joseph porter	2	3	6
Henry Kenny	–	3	6
John Buxton	–	8	–
William Nickols	–	10	–
Jonathan Knight	–	2	3
Thomas Wilknes	–	10	–
Henry Wilknes	–	11	–
Joseph Mazary	–	14	–
John Tarbill	–	3	–
Benjamin Holton	–	6	–
John Darling	–	10	–
Thomas putnam jur	–	1	–

We whose names are underwritten, being chosen by the inhabitants to settle the accounts of disbursements, both debt and credit, which we have done to the best of our understanding.

John Putnam, Senr., Joseph Hutchinson,
Nathaniell Ingersoll, Thomas Fuller

At an adjournment of the meeting from the eighteenth day of this instant December, 1684, to the twenty-ninth day of the same month.

It was voted that we will give Mr. Lawson for the last quarter of this year thirteen pounds, ten shillings in money, and his wood as it is already ordered; and Thomas Putnam, Senr., and Nathanil Ingersoll are chosen to receive the money and pay it to Mr. Lawson.

The 2nd day of February, 1684/85

At a meeting of the inhabitants of Salem Village there was chosen to reckon with Lieut. Nathaniell Putnam: John Putnam, Senr., Joseph Hutchinson, Nathaniell Ingersoll, and Daniell Andrew, or the major part of them.

"The town of Salem, considering of a grant made by the General Court in the year Sixteen Hundred Thirty and Nine unto a Village that the inhabitants of

Salem did intend to plant near the river that runneth to Ipswich. Upon the certain information of several of our ancient inhabitants that do affirm that the town of Salem had agreed to plant a village near the river that runneth to Ipswich, and for more than forty years since; and did grant out lands unto several of our inhabitants upon the place, and our inhabitants did several of them go thither to dwell and have contined their dwelling there, and for many years since we have settled a Village there upon the place above named; upon these grounds above named we do hereby declare that the grant above named doth belong to the Village above expressed, and we do by these presents assign over and give up all our right to the forenamed grant unto this our Village."

At a meeting of the inhabitants of Salem Village the 2nd of February, 1684/85, we do hereby declare by vote that if the town of Salem will vote the above writing and make it their act and gift unto the Village, that then we declare by these presents that what land soever that we have that Salem did grant and lay out to any of us that doth lie within the grant made by the General Court in the year 1639 unto Salem Village, we do hereby engage that if we do lose any of those lands that the loss of them shall be at our own charge, and not require any satisfaction of the town of Salem.

We desire Lt. Thomas Putnam, Lt. Porter, Joseph Porter, Daniell Andrew, Lt. John Putnam, or either of them to deliver this paper to the selectmen of Salem and bring us a return.

The 28th of February, 1684/85

The inhabitants of this Village are desired to meet at the usual place of meeting upon the sixth day of March next to take the old Committee's accounts, and to choose a new Committee and give instructions to them; also to receive the account of the committee chosen to reckon with Lt. Nathaniell Putnam. And to take order about the fencing in of the ministry land and to take order about the galleries for the meetinghouse and better fitting the pulpit.

> Frances Nurs, Thomas Wilknes
> Ezekell Chever

The sixth day of March 1684/85

At a general meeting of the inhabitants of Salem Village there was chosen for a Committee for the year ensuing, viz.: Lt. John Putnam, Jonathan Walcott, John Buxton, William Sibley, and Thomas Putnam, Junr.

2. Voted that the Committee in being shall keep the original papers that the votes are written on, and at the year's end they shall be compared with the book, when the Committee shall give an account of the votes that have passed.

3. Voted that for this year the Committee shall raise our public charges as followeth: that vacant land to be rated at 4 s. per hundred and not doubled, and all land within-fence at one penny per acre and so to be doubled on that as on other estates, and all heads and estates as the law doth direct.

4. Voted that we will set up two end galleries forthwith and finish the galleries, and also set up a canopy over the pulpit; and it is left to the Committee to set men to work, and to agree with men for price and pay, and to make a rate upon the inhabitants to pay for the work.
5. Voted that it is left to the Committee to take care about mending the fence about the ministry land.

The 20th of March, 1684/85, we reckoned with the old Committee and their account is as followeth:

There was a rate made to pay Mr. Epps, and removing of Mr. Lawson and the repairing of the ministry house. The whole rate was 22 pounds, 12 shillings, and 7 pence; Frances Nurs, Thomas Wilknes, Ezekill Chver. There was a quarter rate made for Mr. Burroughs or his order; the whole rate was 14 pounds, 18 shillings, and 10 pence, which were delivered to Constable Daniell Rea; Francis Nurs, Tho. Wilknes, Ezekill Chever. There was a rate made for Mr. Lawson's year salary, 1684; the whole rate was sixty-two pounds, eleven shillings, and five pence; Frances Nurs, Thomas Wilknes, Ezekill Chever.

"Received this 29th of March 1686 [1685?] of Thomas Putnam, Senr. and Nathanael Ingersoll in money and as money sixty pounds, and my wood, being in full of my salary for the year 1684. I say received

per me, Deodat Lawson"

We whose names are underwritten, being formerly chosen a Committee by the inhabitants of New Salem or Salem Village to reckon with Lt. Nathaniell Putnam, have accordingly reckoned with him and do find on stating all accounts to this day there is due to him for balance one pound, sixteen shillings, and six pence from the inhabitants, as witness our hands March the 6th, 1684/85.

John Putnam, Senr., Joseph Hutchinson
Daniell Andrew, Nathal. Ingersoll

Salem Village this 20th of March, 1684/85

The inhabitants of this village are desired to meet at their ordinary place of meeting on the 26th day of this instant March at one of the clock, to choose two men to supply the place of deacons, and to choose men to take an account of men's estates and to consider how the contribution shall be carried on, and to choose men to call the constables to an account.

John Putnam, Senr., Jonathan Walcott
John Buxton, Tho. Putnam, Junr.

The 26th day of March, 1685

At a general meeting of the inhabitants of Salem Village: firstly, voted that we will keep up the contribution.

2. Voted that all our inhabitants shall put their money in papers which they contribute, or else it shall be accounted as strangers' money.
3. Voted that all the money which strangers contribute here shall be Mr. Lawson's.
4. Chosen to supply the place of deacons for the year ensuing were Lt. Thomas Putnam and Sargeant Nathaniell Ingersoll.
5. Chosen to take an account of men's estates in our inhabitants in order to making of rates, and to bring it in to the Committee by the 20th of May next, were William Way and Thomas Kenney.
6. Voted that the Committee in being are hereby empowered to call the several constables to an account for the several sums which have been committed to them by several Committees, and the inhabitants to bear their charge in suit or preparation for suit; and also the Committee in being shall have power to abate rates formerly made where they see reason so to do.

The inhabitants of this village are desired to meet together on this instant day, as soon as lecture is done, to consider how the galleries shall be seated.

Date this third of June, 1685.

> John Putnam, Senr., Jonathan Walcott
> John Buxton, William Sibley, Tho. Putnam, Junr.

The third day of June, 1685

At a meeting of the inhabitants of Salem Village; firstly, it was voted that it is a legal meeting.
2. Voted that all the meetinghouse shall be seated over again.
3. Voted that we will choose seven men for a Committee to seat the meetinghouse over again.
4. Voted that the Committee which shall be chosen to seat the meetinghouse shall have respect first to age, secondly to office, thirdly to rates.
5. Chosen for a Committee to seat the meetinghouse were Lt. Thomas Putnam, Bray Wilknes, Frances Nurs, Joseph Hutchinson, Joseph Herrick, Thomas Flint, and Lt. John Putnam.
6. Voted that these or any five of them agreeing shall be a valid act. Also we desire Mr. Lawson to give his advice to the Committee chosen about seating the meetinghouse.

Salem Village this 14th of November, 1685

The inhabitants of this place are desired to meet together at their ordinary place of meeting on the 18th day of this instant November in the afternoon after lecture, to consider whether or no the Committee shall add those several sums of money which are due from our inhabitants to several persons, into the rate which is to be made for the building [of] the galleries.

> By order of the Committee
>
> Tho. Putnam, Junr., Cler.

The 18th day of November, 1685

At a meeting of the inhabitants of Salem Village; firstly, voted that the Committee shall add that which is due to Lt. Nathaniell Putnam, and that which is due to Corporal Kenny, and that which is due for hanging of casements, and that which is due for making the pulpit, into the rate that is to be made for building the galleries.

2. Voted that the Committee shall add all the righteous debts of the plantation into the rate of the galleries, that every man may be paid—provided every man bring in his account to the Committee the 23rd day of this instant month to Nathanl Ingersoll's house.

The rate which was made for the building [of] the galleries and pulpit and to pay other debts of the plantation: in the year 1685 the whole rate was thirty-one pounds, eleven shillings, and five pence, which rate was to be paid in provision except those to whom it is due will accept of other pay. By order of the Committee.

Tho. Putnam, Jur., Cler.

In the year 1685, paid to Lt. Nathaniell Putnam by his gallery rate one pound, seven shilling, and six pence. Also Job Swinaton: paid to him out of his gallery rate nine shillings, which paid him his 1 p., 16 s., 6 d. By order of the Committee.

Thomas Putnam, Junr., Cler.

The remainder of this rate, being three pounds, four shillings, nine pence, was committed to Constable Henry Kenny, with an order to pay it to the particular persons to whom it was due. Bearing date the third of September, 1686. By order of the Committee.

Tho. Putnam, Cler.

The 16th of March, 1686/87

Constable Henry Kenny is discharged from the bill abovesaid of three pounds, four shillings, and nine pence, and we find the whole rate of the galleries and pulpit paid, except two shillings, six pence, which remains due to Capt. John Putnam, and seven shillings, which remains due to Ensign Thomas Flint. By order of the Committee.

Tho. Putnam, Clr.

The rate which was made for Mr. Lawson's salary in the year 1685: the whole rate was sixty-two pounds, one shilling, and six pence.

Abated out of this rate to Tho. Kenny, 2 s., 6 d.; to William Sheldin, six shillings; paid to James Hadlock, Junr., out of this rate for sweeping the meetinghouse, five shillings; and John Sheepard for sweeping the meetinghouse,

4 s. and 6 d. The remainder of this rate, being six pound, four shillings, and nine pence, was committed to Constable Henry Kenny with a warrant by our order bearing date the 7th of April, 1686. By order of the committee.

Tho. Putnam, Junr., Cler.

The seventh of January, 1686/87. Constable Henry Kenny is discharged from the bill abovesaid of six pounds, four shillings, and nine pence, which was the remainder of Mr. Lawson['s] rate in the year 1685. By order of the Committee.

Tho. Putnam, Cler.

"Received this 19th of January, 1686/87, of Nathaniel Ingesoll and Jonathan Walcutt sixty pounds in and as money, being in full of my salary for the year 1685. I say rec'd

per me, Deodat Lawson"

Salem Village this 6th of March, 1685/86

The inhabitants of this place are desired to meet together there at their ordinary place of meeting on the tenth day of this instant March, in the afternoon after lecture, to receive the old Committee's accounts and to consider what to do concerning the attachments which are laid on the ministry house and land, and to consider what you will do concerning the rates which were committed to the Constable Daniell Rea, Jno. Putnam, Senr., William Sibley, Jona. Walcott, Jno. Buxton, Tho. Putnam, Jun.

The tenth day of March, 1685/86

At a meeting of the inhabitants of Salem Village; it was voted first that Constable Daniell Rea is discharged from the rates which were committed to him by Frances Nurs, Thomas Wilknes, and Ezekill Chever which were on the Committee in the year 1684, and to all the bills charged to him on the book as Constable.

2. Voted that the Committee now in being shall make the rates over again that were committed to Constable Daniell Rea by Frances Nurs, Thomas Wilknes, and Ezekill Chever which were on the Committee in the year 1684, and to demand them and to pay them to whom they were ordered to be paid unto, that is to say, the twenty pound rate and the quarter rate for Mr. Burroughs or his order.

The twelfth of March, 1685/86, there was a quarter rate made for Mr. Burroughs or his order; the whole rate was fourteen pounds, six shillings, and eleven pence, which rate was to be paid in or as money. The remainder of this rate which is not yet paid is six pounds, nine shillings, and ten pence, which was committed to Constable Henry Kenny with a warrant by our order bearing

date the seventh of April, 1686, with an order to pay it to the Committee or to
Lt. Thomas Putnam. By order of the Committee.

Tho. Putnam. Junr., Clerk

The twelfth of March 1685/86, there was a rate made for to pay Mr. Epps
and for the removing of Mr. Lawson from Boston and repairing the ministry
house. The whole rate was twenty pounds, fifteen shillings, and ten pence, which
rate was to be paid one-half in money, the other half in provision. The remainder
of this rate which is not yet paid is two pounds, fourteen shillings, 4 pence in
money, and three pounds, two shillings, five pence provision, which was
committed to Constable Henry Keny with a warrant by our order bearing date
the seventh of April, 1686, with an order to pay it as followeth: to Mr. Daniell
Epps, one pound and five pence in provision; and to Jonathan Walcott, in
provision, 2 p., 2 s., 0 d., and in money, 1 p., 13 s., 6 d.; and to Nathaniell
Ingersoll, in money, one pound and half [?] pence. Remains due yet to
Mr. Epps, as former accounts show that this rate will not pay, in pay, ten
shillings; and to Daniel Rea, in pay, six shillings; and Jonathan Putnam, in pay,
six shillings; and to James Hadlock, Jr., in pay, six shillings. Dated this ninth of
April, 1686. By order of the Committee.

Thomas Putnam, Junr., Cler.

The 7th of January, 1686/87. Constable Henry Keny C^r by Mr. Daniell
Epps: £1, 5 d. in pay; also in the abovesaid £20 rate, by John Sheepard: 1 s.,
3 money [and] 1 s., 3 d. pay; also by abatement to Lt. Nathaniell putnam: 2 s.,
9 d. in pay.

The 16th of March, 1686/87. Constable Henry Keny is discharged from the
bill abovesaid of two pounds, fourteen shillings, four pence in money and three
pounds, two shillings, five pence provision, and we find the whole rate paid,
except one shilling and 6 pence in money, and two shillings in provision, which
remains due to Jona. Walcott. By order of the Committee.

Thomas Putnam, Cler.

An accounts of debts that remain due in Constable Joseph Pope's Bill which
remain due to the several persons hereafter named; also the names of those from
whom it was due: remain due to Lt. Tho. Putnam by William Ierland, 10 s., 3 d.,
by Tho. Haill, 1, 6 s. Remain due to Natha. Ingersoll by Job Swinaton, Senr.,
2 s., 4 d. Remain due to Jonathan Walcott by Joseph Popes, one rate 1 p., 0 s.,
8 d., by abatement to Thomas Preston, 12 s., 4 pence, by abatement to Samuell
Abby, 2 s. Remain due to Lt. John Putnam by Beverly men, 3 s., 6 d., by
abatement to George Jacobs, 3 s., 6 d. Remain due to Joseph Hutchinson by
Beverly men, 4 s., 5 d., by John Upton, 2 s., 7 d. Remain due to Allexander
Osborn by Samuell Cutteller, 5 s. Remain due to Daniell Rea by George Hacker,
10 s., by Jerimy Meacham, Senr., 2 s. Remain due to Thomas Fuller, Junr. by
abatement to Bray Wilknes, 9 s. Remains due to Joshua Rea, Senr. by James
Hadlock, Senr., 6 s., by Hery Renalls, ten pence, by Jno. Felton, 8 pence, by

Natha Felton, 9 d. pence, by william Osborn, 9 pence, by Isaac Cook, 1 s., 6 d. Remain due to Thomas Haines by James Stimson, 3 s. Total sum, 4 p., 2 s., 7 d. Dated the 9th of April, 1686. By order of the Committee.

Tho. Putnam, Junr., Cler.

Salem Village, this second day of April, 1686

The inhabitants of this place are desired to meet together at their ordinary place of meeting on the ninth day of this instant April at nine o'clock in the morning, to receive this present Committee's accounts and to choose a new Committee and give instruction to them; also to choose two men to supply the place of deacons and to consider what to do about the fence of the ministry pasture, and to consider what to do about the meetinghouse land that is fenced in. By order of the Committee.

Thomas Putnam, Junr., Cler.

The ninth day of April, 1686

At a meeting of the inhabitants of Salem Village there was chosen for a Committee for the year ensuing, *viz.*: Lt. Jno. Putnam, William Sibley, Thomas Flint, John Tarbill, and Thomas Putnam, Junr.

1. Voted that the instructions which were given to the Committee in the year 1685 shall be the instructions for the Committee in the year 1686.

2. Chosen to supply the place of deacons for the year ensuing were sargeant Nathaniell Ingersoll and Sargeant Jonathan Walcott.

3. Voted that it is left to the Committee to repair the fence about the ministry pasture, and to agree with Joseph Hutchinson about joining the fence of the pasture on the line.

Salem Village, this seventh of May, 1686

The inhabitants of this place are desired to meet together at their ordinary place of meeting on the tenth day of this instant May at twelve of the clock to choose two men to take an account of men's estates, in order to making of rates and to consider what to do about the grant which was made to the Village of Salem by the honored General Court in the year 1639, which Topsfield men lay claim to. It is desired that all our inhabitants would come to the meeting, for it is a matter of great concernment to us all. By order of the Committee.

Tho. Putnam, Cler.

The tenth day of May, 1686

At a general meeting of the inhabitants of Salem Village there was chosen to take an account of men's estates, in order to making of rates, Joseph Holton, Junr. and Aron Way, and to bring in their accounts to the Committee by the last of this month.

At a general meeting of the inhabitants of Salem Village the 10th of May, 1686, it was considered and agreed upon by a general concurrence that whereas in the year 1639 on a motion of Salem to the General Court for a grant of land additional to their first town grant for their encouragement in settling a Village, the said General Court did for that end grant all the land near their bounds between Salem and Ipswich River that did not belong to any other town or person by any former grant should belong to said Village, and the said Village having been inhabited accordingly above forty years, and it being found needfull to settle a minister in said Village for their accommodation therein, the Town of Salem did in the year 1671/72 for the promotion of the said work make a further addition to the said Village by granting all the land on the northerly side of Ipswich Road to the wooden bridge and so on a west line. We do hereby declare that if the Town of Salem do vote and declare that we are the Village intended by the motion to the General Court, and that the said grant in 1639 is and belongs to us, and that they as a town intend and expect it shall be and belong to us and is included in the grant to the Village in the year 1671/72 as much as any part of the land within said limits for the ends and use prementioned in said grant of 1671/72, that then we do hereby propose and engage for ourselves and our heirs to the said Town of Salem that if we lose any of those lands so granted unto us, by law or other ways, that the loss of them shall be our own and the defense thereof at our own charge, and that we nor our heirs shall not demand or require any satisfaction of the Town aforesaid if any of the said lands be recovered or other ways taken from us or our heirs that was granted to any of us inhabitants of said Village or purchased by any of us of any other person that desired their title from Salem Town grant originally lying within the aforesaid limits or grant of 1639.

The above writing was voted to be our act and deed the tenth of May, 1686, and then we made choice of Lt. Nathaniell Putnam and Sargeant Jonathan Walcott and Corporal Henry Kenny or either of them to present this writing to the Town of Salem and bring us a return.

Salem Village, this 27th of August, 1686

The inhabitants of this place are desired to meet together at their ordinary place of meeting on Friday the third day of September next, at ten of the clock, to receive the return of the Committee which were chosen to bargain with Joseph Hutchinson about the land the meetinghouse stands on and to receive the answer of the Town of Salem concerning the land which Topsfield men lays claim to, and to consider what we shall do further in that matter concerning the title of the land which Topsfield lays claim to which belongs to this Village by the grant of the Hond General Court in the year 1639. All the inhabitants are desired to come to the meeting for it is matter of concernment to us all. By order of the Committee.

Tho. Putnam, Cler.

The third of September, 1686

At a general meeting of the inhabitants of Salem Village it was voted that we will choose men for a Committee to transact with the selectmen of the Town of Salem about the answer to our petition or propositions to the Town of Salem bearing date the tenth of May, 1686, according to the Town of Salem's vote bearing date the eleventh of May, 1686.

Nextly, the men chosen and empowered for a Committee to transact with the selectmen of Salem about the answer to our petition or propositions to the Town of Salem bearing date the tenth of May, 1686, were, *viz.*: Lt. Nathaniell Putnam, Capt Jno. Putnam, Lt. Jonathan Walcott, and Corporal Thomas Flint—these or the major part of them to have full power to transact with the selectmen of Salem about the matter abovesaid and to make return to our next meeting.

"At a meeting of the selectmen of the Town of Salem

September the 21st day, 1686

"The petition of Salem Farmers or inhabitants of Salem Village exhibited at general Town meeting in Salem the eleventh day of May, 1686, being left to the selectmen, and they desired and empowered to transact with them about it. Answer is made hereunto by the selectmen, *viz.*: that according to our understanding the motion of the inhabitants of Salem on which the grant of the General Court was obtained in the year 1639 was for the accommodation of this Village now inhabited by the petitioners and we judge that the land then granted in the year 1639 is included in the Town grant unto them in the year 1671/72 for the ends and uses mentioned in said grant of the Town, each particular person holding their propriety in their lands respectively granted thereupon by the Town of Salem, and that we never knew of any other Village as such settled by the said Town of Salem.

"This is a true copy taken out of Salem Town book, Septem. 22nd day, 1686. Per Tim^o Lindall, Record^r to the selectmen."

Salem Village, this 25th of September, 1686

The inhabitants of this place are desired to meet together at their ordinary place of meeting on Friday the first day of October next, at twelve of the clock, to receive the answer of the selectmen of Salem Town concerning the land which was granted to this Village by the honored General Court in the year 1639 which Topsfield men lay claim to, and to consider what shall be done further in that matter. Also to give answer to a petition of several young men which desire a seat in the west gallery; also to consider what to do about the meetinghouse land that is fenced in. By order of the Committee.

Tho. Putnam, Cler.

The first day of October, 1686

At a general meeting of the inhabitants of Salem Village, it was voted that the young men's petition is granted, and the committee is to order how high they shall set their seat.

The first day of October, 1686

At a general meeting of the inhabitants of Salem Village it was agreed and voted by a general concurrence that whereas some of Salem did make a motion to the General Court in the year 1639 and did obtain a grant from the Court of all the lands that did lie between Salem bounds and Ipswich River not formerly granted, for the accommodation of a Village that Salem did intend to plant near said river, and Salem having declared us to be that Village for whom they did obtain the abovesaid grant; and in consideration that Topsfield men do lay claim unto our land granted unto us above, and we being deprived of our just right by them; therefore we do now make choice of our loving friends, *viz.*: Lt. Nathaniell Putnam, Capt Jno Putnam, Sargeant Natha^l Ingersoll, and William Sibley, or the major part of them for a committee to transact with Topsfield men about the land abovesaid. And do hereby fully empower them in our name and for our use, for to sue at law any of them that lay claim to our land, or otherwise for to agree with Topsfield Town as they shall see cause, either in court or out of court, or to give discharge to them or any of them; and what our loving friends above named shall do in that case shall be holden good by us as if we ourselves had done it, and the inhabitants to bear their charge.

The first day of October, 1686

At a general meeting of the inhabitants of Salem Village it was agreed and voted by a general concurrence that whereas Joseph Hutchinson of Salem Village did give an acre of land unto the inhabitants of the Farms of Salem or Salem Village, for to set our meetinghouse upon, in the year 1673, and write a deed of gift thereof in the Village book of records with his own hand, and doth now refuse to let the Village enjoy the acre of land given as abovesaid, but hath fenced in a great [part] of the land and claimeth the whole acre of land although he did deliver the acre of land by bounds with his own hands; in consideration whereof we do now make choice of our loving friends, *viz.*: Lt. Jonathan Walcott, Ensign Thomas Flentt, and Thomas Putnam, or the major part of them, for a committee to transact with Joseph Hutchinson about the land aforesaid, and do hereby fully empower them in our name and for our use to sue Joseph Hutchinson at law or otherwise for to settle or to agree with him as they shall think meet, and what our loving friends shall do in the case above named shall be accounted and holden good by us in all respects as if we had done it ourselves, and the inhabitant to bear their charge.

[Joseph Hutchinson was sued by Salem Village; in his defense he offered the following deposition, which we insert at this point in the record:

"Joseph Hutchinson's answer is as followeth:—

"First, as to the covenant they spoke of, I conceive it is neither known of me nor them, as will appear by records from the Farmer's book.

"Second, I conceive they have no cause to complain of me for fencing in my own land; for I am sure I fenced in none of theirs. I wish they would not pull down my fences. I am loath to complain, though I have just cause.

"Third, for blocking up the meeting-house, it was they did it, and not I, in the time of the Indian wars, and they made Salem pay for it. I wish they would bring me my rocks they took to do it with, for I want them to make fence with.

"Thus, hoping this honoured Court will see that there was no just cause to complain against me, and that their cause will appear unjust in that they would in an unjust way take away my land, I trust I shall have relief. So I rest, your Honour's servant,

Joseph Hutchinson

November 27, 1686"]

Salem Village, this tenth of December, 1686

The inhabitants of this place are desired to meet together at their ordinary place of meeting on the sixteenth day of this instant month at ten of the clock in the morning to discourse with Mr. Lawson and to agitate amongst ourselves in matters referring to his full settlement with us, also to take order about the transcribing of our book of records. The inhabitants are desired all to come to the meeting, for it is matter of concernment to us all. By order of the Committee.

Tho. Putnam, Cler.

The sixteenth day of December, 1686

At a general meeting of the inhabitants of Salem Village it was agreed and voted by a general concurrence that it was left to the Committee to put it to the vote the next convenient Sabbath day, excepting the next Sabbath day, to know the minds of our inhabitants referring to Mr. Lawson to office in this place.

2. It was agreed and voted by a general concurrence that it was left to the Committee together with Lt. Nathaniell Putnam to take care to transcribe our Village book of records according to their best understanding.

Salem Village, this 14th of January, 1686/87

The inhabitants of this place are desired to take notice that we are informed that Joseph Hutchinson, Job Swinaton, Joseph Porter, and Daniell Andrew do desire that four men may be chosen for to transact with them about their grievances relating to the public affairs of this place, and if they cannot agree among themselves that then they will refer their difference to the honored Major Gidney and John Hathorn, Esqr and to the reverend Elders of the church of

Salem; therefore the inhabitants of this place are hereby desired to meet together at their ordinary place of meeting on the seventeenth day of this instant month at one of the clock in the afternoon for to choose four men for the ends above expressed. By order of the Committee.

Tho. Putnam, Cler.

The 17th day of January, 1686/87

At a public meeting of the inhabitants of Salem Village it was agreed and voted by a general concurrence that we make choice of Capt Jno. Putnam, Lt. Jonathan Walcott, Ensign Thomas Flint, and Corporal Joseph Herrick for to transact with Joseph Hutchinson, Job Swinaton, Joseph Porter, and Daniel Andrew about their grievances relating to the public affairs of this place and if they cannot agree among themselves that then they shall refer their difference to the hono^d Major Gidney and John Hathorn, Esqr and to the reverend Elders of the Salem Church for a full determination of those differences.

Salem Village, this 16th of February, 1686/87

The inhabitants of this Village are hereby required in his Majesty's name to meet together at their ordinary place of meeting on the eighteenth day of this instant month at nine o'clock in the morning to hear and to consider of, to receive and embrace, or to refuse, the advice of the honored Major Gidney and John Hathorn and William Brown, Esqrs. and the reverend Elders of Salem Church. Also to view what is already transcribed of our Village book of records and to give some direction to the Committee and Lt. Nathaniell Putnam about the transcribing of the rest. Also to consider of and make void some votes that have passed amongst us that have been grievous to us for time past or that may be unprofitable to us for time to come. All our inhabitants are desired to come to this meeting, for it is matter of great concernment to us all. By order of the Committee.

Thomas Putnam, Cler.

The eighteenth day of February, 1686/87

At a general meeting of the inhabitants of Salem Village it was first voted that Capt Jno. Putnam is chosen moderator for this meeting.

2. It was agreed and voted by a general concurrence that this meeting is adjourned for one hour and a half and removed to Sargeant Nathaniell Ingersoll's house.

3. It was agreed and voted that we make choice of Mr. Joseph Hutchinson, Mr. Joseph Porter, Mr. Daniell Andrew, Capt. Jno. Putnam, Lt. Jonathan Walcott, and Thomas Putnam for to view our books of records and to copy out any entries that are therein which they conceive have been grievous to any of us in time past or that may be unprofitable to us for time to come

and to bring such entries as they copy out to the inhabitants to the adjournment of this meeting to see which of them they will annul and make void in our book of records.

4. It was agreed and voted by a general concurrence that this meeting is adjourned to the twenty-eighth or last day of this instant month February to ten a'clock in the morning.

[February 28, 1686/87]

At an adjournment of the meeting of the inhabitants of Salem Village from the eighteenth day of February 1686/87 to the twenty-eighth or last day of the same month, it was first voted that the acceptance of the advice of the honored and reverend gentlemen of Salem should be voted in general and not in parts.

2. It was agreed and voted by a general concurrence that we do accept of and embrace the advice of the honored and reverend gentlemen of Salem sent to us under their hands bearing date the 14th of February, 1686/87 and order that it shall be entered in our book of records.

3. It was agreed and voted by a general concurrence that all votes that passed amongst us concerning the building of a ministry house are hereby made void and of none effect.

4. It was agreed and voted by a general concurrence that all votes that have passed amongst us about building a kitchen or lean-to to our ministry house are hereby made void and of none effect.

5. It was agreed and voted by a general concurrence that all the votes that passed amongst us on the fifth day of June, 1683, that are entered in our book of records are hereby made void and of none effect, except it be that vote about warning a public meeting.

6. It was voted that Mr. Lawson's salary is regulated as followeth, and this to continue so long as he continues in the work of the ministry amongst us as now he doth.

7. It was agreed and voted by a general concurrence that we, having viewed our new book of records, we do find it already transcribed so far as it is to the full satisfaction of the whole inhabitants, and Mr. Joseph Hutchinson, Mr. Joseph Porter, and Mr. Daniell Andrew, and Capt Jno. Putnam, Lt. Jonathan Walcott, and Thomas Putnam, having had the perusal of it, they approve of all that is transcribed, except one vote, which vote the people see no cause to annul, and they approve also of the leaving out of all that is left out that is not transcribed, and we finding our book of records already transcribed from the beginning of it to the 24th day of May, 1683, though there are some votes left out that passed in Mr. Bayley's days and some votes left out that passed in Mr. Burroughs' days that are not transcribed, which we conceive will be of no great use us for the time to come which we leave to lie in the old book of records as they are and order that all other votes that have passed amongst us from the 24th day of May, 1683, shall be fairly and fully transcribed according to the advice of the honored and

reverend gentlemen of Salem, except such votes as are or shall be made void and of none effect.

[Letter of Advice to Salem Villagers, February 1686/87]

"To Capt John Putnam, Mr. Joseph Hutchinson, etc.

To be communicated to the rest of the inhabitants of Salem Village. Loving brethren, friends, and neighbors: Upon serious consideration of and mature deliberation upon what hath been offered to us about your calling and transacting in order to the settling and ordaining the Reverend Mr. Deodate Lawson, and the grievances offered by some to obstruct and impede that proceeding, our sense of the matter is:

1. That the affair of calling and transacting in order to the settling and ordaining the reverend Mr. Lawson hath not been so inoffensively managed as might have been, at least not in all the parts and passages of it.
2. That the grievances offered by some among you are not in themselves of sufficient weight to obstruct so great a work and that they have not been improved so peaceably and orderly as Christian prudence and self-denial doth direct.
3. To our grief we observe such uncharitable expressions and uncomely reflections tossed to and fro as look like the effects of settled prejudice and resolved animosity, though we are much rather willing to account them the product of weakness than willfulness. However, we must needs say that come whence they will, they have a tendency to make such a gap as we fear if not timely prevented, will let out peace and order and let in confusion and every evil work.
4. As things drew to a conclusion when you met with us, you did seem on both parts to be under a conviction of the necessity of peace, and there was some promising appearance of mutual condescension, and that for the future you would on all hands study to be quiet, and to that end you desired us to give you such advice as we judged would conduce to the promotion of righteousness, peace and order among you. Thus you have our sense of the matter as to what is past and present, and at your request we shall give you what is with us to direct by way of advice to prevent contention and trouble for the future, that it may not devour forever, and that if the Lord please you may be happier henceforth than to make one another miserable and not make your place uncomfortable to your present and undesirable to any other minister, and the ministry itself in a great measure unprofitable; and that you may not bring impositions on yourselves by convincing all about you that you cannot or will not use your liberty as becomes the gospel, as also in testimony of the care we have of you and our unfeigned desire and endeavour of your peace and welfare.

For these ends we advise you:

1. That you desist at present from urging the ordination of the Reverend Mr. Lawson till your spirits are better quieted and composed.

2. That you encourage him in his ministerial work from time to time by an honest fulfilling of your last agreement with him till such time as he is ordained amongst you unless any juster cause shall appear to the contrary than any yet hath done.

3. That the last agreement about his maintenance be not held binding after the time of his ordination unless that act be again confirmed by full and free consent of the major part of the householders lawfully called together upon sufficient notice of time, place, and end of the meeting; yea, if more than a mere major part should not consent to it, we should be loath to advise our brethren to proceed but rather advise upon that condition that some other way may be propounded as may be acceptable to Mr. Lawson and may be more pleasing to the people, as part money and part as money, or part money and part in pay at common price so as Mr. Lawson be not damaged and the people better pleased; we confiding in Mr. Lawson's readiness to comply with any proposition that will suit with the condition of his family.

4. We advise all possible care be taken for the future to prevent the grievance objected about the choice of the Committee, though we cannot totally comply with that proposition which pretends a court order for choosing a Committee without your own limits, seeing we find no such order, but a Committee nominated and appointed by the court in case of disagreement among yourselves, two of which three are dead. We advise, therefore, that whilst this contention lasts, one at least of the Town of Salem out of your limits be fairly chosen as one of your Committee, and that the householders have liberty to choose the rest of themselves or otherwise as they please.

5. We advise the old book of records be kept in being and that such votes in it as are offensive to any come to a further consideration in some lawful meeting appointed to that end, that all inconvenient votes may be repealed or regulated to satisfaction, and such repeals and regulations be inserted in the new book of records and all other votes fairly, fully, and impartially transcribed, and for the future that no votes be recorded but in the presence of the assembly that votes them, or at least at the next lawful meeting being again publicly read, which if it be done and the vote read publicly after it is recorded will undoubtedly prevent any reflection for the future upon the book or bookkeeper.

Finally, we think peace cheap if it may be procured by complying with the aforementioned particulars, which are few, fair, and easy, and that they will hardly pass for lovers of peace, truth, and ministry and order in the day of the Lord that shall so lean to their own understanding and will that they shall refuse such easy methods for the obtaining of them. And if peace and agreement amongst you be once comfortably obtained, we advise you with all convenient speed to go on with your intended ordination, and so we shall follow our advice with our prayers. But if our advice be rejected we wish you better and hearts to follow it, and only add if you will unreasonably trouble yourselves we pray you not any further to trouble us. We leave all to the blessing of God the wonderful counselor and your own serious consideration. Praying you to read and consider the whole and then act as God shall direct you. Farewell.

Salem, February 14th, 1686/87	Bartholomue Gidney, John Hathorne William Brown, Junr, John Higginson Nickolas Noyes"

Salem Village, this 11th of March 1686/87

The inhabitants of this Village are hereby required in his Majesty's name to meet together at their ordinary place of meeting on the sixteenth day of this instant March in the afternoon as soon as lecture is done, to choose and empower men to join with the gentlemen of Salem to run and settle the west line between the Town of Salem and this Village; also to consider of and make void some votes that have passed amongst us that are offensive to some. By order of the Committee.

Tho. Putnam, Cler.

The 16th day of March, 1686/87

At a general meeting of the inhabitants of Salem Village there was chosen and empowered for a committee to transact with the select gentlemen of Salem Town about the running and settling the west line between the Town of Salem and this Village, *viz.*: Lt. Nathaniell Putnam, Mr. Daniell Andrew, Ensign Thomas Flint, Corporal Henry Keny, and Corporal John Buxton—these or the major part of these men shall have full power to transact about and to do the work abovesaid the best way they may or can, and if they see cause, to hire an artist [*i.e.*, surveyor] and the inhabitants to bear their charge.

2. It was agreed and voted by a general concurrence that whereas on the 9th day of April, 1686, we passed a vote to bargain with Joseph Hutchinson for the land the meetinghouse stands on, and chose men for that end, we do now hereby declare that that vote is hereby made void, and the power given to Daniell Andrew, Jona. Walcott, and Daniell Rea on that account of no effect.

3. It was agreed and voted by a general concurrence that whereas there was a vote passed amongst us on the third day of Septem., 1686, that the return of the committee which were chosen to bargain with Joseph Hutchinson should be entered in the book. We do hereby declare that that vote is hereby made void, and the return of Jonathan Walcott, Daniell Andrew, and Daniell Rea on that account of no effect.

The bill of assessments which was made in Salem Village for to pay Mr. Lawson's salary in the year 1686: the whole bill was sixty-two pounds, ten shillings, and nine pence, besides Topsfield and Beverly men; and the remainder of the sum abovesaid which was not paid the 20th of January, 1686/87 being the sum of seventeen pounds, seven shillings, and eight pence was committed to Constable Henry Kenney with a warrant under Major Gedney's hand and seal bearing date the tenth of February 1686/87 with order to pay it according to the direction of the Committee. Paid out of the sum abovesaid to Major Gidney for signing the remainder of this bill of assessments: two shillings; paid to James Hadlock, Jun[r]., out of the sum abovesaid for sweeping the meetinghouse the last quarter of the year that Mr. Burroughs was here: 1[s] 6[d]; paid and ordered to be paid to John Sheepard out of the sum abovesaid for sweeping the meetinghouse:

1P 1s 6d; abated out of the sum abovesaid to Jacob Fuller: 2s; to Samuell Fuller: 2s; to John Wilknes: 1s; dated this 7th of April, 1687. By order of the Committee.

Tho. Putnam, Cler.

"Rec'd this 18th of January, 1687, of Nathaniel Ing^{r}soll and Jonathan Walcutt, sixty pounds in and as money, being in full of my salary for the year 1686. I say rec'd

per me, Deodat Lawson"

This 25th of January, 1687, Constable Henry Kenny is discharged from the bill abovesaid of seventeen pounds, seven shillings, and eight pence, which was committed to him by Major Gedney, bearing date the tenth of February, 1686/87. By order of the Committee.

Tho. Putnam, Cler.

The inhabitants of this Village are hereby required in his Majesty's name to meet together at their ordinary place of meeting on the 7th day of this instant April at nine of the clock in the morning to compare our Village books of records and to consider what you will pay for transcribing our book of records; also to receive this present Committee's accounts and to choose a new Committee and give instructions to them; also to choose two men to supply the place of deacons; also to choose men to take an account of men's estates in order to making of rates. Dated in Salem Village, by order of the Committee this first day of April, 1687.

Thomas Putnam, Cler.

The above writing is a true copy taken out of the original warrant that was set on the meeting post and that stood there a public day, as attest

Thomas Putnam, Cler.

The 7th day of April, 1687

At a general meeting of the inhabitants of Salem Village

1. It was agreed and voted by a general concurrence that we do approve of the transcribing of our book of records.
2. It was agreed and voted by a general concurrence that we will give Thomas Putnam forty shillings in pay as money for transcribing our book of records.
3. There was chosen for a Committee for the year ensuing, *viz.*: Capt John Putnam, Lt. Isarell Porter, Ensign Thomas Flint, John Tarbill, and Thomas Putnam.

4. Voted that the instructions which were given to the Committee in the year 1685 shall be the instructions for the Committee for this ensuing year.
5. Sargeant Nathaniel Ingersoll and Lt. Jonathan Walcott were chosen to supply the place of deacons for the year ensuing.

The 7th day of April, 1687

At a general meeting of the inhabitants of Salem Village there was chosen to take an account of men's estates, in order to making of rates, Samuell Nurs and James Putnam, and Lt. Fuller was chosen to take an account of those on that side the river and to bring in their accounts to the Committee within a fortnight.

"Rec'd this 3rd of May, 1688, of Nathaniel Ingersol and Jonathan Walcutt the sum of fifty-eight pounds and six shillings in and as money, being in part of my salary for the year last past, *viz.*: 1687. I say rec'd

per me Deod^t Lawson"

At a meeting of the inhabitants of Salem Village on Monday the 21st of May, 1688

There was chosen for overseers for the year ensuing Capt. John Putnam, Ensign Thomas Flent, Joseph Hutchinson, Mr. Danill Andrew to take care of our meetinghouse and other public charge, and to make return according to law.

At a general meeting of the inhabitants of Salem Village the 18th of June, 1689.

There was chosen for a Committee for the year ensuing Capt. John Putnam, Joshua Rea, Senr, Ensign Thomas Flint, Edward Putnam, and Thomas Preston.

At the same meeting the 18th of June, 1689

It was agreed and voted by a general concurrence that for Mr. Parice's encouragement and settlement in the work of the ministry amongst us we will give him sixty-six pounds for his yearly salary; one-third part in money, the other two-third parts in provision at the prices following: wheat at four shillings per bushel, rye and barley malt at three shillings per bushel, indian corn at two shillings per bushel; and beef at three half-pence per pound, pork at two pence per pound, and butter six pence per pound; and Mr. Parice to find himself firewood, and Mr. Parice to keep the ministry house in good repair.

And that Mr. Parice shall also have the use of the ministry pasture and the inhabitants to keep the fence in repair, and that we will keep up our contribution; and our inhabitants to put their money in papers, and this to continue so long as Mr. Parice continues in the work of the ministry amongst us. And all provision to be good and merchantable, and if it please God to bless the inhabitants, we shall be willing to give more, and we expect that if God shall diminish the estate of the people, that then Mr. Parice do abate of his salary according to proportion.

At a general meeting of the inhabitants of Salem Village the 23rd of August, 1689

It was agreed and voted by a general concurrence that we make choice of Left. Nathenell Putnam and Capt. John Putnam, Mr. Joseph Hutchinson and Ensign Thomas Flinte, Joshua Rea, Sen[r] and Francis Nurse and Mr. Daniell Andrew, or the major part of them to present our petition to the Town of Salem that we may have a Township granted to us together with our proper share of common, which belongs to us according to law and equity to the proportion of charges which we have borne in the Town of Salem ever since we were by ourselves, or an addition to be made to us some other way. And we do hereby fully empower and authorize our forenamed friends to transact with the selectmen and Town of Salem about the matter above mentioned, or what they or the major part of them shall do in the case above named shall be accounted legal by us as if we ourselves had done it.

2. Voted that the instructions given to the Committee in the year 1685 shall be the instructions for the Committee this year for the raising of our public charges.

At a general meeting of the inhabitants of Salem Village the 10th of October, 1689

It was agreed and voted that the vote in our book of records of 1681, that lays as some say an entailment upon our ministry house and land, is hereby made void and of no effect; one man only dissenting.

2. It was voted and agreed by a general concurrence that we will give to Mr. Parice our ministry house and barn and two acres of land next adjoining to the house, and that Mr. Parice take office upon him amongst us and live and die in the work of the ministry amongst us.
And if Mr. Parice or his heirs do sell the house and land, that the people may have the first refusal of it, giving as much as other men will.

3. There was chosen to lay out the land and make a conveyance of the house and land and to make the conveyance in the name and in the behalf of the inhabitants unto Mr. Parice and his heirs, viz.: Left. Nathenill Putnam, Capt. John Putnam, Capt. Jonathan Walcutt, and Ensign Thomas Flint, and Left. Nathaniell Ingersoll.

At a meeting of the inhabitants of Salem Village the 22nd day of October, 1689, were chosen 2 men, namely John Tarbul and Benjamin Putnam, to take an account of men's estate and bring it in to the Committee in order to make a rate for the maintenance of our minister and to bring it in by the 19th day of November next.

At a meeting of the inhabitants of Salem Village on the 17th day of December, 1689

1. Upon some objection it was voted by a general concurrence that it was a legal meeting. At the same meeting were 26 men householders.

2. Voted that the power which was given to the seven men the 23rd day August, 1689, is by this meeting made void and of no effect.
3. Voted that we will apply ourselves to the Town of Salem for a Township.
4. Voted the men chosen for that end were Capt. John Putnam, Lieut. Nathaneel Putnam, Ensign Flint.
5. Voted that we give them the same power and privilege the seven men had the 23rd August, 1689.

This is the remainder of the rate which was made for Mr. Paris's salary in the year 1689, which is not yet paid; which rate is to be paid one-third part in money, the other two-thirds in provision as money:

	£	s.	d.
William Buckely	0	8	0
James Smith	0	7	0
Samuell Trask	0	7	0
William Sebley	1	0	0
Thomas Haines	0	8	9
Samll Reay	0	2	6
Samuell Upton	0	3	0
Henry Keney sen	0	6	4
Daniell Eliott	0	8	0
Samll Brabrook	0	6	6
Job Swineton	0	10	0
Benj Stacey	0	5	0
Joseph Hutchinson Ju	0	8	0
Edward Bishop	0	4	0
william Sheldon	0	10	0
Thomas Bayley	0	7	0
Richard williams	0	5	0
Joseph Herick	0	12	0
Thomas Rayment	0	10	0
Samll wilkins widow	0	7	0
Charles Starns	0	5	0
John wilkins	0	12	0
Joseph Sweneton	0	8	0
Benjemin Fuller mas	0	7	0
John Darlin	0	7	6
william Chube	0	5	0
Georg Jacobs	0	5	0
Henery Keney Ju	0	9	0
william Upton	0	3	0
John Dale	0	9	0
John Hadlock	0	7	6
Benj Holton widow	0	6	0
John Houlton	0	6	6
Antony wood	0	5	0
Joseph Manning	0	5	0
James Beale	0	5	0
Joseph Flint	0	8	0
Joshua Rea Jun	0	12	0

To Edward Bishop, Constable:

The persons abovenamed have had their rates demanded but yet have not paid it; therefore by virtue of an order of the General Court bearing date

October, 1672, you are hereby required in their Majesties' names to collect of the several persons the sums annexed to each of their names, and if any refuse to pay, to levy the same by distress and deliver the same to Mr. Parise or to the Committee, according to the Court order, and this shall be your warrant.

Salem Village, this 23rd September, 1690

At a meeting of the inhabitants of this Village 30th September, 1690, there was chosen for a Committee for the year ensuing Le^{ft} Natheniell Putnam, John Tarbell, Thomas Fuller, Junr, Jonathan Putnam, and Joseph Holton, Ju^r.

Salem Village, 24th October 1690

The inhabitants of this Village are desired to meet at their ordinary place of meeting on Tuesday the 28th of this instant October at ten a'clock to hear and give answer to some propositions that Mr. Parris hath made to the people, or that he may make on that day, and to determine upon anything that may be needful to be done upon that account, and to give the Committee instructions, and to choose men to take account of men's estates, and consider what shall be done about repairing of the meetinghouse.

> Jonathan Putnam
> John Tarbell
> Joseph Holton

At a general meeting of the inhabitants of this Village 28th October, 1690, it was agreed and voted by a general concurrence that the instructions for the Committee for this year shall be as followeth:

1. That our Committee shall make a rate of sixty pounds for Mr. Parris's salary for this year already begun, one-third part to be paid in money, the other two-thirds to be in provisions according to the prices set in the vote made by our inhabitants the 18th June, 1689, Mr. Parris having relinquished the six pounds voted there for firewood.

2. Voted that the Committee now in being are empowered to repair our meetinghouse and keep it decent, and the inhabitants to bear the charge of it.

3. Voted that our Committee shall raise our public charge this year according to the instructions given to the Committee in the year 1684.

4. There was chosen to take account of men's estates, in order to make a rate, Joseph Putnam and John Holton, and they to bring in an account within a month to the Committee.

5. At the same meeting Leutt. Nathaniell Putnam, Capt. John Putnam, and Frances Nurse were chosen to go to Joseph Holton, Senr., to discourse with him about the deed of our ministry land which we had from him, and make return to the people the next meeting.

6. Voted that we will keep up the contribution and that our inhabitants shall put their money in papers which they contribute, or else it shall be accounted as strangers' money.

Salem Village, 5th December, 1690

The inhabitants of this Village are desired to meet at their ordinary place of meeting on the 9th of this instant December at ten of the clock in the morning to receive the return of those men that were chosen to discourse with Goodman Holton relating to our ministry land, and to consider what to do about sending to the Court for an explanation of our Court order and to give answer to a petition of some persons for liberty to build a seat in the meetinghouse.

> Nath. Putnam
> John Tarbell
> Joseph Holton
> Jonath Putnam

At a general meeting of the inhabitants of Salem Village on the 9th of December, 1690

1. It was voted that we will send to the General Court for an explanation of our Court order relating to our being freed from bearing charge with Salem relating to the ministry there.
2. Voted that Capt. John Putnam and Lett. Thomas Fuller and Mr. Daniell Andrew and Francis Nurse and Thomas Putnam or the major part of them are chosen to draw up a petition to the honored Court in our behalf for that end.
3. Voted that Le^{tt} Natheniell Putnam and Le^{tt} Thomas Fuller shall present our petition to the Court.
4. Voted that Edward Putnam and Jonathan Putnam and John Putnam and James Putnam and Benjamin Putnam shall have liberty to build a seat for their wives joining to Mr. Paris's pew, and so of the same breadth to the east end of the meetinghouse.
5. Voted that Mr. Joseph Hutchinson and Daniell Andrew and Sargeant Swineton and Ensign Flint and Thomas Putnam and Bray Wilkins and John Buxton and Daniell Rea shall have liberty to enlarge the fore seat on the east end of the meetinghouse to set it forwards to make it a double seat for their wives.
6. Voted that the Committee in being shall place other women in the gallery in those seats where the abovesaid women are taken out.

Salem Village, 30th December, 1690

The inhabitants of this Village are desired to meet at their ordinary place of meeting on the 6th of January ensuing at 12 of the clock to choose some men to discourse with Lt. Ingersall and Joseph Holton, Senr., about a division of land between them on which our ministry house stands.

> Nath. Putnam, Thomas Fuller
> John Tarbill, Joseph Holton, Ju.
> Jonathan Putnam

At a general meeting of the inhabitants of Salem Village the 6th of January 1690/91, there was chosen for a Committee to treat with Joseph Holton, Senr., and Liue^t Nathaniell Ingerson about the land our ministry house stands on; Joseph Hutchinson, Senr., Joseph Porter, Daniell Andrew, Frances Nurs, and Thomas Putnam or the major part of them to have full power in the behalf of the inhabitants to get a full and legal assurance of the land which belongs to our ministry house which the inhabitants have purchased of the men first abovenamed, and to make return to the inhabitants of what they do. What is abovewritten was voted to be the act of the inhabitants.

The rate which was made by us whose names are underwritten for Mr. Parris's salary for the year beginning the first of July, 1689, and ending the first of July, 1690: the whole rate was sixty-six pounds, fifteen shillings, and ten pence.

John Putnam, Sen.
Thomas Flint
Edward Putnam

	£	s.	d.
mrs. mary putnam	1	10	00
Joseph putnam	1	14	00
Lett Nath Putnam	2	0	00
Capt John Putnam	2	0	00
Thomas Flint	1	9	00
william way	0	13	00
Aron way	0	8	00
Bray wilkins	0	8	00
Joseph Houlton sen	0	8	00
Benjemen wilkins	0	16	00
Samll willkins widow	0	4	00
Thomas wilkins	1	3	00
John willkins	0	11	00
Abraham walott	0	8	00
Zachiah Goodale	1	5	00
Joseph Houton Jun	0	15	00
Henery willkins	0	12	00
Thomas Putnam	1	00	00
Thomas Fuller sen	0	8	00
Job Sweneton	1	0	00
Joseph Sweneton	0	7	00
Jacob Fuller	0	12	00
Benjemin Fuller inas[?]	0	7	00
Thomas Fuller Jun	1	5	00
John putnam Jun	1	00	00
James Smith	0	10	00
Benjamin Fuller	0	7	00
John Darlin	0	7	00
Henery Keney sen	0	6	00
Henery Keney Jun	0	8	00
John Dale	0	8	00
Sam^{ll} Sebley	0	8	00
John Hadlock	0	7	00
Benj Houlton widow	0	2	00
Henery Houlton	0	7	00
Capt John walcott	1	1	00

	£	s.	d.
Le^{tt} Nath^{ll} Ingersell	1	0	00
John Houlton	0	6	00
	28	2	0
Thomas Haines	0	19	00
Jesper Sweneton	0	7	00
Joseph Pope	1	15	00
Samuell Abbey	0	7	00
Peter Prescott	0	7	00
John Flint	0	15	00
Edward Bishop	0	14	00
walter phillips	0	12	00
Joseph Flint	0	8	00
Joseph Herick	0	14	00
Thomas Rayment	0	8	00
Daniell Andrew	1	16	00
Joshua Rea sen	1	5	00
Daniell Rea	1	4	6
Joshua Rea Jun	0	12	00
Jonathan putnam	1	3	00
James putnam	0	15	00
Benjamin putnam	1	00	00
Georg Jacobs	0	5	00
Francis Nurs	0	8	00
Samull Nurse	0	15	00
John Tarbell	0	15	00
Thomas preston	0	15	00
Edward putnam	1	00	00
Alexander osburn	0	18	00
william Sebley	0	18	00
Joseph Hutchinson sen	2	00	00
Joseph Hutchinson Jun	0	16	00
John Buxton	1	7	00
Samuell Brabroock	0	6	00
Peter Clayce	0	12	00
Joseph porter	2	10	00
Israell porter	0	5	00
william Sheldon	0	5	00
Samuell Ray	0	5	00
Daniell Eliott	0	5	00
Samull Trask	0	5	00
John walcott	0	16	00
Richard williams	0	4	00
	31	0	6
Charles Starns	00	4	00
Ezekell Chevers	0	10	00
John wheldon	0	16	00
Benjemin Stacey	0	4	00
Benjemin Nurse	0	7	00
william Buckley	0	7	00
william upton	0	4	00
Samuell upton	0	4	00
John Rea	0	7	00
John Putnam Tartus [Tertius, i.e., "the 3rd"]	0	7	00
John willard	0	7	00
william Greggs	0	16	00
Francis Eliott	0	4	00

	£	s.	d.
william Earles	0	3	00
Joseph Trumball	0	3	00
william Small	0	7	00
Samull Barton	0	4	00
william Tayler	0	3	00
Robart murrall	0	3	00
Benjemin Hutchinson	0	16	00
John Lane	0	5	00
Samell Lane	0	5	00
william Beele	0	6	00
	7	12	0

This rate was made for the maintenance of Mr. Parise for the year beginning July the first, 1690.

> Natheniell Putnam
> Thomas Fuller, Jun.
> John Tarbell
> Jonathan Putnam

There is abated out of this rate to Benj. Hutchinson, 0–10–0, and to Joseph Hutchinson, Jun., 0–6–0, to John Walcott, 0–8–0, and to John Weldon, 0–6–0, to Samuell Abbey, 0–4–0.

Paid to old Allen for sweeping the meetinghouse, 1–6–0.

[The following notation is written in the margin at this point in the Book of Record:

"Received of the inhabitants of Salem Village at sundry times and in divers species in part of my salary from 1 July, 1689, to 1 July, 1691, the sum of one-hundred and fifteen pounds and five shillings and eight pence; the remainder due for said two years I hereby acquit said Village from. Witness my hand this 31st October, 1694.]

> Sam. Parris"

At a general meeting of the inhabitants of Salem Village 3 April, 1691

1. It was voted that we will address ourselves to the honored General Court sitting at Boston that they would be pleased some way to order the several families which live adjacent to us and are constant comers to our meetinghouse may be some way helpful to us to maintain our minister and to build and repair our meetinghouse.

2. It was voted that we make choice of Capt John Putnam, Mr. Danell Andrew, Ensign Thomas Flint, and Thomas Putnam, or the major part of them, to draw up a petition to the honored General Court in the name and behalf of the inhabitants for the ends above expressed.

3. Voted that we make choice of Leu^{tt} Nathanell Putnam to present the
   petition that shall be drawn up in the name and in the behalf of the
   inhabitants by the men above expressed to the honored General Court.
   Whereas there was a meeting warned on the 3rd of April, 1691, to hear the
   return of those men that were chosen to discourse with Leu^{tt} Ingersall and
   Joseph Houlton, Senr, about our ministry land, accordingly there was a
   meeting on the day aforementioned. And their return to the people was that
   they had done nothing in that matter but discoursed with the men.

There is committed to Constable Joseph Hericke a bill of the remainder of
the rate made for Mr. Parris for the year beginning July 1, 1690: 18 pounds, 16
shillings, 1 pence, together with 3 pounds, 14 shillings, 6 pence, which is for the
use of the people, with a warrant to gather it.

At a general meeting of the inhabitants of Salem Village the 16th of October,
1691, there was chosen for a Committee for the year ensuing:

Francis Nurse, Joseph Porter, Joseph Hutchinson, Daniell Andrew, and
Joseph Putnam.

The inhabitants of this Village are desired to meet at their ordinary place of
meeting on Friday the 16th of this instant October at 12 of the clock to choose
a Committee for the year ensuing and to give them instructions.

Nathaniell Putnam, John Tarbell,
Jonathan Putnam

The 16th of this instant October, 1691, the inhabitants being met together
according to the warrant; it being then voted whether there should be
instructions given to the Committee then chosen in order to making a rate: it
was voted on the negative.

The inhabitants of this Village are desired to meet at their ordinary places of
meeting on the 1st day of December, 1691, at 10 of the clock in the morning to
consider by what means the inhabitants were covened together on the 18th of
June, 1689 (then there was a Committee chosen and a yearly salary stated to
Mr. Parris that day, but no warrant appearing in the book for it), and to consider
of a vote in the book on the 10th of October, 1689, wherein our right in the
ministry house and land seems to be impaired and made void; also to consider
about our ministry house and 2 acres of land given to Mr. Parris, and a
committee chosen to make conveyances to Mr. Parris in the name of the
inhabitants; and to consider about Mr. Parris's maintenance for this year—
whether by voluntary contributions or by subscription.

Joseph Porter, Daniell Andrew, Frances Nurs, Joseph Hutchinson
Joseph Putnam

The inhabitants of this Village are desired to meet together at their ordinary
places of meeting on the 8th day of this instant January at 2 of the clock in the

afternoon to choose men to discourse with the Town at Salem in respect to a petition now depending in the General Court, and to give them instructions for that end. By order of the Committee.

Joseph Putnam

At a general meeting of the inhabitants of Salem Village the 8th of January, 1691/92, it was agreed and voted by a general concurrence that we make a choice of Nathanell Putnam, John Putnam, Senr., Frances Nurs, Joseph Hutchinson, Sen., Joseph Porter, and Thomas Flint, or the major part of them, for to go to the Town meeting which is warned to be held at Salem on the 11th of this instant January, to discourse with the Town of Salem about our petition now pending in General Court and to make return to the inhabitants.

2. Voted that the instructions given to the men abovementioned for the work abovesaid are as followeth: that the Town of Salem would grant our petition now pending in General Court, or else clear us from all Town charges, and then we will maintain all our own poor and highways and pay our country rates with the Town of Salem.

Salem Village, the 23rd January, 1691/92

The inhabitants of this Village are desired to meet together at their ordinary place of meeting on the 28th day of this instant January after lecture to choose some men to transact with the Town of Salem with respect to our petition now pending in General Court and to give them power and instructions for that end. By order of the Committee.

Joseph Putnam

At a general meeting of the inhabitants of Salem Village the 28th of January, 1691/92, it was agreed and voted by a general concurrence that we make choice of Nathaniell Putnam, John Putnam, Senr., Frances Nurs, Joseph Hutchinson, Senr., Joseph Porter, and Thomas Flint, or the major part of them, for to transact and agree if they see cause with the Town of Salem about our petition now pending in General Court.

2. Voted that the instructions given to the men abovementioned for the work abovesaid are as followeth:

That the Town of Salem would grant our petition now pending in General Court, or else clear us from all Town charges, and then we will maintain all our own poor and highways and pay our country rates with the Town of Salem.

Salem Village, the 27th of January, 1691/92

The inhabitants of this Village are desired to meet together at their ordinary places of meeting on the first day of March next ensuing at one of the clock in the afternoon to receive the return of the men that were chosen to transact with the Town of Salem, and in case the people see not cause to accept of what is done, then to choose some to manage our petition now pending in General Court. By order of the Committee.

Joseph Putnam

At a general meeting of the inhabitants of Salem Village the first day of March, 1691/92, it was agreed and voted by a general concurrence that we do not accept of what the Town of Salem hath proferred us: that is, to be freed from the maintenance of their highways, provided we will maintain all our own poor.

2. Voted that we make choice of Capt John Putnam and his son Jonathan Putnam to manage our petition now pending in General Court.
3. Voted that we make choice of Mr. Daniell Andrew to inform the Town of Salem that we do not accept of what the Town of Salem hath proferred us.

Salem Village, the 7th of December, 1692

The inhabitants of this Village are desired to meet together at their ordinary places of meeting on the 13th day of this instant December at 12 of the clock to choose a Committee for the year ensuing, and to consider what shall be done about our ministry house and land, it seeming to be conveyed away after a fraudulent manner. By order of the Committee.

Joseph Putnam

At a general meeting of the inhabitants of Salem Village the 13th December, 1692

There was chosen for a Committee for the year ensuing Joseph Porter, Joseph Hutchinson, Thomas Willikins, Zacheriah Godell, and Joseph Putnam.

The rates which were made by us whose names are underwritten for Mr. Parris's salary for the years beginning the first of July, 1691, and ending the first of July, 1693: the whole rates were one-hundred thirty-six and four shillings and abated out of the abovesaid sum to Thomas Fuller: 8^S, to George Flint: 5^S, to Isaac Nedom: 5^S, to William Buckly: 6^S, to Joseph Hutchinson, Senr.: 12^S.

John Tarbell
Joseph Pope   Joseph Houlton

At a general meeting of the inhabitants of Salem Village the 15th of January, 1692/93

There was chosen for a Committee for the year ensuing Joseph Pope, John Tarbell, Joseph Holton, Jun., Thomas Preston, and James Smith.

The rate which was made by us whose names are underwritten for Mr. Parris's salary beginning the first day of July, 1693, and ending the first of July, 1694: the whole rate was sixty-seven pounds.

John Tarbell, Joseph Houlton,
Joseph Pope

Salem Village, the 3rd of February 1692/93

The inhabitants of this Village are desired to meet together at their ordinary place of meeting on the 14th day of this instant February at eleven of the clock in the morning to consider and agree and determine who are capable of voting in our public transactions by the power given us by the General Court order at our first settlement, and to consider of and make void a vote in our book of records on the 18th of June, 1689, where there is a salary of sixty-six pounds stated to Mr. Parris, he not complying with it; also to consider of and make void several votes in our book of records on the 10th of October, 1689, where our ministry house and barn and two acres of land seems to be conveyed from us after a fraudulent manner, and to consider of and agree about what shall be done for the reparation of our meetinghouse and ministry fences.

Thomas Preston
Joseph Pope
Joseph Holton
John Tarbell

1. Agreed that all men that are ratable, or hereafter shall be living within that tract of land mentioned in our General Court order [i.e. in Salem Village], shall have liberty in our nominating and appointing a Committee and voting in any of our public concerns.

"At a [Court of] General Sessions of the Peace holden at Ipswich March the 28th, 1693, this Court having viewed and considered the above agreement or vote contained in the last five lines, finding the same to be repugnant to the laws of this province, do declare the same to be null and void, and that this order be recorded with the records of this Court.

attest Stephen Sewall, Cler."

Salem Village, 9th March 1693/94

The inhabitants of this Village are desired to meet together at their ordinary place of meeting on the 20th day of this instant March at 12 of the clock to choose a Committee for the year ensuing.

Thomas Presston   Joseph Pope
Joseph Holton   John Tarbell

At a general meeting of the inhabitants of Salem Village the 20th day of March, 1693/94, there was chosen for a Committee for the year ensuing, *viz.*: Lieut. Nathanill Putnam, Ensign Thomas Flint, Corporal Thomas Fuller, Henry Willknes, and Thomas Putnam.

Salem Village, this 28th of April, 1694

The inhabitants of this Village are desired to meet together at their ordinary place of meeting on Monday next, being the last day of this instant April at eight a clock in the morning to consider of the power which was given to a committee which was chosen by our inhabitants on the first day of October, 1686, to transact with Topsfield about our land which lieth between the bounds of Salem and Ipswich River, which Topsfield men lay claim to, and to give order what shall be further done in that matter By order of the Committee.

Thomas Putnam, Cler.

At a general meeting of the inhabitants of Salem Village the last day of April, 1694, it was agreed and voted by a general concurrence that whereas some of Salem did make a motion to the General Court in the year 1639 and did obtain a grant from the Court of all the lands that did lie between the bounds of Salem and Ipswich River not formerly granted, for the accommodation of a Village that Salem did intend to plant near said River, and Salem having declared us to be that Village for whom they did obtain the abovesaid grant, and in consideration that Topsfield men do lay claim unto our land granted to us as above, and we being deprived of our just right by them; we do by these presents name, ordain, appoint, and make our trusty friends, *viz.*: Liue^t Nathaniell Putnam, Capt. John Putnam, Liuet Nathaniell Ingersoll, Ensign Thomas Flint, and Corporal Joseph Herrick of Salem Village, or the major part of them, our true and lawful attorneys for us and in our name and to our use to demand, sue for, and recover our land abovementioned, which any of Topsfield men lay claim to, or otherwise for to agree with Topsfield Town or any of Topsfield men as they shall see cause either in Court or out of Court; giving and hereby granting unto our said attorneys or the major part of them our full power and authority to use and execute all such acts, things, and devices in the law as shall be necessary for the recovery of the said lands, and acquittances or other discharges in our name to make and give and generally to do and execute in the premises as fully as we ourselves might or could do, being all personally present, ratifying, confirming, and allowing all and whatsoever our said attorneys or the major part of them shall lawfully do or cause to be done therein by these presents. In witness whereof we do hereby order and appoint Thomas Putnam to give our said attorneys this our letter of attorneyship in our name out of our book of records under his hand and seal.

Thomas Preston and Samuell Nurs desired to have their dissent to this vote entered in our book of records.

At a general meeting of the inhabitants of Salem Village the last day of April, 1694, it was agreed and voted by a general concurrence that whereas we have chosen and empowered Liuet. Nathaniell Putnam, Capt. John Putnam, Liuet. Nathaniel Ingersoll, Ensign Thomas Flint, and Corporal Joseph Herrick or the major part of them for to transact with Topsfield men about the land granted to us between the bounds of Salem and Ipswich River, we order them to make return of what they shall do in that case to the inhabitants as soon as conveniently they can.

Salem Village, the 29th of June, 1694

The inhabitants of this Village are desired to meet together at their ordinary place of meeting on Tuesday next, being the third day of July, at two a'clock in the afternoon to choose and fully empower men to take and get legal bills of sale in the name of the inhabitants of this Village, of Joseph Hutchinson, Senr, and Joseph Holton, Senr, and Nathaniell Ingersoll, of that land which the inhabitants of this Village have purchased of them for the use of the ministry amongst us. By order of the Committee.

Tho. Putnam, Cler.

At a general meeting of the inhabitants of Salem Village the third day of July, 1694, it was agreed and voted by a general concurrence that we make choice of Mr. Israell Portor and Thomas Flint and Thomas Putnam, or the major part of them, to get and take legal bills of sale in the name of our inhabitants, of Joseph Hutchinson, Senr., Joseph Holton, Senr., and Nathaniell Ingersoll, of that land which the inhabitants of this Village have purchased of them for the use of the ministry amongst us. And we do hereby fully empower them, or the major part of them, to be our agents and trustees in our name to take, demand, and if need be to sue any of them that shall neglect or refuse to give legal deeds of sale of that land which our inhabitants hath purchased of them for the use of the ministry amongst us; giving, and hereby granting unto our said trustees or the major part of them our full power and authority to use and execute all such acts, things, and devices in the law as shall be necessary for the attaining of the same, and make return to the inhabitants of what they shall do in that matter as soon as conveniently they can.

Salem Village, the 15th Sept., 1694

The inhabitants of this Village are desired to meet together at their ordinary place of meeting on Thursday next, being the twenty day of this instant September, at two a'clock in the afternoon to hear and consider of some propositions which Mr. Parris has to make to our inhabitants relating to our ministry house and land, and also to see if we can possibly agree together in peace and unity to settle peace amongst us by calling a Council or other ways according to the command of God to seek peace and pursue it. By order of the Committee.

Thomas Putnam, Cler.

Salem Village, the 26th of November, 1694

The inhabitants of the proprietors of the lands of this Village are hereby required in their Majesties names to meet together at their ordinary place of meeting on Friday next, being the thirtieth day of this instant November at two a'clock in the afternoon to choose a clerk to keep our books of records, and also hear the return of the men or attorneys that were formerly chosen to transact about the lands which was ordered to this Village by the General Court in the year 1639, and also to give order what shall be further done in that matter.

Nath: Putnam, Tho. Flint, Tho. Fuller, Jun., Henry Wilknes, Thomas Putnam.
The Committee

The 30th of November, 1694

At a general meeting of the inhabitants of the proprietors of the lands of Salem Village it was agreed and voted by a general concurrence that we make choice of Thomas Putnam for our clerk to keep our books of records.

2. It was agreed and voted that we will choose and empower agents or attorneys to transact for us about the land which was granted to this Village by the General Court in the year 1639.

3. It was agreed and voted that we make choice of Nathaniell Putnam, John Putnam, Sen[r], Nathaniell Ingersoll, Thomas Flintt, Sen[r], and Joseph Herrick, Senr., or the major part of them for to transact for us about the land which was ordered to this Village by the General Court in the year 1639.

At a general meeting of the inhabitants and proprietors of the lands of Salem Village the thirtieth day of November, 1694, being orderly warned. Whereas the General Court held at Boston in the year 1639 ordered to Salem Village all the lands near Salem bounds between Salem and the river that runs to Ipswich not belonging to any other town or person by any former grant, and whereas of late several persons have unlawfully entered into part of the said lands and do withhold the same from the said inhabitants to whom they do belong and appertain; the said inhabitants have by these presents chosen and appointed Nathaniell Putnam, John Putnam, Senr., Nathaniell Ingersoll, Thomas Flint, Sen[r] and Joseph Herrick, Senr., all of Salem Village, they or the major part of them, to be their agents or attorneys in the behalf and to the use of the said inhabitants to sue, commence and prosecute any suit or suits, action or actions against any person or persons that have unlawfully entered into, or that do withhold or detain from them, the said inhabitants, any part or parcel of the aforesaid lands. Hereby giving and granting to our aforesaid agents or attorneys, or the major part of them, full power and lawful authority to say, do, perform, and finish all and every act and acts, thing and things, device and devices, which in the law shall be needful or expedient for the better prosecution of the same; attorney or attorneys under them to make and constitute and at pleasure to revoke acquittances or other discharges in our name, to make or give and generally to do and execute in the premises as fully as we ourselves might or could do, being all personally present. And whatsoever our aforesaid agents or attorneys, or the major part of them, shall lawfully do or cause to be done in, about, or concerning the premises, the said inhabitants will allow of and confirm the same. The abovewritten was voted at the abovesaid meeting of the inhabitants and passed in the affirmative.

as attest Thomas Putnam, Clerk.

Joshua Rea, Senr., Frances Nurs, Sen[r], Samuell Nurs, John Tarbill and Thomas Preston desired that their dissent to the abovewritten vote might be entered in our book of records.

Salem Village, the 16th of March, 1694/95

The inhabitants of this Village are hereby required in their Majesties' names to meet together at their usual place of meeting on Thursday next, being the

21st day of this instant March, at twelve of the clock for to choose a Committee of assessors for the year ensuing. By order of the Committee.

Thomas Putnam, Cler.

At a general meeting of the inhabitants of Salem Village the 21st of March, 1694/95, there was chosen for a Committee of assessors for the year ensuing Liuet. Nathaniell Putnam, Ensign Thomas Flint, Henry Wilknes, Thomas Putnam, and Jacob Fuller.

Salem Village, the 18th of January, 1694/1695

The rate which was made for Mr. Parris's salary in Salem Village for the year beginning the first day of July, 1694, and ending the first day of July, 1695:

	£	s.	d.
Daniell Andrew & son	1	6	0
samuell Abby & son	—	7	—
william Alline	—	4	6
John Buxton & son	1	3	—
samuell Braybrook	—	7	—
william Buckly & son	—	5	6
Edward Bishop senr	—	7	—
Edward Bishop Junr	—	7	—
Henry Brown	—	10	6
ezekill Cever	—	10	6
John Darling & son	—	6	—
John Deale	—	7	—
Frances Ellyott	—	3	6
Benjamin Endecott	—	3	—
ensigne Thomas Flint	1	4	—
Thomas Fuller senr	—	5	6
Thomas Fuller Junr	—	18	—
Thomas Fuller Tertius	—	8	—
Jacob Fuller	—	10	6
Benjamin Fuller	—	8	—
Jonathan Fuller	—	4	6
John Flint	—	10	6
Joseph Flint	—	7	—
George Flint Junr	—	3	6
Humphrey French	—	4	—
Zach: Goodell senr & son	—	18	—
Zach: Goodell Junr	—	8	—
Joseph Goodell	—	4	—
Isaac Goodell	—	7	—
Joseph Holton senr	—	5	6
Joseph Holton Junr	—	14	—
Henry Holton	—	7	—
John Holton	—	7	—
John Hadlock	—	7	—
Thomas Haines	—	16	—
Joseph Herrick senr	1	2	—
Joseph Hutchinson senr	1	3	—
Joseph Hutchinson Junr	—	10	6
John Hutchinson	—	7	—
Benjamin Hutchinson	—	8	—
Liuet Nathaniell Ingersoll	—	17	—

	£	s.	d.
Henry Kenny senr	—	5	6
Henry Kenny Junr	—	7	—
samuell Lane	—	4	6
John martin	—	7	—
Roburt morrill	—	7	—
Frances Nurs senr	—	8	—
samuell Nurs	—	13	—
Isaac Neadom	—	5	6
Thomas Nickolls	—	3	6
Allexander osborn	—	15	—
Liut Nathaniell putnam	1	18	—
Capt John Putnam	1	10	—
Joseph putnam	2	4	—
Joseph pope	1	14	—
Thomas putnam	—	18	—
petter prescett	—	9	—
watter phillips	—	9	—
Jonathan putnam	1	6	—
James putnam	—	18	—
Benjamin putnam	—	18	—
John putnam Tirtius	—	16	—
Eliazer putnam	—	9	—
Thomas preston & son	—	14	—
Edward putnam	1	—	—
Joseph portor & sons	2	12	—
Liuet Isarell portor	—	14	—
James Prince	—	9	—
Joseph prince	—	8	—
John putnam Junr & man	1	2	—
Thomas Rayment	—	16	—
Joshua Rea senr	—	16	—
Daniell Rea	1	4	—
Joseph Rea Junr	—	9	—
John Rea	—	10	—
samuell Rea	—	3	6
Johosaphat Rogers	—	3	6
Job Swinerton & son	1	4	—
Jaspar Swinerton	—	9	—
Joseph Swinerton	—	7	—
Abraham Smith	—	4	6
Ephraim Shelden	—	3	6
william smale	—	14	—
Benjamin Stacy	—	4	—
James Smith & son	—	9	—
samuell sibly	—	8	—
John Tarbill and man	—	14	—
John Tree	—	4	—
william Upton	—	9	—
samuell Upton	—	9	—
Capt Jonathan walcott	—	16	—
Abraham walcott	—	7	—
John walcott	—	7	—
Jonathan walcott Junr	—	4	6
John willden	—	7	—
Joseph whiple	—	10	—
Bray wilknes senr	—	5	6
Aaron way	—	10	6
William way	—	10	—

	£.	d.	
Benjamin Wilknes	—	13	—
samuell Wilknes	—	3	6
Thomas Wilknes senr	—	14	—
Henry Wilknes	—	10	—
John Wilknes	—	9	—
Richard Williams	—	3	—

Sum total, errors excepted, is the just sum of sixty pounds, seven shillings. This is a true copy of the original rate that was then made, excepting of those men which were in controversy between Salem Village and the Town of Topsfield.

Nathaniell Putnam ⎫
Thomas Flint   ⎪
Henry Wilkens   ⎬ The Committee of Salem Village in the year 1694
Thomas Fuller   ⎪
Thomas Putnam   ⎭

Salem Village, the 13th of December, 1695

The bill of assessments or the rate which was made in Salem Village for Mr. Parris's salary for the year beginning the first day of July, 1695, and ending the first day of July, 1696, which rate is to be paid one-third part in money and the other two-thirds parts in provisions:

	£	s.	d.
Daniell Andrew and sons	1	18	—
Samuel Abby and son	—	7	—
william Alline	—	8	—
John Buxton and sons	1	4	—
samuell Braybrook	—	7	—
william buckly & son	—	6	—
Edward Bishop senr & son	—	10	—
Edward Bishop Junr	—	7	—
Henry Brown	—	10	6
Ezekill Chever	—	10	—
John Darling & son	—	6	—
John Deale	—	7	—
Frances Elliott	—	3	6
Benjamin endecott	—	3	—
ensigne Thomas Flint	1	2	—
Thomas Fuller senr	—	5	—
Thomas Fuller Junr	—	18	—
Thomas Fuller Tirtius	—	7	—
Jacob Fuller	—	12	—
Benjamin Fuller	—	7	—
Jonathan Fuller	—	4	6
John Flint	—	10	6
Joseph Flint	—	7	—
George Flint junr	—	3	—
Humphrey French	—	4	—
Zach: Goodell senr & son	1	—	—
Zach: Goodell Junr	—	6	—

	£	s.	d.
Joseph Goodell	—	4	—
Isaac Goodell	—	8	—
John Giles	—	6	—
Joseph Holton sen[r] Estate	—	4	—
Joseph Holten Junr	—	14	—
Henry Holton	—	7	—
John Holton	—	7	—
John Hadlock	—	7	—
Thomas Haines	—	14	—
Joseph Herrick sen[r] & son	1	2	—
Joseph Hutchinson senr	1	3	—
Joseph Hutchinson Junr	—	10	—
John Hutchinson	—	7	—
Benjamin Hutchinson	—	8	—
Liuet Nathaniell Ingersoll	—	17	—
Henry Kenny senr	—	6	—
Henry Kenny Junr	—	6	—
Samuell Lane	—	4	—
John Martin	—	7	—
Robart Morrell	—	7	—
samuell Nurs and son	—	16	—
Isaac Neadom	—	5	6
Thomas Nickols	—	3	6
Allexander osburn	—	15	—
Liuet Nathaniell putnam	2	—	—
Capt John putnam	1	10	—
Joseph putnam	2	4	—
Thomas putnam	—	18	—
Joseph pope	1	16	—
peter prescott	—	9	—
walter phillips	—	9	—
Jonathan putnam	1	6	—
James Putnam	—	18	—
Benjamin putnam	—	18	—
John putnam Tirtius	—	15	—
Eliazer putnam	—	9	—
Thomas preston & son	—	14	—
Edward putnam	1	—	—
Joseph Porter and sons	2	18	—
Isarell porter	—	14	—
James prince	—	7	—
Joseph Prince	—	7	—
John putnam junr	1	—	—
Thomas Rayment	—	16	—
Joshua Rea senr	—	12	—
Daniell Rea	1	4	—
Joshua Rea Junr	—	9	—
John Rea	—	9	—
samuell Rea	—	3	6
Job swinerton and son	1	4	—
Jehosaphat Rogers	—	3	6
Jasper swinerton	—	9	—
Joseph swinerton	—	7	—
Abraham smith	—	5	—
Ephraim Shelden	—	3	—
william smale	—	12	—
Benjamin stacy	—	4	—
samuell smith & Farme	—	7	—

	£	s.	d.
samuell sibly	–	7	–
John Tarbill	–	16	–
John Tree	–	4	–
william upton	–	9	–
samuell upton	–	9	–
Capt Jonathan Walcott	–	12	–
Abraham Walcott	–	7	–
John Walcott	–	7	–
Jonathan Walcott Junr	–	4	6
John Wilden	–	5	–
Joseph Whipple	–	10	–
Bray Wilknes	–	5	–
Aaron Way	–	10	–
William Way	–	8	–
Benjamin Wilknes	–	12	–
samuell Wilknes	–	3	–
Thomas Wilknes senr	–	14	–
Henry Wilknes	–	9	–
John Wilknes	–	7	–
Richard williams	–	3	–
	61	1	6

Sum total, errors excepted, is the just sum of sixty-one pounds, one shilling, and six pence. This is a true copy of the original rate that was then made, excepting those men which were then rated, which live between the bounds of Salem and Ipswich River which are yet in controversy.

> Nathanell Putnam
> Thomas Flint
> Henry Wilkens   The Committee of Salem Village in the year 1695
> Jacob Fuller
> Thomas Putnam

[From this point on, for reasons of space, we have left out certain entries from the record. We have indicated these omissions by bracketed entries mentioning the date. The omissions primarily concern the Village's search for a new minister to replace Mr. Parris. At least five men were approached, including the Reverend James Bayley.]

[March 20, 1696: Notice of Meeting]

At a general meeting of the inhabitants of Salem Village, the 24th day of March, 1695/96:

There was chosen for committee for the year ensuing, *viz.,* Capt. John Putnam, Thomas Putnam, John Dale, Benja. Wilkins and John Walcott.

At a general meeting of the inhabitants of Salem Village, the 24th day of March, 1695/96:

It was agreed and voted by a general concurrence that we make choice of Thomas Putnam to be our clerk to keep our Book of Records.

[June 25, 1696: Notice of Meeting]

The 7th day of July, 1696, at a general meeting of the inhabitants of Salem Village, it was agreed and voted by a general concurrence that whereas Mr. Parris has several times declared to the church that he did not intend to continue his stated work of the ministry amongst us no longer than the last Sabbath Day of June, 1696, and accordingly Mr. Parris did also on the two last Sabbath Days of the aforesaid June publicly declare to the whole congregation in this place that he did now intend to desist his stated work of the ministry amongst us, and thereby give way for the bringing in another minister in this place, that might, if it might be, give satisfaction to the whole inhabitants. And accordingly Mr. Parris having now desisted his ministerial work in this place, we do hereby agree to endeavor to get another minister, declaring ourselves also now to be at liberty from Mr. Parris.

The 7th day of July, 1696, at a general meeting of the inhabitants of Salem Village, it was agreed and voted by a general concurrence that whereas Mr. Parris has desisted the work of the ministry amongst us, that we now make choice of Sargent Job Swinnerton and Benjamin Putnam for to go a first time, and Jonathan Putnam and Joseph Putnam for to go a second time, and Lieut. Thomas Fuller and John Tarbell for to go a third time, to endeavor to get a minister to preach the word of God to us, that we may not be destitute of the ministry of the word in this place; and the inhabitants to bear their charge, and they to engage to the minister that shall come and preach to us twenty shillings a day, and they and each of them to take the best counsel and advice they can of the Reverend Elders in the country where they go, about getting a minister for us.

[August 1, 1696: Meeting
August 28, 1696: Notice of Meeting
September 1, 1696: Meeting
September 11, 1696: Meeting]

The 14th of September, 1696, at a general meeting of the inhabitants of Salem Village, it was agreed and voted that whereas Mr. Parris brought a writing into our public meeting on the first day of this instant September to which he desired an answer within a fortnight, we now make choice of Mr. Joseph Hutchinson, Senior; Daniel Andrew; Joseph Herrick, Senior; John Buxton; Joseph Putnam; John Tarbell; and Daniel Rea, or the major part of them, to give answer to Mr. Parris about the aforesaid writing, hereby fully empowering them, or the major part of them, to transact with Mr. Parris in behalf of our inhabitants relating to all differences that are between Mr. Parris and us, by putting our differences to arbitration if they see cause, being fully empowered to enter into bonds of arbitration with Mr. Parris in behalf of our inhabitants and to choose arbitrators for us, and the inhabitants to bear their charge.

[September 16, 1696: Notice of Meeting]

Salem Village, the 28th of September, 1696

At a general meeting of the inhabitants of Salem Village, it was agreed and voted that whereas we did charge and empower men at our last public meeting, on the 14th of this instant, to transact with Mr. Parris relating to all differences that are between him and our inhabitants, we do hereby continue their power, and they or the major part of them to agree or otherwise to transact with Mr. Parris as they shall see cause relating to all differences that are between Mr. Parris and our inhabitants, either in part or in whole.

[October 10, 1696: Notice of Meeting
October 12, 1696: Meeting
October 23, 1696: Notice of Meeting
October 27, 1696: Meeting
November 13, 1696: Notice of Meeting
November 17, 1696: Meeting]

Salem Village, the 3rd of December, 1696

The inhabitants of this Village are hereby required in His Majesty's Name to meet together at their usual place of meeting on Monday next, being the 7th day of this instant December, at eleven a'clock in the forenoon, to give more power to the men formerly chosen to transact with Mr. Parris relating to the differences that are between him and our inhabitants about our ministry house, and also to consider of and agree how to fetch Mr. Broadstreet and where he shall be entertained. By order of the Committee,

Thomas Putnam, clerk

[December 7, 1696: Meeting
February 3, 1697: Notice of Meeting
February 8, 1697: Meeting
February 19, 1697: Notice of Meeting]

Salem Village, the 23rd of February, 1696/97

At a general meeting of the inhabitants of Salem Village, it was agreed and voted by a general concurrence that we make choice of Capt. John Putnam, Capt. Israel Porter, and Capt. Thomas Flint to go and treat with Mr. Parris relating to our ministry house, to know upon what terms he will leave it, and to make return of what they shall have done in that matter at our next public meeting.

At a general meeting of the inhabitants of Salem Village, the second day of March, 1696/97, being adjourned from the 23rd day of February, 1696/97, it was agreed and voted by the said inhabitants, by a general concurrence, that whereas Mr. Samuel Parris, our late minister, hath for these eight months past desisted his stated work of the ministry amongst us, and yet still doth keep the possession of our ministry house, to our great damage, therefore the aforesaid inhabitants have by these presents chosen and appointed Mr. Joseph Hutchinson, Senior; Daniel Andrew, Senior; Thomas Flint, Senior; Joseph Herrick, Senior; and Joseph Putnam, all of Salem Village, they or the major part of them, to be their agents or attorneys in the behalf and to the use of the said inhabitants to compound and agree, or to sue, commence, and prosecute any suit or suits, action or actions against the aforesaid Mr. Samuel Parris for his withholding or unlawfully detaining from them, the said inhabitants, their ministry house; hereby giving and granting to our aforesaid agents or attorneys, or the major part of them, full power and lawful authority to say and perform and finish all and every act and acts, thing and things, device or devices, which in the law may be needful or expedient for the better prosecution of the same; attorney or attorneys under them to make and constitute and at pleasure to revoke acquittances or other discharges in our name; to make or give and generally to do and execute in the premise as fully as we ourselves might or could do, being all personally present. And whatsoever our aforesaid agents or attorneys, or the major part of them, shall lawfully do, or cause to be done, in, about, or concerning the premises, the said inhabitants will allow of and confirm the same.

At a general meeting of the inhabitants of Salem Village the second day of March, 1696/97, it was agreed and voted that we make choice of Joseph Putnam to go to Deacon Ingersoll and Deacon Putnam to desire them to deliver to him what money they have in their hands which belongs to the inhabitants of this Village, that so it may be improved for the use of the said inhabitants, and he to give them or either of them, a receipt of what money he shall receive of either of them on that account.

"Received of Deacon Putnam the 4th day of March, 1696/97, two pounds, and ten shillings, and ten pence of the inhabitants' money. I say received by me, Joseph Putnam."

[March 19, 1697: Notice of Meeting]

At a general meeting of the inhabitants of Salem Village, the 23rd day of March, 1696/97, there was chosen for a committee for the year ensuing, Lieut. Nathaniel Putnam, John Buxton, Thomas Putnam, Jonathan Putnam, and Samuel Nurse.

At a general meeting of the inhabitants of Salem Village, the 23rd day of March, 1696/97, it was considered, agreed, and voted by the aforesaid inhabitants, by a general concurrence, that whereas Mr. Samuel Parris, our late minister, has commenced an action against the inhabitants of this Village at the next Inferior Court of Common Pleas, to be holden for this county at Ipswich the last Tuesday of this instant March; therefore the aforesaid inhabitants have by these presents chosen and appointed Lieut. Nathaniel Putnam; Daniel Andrew, Senior; Thomas Flint, Senior; Joseph Herrick, Senior; Thomas Putnam; and Joseph Putnam, all of Salem Village, they or the major part of them, to be their agents or attorneys to make answer to Mr. Samuel Parris in the case aforesaid. . . .

[There follows a legal form empowering this committee in the same fashion as printed in the entry for March 2, 1697.]

[April 23, 1697: Notice of Meeting]

At a general meeting of the inhabitants of Salem Village the 27th of April [1697], being orderly warned, it was considered and agreed and voted by the said inhabitants by a unanimous consent that whereas Mr. Samuel Parris, our late minister, hath for more than nine months last past desisted his stated work of the ministry amongst us, and yet still he doth keep the possession of our ministry house to our great damage; therefore the aforesaid inhabitants have by these presents chosen and appointed Lieut. Nathaniel Putnam; Daniel Andrew, Senior; Thomas Flint, Senior; Joseph Herrick, Senior; Thomas Putnam; and Joseph Putnam, all of Salem Village, they or the major part of them, to be their agents or attorneys in the behalf and to the use of the said inhabitants, to compound and agree with Mr. Parris themselves if they can, or by leaving it to arbitration if Mr. Parris will join with them therein; or otherwise to sue, commence, and prosecute any suit or suits, action or actions against the aforesaid Mr. Samuel Parris. . . .

[From this point the wording is nearly identical with the previous form.]

[August 27, 1697: Notice of Meeting]

[September 14, 1697: The action taken at this meeting is included in chapter 20, p. 267.]

[October 1, 1697: Notice of Meeting]

At a general meeting of the inhabitants of Salem Village, the 5th day of October, 1697, it was agreed and voted by the aforesaid inhabitants, by a unanimous consent, that we will keep Tuesday, the 12th day of this instant October, as a day of fasting and prayer, to seek direction of the wonderful Counsellor about providing a minister for us. . . . [A] nd we desire the Rev. Mr. Hale, Mr. Noyes, and Mr. Gerrish to come to us and to be helpful to us in carrying on the work of the said day.

At a general meeting of the inhabitants of Salem Village, the 5th day of October, 1697, it was agreed and voted by the aforesaid inhabitants, by a unanimous consent, that we desire the Rev. Mr. Robert Haile to come and preach to us a Sabbath day or two or three, till we can tell what we shall be about getting a minister. Also we make choice of Jonathan Putnam and Benjamin Putnam to entreat Mr. Haile to come and preach with us, and, if they cannot prevail with him, to endeavor to get Mr. Daniel Epps to come and preach with us a day or two.

Epilogue

Salem Village Becomes a Town (1752)

[When the General Court passed the following act of incorporation, the English authorities forbade Massachusetts to create any new towns (which would have enlarged the troublesome General Court). Accordingly, "districts" were being set up rather than towns. These districts were identical to towns, except that they could not elect representatives to the provincial legislature. The "Middle Parish," which is referred to, consisted of lands lying east and south of the old Salem Village bounds.]

An Act for Creating the Village Parish and Middle Parish, So Called, in the Town of Salem into a Distinct and Separate District by the Name of Danvers.

Whereas the Town of Salem is very large and the inhabitants of the Village and Middle Parishes, so-called, within the same (many of them, at least) live at a great distance from that part of Salem where the public affairs of the Town are transacted, and also from the grammer school which is kept in the said First Parish.

And whereas most of the inhabitants of the said first Parish are either merchants, traders, or mechanics, and those of the said Village and Middle Parishes are chiefly husbandmen, by means whereof many disputes and difficulties have arisen and may hereafter arise in the managing their public affairs together, and especially touching the apportioning the public taxes,

For preventing of which inconveniences for the future,

Be it enacted by the Lieut. Governor, Council, and House of Representatives, that that part of the said Town of Salem which now constitutes the Village and Middle Parishes in said Town, according to their boundaries and the inhabitants therein, be erected into a separate and distinct District by the name of Danvers, and that said inhabitants shall do the duties that are required and enjoined· on other towns, and enjoy all the powers, privileges, and immunities that Towns in this province by law enjoy, except that of separately choosing and sending one or more representatives to represent them at the General Assembly. . . .

Jany the 25, 1752.

List of Accused Witches Who Lived in or Around Salem Village

Name	Description*	Date of Warrant
Daniell Andrew		May 14
Bridget Bishop**		April 18
Edward Bishop		April 21
Sarah Bishop		April 21
Mary Black	Nathaniel Putnam's slave	April 21
Sarah Buckley		May 14
George Burroughs**		April 30
Saray Cloyes	Rebecca Nurse's sister	April 4
Giles Cory**		April 18
Martha Cory**	Giles Cory's wife	March 19
Mary DeRich	Daughter of William Bassett of Lynn	May 23
Mary Easty	Rebecca Nurse's sister	May 20
Sarah Good**		Feb. 29
Dorcas Good	Sarah's daughter	March 23
George Jacobs, Sen.**		May 10
George Jacobs, Jun.	George Senior's son	May 14
Margaret Jacobs	George Junior's wife	May 10
Rebecca Jacobs	George Senior's granddaughter	May 14
Rebecca Nurse**		March 23
Sarah Osborne		Feb. 29
John Procter**		April 11
Elizabeth Procter	John's wife	April 8
Benjamin Procter	John's son	May 23
Sarah Procter	John's daughter	May 21
William Procter	John's son	May 28
Tituba Indian	Slave of Samuel Parris	Feb. 29
Mary Warren	John Procter's servant	April 18
John Willard**	Bray Wilkins' grandson-in-law	May 10
Mary Withridge	Sarah Buckley's daughter	May 14

*If not indicated elsewhere in this book.
**Executed.

375

List of All Persons Accused of
Witchcraft in 1692

[The date given is the date of the warrant or complaint. While all of these individuals were accused, not all were actually imprisoned. Where the specific date is unknown, it is probable that the accusation occurred in June 1692 or after.]

Name	Town	Date
Nehemiah Abbot	Topsfield	May 28
Nehemiah Abbot, Jun.	Topsfield	April 21
Capt. John Alden	Boston	May 31
Daniel Andrew	Salem Village	May 14
Abigail Barker	Andover	Sept. 8
Mary Barker	Andover	August 29
William Barker, Sen.	Andover	August 29
William Barker, Jun.	Andover	August 29
Sarah Basset	Lynn	May 21
Bridget Bishop	Salem Village	April 18
Edward Bishop	Salem Village	April 21
Sarah Bishop	Salem Village	April 21
Mary Black	Salem Village	April 21
Mary Bradbury	Salisbury	April 26
Mary Bridges	Andover	July 28
Sarah Bridges	Andover	August 25
Hannah Bromage	Andover	July 30 (examination)
Sarah Buckley	Salem Village	May 14
George Burroughs	Wells, Maine	April 30
Candy (slave)	Salem Town	June 1
Hannah Carrell	Salem Town	September 10
Martha Carrier	Andover	May 28
Andrew Carrier	Andover	July 21
Richard Carrier	Andover	July 21
Sarah Carrier	Andover	—
Thomas Carrier	Andover	July 21
Bethia Carter	Woburn	May 8
Elizabeth Cary	Charlestown	May 28
Mary Clarke	Haverhill	Aug. 3
Rachel Clenton	Ipswich	March 29
Sarah Cloyse	Salem Village	April 4
Sarah Cole [I]	Salem Town	September 10
Sarah Cole [II]	Lynn	October 3
Elizabeth Colson	Reading	May 14
Giles Corey	Salem Village	April 18
Martha Corey	Salem Village	March 19
Deliverance Dane	Andover	—
Mary DeRich	Salem Village	May 23
Rebecca Dike	Gloucester	November 5
Elizabeth Dicer	Gloucester	September 3
Ann Doliver	Gloucester	June 6
Joseph Draper	Andover	September
Lydia Dustin	Reading	April 30
Sarah Dustin	Reading	May 8
Rebecca Eames	Andover	August 19
Mary Easty	Salem Village	April 21
Esther Elwell	Gloucester	November 5

Name	Town	Date
Martha Emerson	Haverhill	July 2
Joseph Emons	Manchester	September 5
Phillip English	Salem Town	April 30
Mary English	Salem Town	April 21
Thomas Farrer, Sen.	Lynn	May 14
Edward Farrington	Andover	September 17
Abigail Faulkner, Senior	Andover	August 11
Abigail Faulkner, Jun.	Andover	September
Dorothy Faulkner	Andover	September 17
Captain John Flood	Rumney Marsh	May 28
Elizabeth Fosdick	Malden	May 28
Elizabeth Fosdick [Jun.?]	Malden	June 2
Ann Foster	Andover	July 15
Nicholas Frost	Manchester	September 5
Eunice Frye	Andover	—
Dorcas Good	Salem Village	March 23
Sarah Good	Salem Village	February 29
Mary Green	Haverhill	—
Elizabeth Hart	Lynn	May 14
Sarah Hawkes	Andover	September 1
Margaret Hawkes	Salem Town	June 1
Dorcas Hoar	Beverly	April 30
Abigail Hobbs	Topsfield	April 18
Deliverance Hobbs	Topsfield	April 21
William Hobbs	Topsfield	April 21
Elizabeth How	Topsfield	May 28
John Howard	Rowley	August 5
Francis Hutchens	Haverhill	August 18
Mary Ireson	Lynn	June 4
John Jackson, Sen.	Rowley	August 5
John Jackson, Jun.	Rowley	August 5
George Jacobs, Sen.	Salem Town	May 10
George Jacobs, Jun.	Salem Village	May 14
Margaret Jacobs	Salem Town	May 10
Rebecca Jacobs	Salem Village	May 14
Abigail Johnson	Andover	August 29
Elizabeth Johnson, Sen.	Andover	August 29
Elizabeth Johnson, Jun.	Andover	August 10
Rebecca Johnson	Andover	January 7, 1693
Stephen Johnson	Andover	September 1
Mary Lacey, Sen.	Andover	July 20
Mary Lacey, Jun.	Andover	—
John Lee	—	April 1 (testimony)
Jane Lilly	Malden	September 5
Mary Marston	Andover	August 29
Susanna Martin	Amesbury	April 30
Mary Morey	Beverly	May
Sarah Morrill	Beverly	—
Rebecca Nurse	Salem Village	March 23
Sarah Osborne	Salem Village	February 29
Mary Osgood	Andover	—
Elizabeth Paine	Charlestown	June 2
Alice Parker	Salem Town	May 12
Mary Parker	Andover	August
Sarah Pease	Salem Town	May 23
Joan Peney	Gloucester	September 20
Hannah Post	Boxford	August 25

Name	Town	Date
Mary Post	Rowley	August 2
Susanna Post	Andover	August 25
Margaret Prince	Gloucester	September 3
Benjamin Proctor	Salem Village	May 23
Elizabeth Proctor	Salem Village	April 8
John Proctor	Salem Village	April 11
Sarah Proctor	Salem Village	—
William Proctor	Salem Village	May 28
Ann Pudeator	Salem Town	May 12
Abigail Roe	Gloucester	November 5
Wilmot Reed	Marblehead	May 28
Sarah Rice	Reading	May 28
Susanna Roots	Beverly	May 21
Henry Salter	Andover	September 7
John Sawdy	Andover	September [?]
Margaret Scott	—	September
Ann Sears	Woburn	May 8
Abigail Soames	Salem Town	May 13
Martha Sparks	Chelmsford	—
Tituba Indian	Salem Village	February 29
Jerson Toothaker	—	—
Mary Toothaker	Billerica	May 28
Roger Toothaker	Billerica	May 18
[Daughter of Roger Toothaker]	Billerica	May 28
Job Tookey	Beverly	—
Hannah Tyler	Andover	September 16
Martha Tyler	Andover	September 16
Mercy Wardwell	Andover	—
Samuel Wardwell	Andover	September 1
Sarah Wardwell	Andover	September 1
Mary Warren	Salem Village	April 18
Sarah Wilds	Topsfield	April 21
Ruth Wilford	Haverhill	August 18
John Willard	Salem Village	May 12
Sarah Wilson, Sen.	Andover	September 17
Sarah Wilson, Jun.	Andover	—
Mary Withridge	Salem Village	May 14

Selected List of Accusers and Persons
Against Whom They Testified

ABBEY, Samuel (Easty, S. Good)

ADAMS, Martha (G. Cory)

ALLEN, William (S. Good, Osborn)

BAILEY, Elizabeth (Willard)

_____ , Thomas (Willard)

BAYLEY, Joseph (E. Procter)

BIBBER, Sarah (Burroughs, G. Cory, Easty, S. Good, Hoar, Martin, Nurse, J. Procter, Pudeator, Tookey, Willard)

BITTFORD, Stephen (E. Procter)

BOOTH, Alice (M. Cory)

_____ , Elizabeth (G. Cory, M. Cory, Derich, E. Procter, J. Procter, S. Procter, Tookey, Warren, Willard)

BRAYBROOK, Samuel (Easty, S. Good, Osborne)

BUXTON, John (COMPLAINTS: N. Abbot, E. Bishop, S. Bishop, Black, Esty, D. Hobbs, W. Hobbs, Wilds)

CHEEVER, Ezekial (Burroughs, M. Cory, Tituba; COMPLAINTS: B. Bishop, G. Cory, A. Hobbs, Warren)

CHILDUN, Johanna (S. Good, Nurse)

CHURCHILL, Sarah (G. Jacobs Senior, Pudeator)

CORY, Giles (M. Cory)

DERITCH, John (G. Cory, G. Jacobs Senior, M. Jacobs)

ENDECOTT, Samuel (Bradbury)

ENDECOTT, Zerubabel Junior (Bradbury)

FERNEAUX, David (S. Procter)

FLINT, Joseph (G. Jacobs Senior)

_____ , Thomas (Willard)

GADGE, Thomas (S. Good)

_____ , Sarah (S. Good)

GOOD, William (S. Good, Osborne)

HERRICK, Henry (S. Good)

_____ , Joseph Senior and wife (S. Good)

HOLTON, James (J. Procter)

_____ , Joseph (COMPLAINTS: Alden, M. Carrier, Flood, Fosdick, How, Read, Rice, M. Toothaker, [?] Toothaker)

_____ , Sarah (Nurse)

HUBBARD, Elizabeth (B. Bishop, Buckley, Burroughs, G. Cory, Easty, S. Good, Hoar, A. Hobbs, G. Jacobs Senior, R. Jacobs, Lacey, Martin, Nurse, Osborne, E. Procter, J. Procter, Pudeater, Read, Tituba, Tookey)

HUGHES, John (S. Good, Osborne)

HUTCHINSON, Benjamin (Buckley, Burroughs, Easty, Withridge; COMPLAINTS: Cary, Easty)

_____ , Joseph (COMPLAINTS: S. Good, Osborne, Tituba)

INGERSOLL, Nathaniel (Cory, Martin, Nurse, J. Procter, Willard; COMPLAINTS: Cloyse, Derich, Pease, B. Procter, E. Procter)

KENNY, Henry (M. Cory)

KETTLE, James (S. Bishop)

KNIGHT, Margaret (A. Hobbs, Willard)

_____ , Phillip (Willard)

LEWIS, Mercy (Buckley, Burroughs, G. Cory, D. Good, A. Hobbs, G. Jacobs Senior, Lacey, Martin, Osborne, E. Procter, Willard)

NICHOLS, Lydia (A. Hobbs, Willard)

_____ , Thomas (Willard)

PARRIS, Samuel (M. Cory, Martin, Nurse, J. Procter, Tituba, Willard)

PRESCOTT, Peter (Burroughs)

PRESTON, Thomas (COMPLAINTS: S. Good, Tituba)

PUTNAM, Ann Senior (M. Cory, Nurse, Willard)

_____ , Ann Junior (Bradbury, Buckley, Burroughs, G. Cory, Esty, Farrer, A. Faulkner, D. Good, S.

List of Defenders Connected
with Salem Village

Included in this list are names of the following:

1. Individuals testifying in defense of those accused witches who lived in Salem Village.

2. Everyone listed on Charles Upham's map (see pp. 394-95), who signed a petition in favor of an accused witch living in Salem Village. (There were *two* petitions circulated in favor of John and Elizabeth Procter. One petition was signed by thirty-two residents of Ipswich, who described themselves as the Procters' former "neighbors." These signatures, all unfamiliar to readers of this book, are *not* included in the following list.)

3. Everyone giving skeptical testimony designed to cast doubt on the credibility of the afflicted girls.

4. Any "defender" not accounted for in the above categories but whose name might be familiar to readers of this book.

Aborn, Samuel (Nurse Petition)
Allen, Rev. James (Bradbury)
Andrew, Daniel (Nurse, Nurse Pet.)
Andrew, Sarah (Nurse Pet.)
Barton, Samuel (E. Procter)
Bishop, Edward Senior (Nurse Pet.)
Bishop, Hannah (Nurse Pet.)
Bishop, Edward Junior (v. Mary Warren)
Bishop, Sarah (v. Mary Warren)
Buxton, Elizabeth (Nurse Pet.)
Cloyse, Peter (Nurse)
Cooke, Isaac (Nurse Pet.)
Cooke, Elizabeth (Nurse Pet.)
Endecott, Samuel (Procter Pet., Nurse Pet.)
Endecott, Hannah (Procter Pet.)
Elliot, Daniel (E. Procter)
Easty, Mary (Mary Warren)
Felton, Nathaniel Senior (Nurse Pet.)
Herrick, Joseph (Nurse Pet.)
Holton, James (Procter Pet.)
Holton, John (Procter Pet.)
Holton, Ruth (Procter Pet.)
Holton, Joseph Senior (Nurse Pet.)
Holton, Sarah (Nurse Pet.)
Holton, Joseph Junior (Nurse Pet.)

Hubbard, William (Buckley)
Hutchinson, Joseph Senior (Nurse Pet.)
Hutchinson, Lydia (Nurse Pet.)
Jacobs, Thomas (v. Sarah Bibber)
Jacobs, Mary (v. Sarah Bibber)
Kettle, James (v. Elizabeth Hubbard)
Leach, Sarah (Nurse Pet.)
Locker, George (Procter Pet.)
Moulton, Robert (v. Susanna Sheldon)
Nurse, Samuel (Nurse)
Nurse, Sarah (v. Sarah Bibber)
Osborne, William (Nurse Pet.)
Osborne, Hannah (Nurse Pet.)
Phillips, Samuel (How)
Phillips, Walter Senior (Nurse Pet.)
Phillips, Margaret (Nurse Pet.)
Phillips, Tabitha (Nurse Pet.)
Porter, Israel (Nurse)
Porter, Elizabeth (Nurse)
Porter, John (v. Sarah Bibber)
Porter, Lydia (v. Sarah Bibber)
Preston, Rebecca (Nurse)
Putnam, Benjamin (Nurse Pet.)
Putnam, John Senior (Nurse, Nurse Pet.)
Putnam, Rebecca (Nurse, Nurse Pet.)
Putnam, Jonathan (Nurse Pet.)

Putnam, Lydia (Nurse Pet.)
Putnam, Nathaniel (Nurse)
Putnam, Sarah (Nurse Pet.)
Putnam, Sarah (Nurse Pet.)
Putnam, Joseph (Nurse Pet.)
Rea, Daniel (Nurse Pet.)
Rea, Hepzibah (Nurse Pet.)
Rea, Joshua (Nurse Pet.)

Rea, Sarah (Nurse Pet.)
Sibley, Samuel (Nurse Pet.)
Stone, Samuel (Procter Pet.)
Swinnerton, Job (Nurse Pet.)
Swinnerton, Esther (Nurse Pet.)
Tarbell, John (Nurse)
Tarbell, Mary (Nurse)
Wilkins, Thomas (Procter Pet.)

Places of Residence of the "Afflicted Girls"

Name	Place of Residence
Bibber, Sarah	Wenham
Booth, Elizabeth	[?]
Churchill, Sarah	George Jacobs, Senior
Hubbard, Elizabeth	Dr. William Griggs
Lewis, Mercy	Thomas Putnam, Junior
Parris, Elizabeth	Samuel Parris
Putnam, Ann, Junior	Thomas Putnam, Junior
Sheldon, Susanna	"The Widow Sheldon" [?]
Warren, Mary	John Proctor
Walcott, Mary	Thomas Putnam, Junior
Williams, Abigail	Samuel Parris

Census of Salem Village in January 1692*

This census is restricted to the population and residences *within the bounds of Salem Village*, as shown on the map in Charles W. Upham's *Salem Witchcraft*. The list of heads of household in 1692 were drawn up from both Upham's map and the Salem Village tax lists. Information on wives and children was obtained from the vital records of Salem and surrounding towns for marriages and births, then cross-checked in the death records, and was further substantiated by the material in Sidney Perley's *History of Salem, Mass.* and the published genealogies of the following families: Abbey, Bailey, Buckley, Case, Cheever, Cloyse, Flint, Fuller, Herrick, Hutchinson, Ingersoll, Kenney, Porter, Preston, Putnam, Sheldon, Sibley, Smith, Swinnerton, Walcott, and Wilkins. Much of the researched material is from the many small publications of the library at the Essex Institute in Salem. The list includes all offspring born to each family prior to January 1692 and not known to have died prior to that date.

Obviously there are problems inherent in this or any other approach. First and foremost there were those individuals for whom information was simply not available. Further there is considerable incidental evidence that a significant number of individuals—boarders, farm hands, slaves, serving girls, indentured servants—were living in Salem Village in 1692 under other people's roofs, but the precise tally of such individuals is impossible to ascertain. (Most of the afflicted girls, for example, were living with other families in 1692, but for the sake of consistency they have not been included in the census.) Some of the older children may have moved out of the village by 1692, and some daughters have probably also been counted again as wives, in cases where a wife's name, or maiden name, is not known. Although the census is not perfect, it is as comprehensive as possible within these limitations.

In the census the family name appears in boldface. Immediately below the family name is the given name of the head of household and his wife, followed by the names of their children as of January 1692, with dates of birth or baptism (which usually occurred shortly after birth) where known.

Compiled by Abbey Miller and Richard Henderson.

Abbey

Samuel (c. 1649) Mary (Knowlton)

Samuel	1675
Thomas	1678
Elizabeth	1680
Ebenezer	1683
Marcy	1684-85
Sarah	1685-86
Hepsibah	1688
Abigail	1690

Allen

William Hannah

Elizabeth	1679

Andrew

Daniel (1643) Sarah (Porter)

Thomas	1678
Samuel	1683
Daniel	1686
Israel	1689
Mehitable	
Sarah	

Bailey

Thomas Elizabeth

Nicholas

Barton

Lydia (widow of John)

Beele

William (married)

daughter	1690
Bridget	1691

Bishop

Edward ("sawyer") Bridget

Christian Oliver

Bishop

Edward (1648) Sarah (Wildes)
("husbandman")

Braybrook

Samuel Mary

Brown

Henry (1659) Hannah (Putnam)

John	1683
Rebecca	1684
Abraham	1686
Hannah	1689
Eleazer	1691

Buckley

William Sarah

William
Mary Whittredge

Buxton

John (1644) Elizabeth (Holton)

*Mary	1669
*Elizabeth	1672
*John	1675
Joseph	1678
Sarah	1681
Anthony	1682
Hannah	1685
Rachel	1688
Ebenezer	1690

*by John Buxton's first wife,
Mary (Small)

Case

Humphrey   (married)

    Humphrey
    Thomas

Cheever

Ezekial (1655)   Abigaile
                  (Lippingwell)

Abigail	1679
Ezekial	1685-86
Samuel	1689-90

Cloyse

Peter (1640)   Sarah (Towne)
                Bridges

James	1679
Benoni	1683
Abigail	1672
Mary	1677
Peter	1677
Alice	
Hepsibah	

Dale

John   Elizabeth

John Jr.	1685
Elizabeth	1687
Ledia	1688
Mary	1691

Darling

John   Mary (Robbins)

    Thomas

De Rich

Michael   Mary

Flint

George Jr. (1653) Elizabeth (Putnam)

Elizabeth	1685
George	1686
Ann	1687
Ebenezer	1689
Mary	1691

Flint

John (1655)   Elizabeth

Samuel	1679
John	1681
Hanna	1685
Stephen	1687
Joshua	1689

Flint

Joseph (1662)   Abigail (Howard)

Joseph Jr.	1686
Nathaniel	1688
Abigail	1690

Flint

Thomas (1646)   Mary (Dounton)

George	1672
Thomas	1678
Mary	1680
Ebenezer	1683
William	1685
Elizabeth	1687
Jonathan	1689
Ann	1691

Fowle

John   (married)

    Peter

Fuller

Benjamin   Sarah (Bacon)

Benjamin	1687
Samuel	1689
Sarah	1690

Fuller

Jacob   Mary (Bacon)

Mary	1684
Elizabeth	1687-88
Jacob	1691

Fuller

Thomas Sr. (c. 1618)   Hannah

Fuller

Thomas Jr. (c. 1657)   Ruth

Jonathan	1673
John	1676
Joseph	1679
William	1685

Good

William   Sarah

Dorcas

Goodell

Patience (widow of Isaac)

Hester	1672
Zachariah	1675
Abigaile	1678

Goodell

Isaac Jr. (1670)   Mary

Jacob	1691

Goodell

Zechariah Sen.   Eliza (Beachem)
(c. 1646)

Zechariah	1667
Samuel	1669
Joseph	1672
Mary	1674
Abraham	1678
David	1689
Elizabeth	1690
Sarah	1690

Hadlock

John (c. 1671)   Sarah

Haines

Thomas (1651)   Sarah (Ray)

John	1678
William	1680
Sarah	1681
Joseph	1683
Benjamin	1685
Hannah	1689
Thomas	1690

Herrick

Joseph (1645)   Mary (Endicott)

Tryphosa	1681
Rufus	1683
Tryphona	1685
Ruth	1688
Elizabeth	1686
Edith	1690

Houlton

Sarah (widow of Benjamin)

Houlton

Henry (1662)	Abigail (Flint)
James	1689

Houlton

John (1667)   Mary (Star)

Houlton

Joseph Sr. (c. 1621)	Sarah (Ingersoll) Haines

Houlton

Joseph Jr. (1652)	Hannah (Eborne)
Joseph III	1673
Hannah	1683
Sarah	1689

Hutchinson

Benjamin (1668)	Jane (Phillips)
Hannah	1692

Hutchinson

John (1666)   Mary (Gold)

Hutchinson

Joseph Sr. (1633)	Lydia (Small)
Abigaile	1679
Richard	1681
Samuel	1682
Ambrose	1684
Lydia	1685
Robert	1687

Hutchinson

Joseph Jr. (1666)	Elizabeth
Joseph III	1689
Ruth	1691

Ingersoll

Nathaniel (1633)	Hanna (Collins)
Sarah	1662

Jacobs

George Jr. (c. 1649)	Rebecca (Frost)
Margaret	1675
George	1677
John	1679
Jonathan	1681
son	1690?

Kenney

Henry Sr. (c. 1624)	Ann
Hannah	1657
Mary	1659
Sarah	1661
Elizabeth	1662
Lidea	1666

Kenney

Henry Jr. (1669)   Priscilla (Lewis)

Kenney

Elizabeth (widow of Thomas)	
Thomas	1678
Joseph	1680
Daniel	1682
Jonathan	1686

Kettle

James (c. 1665)   Elizabeth

    James   1691

Lane

Samuel   Abigail

Martin

John   Abigail

Needham

Isaac (1669)   Sarah (Holton?)

Nurse

Francis (c. 1621)   Rebecca

    Francis   1660-61

Nurse

Benjamin (1665)   Thomasin
                    (Smith)

    Margaret   1691

Nurse

John   Elizabeth (Very)

    Elizabeth   1677
    Samuel   1679
    Sarah   1680
    Jonathan   1682
    Joseph   1683
    Benjamin   1685-86
    Hannah   1687

Nurse

Samuel   Mary (Smith)

    Samuel   1677-78
    Margaret   1679-80
    George   1682
    Mary   1685
    Rebecca   1688

Osborne

Alexander   Sarah (Prince)

Parris

Samuel (1653)   Elizabeth

    Elizabeth

Phillips

Walter   Margaret

    Jane   1689
    James   1691

Pope

Gertrude (widow of Joseph Sr.)

Pope

Joseph (1650)   Bethshaa (Ray)

    Nathanial   1679
    Bethshaa   /   1683
    Gertrude   1685
    Joseph   1688
    Enos   1690

Porter

Benjamin (1639)   (unmarried)

Porter

Joseph (1638) Ann (Hathorn)

Anna	1667
Samuel	1669
Nathanial	1671
William	1674
Abigail	1676
Hepsibah	1678
Joseph	1681
Ruth	1682
Mehitable	1682

Prescott

Peter Elizabeth (Rideington)

Preston

Thomas (1643) Rebecka (Nurse)

Rebecka	1670
Mary	1672
John	1673
Martha	1676
Elizabeth	1677
David	1689
Thomas	16–
Jonathan	16–

Prince

James (c. 1668) Sarah (Rea)
Phillips

Prince

Joseph (c. 1672) Eliza.
(Robinson)

Putnam

Benjamin (1664) Sarah

Nathanial	1686
Tarrent	1688
Elizabeth	1690

Putnam

Edward (1654) Mary (Hale)

Edward	1682
Holyoke	1683
Elisha	1685
Joseph	1687
Mary	1689

Putnam

Eleazer (1665) Hannah
(Boardman)

Putnam

James (1661) Sarah

Sarah	1686
Bartholomew	1688
James	1690

Putnam

John (1667) Hannah

Putnam

Capt. John (1627) Rebecka
(Prince)

Susanna	1670
Ruth	1678

Putnam

John (1657)   Hannah (Cutler)

Elizabeth	1680
Margaret	1683
Samuel	1684
Joshua	1686
Joseph	1687
Mary	1688
Susanna	1690
John	1691
Rebecca	1691

Putnam

Jonathan (1660)   Lydia (Potter)

Ledia	1684
Elizabeth	1686
Ruth	1689
Susanna	1690
Jonathan	1691

Putnam

Joseph (1669)   Elizabeth (Porter)

Mary	1691

Putnam

Lieut. Nathaniel (1619)

Putnam

Mary (widow of Lieut. Thomas)

Putnam

Sgt. Thomas (1653)   Ann (Carr)

Anna	1679
Thomas	1681
Elizabeth	1683
Ebenezer	1685
Deliverance	1687
Timothy	1691

Raymont

Capt. Thomas   Mary

Mary	1684
Thomas	1684
Jonathan	1686
Abigail	1688
Josiah	1690
Mehitable	1691

Rea

Daniel (1654)   Hepzibah (Peabody)

Jemima	1680
Daniel	1682
Zerubabell	1685
Hepzibah	1687
daughter	1690

Rea

John (1666)   Ruth

son	1691

Rea

Joshua Sr. (c. 1629)   Sarah (Waters)

Daniel	1654
Elizabeth	1660
Hannah	1668
John	1666

Rea

Joshua Jr. (1664)   Eliza. (Leach)

Sarah	1686

Rea

Samuel   Mary

Samuel	1687-88
William	1691

Shepard

John   Rebecka

John	1678

Sibley

Samuel (1657)   Mary (Putnam?)

Sibley

Ruth (widow of William)

Sheldon

Ephraim   Rebecca

Mary	1667
Lydia	1669
Sarah	1671
Rebecca	1673
Hepsibah	1675

Sheldon

Widow

Susanna	1674

Small

William (1667)

Smith

Abraham (1670)   Mary

Smith

James   Margaret

Samuel	1676
Elizabeth	1678
John	1689-90
Sarah	1691

Smith

John   Ann (Skerry)

Stacey

Benjamin   Anna (Hardin)

Swinnerton

Jasper (1659)

Swinnerton

Job Jr. (c. 1630)   Hester (Baker)

*Ruth	1664
*Mary	1670
Benjamin	1682
Esther	1682
James	1687
Abigail	1690

Swinnerton

Joseph (1660)   Mary

Tarbell

John (c. 1653)   Mary (Nurse)

John	1680
Mary	1688
Cornelius	1690
Jonathan	1691

*By Job's first wife, Ruth Symonds.

Trask

    Samuel   Susannah

          Samuel   1690

Upton

    Samuel (1664)

Upton

    William (1663)

Walcott

    Abraham (1636)   Abigail

        Abigail   1689

Walcott

    Jonathan (c. 1639)   Deliverance
                          (Putnam)

        Hannah   1667
        Jonathan   1670
        Mary   1675
        Samuel   1678
        Ann   1685
        Thomas   1689
        William   1691

Walcott

    John (1666)   Mary

Watts

    Jeremiah   (married)

Way

    Aaron (1651)   Mary

        Aaron   1674
        Mary   1677
        Elizabeth   1678
        Thomas   1683
        Ruth   1685

Way

    William   Persis

        Mary   1690
        Moses   1690
        Samuel   1690

Welton

    John (c. 1657)   Mary

Whipple

    Joseph (1666)   Sarah
                    (Hutchinson)

Wilkins

    Benjamin (c. 1640)   Priscilla
                         (Baxter)

        Benjamin   1679
        Anna   1681
        Jonathan   1683
        Sarah   1686
        Abigail   1688
        Priscilla   1691

Wilkins

    Bray (1610)   Anna

Wilkins

Henry (c. 1638)   Ruth

Samuel	1673
*Daniel	1675
Nehimiah	1683
Susanna	1684
Henry	1684-85
Aquilla	1684-85
Elizabeth	1684-85
Rebecca	1684-85
John	1686
Ebenezer	1688
Ruth	1690

*Died May 16, 1692.

Wilkins

John (c. 1650)   Betty (Southwick)

John	1689
Esther	1690

Wilkins

Samuel   Priscilla (Parker)

Wilkins

Thomas Sr.   Hannah (Nichols)

Thomas	1669
Elizabeth	1673
Hannah	1678
Bray	1678
Joseph	1690
Isaac	1690

A Map of Salem Village in 1692*

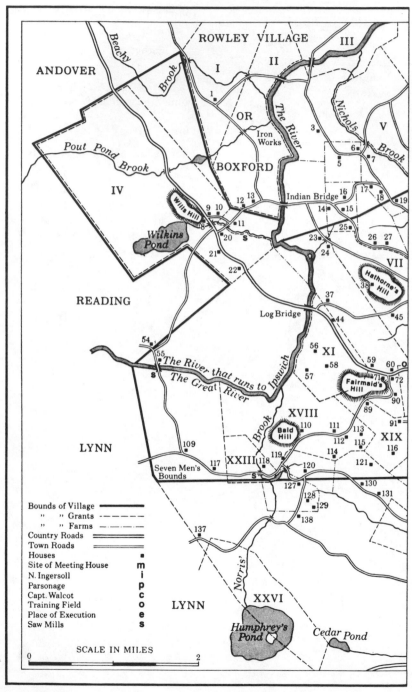

Adapted from Charles W. Upham, Salem Witchcraft, 2 vols., Boston, 1867.

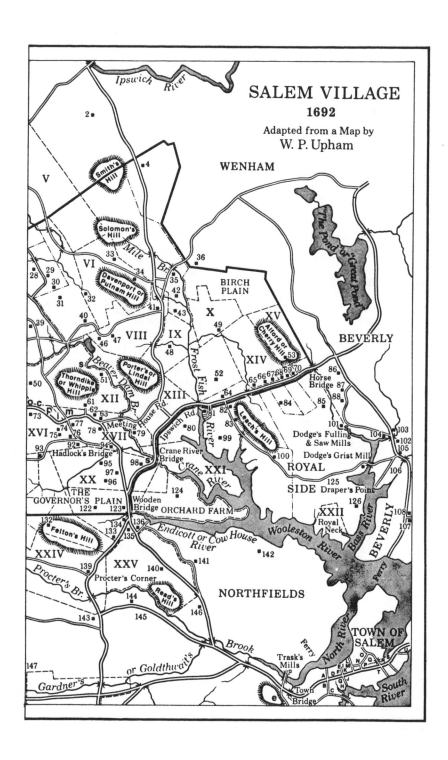

SALEM VILLAGE
1692
Adapted from a Map by
W. P. Upham

Numerical Index to Upham's Map

Upham's map indicates all the houses standing in 1692 within the bounds of Salem Village as well as some others in the vicinity. The houses are numbered on the map with arabic figures 1, 2, 3, and so on, beginning at the top and moving from left to right. The name given is that of the head of household in 1692. The letter *c* following the name indicates that the site given is conjectural.

1. John Willard. c.
2. Isaac Easty.
3. Francis Peabody. c.
4. Joseph Porter.
5. William Hobbs.
6. John Robinson.
7. William Nichols.
8. Bray Wilkins. c.
9. Aaron Way.
10. Thomas Bailey.
11. Thomas Fuller, Sr.
12. William Way.
13. Francis Elliot. c.
14. Jonathan Knight. c.
15. Thomas Cave.
16. Phillip Knight.
17. Isaac Burton.
18. John Nichols, Jr.
19. Humphrey Case.
20. Thomas Fuller, Jr.
21. Jacob Fuller.
22. Benjamin Fuller.
23. Deacon Edward Putnam.
24. Sergeant Thomas Putnam.
25. Peter Prescott.
26. Ezekiel Cheever.
27. Eleazer Putnam.
28. Henry Kenny.
29. John Martin.
30. John Dale.
31. Joseph Prince.
32. Joseph Putnam.
33. John Putnam 3d.
34. Benjamin Putnam.
35. Daniel Andrew.
36. John Leach, Jr. c.
37. John Putnam, Jr.
38. Joshua Rea.
39. Mary, wid. of Thos. Putnam.
40. Alexander Osburn and James Prince.
41. Jonathan Putnam.
42. George Jacobs, Jr.
43. Peter Cloyse.
44. William Small.
45. John Darling.
46. James Putnam.
47. Capt. John Putnam.
48. Daniel Rea.
49. Henry Brown.
50. John Hutchinson.
51. Joseph Whipple
52. Benjamin Porter.
53. Joseph Herrick.
54. John Phelps. c.
55. George Flint. c.
56. Ruth Sibley.
57. John Buxton.
58. William Allin.
59. Samuel Braybrook. c.
60. James Smith.
61. Samuel Sibley.
62. Rev. James Bayley.
63. John Shepard.
64. John Flint.
65. John Rea.
66. Joshua Rea.
67. Jeremiah Watts.
68. Edward Bishop, the sawyer.
69. Edward Bishop, husbandman.
70. Capt. Thomas Raiment.
71. Joseph Hutchinson, Jr.
72. William Buckley.
73. Joseph Houlton, Jr.
74. Thomas Haines.
75. John Houlton.
76. Joseph Houlton, Sr.
77. Joseph Hutchinson, Sr.
78. John Hadlock.
79. Nathaniel Putnam.
80. Israel Porter.
81. James Kettle.
82. Royal Side Schoolhouse.
83. Dr. William Griggs.
84. John Trask.
85. Cornelius Baker.
86. Exercise Conant.
87. Deacon Peter Woodberry.
88. John Raiment, Sr.
89. Joseph Swinnerton.
90. Benjamin Hutchinson.
91. Job Swinnerton.
92. Henry Houlton.
93. Sarah, widow of Benjamin Houlton.
94. Samuel Rea.
95. Francis Nurse.
96. Samuel Nurse.
97. John Tarbell.
98. Thomas Preston.

99. Jacob Barney.
100. Sergeant John Leach, Sr.
101. Capt. John Dodge, Jr.
102. Henry Herrick.
    [This had been the homestead of his father, Henry Herrick.]
103. Lot Conant.
    [This was the homestead of his father, Roger Conant.]
104. Benjamin Balch, Sr.
    [This was the homestead of his father, John Balch.]
105. Thomas Gage.
106. Families of Trask, Grover, Haskell, and Elliott.
107. Rev. John Hale.
108. Dorcas, widow of William Hoar.
109. William and Samuel Upton. c.
110. Abraham and John Smith.
    [This had been the homestead of Robert Goodell.]
111. Isaac Goodell.
112. Abraham Walcott.
113. Zachariah Goodell.
114. Samuel Abbey.
115. John Walcott.
116. Jasper Swinnerton.
117. John Weldon. Captain Samuel Gardner's farm.
118. Gertrude, widow of Joseph Pope.
119. Capt. Thomas Flint.
120. Joseph Flint.

121. Isaac Needham. c.
122. The widow Sheldon and her daughter Susannah.
123. Walter Phillips.
124. Samuel Endicott.
125. Families of Creasy, King, Batchelder, and Howard.
126. John Green.
127. John Parker.
128. Giles Cory.
129. Henry Crosby.
130. Anthony Needham, Jr.
131. Anthony Needham, Sr.
132. Nathaniel Felton
133. James Houlton.
134. John Felton.
135. Sarah Phillips.
136. Benjamin Scarlett.
137. Benjamin Pope.
138. Robert Moulton. c
139. John Procter.
140. Daniel Epps. c.
141. Joseph Buxton. c
142. George Jacobs, Sr.
143. William Shaw.
144. Alice, widow of Michael Shaflin.
145. Families of Buffington, Stone, and Southwick.
146. William Osborne.
147. Families of Very, Gould, Follet, and Meacham.

i Nathaniel Ingersoll.
p Rev. Samuel Parris.
c Captain Jonathan Walcott.

Alphabetical Index to Upham's Map

Guide to Grants of Land in Salem Village

The following guide includes a brief history of the land after the time of the original grants, all of which were made by the town of Salem unless otherwise stated. The grants are indicated on Upham's map by Roman numerals; the bounds, by broken lines.

I. John Gould

Sold by him to Capt. George Corwin, March 29, 1674; and by Capt. Corwin's widow sold to Philip Knight, Thomas Wilkins, Sr., Henry Wilkins, and John Willard, March 1, 1690.

II. Zaccheus Gould

Sold by him to Capt. John Putnam before 1662; owned in 1692 by Capt. Putnam, Thomas Cave, Francis Elliot, John Nichols, Jr., Thomas Nichols, and William Way.

The above, together, comprised land granted by the General Court to Rowley, May 31, 1652, and laid out by Rowley to John and Zaccheus Gould.

III. Gov. John Endicott

Ipswich-river Farm, 550 acres, granted by the General Court, Nov. 5, 1639; owned in 1692 by his grandsons, Zerubbabel, Benjamin, and Joseph.

The General Court, Oct. 14, 1651, also granted to Gov. Endicott 300 acres on the southerly side of this farm, in "Blind Hole," on condition that he would set up copper-works. As the land appears afterwards to have been owned by John Porter, it is probable that the copper-mine was soon abandoned.

IV. Gov. Richard Bellingham

Granted by the General Court, Nov. 5, 1639.

V. Farmer John Porter

Owned in 1692 by his son, Benjamin Porter. This includes a grant to Townsend Bishop, sold to John Porter in 1648; also 200 acres granted to John Porter, Sept. 30, 1647. That part in Topsfield was released by Topsfield to Benjamin Porter, May 2, 1687.

VI. Capt. Richard Davenport

Granted Feb. 20, 1637, and Nov. 26, 1638; sold, with the Hathorne farm, to John Putnam, John Hathorne, Richard Hutchinson, and Daniel Rea, April 17, 1662.

VII. Capt. William Hathorne

Granted Feb. 17, 1637; sold with the above.

VIII. John Putnam the Elder

This comprises a grant of 100 acres to John Putnam, Jan. 20, 1641; 80 acres to Ralph Fogg, in 1636; 40 acres (formerly Richard Waterman's) to Thomas Lothrop, Nov. 29, 1642; and 30 acres to Ann Scarlett, in 1636. The whole owned by James and Jonathan Putnam in 1692.

IX. Daniel Rea

Granted to him in 1636; owned by his grandson, Daniel Rea, in 1692.

X. Rev. Hugh Peters

Granted Nov. 12, 1638; laid out June 15, 1674, being then in the possession of Capt. John Corwin; sold by Mrs. Margaret Corwin to Henry Brown, May 22, 1693.

XI. Capt. George Corwin

Granted Aug. 21, 1648; sold (including 30 acres formerly John Bridgman's) to Job Swinnerton, Jr., and William Cantlebury, Jan. 18, 1661.

XII. Richard Hutchinson, John Thorndike, and Mr. Freeman

Granted in 1636 and 1637; owned in 1692 by Joseph, son of Richard Hutchinson, and by Sarah, wife of Joseph Whipple, daughter of John, and grand-daughter of Richard Hutchinson.

XIII. Samuel Sharpe

Granted Jan. 23, 1637; sold to John Porter, May 10, 1643; owned by his son, Israel Porter, in 1692.

XIV. John Holgrave

Granted Nov. 26, 1638; sold to Jeffry Massey and Nicholas Woodberry, April 2, 1652; and to Joshua Rea, Jan. 1, 1657.

XV. William Alford

Granted in 1636; sold to Henry Herrick before 1653.

XVI. Francis Weston

Granted in 1636; sold by John Pease to Richard Ingersoll and William Haynes, in 1644.

XVII. Elias Stileman

Granted in 1636; sold to Richard Hutchinson, June 1, 1648.

XVIII.   Robert Goodell

504 acres laid out to him, Feb. 13, 1652: comprising 40 acres granted to him "long since," and other parcels bought by him of the original grantees; *viz.*, Joseph Grafton, John Sanders, Henry Herrick, William Bound, Robert Pease and his brother, Robert Cotta, William Walcott, Edmund Marshall, Thomas Antrum, Michael Shaflin, Thomas Venner, John Barber, Philemon Dickenson, and William Goose.

XIX.   Job Swinnerton

300 acres laid out, Jan. 5, 1697, to Job Swinnerton, Jr.; having been owned by his father, by grant and purchase, as early as 1650.

XX.   Townsend Bishop

Granted Jan. 11, 1636; sold to Francis Nurse, April 29, 1678.

XXI.   Rev. Samuel Skelton

Granted by the General Court, July 3, 1632; sold to John Porter, March 8, 1649; owned by the heirs of John Porter in 1692. "Skelton's Neck."

XXII.   John Winthrop, Jr.

Granted June 25, 1638; sold by his daughter to John Green, Aug. 9, 1683.

XXIII.   Rev. Edward Norris

Granted Jan. 21, 1640: sold to Eleanor Trusler, Aug. 7, 1654; to Joseph Pope, July 18, 1664.

XXIV.   Robert Cole

Granted Dec. 21, 1635; sold to Emanuel Downing before July 16th, 1638; conveyed by him to John and Adam Winthrop, in trust for himself and wife during their lives, and then for his son, George Downing, July 23, 1644; leased to John Procter in 1666; occupied by him and his son Benjamin in 1692.

XXV.   Col. Thomas Reed

Granted Feb. 16, 1636; sold to Daniel Epps, June 28, 1701, by Wait Winthrop, as attorney to Samuel Reed, only son and heir of Thomas Reed.

XXVI.   John Humphrey

Granted by the General Court, Nov. 7, 1632, May 6, 1635, and March 12, 1638, 1,500 acres, part in Salem and part in Lynn; sold, on execution, to Robert Saltonstall, Dec. 6, 1642, and by him sold to Stephen Winthrop, June 7, 1645, whose daughters—Margaret Willie and Judith Hancock—owned it in 1692: that part within the bounds of Salem is given in the Map according to the report of a committee, July 11, 1695.

Orchard Farm

Granted by the General Court to Gov. Endicott; owned by his grandsons, John and Samuel, in 1692.

The Governor's Plain

Granted to Gov. Endicott, Jan. 27, 1637, Dec. 23, 1639, and Feb. 5, 1644; including land granted under the name of "small lots."

Johnson's Plain

Granted to Francis Johnson, Jan. 23, 1637.

[This guide, which we have modified slightly, was originally published in Upham's Salem Witchcraft.*]*

Guide to the Farms of Salem Village

The following bounds are indicated on Upham's map by dotted lines except where they coincide with the bounds of grants.

1st, Between grants No. XL and VII., and extending north of the Village bounds, and south as far as Andover Road,—about 500 acres; bought by Thomas and Nathaniel Putnam of Phillip Cromwell, Walter Price and Thomas Cole, Jeffry Massey, John Reaves, Joseph and John Gardner, and Giles Corey; owned, in 1692, by Edward Putnam, Thomas Putnam, and John Putnam, Jr. This includes also 50 acres granted to Nathaniel Putnam, Nov. 19, 1649.

2d, At the northerly end of Grant No. VII., and extending north of the Village bounds,—100 acres, known as the "Ruck Farm"; granted to Thomas Ruck, May 27, 1654, and sold to Philip Knight and Thomas Cave, July 24, 1672.

3d, North of the "Ruck Farm,"—100 acres; sold by William Robinson to Richard Richards and William Hobbs, Jan. 1, 1660, and owned, in 1692, by William Hobbs and John Robinson.

4th, Next east, bounded northeast by Nichols Brook, and extending within the Village bounds,—200 acres; granted to Henry Bartholomew, and sold by him to William Nichols before 1652.

5th, East of the "Ruck Farm," and extending across the Village bounds, —about 150 acres; granted to John Putnam and Richard Graves. Part of this was sold by John Putnam to Capt. Thomas Lothrop, June 2, 1669, and was owned by Ezekiel Cheever in 1692: the rest was owned by John Putnam.

6th, East of the above, and south of the Nichols Farm,—60 acres, owned by Henry Kenny; also 50 acres granted to Job Swinnerton, given by him to his son, Dr. John Swinnerton, and sold to John Martin and John Dale, March 20, 1693.

7th, South of the above, and east of Grant No. VII.,—150 acres; granted to William Pester, July 16, 1638, and sold by Capt. William Trask to Robert Prince, Dec. 20, 1655.

8th, East of Grant No. VI., and extending north to Smith's Hill and south to Grant No. IX.,—about 400 acres; granted to Allen Kenniston, John Porter, and Thomas Smith, and owned, in 1692, by Daniel Andrew and Peter Cloyse.

9th, East and southeast of Smith's Hill,—500 acres; granted to Emanuel Downing in 1638 and 1649, and sold by him to John Porter, April 15, 1650. John Porter gave this farm to his son Joseph, upon his marriage with Anna, daughter of William Hathorne.

10th, East of Frost-fish River, including the northerly end of Leach's Hill, and extending across Ipswich Road,—about 250 acres, known as the "Barney Farm;" originally granted to Richard Ingersoll, Jacob Barney, and Pascha Foote.

11th, South of the "Barney Farm,"—about 200 acres; granted to Lawrence, Richard, and John Leach; owned, in 1692, by John Leach.

12th, North of the "Barney Farm," and between grants No. XIII and XIV.,—about 250 acres, known as "Gott's Corner"; granted to Charles Gott, Jeffry Massey, Thomas Watson, John Pickard, and Jacob Barney, and by them sold to John Porter.

13*th*, Eastward of the "Barney Farm,"—40 acres; originally granted to George Harris, and afterwards to Osmond Trask; owned, in 1692, by his son, John Trask.

14*th*, Next east, and extending across Ipswich Road,—40 acres; granted to Edward Bishop, Dec. 28, 1646; owned, in 1692, by his son, Edward Bishop, "the sawyer."

15*th*, At the northwest end of Felton's Hill, and extending across the Village line,—about 60 acres; owned by Nathaniel Putnam.

16*th*, Southeast of Grant No. XXIII.,—a farm of about 150 acres; owned by Giles Corey, including 50 acres bought by him of Robert Goodell, March 15, 1660, and 50 acres bought by him of Ezra and Nathaniel Clapp, of Dorchester, heirs of John Alderman, July 4, 1663.

17*th*, Northeast of the above,—150 acres granted to Mrs. Anna Higginson in 1636; sold by Rev. John Higginson to John Pickering, March 23, 1652; and by him to John Woody and Thomas Flint, Oct. 18, 1654; owned in 1692 by Thomas and Joseph Flint.

[This guide, like the preceding one, was originally published in Upham's Salem Witchcraft.]

Nine Sectional Maps of Salem Village in 1700*

[These nine maps show the ownership of nearly every plot of land in Salem Village. They are adapted from the originals by Sidney Perley published in the Essex Institute Historical Collections (Salem, Massachusetts) in April, July, and October 1915; April 1916; October 1917; April, July, and October 1918; and January 1919. Accompanying each original map was a detailed lot-by-lot real-estate history of that section of the Village, and these maps become even more valuable if used in conjunction with that material.

Note that these maps show the Village in 1700, eight years after the witchcraft episode. In some instances we have added in parentheses the name of a 1692 owner. Squares indicate houses, unless otherwise noted. Properties on the periphery of one map are usually shown in more detail on another. In some small details (particularly on the precise location of roads) these sectional maps do not agree with W. P. Upham's Salem Village map. We have not tried to resolve such disagreements.]

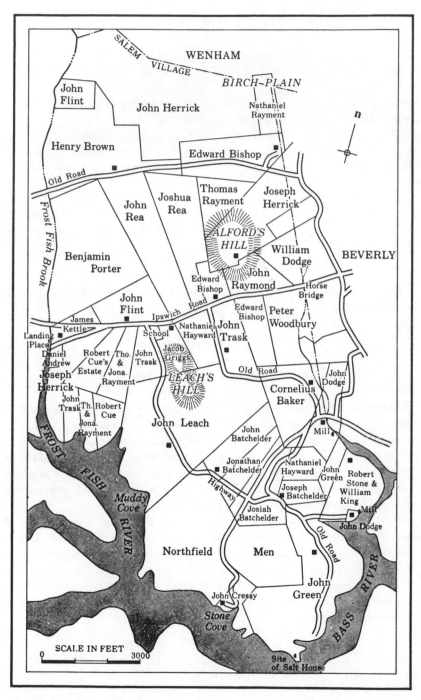

WENHAM

SALEM VILLAGE

BIRCH-PLAIN

John Flint

John Herrick

Nathaniel Rayment

Henry Brown

Edward Bishop

n

Old Road

Frost Fish Brook

John Rea

Joshua Rea

Thomas Rayment

Joseph Herrick

ALFORD'S HILL

BEVERLY

Benjamin Porter

William Dodge

Edward Bishop

John Raymond

Horse Bridge

John Flint

Ipswich Road

Edward Bishop

Peter Woodbury

James Kettle

School

Nathaniel Hayward

John Trask

Landing Place

Daniel Andrew

Robert Cue's Estate

Tho. & Jona. Rayment

John Trask

Jacob Griggs

Old Road

John Dodge

Joseph Herrick

LEACH'S HILL

Cornelius Baker

John Trask

Th. & Jona. Rayment

Robert Cue

John Leach

Mill

FROST FISH RIVER

John Batchelder

Muddy Cove

Jonathan Batchelder

Nathaniel Hayward

John Green

Robert Stone & William King

Highway

Joseph Batchelder

Mill

John Dodge

Josiah Batchelder

Northfield

Men

Old Road

John Green

John Cressy

BASS RIVER

Stone Cove

SCALE IN FEET

0   3000

Site of Salt House

*Adapted from maps by Sidney Perley.

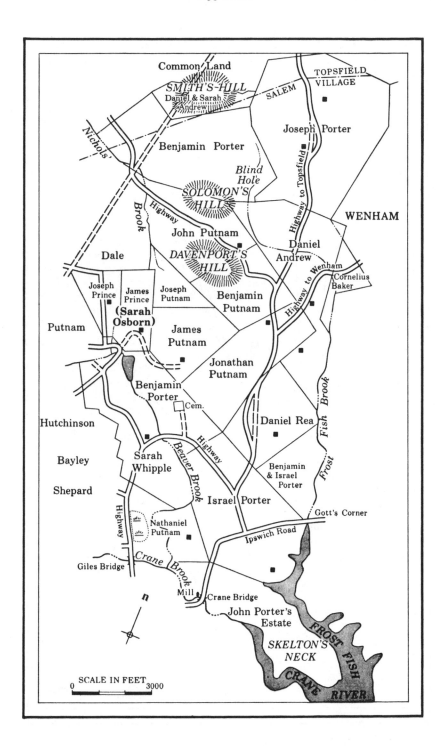

Common Land

SMITH'S-HILL
Daniel & Sarah
Andrew

TOPSFIELD
VILLAGE

SALEM

Nichols'

Benjamin Porter

Joseph Porter

Blind
Hole

SOLOMON'S
HILL

WENHAM

Brook

Highway

John Putnam

Daniel
Andrew

Highway to Topsfield

Dale

DAVENPORT'S
HILL

Joseph
Prince

James
Prince

Joseph
Putnam

Benjamin
Putnam

Highway to Wenham

Cornelius
Baker

Putnam

(Sarah
Osborn)

James
Putnam

Jonathan
Putnam

Benjamin
Porter

Cem.

Daniel Rea

Fish Brook

Hutchinson

Sarah
Whipple

Beaver Brook

Highway

Frost

Bayley

Benjamin
& Israel
Porter

Shepard

Israel Porter

Highway

Nathaniel
Putnam

Gott's Corner

Ipswich Road

Giles Bridge

Crane Brook

Mill

Crane Bridge

John Porter's
Estate

SKELTON'S
NECK

FROST FISH

CRANE RIVER

n

SCALE IN FEET
0   3000

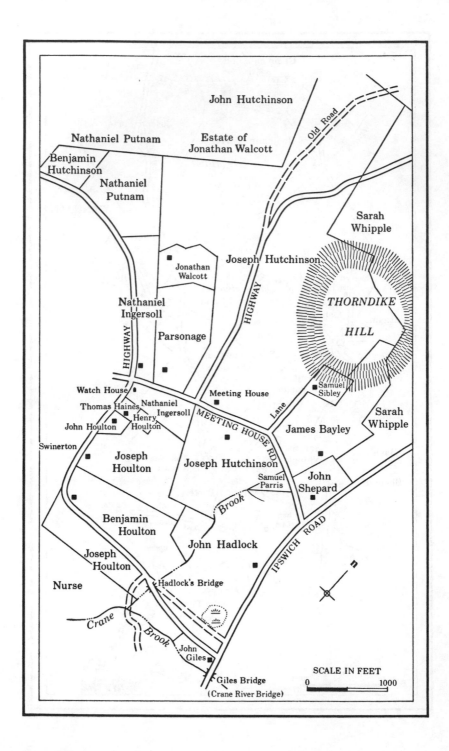

John Hutchinson

Nathaniel Putnam

Estate of
Jonathan Walcott

Old Road

Benjamin
Hutchinson

Nathaniel
Putnam

Sarah
Whipple

Jonathan
Walcott

Joseph Hutchinson

HIGHWAY

THORNDIKE

HILL

Nathaniel
Ingersoll

Parsonage

HIGHWAY

Watch House

Meeting House

Samuel
Sibley

Thomas Haines

Nathaniel
Ingersoll

MEETING HOUSE RD.

Lane

Sarah
Whipple

Henry
Houlton

John Houlton

James Bayley

Swinerton

Joseph
Houlton

Joseph Hutchinson

Samuel
Parris

John
Shepard

Benjamin
Houlton

Brook

IPSWICH ROAD

Joseph
Houlton

John Hadlock

Nurse

Hadlock's Bridge

Crane

Brook

John
Giles

Giles Bridge
(Crane River Bridge)

SCALE IN FEET

0   1000

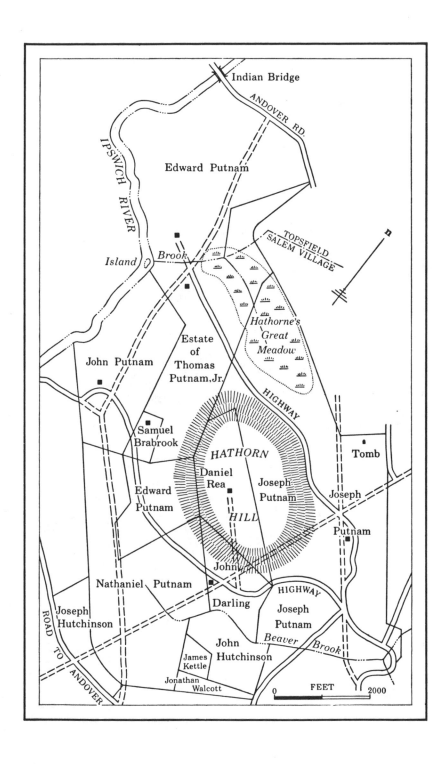

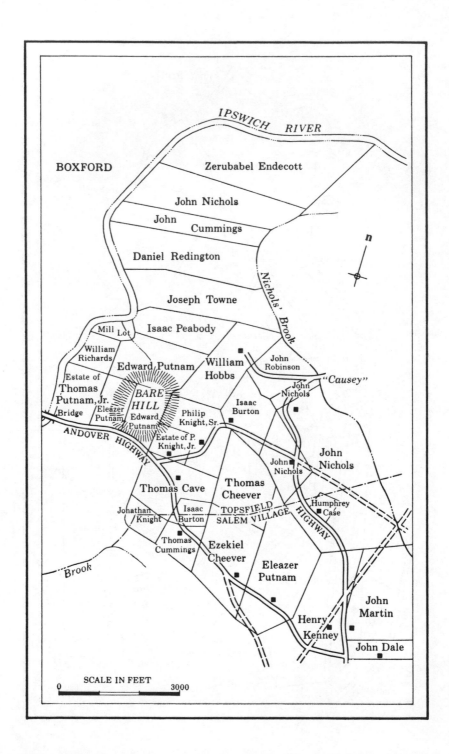

BOXFORD

IPSWICH RIVER

Zerubabel Endecott

John Nichols

John Cummings

Daniel Redington

Joseph Towne

Mill Lot

Isaac Peabody

William Richards

Edward Putnam

William Hobbs

John Robinson

Nichols' Brook

"Causey"

Estate of Thomas Putnam, Jr.

BARE HILL

Eleazer Putnam

Bridge

Edward Putnam

Philip Knight, Sr.

Isaac Burton

John Nichols

ANDOVER HIGHWAY

Estate of P. Knight, Jr.

John Nichols

John Nichols

n

John Nichols

Thomas Cave

Thomas Cheever

Humphrey Case

Jonathan Knight

Isaac Burton

TOPSFIELD SALEM VILLAGE HIGHWAY

Thomas Cummings

Ezekiel Cheever

Eleazer Putnam

Brook

Henry Kenney

John Martin

John Dale

SCALE IN FEET

0   3000

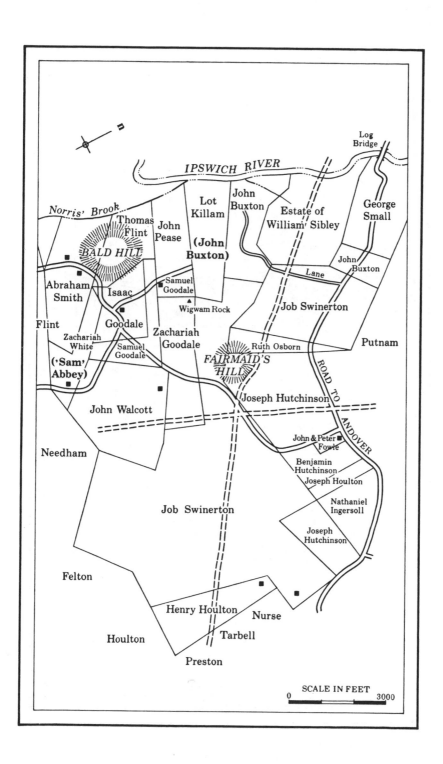

IPSWICH RIVER

Log Bridge

Norris' Brook

John Buxton

Lot Killam

Estate of William Sibley

George Small

Thomas Flint

John Pease

(John Buxton)

BALD HILL

John Buxton

Lane

Abraham Smith

Isaac

Samuel Goodale

Job Swinerton

Flint

Goodale

Wigwam Rock

Zachariah White

Samuel Goodale

Zachariah Goodale

Ruth Osborn

Putnam

('Sam' Abbey)

FAIRMAID'S HILL

ROAD TO ANDOVER

Joseph Hutchinson

John Walcott

John & Peter Fowle

Needham

Benjamin Hutchinson

Joseph Houlton

Nathaniel Ingersoll

Job Swinerton

Joseph Hutchinson

Felton

Henry Houlton

Nurse

Houlton

Tarbell

Preston

SCALE IN FEET

0   3000

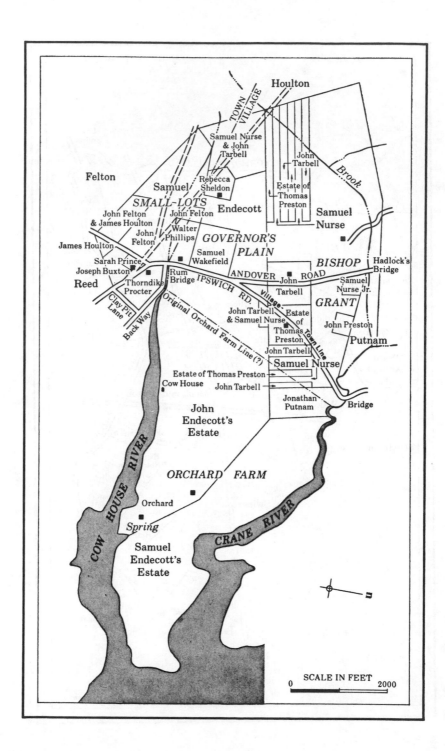

SCALE IN FEET

0   2000

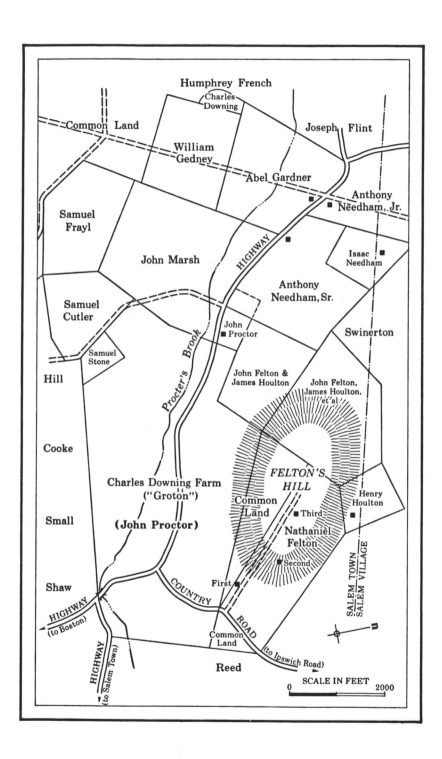

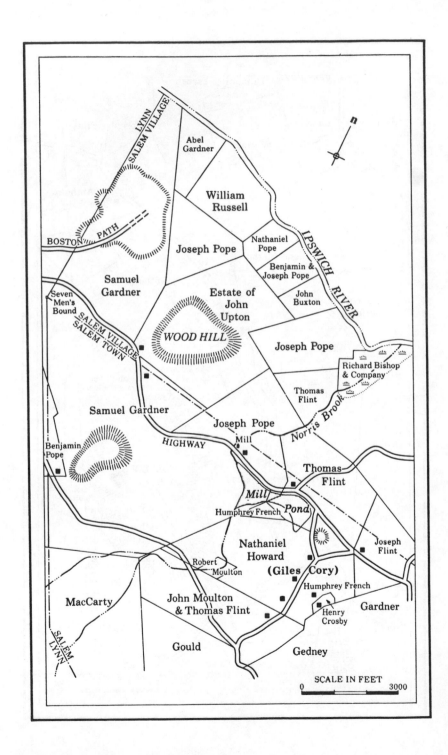

n

LYNN / SALEM VILLAGE

Abel Gardner

William Russell

BOSTON PATH

Joseph Pope

Nathaniel Pope

IPSWICH RIVER

Samuel Gardner

Benjamin & Joseph Pope

John Buxton

Seven Men's Bound

SALEM VILLAGE / SALEM TOWN

Estate of John Upton

WOOD HILL

Joseph Pope

Richard Bishop & Company

Thomas Flint

Norris Brook

Samuel Gardner

HIGHWAY

Joseph Pope
Mill

Benjamin Pope

Thomas Flint

Mill Pond

Humphrey French

Joseph Flint

Nathaniel Howard

(Giles Cory)

Robert Moulton

Humphrey French

MacCarty

Gardner

John Moulton & Thomas Flint

Henry Crosby

SALEM / LYNN

Gould

Gedney

SCALE IN FEET
0   3000

Additional Genealogies of Some
Salem-Village Families

[The following genealogies are not complete. Rather, their purpose is to clarify the relationship of a few individuals whose names occur frequently in this book. Catherine Leonard Hopkins assisted in the compilation of these genealogies.]

Flint Family

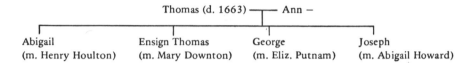

Thomas (d. 1663) ——— Ann —

Abigail	Ensign Thomas	George	Joseph
(m. Henry Houlton)	(m. Mary Downton)	(m. Eliz. Putnam)	(m. Abigail Howard)

Fuller Family

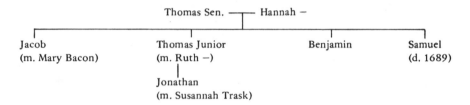

Thomas Sen. ——— Hannah —

Jacob	Thomas Junior	Benjamin	Samuel
(m. Mary Bacon)	(m. Ruth —)		(d. 1689)

Jonathan
(m. Susannah Trask)

Goodale Family

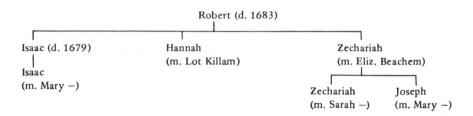

Robert (d. 1683)

Isaac (d. 1679)   Hannah   Zechariah
                   (m. Lot Killam)   (m. Eliz. Beachem)

Isaac
(m. Mary —)

Zechariah   Joseph
(m. Sarah —)   (m. Mary —)

Houlton Family

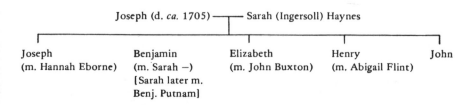

Joseph (d. *ca.* 1705) ——— Sarah (Ingersoll) Haynes

Joseph	Benjamin	Elizabeth	Henry	John
(m. Hannah Eborne)	(m. Sarah —) [Sarah later m. Benj. Putnam]	(m. John Buxton)	(m. Abigail Flint)	

Hutchinson Family

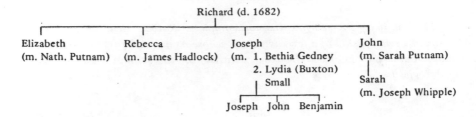

Richard (d. 1682)

Elizabeth	Rebecca	Joseph	John
(m. Nath. Putnam)	(m. James Hadlock)	(m. 1. Bethia Gedney	(m. Sarah Putnam)
		2. Lydia (Buxton)	
		Small	Sarah
		Joseph John Benjamin	(m. Joseph Whipple)

Porter Family

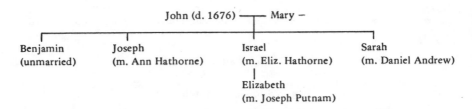

John (d. 1676) —— Mary —

Benjamin	Joseph	Israel	Sarah
(unmarried)	(m. Ann Hathorne)	(m. Eliz. Hathorne)	(m. Daniel Andrew)
		Elizabeth	
		(m. Joseph Putnam)	

Swinnerton Family

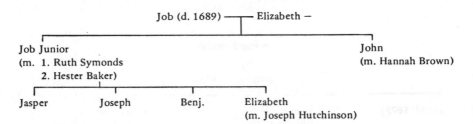

Job (d. 1689) —— Elizabeth —

Job Junior   John
(m. 1. Ruth Symonds   (m. Hannah Brown)
    2. Hester Baker)

Jasper   Joseph   Benj.   Elizabeth
                                                               (m. Joseph Hutchinson)

Walcott Family

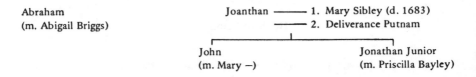

Abraham   Joanthan —— 1. Mary Sibley (d. 1683)
(m. Abigail Briggs)   —— 2. Deliverance Putnam

John   Jonathan Junior
(m. Mary —)   (m. Priscilla Bayley)